River Voices

Perspectives on the Presumpscot

ROBERT M. SANFORD
and
WILLIAM S. PLUMLEY

MICHAEL SHAUGHNESSY
Art Editor

North
Country
Press

River Voices: Perspectives on the Presumpscot

Cover image: *Presumpscot Falls looking toward Blackstrap* Charles Frederick Kimball, 1860, oil on canvas, 22" x 32 1/8", Portland Museum of Art, Gift of Maine National Bank

Back cover image: Aebel Shaughnessy placing a stone at the Chief Polin Memorial, 2018

ISBN 978-1-943424-61-0

LCCN 2020939742

North Country Press
Unity, Maine

About the Art

The images in this book come from a variety of artists who live and work around the Presumpscot River. Each takes various points of inspiration from the serenity, vibrancy, and power of rivers. There is the strong brushwork and bold colors of Caren-Marie Michel, a Westbrook artist who often focusses on the contrasting forms of the river, incorporating the geologic and built environment. She sometimes works in series from the same location, capturing the changes of season, time, and atmosphere. In contrast, Mary Brooking, another Westbrook artist, considers the more ethereal conditions of water, land, and sky. Using a limited palette, she evokes a soft mysticism with subtle blending and precise but intuitively dappled brushstrokes. Whereas Caren-Marie and Mary take a wider view of the river and its contexts, Michelle Stuckey's work is more intimate, with an eye toward plants and tightly framed areas that might well go unnoticed by others. Her use of color and light give a soft romantic and melancholic feeling. Another close view is offered by David Little, with emphasis on the robustness of rushing water. His palette is darkened, reflecting the influence of artists of the nineteenth-century Barbizon School. Muted colors and oil paints render his interpretation of water and stone highly physical and fluid. Andy Curran's palette is lighter and more animated than David's. With a similar concentration and strongly assured brush strokes, he is drawn to the play of color and light on the open and intimate areas of the river. Barbie DelCamp, on the other hand, uses digitally enhanced photographs of various moments she experiences along the river. She is a keen observer of nature. Although her images are from nature and direct experience, once digitally worked, they have a sense of magnified realism that borders on the surreal.

Artists also gain inspiration from the river for three-dimensional works. Anne Alexander lives and works along the river. Her work is elegantly simple and often based on direct interpretations of natural forms—in this case, a small snail found along the river. Pamela Slaughter creates a refined interpretation of the way stones descend into and rise out of soil or sand as water ebbs and flows. Michael Shaughnessy works in installations in hay. His art is often inspired by the roll and flow of rivers. His work creates homage to the Presumpscot and its many falls and rapids lost to dams.

The chapter images by Portland, Maine, artist Jennifer Christian are inspired by the flow and forms of rivers. Images bear hints of their references but only go so far in what they reveal. Only a lone oar in the water and a few flowers have direct references. Her work is subtle and nuanced but active, like the rocks with water dancing around and over them.

The poet Mihku Paul draws on her traditional indigenous education from her Wolastoqiyik grandfather. Her poems are intimate renditions of rivers and waters from a particularly indigenous perspective. Her creative work and activism, as the poem illuminates, help people understand that "human beings are simply part of the great web of life, and that all earth's inhabitants have the right to live and thrive on our precious planet."

Ecological and historical stories can impart much about the river, but the hand and eye of the artist bring to the fore that which can only be felt.

Acknowledgments

The concept for this book began over twenty years ago when the co-editors, after a board meeting of the Friends of Presumpscot River, were discussing the concept of stewardship and what it means to "care for a river." They noted the importance of learning about a river in myriad aspects: archaeology, geology, biology, ecology, history, economics, and politics, to name a few, in gaining a proper understanding for the basis of effective stewardship. Over ten years ago, we made an initial foray into collecting potential chapters. But life has a way of intervening, and it was some time until we were able to pick up the reins on this project again.

We are deeply grateful to the chapter authors, some of whom had to wait many years for us to make downstream progress. The river's voice is strengthened by their writing. We had to make some tough choices in assembling the chapters; we could have easily doubled the size but wanted to make a manageable document that conveyed a reasonable variety of subjects associated with the river. Many artists also responded to our call for artwork. We only regret that we could not use everything we received, for the watershed has a fabulous cadre of artists who offer another way of knowing: an emersion of the senses into the river's cool depths. Patricia Newell of North Country Press instantly and durably signed onto and supported this endeavor. Wanda Whitten, our technical editor, did so much more than we could ask for, donating many hours of her time, talents, and humor. We could not have done this without you, Wanda, and those editing sessions; I would happily sneak your dog onto campus any day.

We profoundly appreciate the Friends of the Presumpscot Board and members, many of whom are chapter authors. The Friends are a group of deeply committed and conscientious environmental activists who care about truth and public processes in addition to the river itself and Maine in general. Members have given generously of their time and support. One, Alison Graham Linsley, so loved the river that she left the Friends as a beneficiary. Sadly, she passed away in 2019 but throughout her life was actively engaged in the outdoors and environmental advocacy and found much peace and serenity in paddling Presumpscot's waters.

We think that every river deserves a gathering of works about it, and we hope that this publication is a reasonable testimony of stewardship, caring, and expression.

Contributors

Anne Alexander has lived along the Presumpscot River for 25 years. She is a sculptor who works in the mediums of clay, wood, and stone. Her sculpture is organic in form. It is inspired by small natural specimens observed when she explores her surrounding environment. Anne exhibits her sculpture in numerous galleries and outdoor sited sculpture shows in Maine, New England, and beyond. She has received grants from The Maine Arts Commission; The Pollack Krasner Foundation; a Fulbright to The Dominican Republic; and several artist residencies, including at the Maine Farmland Trust Joseph and Monson Arts.

Libby Bischof is Executive Director of the Osher Map Library and Smith Center for Cartographic Education at the University of Southern Maine, where she is also a professor of history. She really, really likes postcards and all things Maine history. She lives in the White Rock neighborhood of Gorham with her husband and two children. She is inordinately fond of wild Maine blueberries and loves exploring the trails surrounding the Presumpscot River.

Rachel Bouvier, Principal of rbouvier consulting, is an environmental economist and a former board member of the Friends of the Presumpscot River. She also teaches at the University of Southern Maine.

Mary Brooking is an artist, teacher, and gallerist living in Westbrook, Maine. Her work is rooted in the natural and built environment. She is known for beautifully colored atmospheric impressions of land, sky, and water. Her work has been widely exhibited in Southern Maine, as well as in New Hampshire, Connecticut, Ohio, and New Mexico. She has had numerous commissions and teaches acrylic painting at her arts space in Westbrook, Continuum For Creativity. She regularly exhibits her work there, as well as at Casco Bay Artisans in Portland, Maine and Art 3 Gallery in Manchester, NH. Her paintings are in collections in the United States and Canada.

Jennifer Eve Christian's art is based on natural patterns observed, blurring the line between the micro and the macro point of view. Much of Jennifer's work, including the drawings in this publication, represent a re-remembering of experience and memory. The drawings play with scale, perspective, and repetition of form and build structural armature through the accumulation of marks. The drawings in this publication are directly inspired by the Presumpscot River and its flora, fauna, and flow. Jennifer has studied in both the UK and the USA, and her work is part of both public and private collections throughout both countries. Jennifer currently lives and works in Portland, Maine.

Wayne Cobb is a retired engineer living near his boyhood home in the North Deering section of Portland. His lifelong interest in history found a focus when he learned that a portion of the street he lived on, Washington Avenue, was once called Quaker Lane. His historical research led him to become a member of the Portland Society of Friends. He can be reached at Wcobb2@gmail.com

Sandy Cort is a founding member and current treasurer of the Friends of the Presumpscot River (FOPR), a local river advocacy organization. Her volunteer efforts with FOPR have included successful efforts to upgrade the water-quality classification of a section of the river through the Maine Legislature and participation in FOPR's successful efforts to achieve fish passage at the Cumberland Mills dam on the Presumpscot River through a never-before-used state proceeding. As a volunteer with FOPR, she has worked to obtain orders for the installation of fish passage at several dams through the Federal Energy Regulatory Commission process. Sandy also served on the advisory board of the Environmental Health Strategy Center and was an active volunteer with the Alliance for a Clean and Healthy Maine coalition. She is a past president and board member of the Learning Disabilities Association of Maine and served on the executive board of the Learning Disabilities Association of America. She graduated from the University of Southern Maine with a B.S. in Art Education. Sandy lives with her husband Bruce in Westbrook, Maine, and can be reached at sjcort@maine.rr.com.

Andy Curran grew up in the Prides Corner area of Westbrook near Millbrook, a tributary of the Presumpscot River. He studied art at the study the health of this waterway by gathering data on the macro-invertebrates found there. He can be reached at robert.kuech@maine.edu.

David Little is the author of *Art of Katahdin* (2013), winner of the Boston Globe's "Best of New England" award for non-fiction. With his brother Carl, he has co-authored *Art of Acadia* (2016) and *Paintings of Portland* (2018). He has co-curated exhibitions at Bates College Museum of Art and the University of New England Art Gallery. Little attended the Skowhegan School of Painting and Sculpture, where he became interested in the beauty, diversity, and challenge of painting water and light. He has had residencies at the Carina House on Monhegan Island and the Virginia Center for the Creative Arts. His paintings have been shown in galleries and museums across New England. He lives with his wife Mikki in Portland, Maine.

Timothy Lynch is a reference librarian at the University of Southern Maine, where he is known for his eclectic interests and for his approachability in working with students, faculty, and other library patrons. His professional interests include media literacy, active learning in information-literacy instruction, and research support for humanities and social sciences. He has lived in Maine since 2001.

Tracy S. Michaud, PhD is Assistant Professor and Chair of the Tourism and Hospitality program at the University of Southern Maine. She joined the faculty at USM after a decade of working in rural Maine doing anthropologically based community tourism development. Having grown up on a "Mill Town" river in Maine that is now in transition, she focuses her teaching and research on tourism and sustainable community development, cultural and culinary tourism, and tourism entrepreneurship in Maine and Iceland. She recently received the *ICHRIE NENA Best Research Poster Award on Engaged Learning in Tourism Education, Outstanding Faculty Involvement Award* and an *Engaged Faculty Teaching Fellowship* at USM as a result of teaching classes that incorporate mutually beneficial partnerships and learning activities among students, the tourism industry, and local communities.

Caren-Marie Sargent Michel was born in Portland, Maine, and lives in Westbrook, Maine. Michel's work explores the urban, industrial, and

11

pastoral images of Maine and documents the ever-changing landscape in paint. Michel is a devoted plein air painter working in acrylic and pastel on locations all over Maine, New Brunswick, and Nova Scotia, Canada. Michel often portrays a location through series, capturing different seasons or times of day with changing light and color. She has shown locally, regionally, and nationally as well as in the Canadian Maritimes. Her work is known for vibrant colors, strong brushwork, and unique formats. She often draws on depictions of her city of residence and the Presumpscot River and its mills.

Alvin H. Morrison is Emeritus Professor of Anthropology at the State University of New York College at Fredonia. He received his PhD in Anthropology from SUNY Center at Buffalo, his MA in Sociology & Anthropology from Boston University, and a BA in History from Dartmouth. He was a researcher for the 1980 Maine Indian Recognition & Land Claims Settlement and in 1990 for the Aroostook Band of Micmacs Recognition & Land Claims Settlement. He is a frequent contributor to Papers of the Algonquian Conferences, published annually in Canada since 1975.

Irwin Novak is Professor Emeritus of Geology at the University of Southern Maine. His teaching focused on Oceanography, Geomorphology, and Glacial Geology. He was at one time the Associate Dean of the College of Arts and Sciences and a member of the Russell Scholars Faculty. His research focused on the geology of Maine and of Greece as viewed from space using satellite imagery. He earned his PhD from Cornell University, M.S. from the University of Florida, and B.A. from Hunter College of the City University of New York. He taught summer courses for many at Cornell's Shoals Marine Laboratory on Appledore Island, Maine, as well as a variety of courses offered by USM on Lesvos island, Greece. An avid film buff, he coordinates the annual Greek film series for the Hellenic Society of Maine, of which he is a board member.

Mikhu Paul is a Wolastoqeyik poet, writer and visual artist raised along the Penobscot River in Old Town. She is an enrolled member of Kingsclear First Nations, N.B. Canada. Mihku's art and writing are shaped by her cultural identity and work as a longtime activist for diversity and environmental concerns. Her art has been published on the cover of MELUS, and in the international journal POEISIS, and her one woman mixed media exhibit, *Look Twice: The Waponaki in Image & Verse*, was shown at the Abbe Museum in Bar Harbor, as well as the Glickman Library at USM. Her first book, *20th Century PowWow Playland*, was published in 2012 (Greenfield Review Press). She is currently finishing a new manuscript on the waters. Mihku lives and works in a historic community along the Stroudwater River in Portland.

Firooza Pavri is Director of the Muskie School of Public Service and Professor of Geography at the University of Southern Maine. She teaches and conducts research in the area of environmental geography, with a focus on society-environment interactions; natural resource conservation & policy; sustainable development; and geospatial technologies, including remote sensing. Her research uses satellite imaging and other geospatial tools and techniques to monitor landscape changes across wetland, fresh-water, and forested ecosystems.

William (Will) Plumley is a marketing strategist at VONT, a digital marketing agency in Westbrook, Maine, and also member of the company's board of directors. He is a founding board member of the Friends of the Presumpscot, which he led for many years. He has also held leadership roles in the Presumpscot Regional Land Trust, the Presumpscot River Watershed Coalition, and the Northern Forest Canoe Trail.

Robert (Rob) Sanford is Professor of Environmental Science & Policy at the University of Southern Maine. He is a former board member of the Friends of the Presumpscot. His previous books include *Reading Rural Landscapes* and *Environmental Site Plans and Development Review*. Living just a block or two from the Presumpscot with his wife and son, he is on or at the river on a weekly basis if not more frequently.

Ciaran Shaughnessy grew up in Windham, Maine, making frequent use of the many paddling, swimming, and fishing opportunities along the Pre-sumpscot River. Ciaran completed a PhD in Organismic and Evolutionary Biology at the University of Massachusetts Amherst in 2019. He is a research physiologist at National Jewish Health hospital in Denver, Colorado. Ciaran has served in a science advisory capacity for the Friends of the Presumpscot River for many years.

Michael Shaughnessy is a founding member and President of the Board of the Friends of the Presumpscot River. He is a sculptor, small entrepreneur, and faculty member at the University of Southern Maine, where he teaches Drawing, Design and Sculpture. For over thirty-five years, he has shown his work nationally at Museums, Contemporary Art Centers, Universities, Galleries, and one in particular on the top of his car. His primary material has been hay that is gathered, bound, and woven into large-scale installations and sculptures. He lives in a four-generation household and small farm along the banks of the Presumpscot River above Saccarappa Falls in Westbrook, Maine.

Pamela Slaughter is a Portland area sculptor who is known for her elegant vessels and totems in richly surfaced, formed, and transformed paper and cardboard. She has shown her work throughout New England and in Portland. She says of her connection to the Presumpscot River: "I am sure I had experienced the Presumpscot River, but, before I moved my studio into the river side of the Dana Warp Mill, I was not as attentive to it. The river that ran below my windows changed me. Its sounds and seasons, its daytime and night were a comfort and encouragement." While much of her work is in paper and cardboard, the piece pictured in this publication is her first exploration into stone.

Michelle Stuckey's home and studio overlook the mouth of the Presumpscot River as it flows into Casco Bay. Her work often references the elemental aspects alive on the river where she has lived with her family for 45 years. Michelle is a dancer, painter, and educator. She is a certified Waldorf Teacher and holds a BFA from the Maine College of Art. Much of her work is inspired by her belief in the resiliency and beauty of nature and its restorative powers when given the chance to reestablish influence in our world. Her paintings are often atmospheric and a bit mysterious and give an intimate sense that you are within the picture. Michelle shows her paintings regionally and in California. She had her first solo show at the Frost Farm Gallery in 2014.

Maurice M. Whitten is Professor Emeritus of Chemistry at the University of Southern Maine and author of *The Gunpowder Mills of Maine*. While on a bus tour during Gorham's bicentennial anniversary of incorporation in

1964, the bus stopped where the old Cumberland & Oxford Canal once crossed Gambo Road. In describing the canal, the tour guide added as an afterthought: "There was an old gunpowder mill somewhere in this area, but I don't know much about it." This comment triggered Whitten's curiosity and resulted in his extensive research on the gunpowder mills of Maine.

Wanda Poore Whitten is a freelance editor who, for nearly 20 years, served as the Managing Editor for the University of Maine System's interdisciplinary journal *The Maine Scholar*. She lives in Limington with her Associate Editor Miss Brit, a schnauzer-beagle mix who also serves as Playtime Coordinator. When their noses are not in manuscripts, they enjoy digging in the garden. They can be reached at wwhitten@roadrunner.com

Table of Contents

Introduction

If you want, you can scroll through River Network's interactive map and see which one of the quarter million American rivers is the one that flows through your watershed. The site promises information about "who is protecting your water."[1] This book concerns one particular river in Maine. The Presumpscot River is a 25.8-mile outlet of Sebago Lake that flows across many dams; through a watershed of 648 square miles; and past thousands of people to Casco Bay, along the coast of Maine. It is not the widest, the most scenic, or the biggest river. But its watershed is our watershed; it is our place.

Rivers have inspired writers since long before Herodotus (485-425 BC) referred to Egypt as "the gift of the Nile" and described the Euphrates as the lifeblood of merchants. Who among us cannot recall to mind the adventures of Huckleberry Finn and Jim finding freedom and refuge on the Mississippi? Hemingway reflected the voices of rivers and streams in his Nick Adams stories and even titled a book *Across the River and into the Trees*;[2] just the title is enough for that powerful, deceptively simple writer to convey the strength of physical landscape in the manifestation of personal character. Nonfiction exudes the strong metaphor of rivers, their voices, their mouths, and even their teeth (see, for example, *River Teeth: A Journal of Nonfiction Narrative*).[3]

Thoreau always had at least two voices when he spoke of rivers and nature: that of the naturalist and that of the poet (see his classic *A Week on the Concord and Merrimack Rivers*).[4] Long after his death, *The River*[5] was published from segments of his *Journal*, reflecting his meanderings along the Concord River.[6] Closer to home, he makes reference to the Penobscot, Allagash, and other Maine rivers in his travels to Katahdin in *The Maine Woods*.[7] The legacy of Thoreau permeates our notions of river stewardship.

Perhaps the greatest literary work specific to the Presumpscot River is a lengthy poem by John Greenleaf Whittier titled *Funeral Tree of the Sokokis*.[8] It is Whittier's lament and homage to Chief Polin, an early proponent and protector of the Presumpscot, who called it "The River which I belong to."[9] Although Whittier mistakenly refers to the Presumpscot as the Saco, the story he tells of Polin's burial in a hidden grave along Sebago Lake is consistent with the known history of the day Polin was shot dead in Windham (May 14, 1756), as a result of continued conflict with local white settlers. (For more on the relationship between the river and literature see Chapter 7, by Lisa Hibl.)

Originally conceived of as statements of individual "voices" of people who care for the Presumpscot River and its watershed, this project took quite a few years to come together. The authors have generously contributed their own voices, which collectively contribute to a larger chorus of the river itself. This publication is a statement of stewardship on behalf of and by people who know and care for the river. We invited each author to write about the river from the perspective of their own experience and expertise. A river can be many different things to many different people (and other living things), and we may have no easy way to capture all of these values and meanings. So we gave each author only the broadest guidelines, in the interest of conveying their individual style as much as possible. We figured that a range of perspectives on the river might reflect the depth and range of components we see in our stewardship of it. We acknowledge and value the history of the river and the natural and cultural aspects of the systems and peoples who have existed here from long before Chief Polin, through to present times, a river held in trust for future generations.

There are many different ways to perceive, value, and relate to a river. Some of us are academics who relate to the river from a particular field of study. Others are not. Further, for some of us, the river is a complete being that we must *not* break down into components for analysis. For many of us, it is a place we try to be on or near every day that we can. Some of us relate to it from multiple perspectives. Our relationship to the river is a complex thing. Many of the authors have a past or present association to the river through the activist group Friends of the Presumpscot River (FOPR), which has provided advocacy and stewardship on behalf of the river for more than 25 years, via activities ranging from participation in dam license renewals in support of restoration of fish passage to water-quality-improvement initiatives, films, lectures, fundraising dinners, celebrations of the river and its history, and community paddling events. For many of us, stewardship means increasing our understanding of the river and actively investing ourselves in its protection. This stewardship may be a public set of values and behaviors, or it may be private, in accordance with our individual natures, but it is often deeply personal.

We can interpret the concept of "river voices" as the many voices a river has, and as the many voices of the people who speak about it. Indeed, the River Network, established in 1988, is a nationally based organization with its own *River Voices* digital newsletter, linking nongovernment organizations (NGOs), supporters, and partners through the network. River voices remind us of the value of place and of being outside. They can also be a collective response to the sort of nature-deficit disorder articulated by Richard Louv, with the accompanying dangers of depression; sedentariness; and attention disorders associated with seeing nature as a danger, and rivers as mere flowing riskiness.[10]

Many rivers have had their own particular stories told, especially the stories of stewardship groups who have struggled to protect a particular river. One example among hundreds is Stephen Most's *River of Renewal*, which deals with the controversy of over-allocation of the Klamath River in the northwest.[11] New England has water-rich states with a long history of river use in transportation, manufacturing, recreation, and power generation, among other activities. When we needed them less, we turned our backs on them; entire urban neighborhoods faced away from the river. Water quality degraded; fumes off-gassing from the river as it flowed through Westbrook notoriously shucked the paint off adjacent houses in the 1960s and early 1970s.[12] Federal legislation began to turn things around in the 1970s, notably the Clean Water Act. The early 1990s saw the formation of the non-profit Friends of Presumpscot River, in response to the environmental threat of a proposed de-inking plant (discussed in Dusti Faucher's and Sandy Cort's chapters). The plant proposal did not go.

We begin with Irwin Novak's chapter on the geology of the river, as that reflects the chronologically deepest-reaching aspects of our appreciation. Geologists often see things from the perspective of millennia; to them, a river might be a very temporary entity, even if it dates to before the last ice age. We progress to Al Morrison's piece on Native Americans, which sets a linguistic basis for the historical context of the river to its original people. The influx of white European-descended people to the watershed is an archaeologically recent event for peoples now in a position to influence the river's present and future. This chapter reminds us that we were not the first people here nor the first people to care about, live off of, and center our lives on (literally and figuratively) this river.

Figure 1: *Dana Warp 6* (Caren-Marie Michel, 2017, 30" x 30", acrylic on canvas, private collection. Photo by Jay York Photography)

We move forward in history to the role of the river in more recent times, especially its 19th-century industrial role. Wayne Cobb writes in Chapter 4 about the Quaker community adjacent to the Presumpscot. It is a fascinating story about Yankee ingenuity and the connection of these Quakers to the world. Maine historian and Osher Map Library Director Libby Bischof's chapter on postcards (Chapter 5) reflects the late-19th- to early- 20th-century period in Westbrook's history; the predominant source of era postcards that involve the Presumpscot. Chapter 6 was drawn from Maurice Whitten's book on gunpowder mills of Maine. It focuses on the Presumpscot River's association with the manufacture of gunpowder, including production of 25% of all the gunpowder used by the Union army in the Civil War.

From a grounding in history, we progress to Lisa Hibl's Chapter 7, "The River in Literature," in which she draws upon the historical context through current explorations and reflection upon the Presumpscot. In chapter 8, Firooza Pavri and Timothy Lynch discuss land use in the Presumpscot river corridor, which forms a basis for understanding the river's past relationship with people and its potential future interactions. Research fisheries biologists Ciaran Shaughnessy and Daniel Hall write about the fish of the Presumpscot, a reflection of man-made and natural systems of the river and its fisheries. We can hardly imagine today the incredible abundance of life in and around the river just a few hundred years ago, especially given the abysmal condition of the lower Presumpscot a mere 40 years ago, but their chapter shows us what is still possible.

Next, we arrive at two chapters on dams and citizen activism on behalf of the river—the very concept that gave birth to the idea of this publication. It is the story of a grassroots effort to rebalance the ways that we use the river that managed to restore much of its greatly depleted natural functions for the benefit of all of its communities. This story is what made us realize that we could not understand our own roles in stewardship without exploring our own voices and the many voices of the river itself. Dusti Faucher, a founder and board member of the Friends of the Presumpscot River, gives us the early history of this non-profit activist group in Chapter 10. Another founder and board member, Sandy Cort, brings the history of FOPR forward to the present day in Chapter 11.

The Presumpscot River watershed has experienced dramatic human-led changes in what has become the most densely populated place in Maine—Greater Portland. Chapter 12, by consulting economist and economics professor Rachel Bouvier, provides an economics perspective in the growth of river use by area communities and commerce. Author and river adventurer Zip Kellog brings us in a different direction to the simple and joyful use of the river as a place to paddle upon in Chapter 13, "Why Paddle the Presumpscot When the Allagash is in Your Backyard?"

Looking from the present toward the future, science education professor Bob Kuech discusses the river in terms of environmental education (Chapter 14). Finally, from an even broader perspective than education, Tracy Michaud's chapter, "We Now Face the River: Tourism on the

Presumpscot River," documents how Westbrook now more fully appreciates its river.

This book is a manifestation of the many different aspects of "knowing" a river and the many ways that awareness informs our stewardship. We hope that it is a very public statement of deeply felt values. We hope that it is a poignant statement of what caring for a river means to us and how a few voices can express themselves. We hope that each river gets its set of spokespeople and that this publication can exemplify one set of expressions as part of a collective whole. In the Adirondacks, Helene Gibbons[13] likens the Japanese concept of *Shinrin-yoku* ("forest bathing"[14]) to "river-walking"; a mindful river-sensing and experiencing version of this yogi-like practice. It is a response to nature-deficit disorder. Research indicates that forest bathing increases cortisol and reduces blood pressure and stress.[15] We have no reason to think that river-walking will not do the same. May you all be river-walking in your own way, informed by the following chapters.

---

[1] River network. (2018). https://www.rivernetwork.org/

[2] Hemingway, E. (1950). *Across the river and into the trees*. New York: Charles Scribner's Sons.

[3] Ashland University, Bixler Center for the Humanities. *River Teeth: A Journal of Nonfiction Narrative*. http://www.riverteethjournal.com/

[4] Thoreau, H. D. (1998 [1849]). *A week on the Concord and Merrimack Rivers*. H. D. Peck (Ed.). New York: Penguin.

[5] Thoreau, H. D. (1963). *The river*. Bramhall House: New York.

[6] Thoreau, H. D. (2009). *The journal of Henry David Thoreau, 1837-1861*. New York: Review Books.

[7] Thoreau, H. D. (1906 [1864]). *The Maine woods*. Boston and New York: Houghton Mifflin.

[8] Whittier, J. G. (1888-89 [written 1841]). *Funeral tree of the Sokokis*. New York and Boston: Houghton, Mifflin and Company.

9 Massachusetts Colony records, 1739. Massachusetts Archives Collection, records 1629-1799 (328 volumes) https://www.sec.state.ma.us/arc/arccol/colmac.htm

10 Louv, R. (2008). *Last child in the woods: Saving our children from Nature-Deficit Disorder*. Chapel Hill, NC: Algonquin Books.

11 Most, S. (2006). *River of Renewal*. Seattle: University of Washington Press.

12 Casco Bay Estuary Project. (1996). *Casco Bay plan*. https://www.cascobayestuary.org/publication/casco-bay-plan-1996/; Deans, E. (2013). *River of rough places*. http://www.presumpscot.com/story/

13 In Duvall, L. (2017, July 30). Being there: Forest bathing and river walking. *Adirondack Almanack: Adirondack Explorer's Online News Journal*. https://www.adirondackalmanack.com/2017/07/forest-bathing-river-walking.html

14 Li, Q. (2018). *Forest bathing: How trees can help you find health and happiness*. New York: Viking.

15 Whitmore, N. & Sachiko, A. (2018, April 18). Forest bathing: Introduction to *Shinrin-yoku*. *The River Reporter*. https://riverreporter.com/community-living-community-stories/forest-bathing

Geology of the Presumpscot River Valley of Maine

Introduction

The Presumpscot River drains Sebago Lake, Maine's second largest lake, and carries its waters into Casco Bay (Fig.1). The river and its tributaries flow over and through rocks and materials produced over widely separated time periods and shaped by two distinctly different groups of geological processes. In order to appreciate the timeframe involved in the geologic evolution of the region, it is worthwhile taking a look at the Geologic Time Scale.[1]

Figure 1: The Presumpscot River (black line) is the outlet for Sebago Lake (upper left). The river flows south-southeast through the towns of Windham and Gorham and is dammed in numerous places along its course, forming a series of lakes. At Westbrook, the river turns northeasterly toward Falmouth, then east, and finally discharges into Casco Bay. North is at the top (source: State of Maine Office of GIS, 2011) https://www.maine.gov/megis/

The Geologic Time Scale

Geologists strive to unravel the events that have shaped a region. They clamber over bedrock exposures (outcrops) wherever nature or human activity has uncovered them. With their ever-present hammers, they chip away, collecting samples in order to determine the mineral content, rock type, structure, and age relationships of the land. Sometimes they scurry through sand, gravel, or clay pits to view the formations of deposits that have yet to form into rocks. From study results on the origin of various kinds of rocks (petrology), coupled with studies of rock layering (stratigraphy) and the evolution of life (paleontology), geologists reconstruct the sequence of events that have shaped the Earth's surface. Their studies show that during some periods in the geologic past, the land surface was raised in one part of the world to form high plateaus and mountain ranges. Following this uplift of land, the forces of erosion attacked the highlands and transported and redeposited the eroded rock debris into the lowlands. During the same interval of time in another part of the world, the land surface subsided and was covered by the seas. Rivers carried debris to the oceans, where it combined with dead marine organisms to form sediments on the sea floor. Evidence for the pre-existence of ancient mountain ranges lies in the nature of the eroded rock debris, and evidence of the seas' former presence is, in part, the fossil forms of marine life that accumulated with the bottom sediments.

Such recurring events—mountain building and sea encroachment, of which the rocks themselves are records—comprise units of geologic time, even though the actual dates of the events are unknown. Geologists divide the Earth's history into Eras—broad spans based on the general character of the life that existed during these times—and Periods—shorter spans based partly on evidence of major disturbances of the Earth's crust. The Geologic Time Scale (Fig. 2) shows the major divisions arranged in chronological order, with the oldest division at the bottom, and the youngest at the top.

The discovery of the natural radioactivity of uranium eventually led to the development of techniques for measuring the absolute ages of Earth materials. Now geologists can determine, within certain limits, how long ago an event occurred. Prior to the advent of radiometric dating techniques, geologists concentrated on unraveling the order in which events took place.

Phanerozoic Eon (544 to present)	Cenozoic Era ((65 to today)	Quaternary (1.8 to today)
		  Holocene (11,000 BP years to today)
		  Pleistocene (1.8 to 11,000 yrs BP)
		Tertiary (65 to 1.8)
		  Pliocene (5 to 1.8) $\Big\}$ Neogene
		  Miocene (23 to 5)
		  Oligocene (38 to 23)
		  Eocene (54 to 38) $\Big\}$ Paleogene
		  Paleocene (65 to 54)

	Mesozoic Era (245 to 65)	Cretaceous (146 to 65 Jurassic (208 to 146) Triassic (245 to 208)

	Paleozoic Era (544 to 245)	Permian (286 to 245)
		Carboniferous (360 to 286)
		  Pennsylvanian (325 to 286)
		  Mississippian (360 to 325)
		Devonian (410 to 360)
		Silurian (440 to 410)
		Ordovician (505 to 440)
		Cambrian (544 to 505)
		  Tommotian (530 to 527)

Precambrian Time (4,500 to 544)	Proterozoic Era (2500 to 544)	Neoproterozoic (900 to 544) Vendian (650 to 544) Mesoproterozoic (1600 to 900) Paleoproterozoic (2500 to 1600)
	Archaean (3800 to 2500)	
	Hadean (4500 to 3800)	

Figure 2: The Geologic Time Scale. Note: dates are millions of years before the present (source: Geological Society of America)

Rocks and Mineral Types in Southern Maine

Before we take a look at the detailed geologic history of the Presumpscot region, it is important to understand how various rock types form and what rock types are present there. Rocks are made up of combinations of minerals (although some rocks are composed of only one mineral). Minerals are naturally occurring compounds formed by a specific combination of elements. Minerals have a specific set of physical and chemical properties that help to differentiate one from another. Three rock groups or families are classified by their common origin: the igneous, sedimentary, and metamorphic. Almost all of the bedrock in the Presumpscot River area is of a metamorphic origin (Fig. 3), but it is important to remember that this rock type is, in turn, composed of pre-existing sedimentary and igneous rock formed during an even older time.

27

Igneous Rocks
Igneous rocks are those that cool from molten material. If the liquid rock (magma) cools below the Earth's surface, we call it intrusive igneous rock. If the liquid rock flows out onto the surface as lava, then we call it extrusive igneous rock. Examples of igneous rocks in the area are limited to narrow intrusive formations called dikes made of basalt and to moderate to small intrusive formations that cooled at depth to form granite.

Sedimentary Rocks
Sedimentary rocks are formed by accumulation, compaction, and cementation of material derived from the erosion of other preexisting rocks. Sands, gravels, and mud form the basic ingredients that subsequently become sedimentary rocks. These rocks are classified by size and mineral fragments of which they are composed.

One of the most interesting and valuable features of sedimentary rocks is the presence of fossils in many of them. A fossil is any recognizable trace of life that existed before historic times. A geologist uses fossils to reconstruct geologic history. The Geologic Time Scale is primarily based on fossil evidence and, for the timeframe in our area, fossil evidence comes from other locales or has been radiometrically dated. No examples of sedimentary rocks exist in the Presumpscot area.

Metamorphic Rocks
Metamorphic rocks are far and away the dominant rock type here. Metamorphic means "changed form." As stated above, metamorphic rocks were once some other types of rocks: igneous, sedimentary, or even other metamorphic rocks. The change from their pre-existing form to a metamorphic rock is a consequence of being subjected to great pressure, heat, and chemically active fluids. Examples of metamorphic rocks underlying the area include gneiss, schist, marble, phyllite, and meta-sandstones (quartzite).

Timeframe of the Bedrock Geology in the Presumpscot River Basin
The first group of processes that we will investigate was involved in mountain building and produced the underlying metamorphic and igneous bedrock. These rock types formed in a number of mountain-building episodes beginning between 480-440 million years ago (rocks of the Ordovician Age) and culminated in the assembly of the Pangean supercon-

tinent and the formation of the Appalachian Mountains around 225 million years ago. During the Triassic Period (210 million years ago), the Earth's crust began to pull apart and Pangea started to break up, ultimately forming the Atlantic Ocean basin. Overlapping this process, and extending over the last 200 million years or so, a long and continuous period of erosion wore down the mountains on the land, exposing the metamorphic and igneous rocks below while carrying the derived sediments to the continental margins via a series of rivers that were the ancestors of present-day river systems.

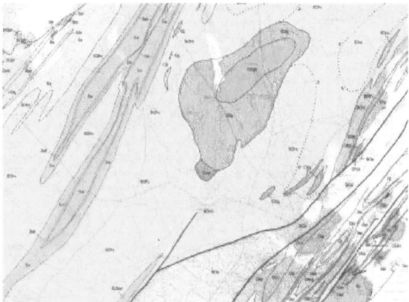

Figure 3: Bedrock geologic map of the Presumpscot River area. Color key: pale and darker greens are schists, and the pinks are granites (source: Berry, H. N., IV & Hussey, A. M., II., 1998. Bedrock geology of the Portland 1:100,000 quadrangle, Maine and New Hampshire: Maine Geological Survey, Open-File Map 98-1, 1 plate, color map, scale 1:100,000. *Maine Geological Survey Maps. 228.*)
http://digitalmaine.com/mgs_maps/228

Glaciation

Following the mountain-building and ocean-basin-forming events, the next major geologic event was glaciation. As the climate cooled during this period, vast glaciers covered the northern half of North America and much of Eastern Europe in the northern hemisphere. Growth and shrinkage, erosion, and deposition associated with glaciation is responsible for the present-day landscape. Repeated continental glaciations during the past one to two million years, perhaps as many as four or six, further eroded the land. The most recent of these glacial periods, the Wisconsin Glaciation, covered Maine out to and over the Gulf of Maine to the edge of the continental shelf with a mass of ice perhaps one mile thick some 18,000-20,000 years ago. The ice deepened the underlying valleys. As it retreated, the melting ice laid down a blanket of glacial gravels and sands that filled the pre-existing valleys and covered much of the upland areas. In addition to these sediments, a cover of blue-gray glacio-marine clay, known as the Presumpscot Formation, was laid down as the finest sediments were deposited in the ice-marginal ocean. This sea covered about one-third of the state (except for mountains, which stuck up out of the sea like the islands of Casco Bay), and it extended even further inland along the major valleys.

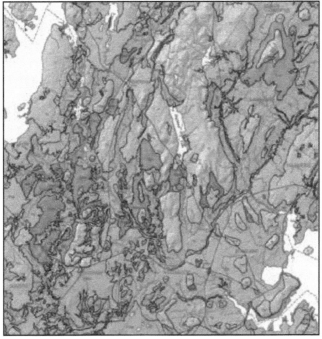

Figure 4: Surficial geologic map of the Presumpscot River area. Color key: greens are morainal materials, purples are stream-derived deposits, and tans are marine silts and clays (source: Tolman, S.S. (Comp.), 2006. Surficial geology of the Portland 1:100,000 quadrangle, Maine: Maine Geological Survey, Open-File Map 06-1, map, scale 1:100,000. *Maine Geological Survey Maps*. 1508.)
http://digitalmaine.com/mgs_maps/1508

As the land began to emerge from this ocean about 13,000 years ago, processes of weathering and erosion like those we see in Maine today began to shape the landscape even further—though the landscape is decidedly dominated by glacial processes. Streams started down-cutting into the underlying materials. Early on, the water discharge from melting glaciers into the streams was significantly more than it is today. Sometimes these rivers exhumed the materials that had filled the pre-glacial bedrock valleys, and sometimes they cut a new valley altogether in either bedrock or the glacial cover.

Geomorphic Features of the Presumpscot River Valley

The pre-glacial Presumpscot River cut a much deeper valley into the bedrock than the one we see now. Detailed studies made in preparation for the I-295 highway crossing over the river in Falmouth and at the Fore River crossing near Thompson's Point reveal that the pre-glacial valley was cut some 130 feet deep into bedrock.[2] That ancestral Presumpscot valley was subsequently filled with glacial and glacio-marine sediments as the ice receded and melted downward. The waterfalls along the river attest to its relative newness; old streams are relatively devoid of falls. Geomorphologists refer to the Presumpscot's overall drainage pattern as "deranged," that is, a disordered arrangement imposed on it by glaciation and deglaciation. The ancestral valley flowed out into Casco Bay via the Fore River, but the present valley mouth is a new location for this stream, as the Presumpscot's flow was diverted northeastward at Westbrook by a massive landslide.

Now, as the Presumpscot leaves Sebago Lake, it flows through mostly sands and gravels deposited by glacial-melt water. Occasionally, the river cuts through underlying bedrock. Downstream of Westbrook, it flows mainly through the silty-clayey glacio-marine Presumpscot Formation and, occasionally, sandy to gravelly deltaic deposits left by rivers extending from the former glacier's margins into the sea. Here, too, are interspersed bedrock exposures. Sand and gravel pits adjacent to the river, and within its valley, attest to the interrelationship between glacial, marine, and stream process and materials.

Damming of the Presumpscot River has drowned many bedrock exposures and natural waterfalls. The dominantly metamorphic rocks (with some igneous) that underlie the glacial and glacio-marine materials are still apparent in a few places, especially adjacent to dam sites. Examples include the small falls where the river joins the Eel Weir Canal at the Covered

Bridge off Hurricane Road, and where the Little River (a major tributary of the Presumpscot) crosses under Route 114 in Gorham. Bedrock is also present at Mallison Falls, off Bridge Street in downtown Westbrook; one-eighth mile above the Smelt Hill Dam; and at the dam itself, just above where the river joins Casco Bay and becomes an estuary.

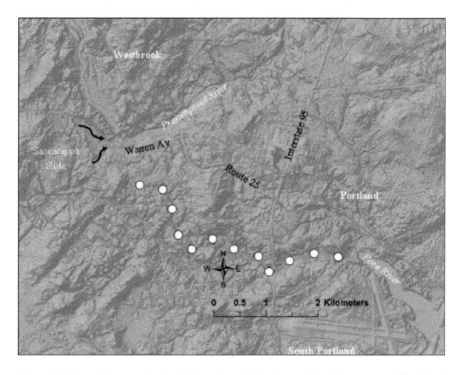

Figure 5: Map of greater Portland showing the location of the Saccarappa Slide (black arrows), where the Presumpscot River abruptly changes course from SSE to ENE in Westbrook. This Lidar relief image indicates the Stroudwater River channel location (white circles) that could have connected the Presumpscot River to the Fore River prior to the landslide (source: Dickson, S. M., & Johnston, R. A. (2015). Geomorphology of Presumpscot Formation landslides. In M. E. Landon & C. Nickerson (Eds.), *The Symposium on the Presumpscot Formation.* https://umaine.edu/presumpscot-symposium/2015-symposium-proceedings/

Landslides and the Course of the River Valley

Another geologic process that has contributed to the river's shape is landsliding or slope failure, which has occurred mostly in the glacio-marine deposits of the Presumpscot Formation. In 1868, a major slope failure downstream of the S. D. Warren Mill (now Sappi papermill) created a dam that flooded the lower floors of the mill itself.[3] According to newspaper accounts at that time, the mill was closed for two weeks while the dam was excavated by horse-drawn draglines. Many other failures have occurred in historic time. In fact, a pre-historic landslide, the Saccarappa Slide, may be the major reason why the river turns northeastward from its southeastward flow at Westbrook (Fig. 5).[4]

Landslides along the river may be the prime reason why the Presumpscot has a meandering pattern along many parts of its course. The slope failure relocated the river channel in the direction of the slide. Detailed aerial photo analysis has revealed many landslides at river bends, particularly downstream of Westbrook, where the river flows through more clayey and silty sediments. Larger, more open meanders characterize the river above Westbrook. There it generally flows through more sandy sediments left by glacial streams and deltas.

Conclusion

The Presumpscot River is easily accessible: by foot; by canoe; and, in some places, by bicycle. This access allows for multiple opportunities to view the geology of the area and link it to the geologic forces and processes that shaped the local, state, and northeastern United States landscape.

Figure 6: *Thanksgiving* (Michelle Stuckey, 2014, oil on canvas, 24" x 16")

[1] Geological Society of America (2018, August). *GSA Geological Time Scale* v. 5.0. https://www.geosociety.org/GSA/Education_Careers/Geologic_Time_Scale/GSA/timescale/home.aspx

[2] Upson, J. E., & Spencer, C. W. (1964). *Bedrock valleys of the New England coast as related to fluctuations of sea level.* (Geological Survey Professional Paper), 454-M.

[3] Dickson, S. M. (2014). *The Great Landslide of 1868, Westbrook, Maine.* Maine Geological Survey website. https://umaine.edu/presumpscot-symposium/wp-content/upload/sites/425/2015/10/dickson_johnston_2015_presunpscot.pdf

[4] Novak, I. D. (1987). *Inventory and bibliography of Maine landslides.* Maine Geological Survey Open-File Report 87-3, 27 p., 1 map; Novak, I. D. (1990). *Air photo reconnaissance of slope failures in the Presumpscot Formation, Cumberland County, Maine.* Maine Geological Survey Open-File Report and Map No. 90-22, 4 p., 1 map; Dickson & Johnston, Geomorphology; Thompson, W.B. 2008. *Surficial geology of the Portland West quadrangle, Maine.* Maine Geological Survey Open-File Map 08-16.

Ethnohistory of the Presumpscot Wabanakis

Figure 1: *Abenaki Couple*, an 18th-century watercolor by an unknown artist. Courtesy of the City of Montreal Records Management & Archives, Montreal, Canada.

"What's in a Name?"

In ca. 1595, Shakespeare scripted Juliet's primeval question to Romeo. A few years later, some of his contemporaries dropped us an enigmatic place-name to ponder–Ashamahaga–in a context that implied it was then a label for today's Presumpscot River, although its true meaning is now unknown to us. I shall describe that context shortly but first must present some general facts about Indian place-naming, especially as it applies to rivers, the all-important lifelines of our First Nations Peoples.[1]

Wise Wabanaki[2] traditionalists remind us that Native American place-names were *received from* the land and water, not *bestowed upon* them as were/are the European Newcomers' names. Also, even beyond general Indian names for any contributing river branches, specific features of any parts or stretches of a river may have separate names. Furthermore, no overall single name may exist for an entire river–even if it did, we may be unwise to consider it as a singular "Proper Noun." Similarities of place-descriptive names, because of similarities in geographical features, inevitably led to often-repeated "common noun" place-names, even for those located close by each other. This open-ended American Indian style of nomenclature contrasts sharply with the more restrictive European style, frequently causing confusion.

"Whatever words the Natives used for place-names . . . fell heavily on the tin ears of the Newcomers"—English or French—who, at best, often used idiosyncratic and inconsistent spellings of any word, familiar or unfamiliar.[3] Today, we are the inheritors of their clumsy attempts at catching the Natives' exotic pitches. We also must realize that changes in dialects and pronunciation have occurred since the 1600s, among both Natives and Newcomers, so the "real" place-names may be far beyond recall today. So, whenever the current name for our river came into use, did it always lack the second-letter "R," as in P_ESUMPSK in the 1636 grant from Gorges to Cleeve? If so, when was it added, as in PRESUMPSCOTT in Sullivan's 1795 *History of the District of Maine*?[4] Far too specific, we may never find satisfactory answers to these questions.

Fannie Hardy Eckstorm is my choice of the best interpreter for most Maine Indian place-name questions. As her "Indian Place-Names of the Penobscot Valley and the Maine Coast" tells us, Presumpscot's "early forms do not begin with *pre-* but with *pes-* or *pas-*, prefixes that denote something split up, or divided." She then sees *ompsk* as "rock" or "stone" and finally implies that "rough places river" is at least an "apt characterization" of the name's intent, even if not an exact translation.[5] Eckstorm lived from 1865 to 1946, mostly in the Bangor area, at a time and place well suited to gain linguistic insights from still-fluent Maine Indian consultants, as well as her wide network of scholarly correspondents. Among many other accomplishments, she was Maine's first practitioner of what we now call ethnohistory.[6] But, alas, she seems not to have given us any help at all with the name Ashamahaga, linguistically or even geographically.

Ashamahaga's Context

Ashamahaga, sole-alone between Sagadahoc and Shawakotoc in two early-published (1614 and 1625) accounts of Maine rivers, clearly implies that it must be the Presumpscot River.[7] Indeed, no likely alternative exists between the joint Kennebec-Androscoggin Rivers' estuary (often termed the Sagadahoc River) and the Saco River. The 1614 report gives only the list of river names, but the 1625 chronicle adds tantalizing details. Both accounts resulted from debriefing five Wabanaki men whom Captain George Waymouth kidnapped from Muscongus Bay (north of Monhegan Island) in 1605, when his expedition came to the Maine coast to find a suitable location for an English colony.

Waymouth took the Wabanaki captives to England; they would later return as guides for other English voyages. Three were assigned to Sir Ferdinando Gorges (who would soon become the absentee landlord of southwestern Maine), and two went to Sir John Popham (the first major financer of the Popham-Gorges colonial endeavors, who died in 1607, very soon after his short-lived Sagadahoc Colony had started out from England).

The detailed account, published in 1625, "The Description of the Countrey of Mawooshen, Discovered by the English in the Yeere 1602,"[8] presents the first known Wabanaki human-geography data, naming (from east to west) ten rivers and the Native communities and leaders living thereon. "The Mawooshen Description" was likely the composite product of both the 1605 debriefing and some other data, but we have no way now of telling which is which. However, it makes absolutely no mention at all that the peaceful theme described therein–a Wabanaki political alliance along the Maine coast from today's Ellsworth to Biddeford, under para-mount-sakamo/super-chief Bashaba (*Mawooshen* apparently meaning "walk together")—had begun to unravel with ongoing intergroup warfare by 1607; collapsing by 1615, with Bashaba's murder; and followed by a pandemic of European disease during 1616-1619. So, Waymouth's five captives must have been the major raconteurs of this early version of "Maine: the way life *should* be."

Of course, by the 1625 publication, many of the persons and groups named in 1605 had either died or regrouped. Yet the English general public relished hearing *any* tales of exploration and discovery, and the specific target of publishing them was to lure potential investors into further overseas affairs. National pride was the common issue during that internationally competitive and still-open-ended Age of Discovery. J. A. Froude rightly called the collective series of travelog publications by both Richard Hakluyt[9] and Samuel Purchas[10] "the great prose epic of the English nation." Even after we discount it for potential propaganda (from captive Indians seeking early return, through English naivete, to huckster hype), and for misunderstandings and mistakes, it all helps us better understand the spirit of its time. And even for our purposes here, reading about Ashamahaga and Shawakotoc is still fascinating:

> To the Westward of Sagadahoc, foure dayes iourney there is another Riuer called Ashamahaga, which hath at the entrance six fathoms water, and is halfe a quarter of a mile broad: it runneth into the Land two dayes iourney: and on the East side there is one Towne called Agnagebcoc, wherein are seuentie houses, and two hundred and fortie men, with two Sagamos, the one called Maurmet, the other Casherokenit. Seuen dayes iourney to the South-west of Ashamahaga there is another Riuer, that is six fathoms to the entrance: This Riuer is named Shawakotoc, and is halfe a myle broad: it runneth into the Land fiftie dayes iourney, but foure dayes from the entrance it is so narrow, that the Trees growing on each side doe so crosse with their boughes and bodies on the other, as it permitteth not any meanes to passe with Boates that way: for which cause the Inhabitants that on any occasion are to trauell to the head, are forced to go by Land, taking their way vpon the West side. At the end of this Riuer there is a Lake of foure dayes iourney long, and two dayes broad, wherein are two Ilands. To the North-West foure daies iourney from this Lake, at the head of this Riuer Shawakatoc there is a small Prouince, which they call Crokemago, wherein is one Towne. This is the Westermost Riuer of the Dominions of Basshabez, and Quibiquisso [= today's Union River at Ellsworth, Maine] the Westermost [sic–obviously meaning easternmost].[11]

That quotation is the entirety of the last two paragraphs of the 1625 "Mawooshen Description," and the only two that need concern us. How much of it can or should we believe? Certainly not all, but at least some. Clearly, the Presumpscot River's Sebago Lake attributes are bestowed here upon the Saco River. But "Crokemago" does belong on the Saco, because it seems to be a version of "Narracomecock"—the name of the Wabanaki fort at Pigwacket/Pequawket—now Fryeburg (which one should not confuse with a place of similar name [Rocameca] on the Androscoggin River). The importance of Crokemago/Pigwacket to the Presumpscot's Wabanakis is nonetheless a key issue for us to consider later. The basic question for us now, though, is about "Agnagebcoc Towne": Where could A-Towne's remains now be hiding?

Agnagebcoc's Siting

Perhaps the town's name itself holds information pertinent to locating it. However, even though Eckstorm suggests meanings for a few of the names of rivers and towns in the "Mawooshen Description," she seemingly ignores Ashamahaga and Agnagebcoc–and I know of no other properly grounded scholar who has attempted them. So, we are left with only the following barest "facts" (if we can believe them) and theories.

> Description: A-Towne = 1 Towne of 70 Houses and 240 Men.
> Extension: One community averaging 3.4 men (warriors) per household of at least 9 persons each, = a minimum of 630 total population.
> Comments: Not easy to hide big A-Towne; not easy to feed its big population. In wartime, protection by location is adaptive for both people and crops.

The following ethnohistorical accounts by de Champlain and Levett contrast the Native foodways on the major river-mouths east and west of the Presumpscot and thus suggest a potential profile of the lost community of A-Towne. Note that these accounts mention a wartime setting ignored by the "Mawooshen Description" of essentially the very same date (1605).

French explorer Samuel de Champlain cruised along the Maine coast from the French colonial outpost of Port Royal (now Annapolis Royal in Nova Scotia) in summer 1605—the same year that Waymouth kidnapped the five Wabanaki men from Muscongus Bay. About the Sagadahoc Estuary (lower Kennebec River) Indians, Champlain wrote:

> The [Native] people live like those near our settlement [Port Royal NS–i.e., by hunting, fishing, gathering], and they informed us that the Indians who cultivated Indian corn lived far inland, and had

ceased to grow it on the coasts on account of the war they used to wage with others who came [by sea] and seized it.[12]

Of the Saco River-mouth Indians, he stated, "They till and cultivate the land, a practice we [coming from the northeast, in today's western Nova Scotia] had not seen previously"[13] and said of the Saco Indians' Biddeford-Pool-vicinity village of Chouacoe: "The Indians remain permanently in this place, and have a large wigwam surrounded by palisades formed of rather large trees placed one against the other; and into this they retire when their enemies come to make war against them."[14]

The bottom line: maize gardening (corn cultivation) is necessary for feeding larger populations, but it is labor intensive, requires sedentary attendance, and is often too risky (climate, weather, predators, etc.). The sea-going "Tarentines" were Micmacs and Eastern-Etchemins who lived too far to the colder northeast to grow maize securely and, therefore, had to either trade or raid for it across the Gulf of Maine. The closer that potential producers lived to the Bay of Fundy (from which the Tarentines came), the less sensible it was to tempt maize-raiding by growing their corn near the coast.

So, because A-Towne likely required maize to feed its multitude, the town (or at least its maize garden) was unlikely near the mouth of the Presumpscot River in 1605. The upstream side of at least one if not two or more waterfalls seems to me the most probable place to expect to find it (or its garden).

The Lowest/"Last" waterfall on the Presumpscot River (i.e., the closest to the sea, which for our purpose of going *upstream* we must call the "First" Fall) is at or near the recently removed Smelt-Hill Dam in Falmouth. From the seaside at Martins Point Bridge (US Route 1) to this First Fall is approximately two and one-half miles upstream, much of it mudflats at low tide. Of this place in 1623-1624, Englishman Christopher Levett stated, "Just at this fall of water the sagamore or king of that place hath a house, where I was one day when there were two sagamores more, their wives and children, in all about fifty, and we were but seven."[15]

Clearly, "about fifty" is not A-Town, and archaeological evidence indicates that this First Fall area was only a regular seasonal fishing camp. However, Levett's trip to Maine was *after* the end of the Native warfare that crescendoed in the destruction of Bashaba and his Mawooshen alliance by 1615 and was followed by the devastating "plague" of 1616-1619, which caused up to 90% depopulation among the Indians and led to major removals/regroupings of survivors throughout the entire region, stretching from Cape Cod to Penobscot Bay. That plague did not affect the few Europeans present; whatever the disease was, the Europeans had inherited immunity to it. The 1634 encore epidemic was identifiably smallpox, which again harmed the Natives severely.

No detailed account of the Presumpscot First Fall area dating earlier than Levett's in 1624 is available today, if ever it was, for a comparison of conditions pre- and post-disasters. Captain John Smith's account of his 1614 cruise along the Maine coast, like the 1605/1625 "Mawooshen Description," by default describes a peaceful region (both accounts were promotional propaganda). Smith mentions warfare only in the past tense and states nothing more specific about the Portland area than "westward of this Riuer [Sagadahock] is the Country of Aucocisco, in the bottome of a large deepe Bay, full of many great Iles, which diuides it into many good Harbours."

Like the name "New England," which we know Smith coined, his use of Aucocisco seems to be a first in known records. That he meant it for more than just Portland seems clear from its use again a few pages later, when he lists among "the chiefe Mountains" he saw along the Maine coast, "the twinkling Mountaine of Acocisco"—Mount Washington seen from Casco Bay. Smith starts his *Description of New England* with a list of Native "Countries . . . alied in confederacy" with Bashaba "the chiefe and greatest [leader] amongst them"—a list including "Ancocisco"—a third spelling.[16]

Fannie Eckstorm (my guru of place-naming) claims that *Aucocisco* is Micmac for "muddy-bay" and refers specifically to Back Cove in Portland. Eckstorm sees *Casco* as an Abenaki word for "heron" (a large water bird) and suggests that *Casco* somehow replaced *Aucocisco* as an early name for Portland. She does not comment about how or why one small, muddy bay's name could stretch to include a faraway tall mountain in the same "Country" with it.[17]

So, conceivably, before the time of Tarentine maize raiding, A-Towne might have been on or close to the seashore in today's East Deering section of Portland, a peninsula facing the harbor but on a narrow neck between both Back Cove and the Presumpscot River mouth, both of which are very muddy bays at low tide. In 1614, Smith may have heard an antique name for that *place* that still applied, generally, to its wider spread *people*: Aucocisco later somehow becoming Casco, for both the English colonial town and its bay region.

The Second Fall upstream is Ammoncongin Fall at Cumberland Mills in Westbrook, at or near the S.D. Warren/Sappi (South African Pulp and Paper Industry) papermill's dam. It is over six miles upstream from First Fall, and over eight and one-half miles upstream from seaside at Martins Point Bridge—well away from the sea-going Tarentines. Also, it is only around one mile downstream from the Third Fall, Saccarappa, at the old Dana Warp Mill on Bridge Street in Westbrook.

In my estimation, this is a wise locale to look for A-Towne: a mile-wide ribbon on each side along the river, starting at the Portland-Westbrook boundary below Second Fall (an area relatively "undeveloped" today) and extending upstream to above Third Fall. No luck? Extend yet more easterly to the Westbrook-Falmouth boundary (also a less-developed area). My reasoning comes from reading several nineteenth- and twentieth-century comments about local historical and geological events—comments that may seem less than best today but nonetheless emerge from old-time field experiences and folk knowledge largely overlooked today, if remembered at all. Let's consider one such historical comment.

In his 1623-1624 explorations, Christopher Levett states that he "went about three miles" up the Presumpscot. (From seaside at US 1 to First Fall, I measure two and one-half miles.) Yet he also states, regarding First Fall, "further a boat cannot go, but above the fall the river runs smooth again."[18] Earlier, Levett may have been farther up the Presumpscot by another route, as Charles S. Forbes suggests in "The Story of the Presumpscot," namely, via the Fore and/or Capisic and/or Stroudwater Rivers.[19] Levett states that he went "six miles up" the Fore River, which probably means inclusive of its Capisic or Stroudwater neighbors. Forbes wrote:

> When Levett explored the [Fore] river . . . he must have found the *Indian planting ground which was a short distance below the* [Presumpscot Second] *falls at Cumberland Mills* [by walking to it from the south-west]. . . . George Munjoy . . . had found his way to that part of the Presumpscot and in 1666 bought of the sagamores Nunateconett and Warabitta the land which was "to begin on the other side of the Ammoncongin [Presumpscot] river at the great falls, and go down the riverside to *the lowermost planting ground*," etc. This was the deed of the famous *mile square*.[20]

An Indian planting ground may or may not mean that an Indian village was nearby. It may have been important both to hide the corn from raiders and to keep the village nearer the coast for traders. However, even if A-Towne was nearby and is lost to us today, we may still account for it (either here or elsewhere on the lower Presumpscot), theoretically at least, given some geological information about the "Presumpscot Formation" of slippery glacial marine clay (named for this very region), combined with local historical information of known stream-bank collapses and mudslides resulting from the Presumpscot Formation. In his 1987 book on Maine geology, David L. Kendall states:

> At Gorham in September 1983, nearly seven acres of land slid into the Stroudwater River and Indian Creek. It . . . . all happened in just a few moments. . . . Landslides like this are not frequent in Maine but they all seem to involve the glacial marine clay.[21]

My maps call it "Indian Camp Brook," instead of Indian Creek (which makes it seem named from only limited Native use), but it makes the point that A-Towne understandably could have been buried in the same way. And Forbes, who does not mention any Indian village in his 1894 paper, devotes almost two full pages to mudslides in Westbrook, parts of which include these excerpts:

> Saccarappa is built upon a great landslide, or rather it was in part a slide and in part a subsidence. An area of this character of about two hundred acres is marked by abrupt embankments, whose height varies from ten to thirty feet.[22]

> May 5, 1831, a large slide occurred on the north side of the [Pre-sumpscot] river near Pride's Bridge [on US Route 302 in Riverton. However, the] greatest of the slides within historic days took place . . . [upstream] about one third of a mile below the village of Cum-berland Mills [at Ammoncongin Fall, the Second Fall], on November 22, 1868. The bed of the river some two hundred feet in width was filled for half a mile with debris.[23]

Undoubtedly, besides those mudslides that Forbes and Kendall mention, others must have occurred on the Presumpscot between 1605 and the present, at least one of which could have buried and/or scattered whatever evidence was left of A-Towne, wherever it was. Someone(s) may have found and kept some bits of evidence that may yet come out of storage, or the less-developed Westbrook-Portland-Falmouth area may yet yield some unexpected pay dirt. So, in sum, I suggest that we may yet be able to *site* Agnagebcoc Towne, even if we cannot truly *sight* it.

Naming A-Towne's people also is problematic. Today, we have no way of knowing what they named themselves collectively and at however many levels of social organization. Nor do we know the geographic extent of whatever names they did use at that time. The best that we can do is to consider them simply as Presumpscot River Wabanaki and part of the Abenaki-Pennacook group of the Wabanaki peoples. We have the very same problem as with the Saco River Wabanaki, whose own name we also do not know—only that they were *not* Sokoki, despite that common misconception.[24]

Wabanaki Social Organization and Leadership

Wabanaki survival has long depended upon fluid social organization and flexible leadership. The Wabanakis' Dawnland Diaspora and Mobile Managers have befuddled English and American Newcomers from the early contact period to the present day, as being "improper" by Euro-American standards. However, the Wabanakis are still around today, their continuing presence a testimony to the effectiveness of their adaptively advantageous social structure, which they cleverly and dynamically employed to organize potentially chaotic events.

Wabanaki society could shrink or swell its groupings as occasions required; leadership lacked strict authority and was plural; and both groups and leaders could relocate and return, repeatedly. Even in battle, and when Wabanakis outnumbered their English opponents, if casualties got too high, the Wabanakis might leave the field to fight elsewhere another day. "Improper" this tactic may have seemed, but it also was wise, even if the English proclaimed each such event a "victory." The Newcomers' idea of their God-given "inevitability" of conquering the Natives was stymied by the Wabanakis' equally spiritual response: "We and Our Dawnland are ONE!" Weapons may have changed, but the old ideas remain on both sides.

Anthropological three-category typology of sociopolitical organization puts traditional Wabanaki society in the middle level of complexity: it is not Level 1 "Egalitarian" (no real prestige differential, and no economic differential); nor is it Level 3 "Stratified" (both prestige and economic differentials); it is Level 2 "Rank" (prestige differential and, maybe, but not necessarily, some economic differential, among either individual members of society or their family groups). By contrast, European societies were both technologically and socially more complex at Level 3. And each European society had only one monarch at a time, with all other leaders obedient subordinates (in theory!).

Each Wabanaki group had several sakamos at any one time, but all led without real authority—they had to lead by persuasion to carry out their real responsibilities to the group of persons who voluntarily chose them to lead and who could vote with their feet to go live in another community led by other sakamos. Prestige differentials made the true power base of any sakamo and kept each community's membership fluid. Because kinfolk lived in other communities, too, such fluidity did not mean isolation of individuals or families. Frequent intercommunity visitations kept family communications fresh.

Community members may first look to a few families who had produced past leaders for new leadership, but any potential candidate, male or female, whether for sakamo or shaman (medicine person), had to prove personal capability. Members also did not overlook new sources of leadership; adoptees with obvious talents, and even French priests and English captives were occasionally admired choices for leadership among the Wabanaki peoples.

The Wabanaki did differentiate levels of sakamos, depending on age, experience, talents, needs, and events. Having shamanic spirit powers doubled a person's credentials for leadership positions. In some families, and for individuals, a reputation for having power *is* power itself.

The 1600s produced at least four Wabanaki paramount-sakamos (super-chiefs of super-alliances), who must have had extraordinary leadership talents themselves and also had married off their kinfolk to further extend their webs of influence:

1. Souriquois Micmac Membertou (died 1611), but whose Micmac & Eastern-Etchemin "Tarentine" Alliance outlived him to crush Bashaba's alliance. A former shaman as well, Membertou was the first Native leader in the northeast to convert to Christianity, raising his own power by making a lasting French connection as "Hereditary Grand Chief."

2. Western-Etchemin Bashaba (died 1615) headed the Western-Etchemin & Abenaki-Pennacook "Mawooshen" Alliance, whose influence (some say) extended westward to the Saco River (thus including the Presumpscot River), until it was destroyed by Tarentines. Bashaba's death and resulting realignments were soon followed by the 1616-1619 plague.

3. Pennacook Passaconaway (died c.1665) built a Pawtucket/ Pennacook-Abenaki Alliance centered on the Merrimack River of today's

New Hampshire and Massachusetts but extended into Maine to the eastern end of Casco Bay by himself and skillfully married-out kin. Also a noted shaman, he never converted but promoted peace with the English. His own influence and that of his relatives on the Sebago-Presumpscot region need closer study.

4. Western-Etchemin Madockawando (died c.1698) was based on Penobscot Bay, near his son-in-law, French Baron de St. Castin (aka "Castine"). He wanted to make English connections as well as French, but French Governor Villebon of Acadia denied him that desire. He was both a shaman and a *kinap* (war-chief) as well as the last Wabanaki super-chief.

Sakamos (aka sagamores, sachems) also could become Mobile Managers, traveling far in some cases. Famous examples are Wabanaki Samoset of Pemaquid, Maine, welcoming the Pilgrims in Plymouth, Massachusetts (1621), and Mahican Paugas of Scaticook, New York, acting as warchief at Pigwacket (now Fryeburg, Maine) in Lovewell's Fight (1725). Kinfolk in some communities called in new leadership as needed, even going outside their own "home tribe" (especially after Native warfare, disease epidemics, English push, and French pull caused removals and regroupings). So, when opportunity knocked: "Have Skills, Will Travel."

The ever-increasing and -encroaching English colonials and their European-minded leaders never fully understood the Dawnland Diaspora for Wabanaki survival and saw it only as further "treachery." The English viewed repeated Wabanaki tactical retreats to French missionary stations in Canada (especially Odanak on the St. Francis River near the St. Lawrence) as strategic abandonment of "former" Native territory and French-inspired invasions, ergo intolerable. Caught in the middle, the Wabanakis preferred French pull to English push yet still tried to maintain autonomy. Wabanakis were not mere European pawns. They still needed their traditional natural resources (now English-held), and preferred English trade goods. My own research of Wabanaki frontier encounters leads me to believe that, with the French for "friends," the Wabanakis really did not need the English for "enemies." I believe that the Wabanakis knew and acted upon all of that information. Their encounter dynamics on the Presumpscot River seem to me to reflect all of the above.

Encounter Dynamics on and Around the Presumpscot, 1623-1756

During the 133-year span between 1623 and 1756, only two Presumpscot Wabanaki sakamos seem sufficiently well known to discuss in any detail. In between, of course, were innumerable Anglo-Wabanaki encounters—some very worthy of note—whose casts of characters are either anonymous or nearly so. In what follows, I will begin with sakamo Skitterygusset (fl. 1623-1657); end with Chief Polin (d. 1756); and, in between, selectively outline chronologically some of the more significant local encounters.

In 1623, English entrepreneurial agent Christopher Levett met, liked, and was liked by sakamo "Skedraguscett," who "hath a house" (and 50-odd guests) at Presumpscot First Fall. This sakamo and others adopted Levett as their "cousin." After fond farewells, Levett went back to England, where unforeseen circumstances prevented his promised return. Thus ended a rare opportunity for peaceful cooperation between Natives and Newcomers.

The next we hear of Skitterygusset, he was under accusation of leading a murderous gang against the dishonest English fur trader Walter (Great Watt) Bagnell, in 1631 at Richmond Island (off Cape Elizabeth), where Bagnell had set up his trading-post (English goods for Indian furs). Two years later, an English expedition, unsuccessfully hunting pirates, put in at Richmond Island, where they found and lynch-hanged another sakamo, Black Will (guilty or innocent), in revenge for Bagnell's murder.

Some interesting points: (a) Black Will most probably was Black William/Poquanum, a sakamo of Nahant, Massachusetts; (b) Fannie Eckstorm, without any comment, calls Skitterygusset "a sachem of Lynn Mass." in her place-name entry for 'Skitterygusset: a creek near the mouth of the Presumpscot [in Falmouth, Maine]."[25] Lynn and Nahant are two abutting communities on the North Shore of the greater Boston area. Here we seem to have Mobile Managers at work in a Native Maine-Massachusetts (Passaconaway?) connection.

Perhaps it was to Massachusetts that Skitterygusset went in 1634, during the second major epidemic (smallpox this time). He seems not to have been at Presumpscot then, because John Winter, the new trade agent in residence at Richmond Island, wrote to Robert Trelawney (his boss in England) in April 1634:

> The trading heare abouts with the Indians is not worth any thing, for heare is no Indian lives nearer unto us then 40 or 50 myles, except a few about the River of Salko . . . ; [and again in August:]

Theris a great many of the Indyans dead this yeere, both east and west from us & a great many dyes still to the eastward from us.[26] Wherever he was in 1634, Skitterygusset outlived the epidemic and still belonged to the Presumpscot. On 27 July 1657, "Scitterygusett of Casco Bay, Sagamore," signed a deed with fisherman Francis Small of Casco Bay (to share? or abandon?) a very large tract of land on the Presumpscot River, in return for "one trading coat a year for Capisic, and one gallon a year of liquor for Ammoncongan."[27] Seeming more like rent or lease amounts, those petty payments imply that Skitterygusset thought he was making a personal alliance with the Newcomer for sharing, not selling out. But was Francis Small's intention the smaller or the larger of those possibilities?

[LAND-DEED of SCITTERYGUSETT to FRANCIS SMALL]

Casco Bay 27: day of July 1657:

Bee it knowne vnto all men by these prsents, that I Scitterygusett of Casco
Bay Sagamore, do hereby firmely Couenant bargan, grant, & sell vnto
Francis Small of the sd Casco bay fisherman, his heyres, executors,
Administrators, & assignes, all that vpland & Marshes at Capissicke,
Lijing vp along the Northerne side of the riuer, vnto the head yr of, & soe
to reach & extend vnto ye river side of Ammecungan/ To haue & to hould
& peaceably to possesse & Injoy all the aboue sd Tract of Land with all
manner of Royaltys, of Mines, Mineralls, fishings, fowlings, Hawkines,
huntings, Immunjtys profetts, Comoditys, libertys, & priuiledges
wtsoeuer, for the same for euer to abide, & remajne, to the soole & onely
pper vsse, & behoofe of him the abouesd Fran: Smale, his heyres,
executors Administrators & assigns for euer; In witnesse wrof I haue
here vnto sett my hand & seale the day & yeare aboue written/

Signed sealed & Deliuerd   The marke of
  In the psence of,   Scitterygussett/
  Payton Cooke/
  Nathanjell Wallis/   Vera Copia Transcribed, & Compared
  The marke of   by ye original July : 8 : 59 : Edw:
  Peter Indean/   Rishworth Re: Cor:

Memorandum yt I Francis Smale do bind my selfe yearly to pay unto
ye sd Scittergussett Sagamore during his life one Trading Coate for
Capussicke & one Gallone of Lyquor for Ammomingan/   Francis Smale
              Transcribed out of ye originall
              Edw: Rishworth Re: Cor:

(Source: *York Deeds* Book I / Part I / Fol. 83, 1887, Portland, Maine)

Figure 2.

Nagging questions of Natives' sharing or abandoning land via New-comers' "deeds" afflict all such early colonial transactions—and "Scit-terygusett to Small" seems to be the first such on the Presumpscot.[28] Native bands held property in common, and any sakamo supposedly lacked authority; any of his followers who disliked his decisions were free to leave him and go elsewhere. Would he have consulted his people about either a personal alliance for *sharing* their land, or about their outright *abandonment* of it? In other words: How far apart were the theory and the practice of sakamoship? What, if any, agency for making decisions about land did Wabanaki followers have relative to that of their leaders? The ethnohistori-cal jury is still out for a verdict on most of these questions.

The "meaning" of Indian-land deeds varied in different regions of the continent and clearly evolved over time everywhere. At first, the Wabanakis could not have known the English concept of private alienation by sale. Their concept of land was joint usage and shared beyond the "in" group by alliance. Initially, the Natives welcomed the few English, but the latter wore out their welcome by overcrowding and land grabbing beyond toleration. Just after 1700, the population of New France was 15,000 French, while that of New England was 100,000 English. Furthermore, by then, the Newcomers had set patterns of the French wanting Indians *on* the land for trading, and the English wanting them *off* the land for farming.

These ever-increasing pressures were greatest in New England, and, in 1675, the lid finally blew off the pot with the onset of King Philip's War. By then, the Massachusetts Colony government controlled what is now Maine and, to "protect" themselves from the north, started an unwise policy of demanding that all Maine Wabanakis turn in their firearms, which had become their tools of choice for subsistence hunting. That intolerable policy, Southern New England Indians fleeing northward, plus a Saco River sakamo's child being killed by callous Englishmen touched off a separate new region of the war: King Philip's War: Northern Front (Anglo-Wabanaki War #1).

In Maine, Wabanaki wrath against English encroachment turned to vio-lence early in September 1675, first near Brunswick, with Indians burning the homestead of Thomas Purchas, who had (overly?) enriched himself by privately trading for furs from the Natives. No English lives were lost there, but the marauders declared it a warning that much worse was to come. Indeed, a few days later, the full horrors of the deadly hit-and-run raids began in today's Falmouth, on the east bank of the Presumpscot, just north of today's Middle Road (Route 9) bridge, between Merrill Road and the river.

```
┌─────────────────────────────────────────────────────────────────────┐
│                    THE SIX ANGLO-WABANAKI WARS                        │
│                                                                       │
│        From east to west, the WABANAKI Peoples (= Dawnlanders) at one │
│          time or another collectively included the MICMAC, MALISEET,  │
│            PASSAMAQUODDY, PENOBSCOT, ABENAKI, and PENNACOOK, and the   │
│                       various divisions thereof.                      │
│                                                                       │
│      1. KING PHILIP'S WAR                        1675 — 1678          │
│             NORTHERN FRONT                                            │
│          (No European Counterpart)                                    │
│                                                                       │
│      2. KING WILLIAM'S WAR                       1688 — 1699          │
│          St-Castin's War                                              │
│          (War of the League of Augsburg)                             │
│          (War of the Grand Alliance)                                 │
│                                                                       │
│      3. QUEEN ANNE'S WAR                         1702 — 1714          │
│          (War of the Spanish Succession)                              │
│                                                                       │
│      4. ABENAKI WAR                              1721 — 1726          │
│          Governor Dummer's War                                        │
│          Rale's War                                                   │
│          Lovewell's War                                               │
│          Grey-Lock's War                                              │
│          (No European Counterpart)                                    │
│                                                                       │
│      5. KING GEORGE'S WAR                        1744 — 1749          │
│          Governor Shirley's War                                       │
│          (War of the Austrian Succession)                             │
│                                                                       │
│      6. THE FRENCH & INDIAN WAR                  1754 — 1763          │
│          (Seven Years War)                                            │
│                                                                       │
│ PLUS TWO MORE POTENTIAL WARS, WHEN WABANAKI AFFAIRS WERE STILL VERY   │
│ VOLATILE:                                                             │
│                                                                       │
│      7. AMERICAN REVOLUTION                      1775 — 1783          │
│          First War for American Independence                          │
│                                                                       │
│      8. WAR OF 1812                              1812 — 1815          │
└─────────────────────────────────────────────────────────────────────┘
```

Figure 3

51

The extended family of John Wakely (four adults, three children) were surprised at home and butchered there, except 11-year-old Elizabeth. She was taken captive and held for nine months, before Sakamo Squando released her at Cocheco (Dover, NH). Squando's own infant son had died after a prank by Englishmen on the Saco River to see if Indian children could swim instinctively.

For Maine, the Wakely massacre and captivity provided the first English war casualties in the first of six Anglo-Wabanaki Wars and set a gruesome pattern for decades to come: English push and Wabanaki retaliation, stretching from 1675 to 1763 and frequently fired by French involvement, too, both political and religious (French pull).

For the high number of casualties (killed, wounded, captured) relative to the small New England population, this war was extremely costly—and to the Natives also. Both sides lost, in too many ways to count. The war "settled" nothing except each side's mind against the other, and each causal issue would erupt again and again. All along the Maine coast's thin ribbon of settlements, from the Piscataqua River to Pemaquid Point, the homeless surviving colonists fled southward to the Massachusetts Bay Colony heartland. The greater Portland area (including the small settlements on the Presumpscot River), known as Falmouth since 1658, was so hard-hit that its survivors first fled to the islands of Casco Bay, but even there the Natives still attacked. This war signaled the *first* destruction of "Portland"—and all other Maine coastal communities.

Green colonial militia units were ineffective protectors, even of themselves—thus, during repeated attacks on Black Point (in Scarborough), an ambush led to the name "Massacre Pond." Moreover, from Black Point on 15 September 1676, two leading citizens wrote to the Massachusetts governor that they had seen "two or three Frenchmen" with the Indian attackers. Some historians claim no French involvement in King Philip's War, but the Northern Front had at least French "observers" (as we term them today).

In southern New England, the war ended soon after the killing of Pokanoket Wampanoag sakamo Metacom/King Philip by the English-allied Pocasset Alderman, in August 1676. Yet in Maine, the Northern Front continued until 1678, when the real threat that the English would call in Mohawk allies from New York tipped the balance. (Earlier, raiding Mohawks hit the Wabanakis repeatedly—on the Penobscot and Kennebec Rivers as recently as 1662. These were the "traditional" Iroquois-League

Mohawks of today's New York state, who were long-term enemies of the Wabanakis and had become English allies, *not* the "separatist" French-Catholic Mohawks who, after 1668, lived in the Montreal area and be-friended the Wabanakis, with whom they raided the New England frontier and fought English armies as French allies.)

New England's colonial militiamen did not receive money for their military service, because the Colonies had too little cash, or anything else of value except land—much of Massachusetts' land being to the north in today's Maine and New Hampshire, both of which needed resettlement after the war. So, the Colony planned to pay veterans with land grants for "Narragansett Towns," named after a major campaign of the war's initial southern front.

No new northern towns actually came into existence at that time, however, because a *new* war soon started: King William's War. So, veterans received paper land-grant IOUs, which many eventually sold cheaply to speculators to get any immediately useful compensation at all. And, with every war thereafter, this unfortunate pattern repeated itself: "Canada Towns" were the second paper-land batch, named for a major campaign of 1690. Later towns often took on the surnames of the veterans' military-unit officers, or simply the names of the veterans' hometowns.

After the Treaty of Casco Bay in April 1678 officially ended War #1, many evacuees returned to their ruins in Falmouth, accompanied by newcomers. The Colony respected old land titles and granted new ones; within a decade, the area redeveloped considerable prosperity. Yet, inasmuch as the war had not addressed the real issue of English encroachment on Wabanaki lands and lifeways (indeed, it continued to increase and creep ever-farther eastward), by August-September 1688, Wabanaki patience was gone and Anglo-Wabanaki War #2 (King William's War) started with a vengeance.

This war saw full French involvement, because it had a counterpart in Europe known as both the War of the League of Augsburg and the War of the Grand Alliance. In Maine, frequent results were joint raids by large numbers of French and Indians, although Indians still continued their solo raids with smaller war parties. Herein, I limit consideration to two raids on Falmouth ("Portland")—in 1689 and again in 1690—and their consequences.

Massachusetts officials deemed Falmouth important enough to Boston commerce that, in 1680, they ordered the construction of Fort Loyal, on the (Portland) waterfront at the foot of today's India Street. They also sent troops under one of their better military commanders, Major Ben Church (whose Indian scout had shot King Philip in 1676), northward on patrol after the destruction of Pemaquid in August 1689. Church's men arrived in Falmouth almost simultaneously with a larger force of French and Indians coming to destroy the town. After a six-hour battle in Deering Oaks on 28 September1689, the enemy withdrew. Major Church would make four more expeditions to Maine, but none so fortunate as his first.

Quebec's French government planned a three-pronged 1690 campaign against the English colonies: Schenectady, New York; Salmon Falls (Rollinsford), New Hampshire; and Falmouth, Maine. Joint forces hit Schenectady on 8 February 1690; Salmon Falls on 18 March; and Falmouth not until mid-May, but with larger forces of French and Indians than the other two targets. The goal was to destroy each town, and all three certainly were; hence, the *second* destruction of "Portland."

Ten-year-old Fort Loyal was the very last stronghold for those survivors of the first-stop local garrisons who were lucky enough to escape the one and reach the other. The Fort held out from 16 to 20 May 1690, when casualties reached a tipping point, and Fort Loyal's acting commander Captain Sylvanus Davis sought fair surrender terms. French force commander Portneuf pledged terms of "good quarter" but certainly did *not* deliver such. Those English colonists whom French-Indian forces did not immediately kill and scalp, they captured and marched to Quebec. Among them were Captain Davis, who had been wounded in an Indian raid in King Philip's War, and Mrs. Hannah Swarton, a Falmouth frontier housewife. Their stories concern us next.

The Massacre at Fort Loyal was but an early case of European officers being unable to convince their Indian allies to obey European terms of surrender, because the Indians expected the Right of Plunder in payment for their services: looting goods; taking scalps for both war-rituals and bounties; and taking captives for adoption, marriage, servants, or sale-money. Both the French and English had, and suffered from, this problem with Indian allies, but the French are remembered in the northeastern USA today (by English speakers, at least) as being "infamous" for it—not only by history buffs (Fort Loyal 1690, Fort Oswego 1756, Fort William-Henry 1757), but especially by American literature buffs, because of James Fenimore Cooper's 1826 novel *Last of the Mohicans*.

The Rhetoric and Iconography of Encounter is a fascinating aspect of both ethnohistory and the anthropology of literature. Indeed, a special genre of American literature is "Indian Captivity Narratives (ICNs)" (real adventure stories, popular in earlier centuries), and several came from King William's War (War #2) and from Maine at least three: John Gyles (Pemaquid 1689); Sylvanus Davis (Falmouth 1690); and Hannah Swarton (Falmouth 1690). Only two of these three pertain to "Portland," so I consider only them here.

As acting commander of Fort Loyal, Captain Sylvanus Davis had to make a report to his military superiors upon his release after four months as a military prisoner in Quebec City. His report is not a typical captivity narrative by any means, but neither were his conditions. As an officer, he was accorded special favor, so he underwent absolutely no Indian encounters except on his 24-day march overland with his French and Indian captors. However, his candor and relative informality make his report interesting anthropologically. Davis had a particularly tinny tin-ear for French names, seemingly not caring much about accommodation to making the best of his foreign surroundings. Yet his encounters with his French military counterparts give us a rare view of them that is totally absent from most "ICNs."[29]

Colonial period mores of "women's place" put an extremely biased filter on early captivity narratives *about* women, although supposedly *by* them. The first northeastern case was from after King Philip's War (War #1) and tells *about* Mrs. Mary Rowlandson's captivity, through the narration of Increase Mather, a prominent Massachusetts Puritan clergyman.[30] He was also the father and mentor of Cotton Mather, an even more prominent Massachusetts Puritan clergyman, who played the same role of telling *about* Hannah Swarton's captivity.[31]

Both Mathers milked their respective cases for sermon materials and clearly put Puritan dogma into captives' mouths throughout, especially regarding their respective "Redemptions" (which did not just mean being sprung from foreign captivity). Mather clearly believed that when Hannah Swarton left the Communion-ity of Puritan orthodoxy in Beverly, Massachusetts, to go into the wilderness to live in Falmouth, she had asked for trouble; yet, nonetheless, she was "Redeemed." Here was a cautionary tale for Puritans to think upon, if ever there was one.

Almost a century and a half later, in 1837, the Massachusetts Sabbath School Society in Boston published a further twist to the Hannah Swarton captivity story, altering her name just slightly to *Hannah Swanton, the Casco Captive: or, the Catholic Religion in Canada, and its Influence on the Indians in Maine.*[32] Yet another cautionary tale, updated, but taking us further from Hannah, on yet another's errand.

So, from War #1 onward, the trend became for clergymen (who were the only trained writers in some frontier communities) to publish women's Indian Captivity Narratives and pack them with the religious overtones that are less frequent in men's. Men also tended to write their own narratives, often later in life. Anthropologists seeking first-hand tales of Indian cultures thus usually prefer men's narratives but have to take whatever is available.

Cotton Mather called the 1690s the "Mournful Decade" but nonetheless took advantage of the fine opportunities it gave him to study victims' case-histories. One such case was that of Mercy Short, in today's terms a Post-Traumatic Stress Disorder victim of the March 1690 Salmon Falls Raid. She early became linked to the 1692 Salem Witchcraft hysteria by claiming to have been evil-eyed and cursed by Sarah Good, a poor loner who already was in jail as a suspect. Mather saw connections between and among the Puritans' backsliding from former Orthodoxy, Devilish French and Indian attacks, and Witchcraft. In Mather's mind, God was punishing Massachusetts Colony. (Or was it self-punishment?)

Many Falmouth refugees from both wars had fled to Salem and other North-Shore communities in which they had families or friends. Those who had not returned after War #1 had considered selling their land-titles in Maine to a number of Boston-area businessmen who took advantage of this new windfall opportunity to buy up cheaply whatever lands in Maine that they could acquire, as long-term investments. After 1690, during the War #2 rush to sell, buyers could get much for little, with inevitable interfamily feuds resulting. In 1692 Salem and neighboring towns, when the "Afflicted Girls" who made the Witchcraft accusations ran out of loners and deviants to target, they went into interfamily politics to find new fodder. Under law, a witch-finder could claim a witch's property—indeed, a temptation to accuse. Eventually, even Governor Phipps' wife was accused, and the nonsense finally stopped. But these added insults following the initial injury of warfare were to remain problematic.

After the Massacre at Fort Loyal in May 1690, on "the Neck" (today's intown Portland from East End to West End) called *Machegonne* (meaning "knee"?), all the satellite settlements of Falmouth, and even as far as Saco, were empty. Not until August 1692, when Major Church returned on his third expedition—accompanied by Sir William Phipps, the Governor—were the bones of the 1690 raid victims buried. As if it were haunted, the Neck lay vacant of English resettlement until after War #3.

War #2 ended in Europe with the Treaty of Ryswick in 1697, but in Maine not until the Treaty of Mare Point, in Casco Bay, 7 January 1699. What is now Falmouth became the new focus of resettlement, starting in 1700 with the building of Fort New Casco, near Waites Landing today. This fort was a truck-house (trading post) for the Wabanakis as much as it was a stronghold for the English. It was right around the corner from, and to the east of, the mouth of the Presumpscot River.

After the War of the Spanish Succession broke out in Europe, Massachusetts Colony Governor Dudley held a 20 June 1703 council at Fort New Casco with all the Wabanakis he could contact. Sakamos present promised peace to the Governor, but *two months later*, 500 French and Indians attacked all the Maine settlements from New Casco to Wells. So, August 1703 marked the start of Anglo-Wabanaki War #3 (Queen Anne's War).

The Siege of Fort New Casco started with a truce parley faked by the attackers, which, when it failed to take the fort off-guard, led to the destruction of all the homes in the area. The English hero of the failure of the Indian-truce hoax was Major John March, the colonial military officer commanding the fort and a resident of the area. Then, as the fort was being undermined on the water side, the lucky arrival of the Colony warship not only raised the siege but destroyed 200 canoes. While this was an English tactical victory, it kept the attackers in the area, where they continued their depredations, especially upon English boats in Casco Bay.

Later in the war, which lasted a decade, harassment of Scarborough, Saco, and settlements westward was continual. So pressed were the Colony's armed forces that the Massachusetts government proclaimed a bounty of £40 for each Indian scalp, to encourage the formation of Bounty Parties as a means of better patrolling the frontiers.

The war in Europe ended with the Treaty of Utrecht in 1713, and War #3 in New England with the Treaty of Portsmouth on 13 July 1713. Yet both there and here, the wars and treaties resolved few if any real issues.

With "peace" restored, the English kept pushing ever eastward, taking their military posts with them. Therefore, Fort New Casco in Falmouth was now irrelevant and was torn down in 1716. The French, who claimed that their Acadia Province extended west to Kennebec River, countered English expansion there by prompting Jesuit missionaries Rale and LaChasse to exhort the Wabanakis to resist such intrusion. Massachusetts Colony Governor Shute contra-countered by calling a council with Wabanaki leaders at Arrowsick Island (east of Sagadahoc Estuary) in 1717. There, he heard first-hand accounts of Native concerns.

In 1720, the French stimulated Wabanakis from Norridgewock and Penobscot, and even those in Nova Scotia, to start depredations against English intruders. The English countered in force, so that, inevitably and eventually, War #4 (The Abenaki War, aka Governor Dummer's War, etc.) roared through the northeast. This time, Europe had no counterpart; therefore, direct French participation was not "official"—but Jesuit missionaries had such high profiles that the English targeted them specifically. Colonel Thomas Westbrook led troops to Norridgewock to capture Father Sebastien Rale in 1722. Rale fled before the English arrived but left behind papers said to implicate French involvement in the Wabanakis' attacks.

The English kept up their military offensives in War #4, successfully (at last) in the east; but in the Connecticut River Valley, Western Abenaki Chief Greylock harried English settlements repeatedly, at will. Maine historians seldom mention Greylock's name, but the Western Abenakis still count him as a freedom fighter extraordinaire. In Maine, historians tend to emphasize the importance of two English blows struck against the Wabanakis:

1. In August 1724, after unsuccessful attempts by others, Captain Jeremiah Moulton (who at age four, 32 years before, had seen both his parents killed and scalped in an Indian raid on York in 1692) led a truly surprise attack on Norridgewock village and mission on the Kennebec River (near today's Skowhegan). This time, Father Rale and some sakamos were killed and scalped, many Wabanakis of all ages and both genders died, and the entire community was burned and abandoned. Survivors regrouped and moved to recently abandoned, then fully destroyed, Indian Old Town on the Penobscot River, further from the English.

2. In May 1725, after the Massachusetts government offered £100 scalp bounties, Captain John Lovewell led a bounty party to Pigwacket village (at present Fryeburg) but was ambushed nearby the village. Lovewell and 14 of his men died, but their survivors held their position and outgunned twice their number. After their war-chief Paugus (a borrowed Mahican sakamo)

was killed, the Natives withdrew, not only from the battlefield but from their village as well, at least temporarily. It was a Pyrrhic victory for the English, but it did seem to shut down the Pigwacket fort of Narrocke-mecock on the Saco River. That fort-village on the Saco River seems to have been the base, along with Odanak /St- Francis on Arsikontegok/St-Francois River in Quebec, for those Wabanakis who were at least seasonal-ly using the Presumpscot River from at least c.1700 onward.

War #4 officially ended in July 1727, in a tent on Munjoy Hill, with the signing of the Treaty of Falmouth, but the Wabanakis soon complained that it was mistranslated to them. The idea that Wabanakis were to be loyal subjects of the British Crown and thus guilty of treason if they had "unlaw-ful" dealings with the French, and that the British Crown itself owned all of the "once"-Wabanaki land not already specifically "deeded" to Englishmen, made little if any sense to the fluid-structured Wabanakis, even when translated perfectly.

By the end of War #4, the Wabanakis had undergone massive removals and regroupings. Many moved north to French mission-stations in Quebec at Odanak/St. Francis and Wolinak/Becancour; many others moved eastward to form the Eastern Abenaki Penobscot community and the Etchemin Passamaquoddy and Maliseet communities that we know today. War #4 was a definite turning point in the Dawnland Diaspora for Surviv-al, but the Wabanakis' seasonal returns to traditional hunting-fishing-gathering places befuddled and angered the English expansionists. Real issues still were unresolved, and the French still wanted a Wabanaki buffer zone between Canada-Acadia and the English settlements.

With the wisdom of hindsight, we can see what the growing English population in the thin ribbon of coastal settlements could not see—that it really was not yet safe enough to go upriver inland to found new townships and gradually turn that thin ribbon into an ever-broadening sash. Yet the 1730s was when the English push inland started. That also was the time of industrial development, which fostered it: dam and mill construction blossomed on many rivers and streams, financed by both local and Massa-chusetts wealth.

A prominent developer in the now-Portland area was Colonel Thomas Westbrook, who had been commander of eastern frontier troops in War #4. In 1727, he moved from Portsmouth to (Old) Falmouth, where he gave the name Stroudwater to that suburb of today's Portland and eventu-ally lent his name to today's city of Westbrook. Besides being Mast-Agent for the Royal Navy, he was an entrepreneur on his own account and with partners. His 1734-1735 construction of a "great dam" on the Presumpscot was the largest project yet in the area.

Whether that dam was at First Fall (as William Willis states[33]) or at Second Fall—apparently Westbrook had a dam at each—is irrelevant to us, because the Wabanakis blamed the Colonel for not opening the dam's fishway seasonally, as he was supposed to do (and originally had done, according to one complaint) during the fish migrations upstream, upon which the Wabanakis depended, both for food and as fertilizer for crops. The first complaint to the Massachusetts government by three unnamed Wabanakis "belonging to Ammiscogan River" [i.e., Presumpscot], was in 1736.

The first two new upstream Presumpscot River towns were Narragansett #7 (now Gorham) and New Marblehead (now Windham). In 1736, John Phinney (son of a veteran of War #1's Narragansett Campaign) canoed up the Presumpscot with his son Edmund to be the first settlers of today's Gorham. In 1737, after commuting from (Old) Falmouth until he had readied his land, Thomas Chute of Marblehead, MA, moved his family to become the first settlers of today's Windham. Other settlers soon followed in both communities.

In 1739, after the Presumpscot Wabanakis had received no positive response about the seasonal opening of fishways in dams, their last sakamo known to us by name, Polin, went to Boston to appeal to the Governor and Council. The official records of their talk include this question and answer about the size of Polin's band on the Presumpscot:

Governor Belcher: "How many Familys have you att Pesumpscot?"
Chief Polin: "About 25 Men besides Women & children."[34]

This number projects to between 75 and 100 or more persons, of all ages and both genders—but he said nothing about where they were based, and if they were seasonal or year-round.

The Governor and Council agreed with Polin that fishways should be opened on dams wherever Native fishing took place, and decreed so. However, they had no sure way to enforce that decree, especially in Maine. So, although Polin won the round, he lost the fight. And, understandably, he also lost his will to respect Englishmen and their laws. After trying in vain to play by their rules, he was left with no choice but to try to get even.

Before very long, Wabanakis began troubling the new towns. They were both reacting to local pressures and hearing rumors of yet another

European war: England's 1739 war with Spain morphed in 1740 into the full continental War of the Austrian Succession. So, in 1743, the Massachusetts government ordered the building of a line of defensive forts against future French and Indian attacks and funded both Gorham and Windham to do so. In 1744, each town built a Province Fort, supposedly big enough to enclose the community's evacuated citizens during an attack. In Gorham, the fort was on Fort Hill (west side of Fort Hill Road, just north of the cemetery); in Windham, it was on Anderson Hill (north side of Anderson Road at the intersection with River Road).

Anglo-Wabanaki War #5 (King George's War) began in June 1744. In 1745, New England militias had their finest hour by capturing the largest stone fort in North America, the French Fortress of Louisbourg on Cape Breton Island, Nova Scotia. The 4000 New Englanders were led by Colonel William Pepperell of Kittery, who was made a baronet for his/their efforts. One of his officers was Moses Pearson of (Old) Falmouth, whose Portland-area veterans eventually (really *after* War #6) became the owners of Pearsontown (now Standish) for their military service. Also, a group of Pigwacket warriors who chose to side with the English and moved to Boston was also under Pepperell at Louisbourg—proving that Wabanaki flexibility in choosing leadership (and the Pigwackets themselves) still thrived.

But that was the good news. The bad news was that English treaty-makers gave Louisbourg back to the French in 1748, much to the ire of New Englanders. And in the new inland towns of Maine (Gorham and Windham), homelife during War #5 was grim.

Of the18 families in Gorham, 9 decided to stay on throughout the war; the rest left the new town temporarily for coastal communities. In April 1746, Gorham was fatally raided, one house at a time, so unless other families saw or heard mayhem or received refugees before raiders, they had little time for either home defense or evacuation to the Fort. Moreover, whenever rumors of imminent raids made it seem wise to live at the Fort, proper care for livestock and crops suffered neglect. A tradeoff was for men to form collective guarded work parties that moved from farm to farm during daylight, while the women and children stayed in the Fort. Still, livestock and crops often were destroyed, and the "skulkers" could easily capture or kill any person momentarily separated from any group.

Even the coastal community of (Old) Falmouth had a terrible scare in September-October 1746. Furious over their loss of Louisbourg, the

French Navy planned a bombardment and invasion of New England ports, Falmouth included. A large French fleet and over 3000 troops arrived in Nova Scotia, but it was hit by an epidemic, which killed the admiral. Then a violent gale scattered the fleet and destroyed many ships—much like the so-called "Protestant Wind" that broke up the Spanish Armada in its 1558 attempt to invade England. New England offered thanksgiving for its deliverance, especially given that Old England sent no Royal Navy squadron to help defend the Colonies against the French fleet's planned attack.

Spring and summer 1747 found Presumpscot communities under attacks again. Saccarrapa and Windham suffered multiple deaths and captures—one captive was young Joseph Knights, who would again be captured in War #6. Two whaleboats were sent from (Old) Falmouth to Sebago Lake to pursue raiding parties, although pursuit sometimes meant that the raiders would kill their least-fit captives, who might delay the resulting necessarily speedier flight from pursuers, posing another tradeoff decision.

"Pooran, Chief of the St. François" was supposed to attend a Treaty Conference at Falmouth in October 1749 but apparently did not go.[35] However, the wording of that comment tells us that Polin was then a sakamo in residence at Odanak/St. Francis, the large Wabanaki village and French mission-station on the Arsikontegok/St. François River, near its junction with the St. Lawrence River, in southern Quebec. Mention of the area suggests that he seems to have given up entirely on diplomatic approaches to his grievances about English intrusions on the Presumpscot, as Odanak was a major new base for many displaced Maine Wabanakis.

In Europe, the War of the Austrian Succession ended with the Treaty of Aix-la-Chapelle in October 1748. London celebrated it with Handel's *Music for the Royal Fireworks*, etc. But in New England, despite Massachusetts Governor Phipps' proclamation of November 1749 to "require all his Majesty's good Subjects to live in Peace with the Indians," they did not do so, nor did the Wabanakis do so with them.[36] Different accounts give different dates, depending on local circumstances, as to when War #5 (King George's War) really did end, but I suggest that, despite the Conferences of 1752, 1753, 1754 with different groups of Wabanakis, War #5 simply morphed into War #6 (*The* French & Indian War), which was part of the so-called Seven Years War between Britain and France for world empire. On the Wabanaki frontier in Maine, the same old grudges defied any sort of diplomacy.

I will only consider local affairs regarding War #6, starting with geography. A glance at adjoining Maps 4 and 5 of Delorme's Maine Atlas shows the closeness of the Saco River to the Presumpscot River at the south end of Sebago Lake: straight-line ten miles between Steep Falls (in today's Standish) to White's Bridge (Standish-Windham line), and straight-line twelve miles between East Limington (where the Little Ossipee River meets the Saco) and South Windham (Gorham-Windham line at Little Falls).

Local histories mention Indian trails between the Saco and the Presumpscot, and, in my opinion, it seems probable that considerable interaction between Wabanaki bands based on either or both rivers did, indeed, occur—more so than (but not totally excluding) between those of the Sebago-Presumpscot drainage and the Androscoggin River. Thus, Pigwacket village in today's Fryeburg (on the upper Saco) logically would be the main near-base for Presumpscot-using Wabanakis, and, unquestionably, Odanak/St. Francis was the far-base. Wabanakis living on the Presumpscot would have been as endangered as were the English during War #6—even *using* the Presumpscot would have been hazardous for them.

In Pearsontown (now Standish)—the still more theoretical than actual newest town on the Presumpscot (also on the Saco)—a fort was built in 1754, long before actual settlers came to live. Workers had it almost completed and had gone to (Old) Falmouth for supplies, when an Indian raid set it afire. Other raids kept the workers inside the fort for days on end.

Notes from the 25 July 1754 meeting of Governor Shirley's Council in Boston state:

His Excellency mentioning to the Board the many Outrages & Hostilities suppos'd to be done by one Polan an Arssagunticook Indian [meaning Odanak/St. Francis]. Unanimously advised that his Excellency be desir'd to pursue such measures as he shall think most proper for taking & securing the said Indian so that any further mischief may be prevented being done by the said Indian.[37]

Showing the rising desperation (and inflation?) during the colonial period in New England, the Massachusetts government offered bounties for (enemy) Indian scalps, starting with £3 each during War #1 and ending with £300 each during War #6. In some cases, counterfeiting occurred by substituting friendly Indians' scalps, which understandably hastened a new outbreak of hostility in 1755 in Maine. The bounties not only stimulated in-person scalp hunters but also stay-at-home investors who outfitted bounty parties for profit—somewhat comparable to US citizens investing in Government War Bonds in World War 2.

One such investor was (Old) Falmouth's leading clergyman, Harvard graduate Parson Thomas Smith, whose father, Thomas Sr., was Truckmaster (Indian-trading-post manager) on the Saco at Union Falls in today's Dayton, Maine, and whose son became Parson Peter Smith in New Marblehead (Windham). Thomas Jr. wrote in his diary for 18 June 1757: "I received £165, 3s, 3d of Cox for my part of scalp money."[38] His salary that year, he reports elsewhere, was £800. From Parson Thomas Smith's diary, we learn details about events leading to and including Chief Polin's last raid of revenge, which was on Windham in 1756:

May 10. This morning we are alarmed with young [Joseph] Knights, who escaped [his second captivity] from the Indians three days ago and got to North Yarmouth this morning, who brings news of 120 Indians coming upon the frontier who are to spread themselves in small scouts [scouting parties] from Brunswick to Saco.[39]

May 14. This morning, one Brown was killed and Winship was wounded and scalped at [New] Marblehead [Windham]. Manchester fired upon them, and we hope killed an Indian [He did; it was Polin!], as did Capt Skillin another. The Indians fled affrighted and left five packs, a bow and a bunch of arrows, and several other things.

Brown and Winship were going with a guard of four men and four lads to work upon Brown's Place, about a mile from the fort . . . and the Indians fired on them; whereupon Manchester fired once, but Farrow and Sterling with the other two lads run away home, and the Indians fled also in great haste. Capt Skillin with a company being gone out in the woods about a mile, were called back and with Capt Brown's scout (that happened also to be there) pursued the Indians and fired on one, and then all shouted for victory. Manchester was the hero of the action, but Anderson behaved gallantly calling, follow on my lads; or the English, perhaps all of them, would have been killed.[40]

Only accounts from decades later tell the follow up: The Wabanakis supposedly carried away Polin's body, went up the Presumpscot, and buried (most of) him, under the roots of a tree that they partly bent over and set straight again. Some say one of Polin's legs was taken back to Canada for Catholic burial. Some say that, decades later still, workmen by the Songo Lock dug up bones that were considered Polin's—including a huge mandible (lower jaw) that could surround a normal sized one. If it were indeed Polin's jaw, it could indicate that he had *acromegaly*, a form of gigantism, probably hereditary, that other Natives could have seen as a supernatural distinction for himself, and his lineage, and would give them chiefly status by default. Some persons claim to have seen these bones; some claim to know where they are now. Others claim that Polin's descendants are alive and well. Cooperation and DNA testing perhaps could tell us much more about the last known sakamo of the Presumpscot, who truly deserves respect as the Last Freedom Fighter of the Native Period of the River.[41] Currently, one cannot easily separate facts about Polin from fables.

Figure 4: *Golden Canoe II* (Mary Brooking, 2018, acrylic on paper mounted on panel, 8"x10")

The nineteenth-century American poet John Greenleaf Whittier wrote Polin a sort of eulogy in 1841 but got both the geography and the ethnicity wrong in *The Funeral Tree of the Sokokis*.[42] The Saco River Wabanakis were just that, *not* Sokokis (who lived on the middle Connecticut River). And the Saco River does *not* drain Sebago Lake—the Presumpscot River does. That much we do know, along with the sad fact borne out by this sad story: that Indian treaties have been mostly pothole patches *at best*, not by any means making for smooth roads forward.

The term "Freedom Fighter" is difficult for us to understand. We can only marvel at English statesman William Pitt Sr, who, in 1777, during the American Revolution, told the English Parliament 'While a foreign troop was landed in my country, I never would lay down my arms, never! Never! Never!"[43] He could grasp the validity of the Americans' desire to expel the English. But a decade earlier, very few if any of those same Americans could have grasped the validity of the Indians' desire to expel the American English invaders of their homeland. And we today still seem to have that same non-relativism in world affairs.

Ethnohistory reminds us that our ancestors were *not* ourselves by candlelight—their world and worldview then were very different from our world and worldview now. But once in a while we can find a "positive?" value in common that inspires across the time gap. In the case of Elizabeth McLellan McLellan (she and her husband Hugh were distant cousins), I find a sort of role model for the ages, and a fascinating tale of encounter dynamics on the Wabanaki Frontier. Hugh and Elizabeth were Ulster Scots ("Scots-Irish") who came to settle in Narragansett #7 (Gorham) in the winter of 1738-1739 and lived there through Wars #5 & #6 and beyond. Their descendent Hugh D. McLellan tells their story in his 1903 *History of Gorham*—admittedly, a potentially biased account but still valuable to consider.[44] My next paragraph below sets the stage for the final paragraph's quoted coda.

The McLellan family went to the Fort (on Fort Hill) to live in it, the day after a truly brutal massacre of the Bryant family in the Indian raid of April 1746, and 'in about seven years, they returned to their log-house!"[45] In autumn 1750, during the theoretical "peace" between Wars #5 & #6 and while all the men and boys were collectively harvesting the fields, the women and children were in the fort without any guard but their own wits—and old Bose, Elizabeth's dog. Bose's sudden growling sent Elizabeth to bar the fort's gate and climb to the watch-box with a rifle she knew how to use well. While the other women present, except one, refused to believe her, a lengthy wait and watch finally produced a "skulking" Indian, whom Elizabeth shot and mortally wounded. Later, captives from isolated Gorham homes eventually reported that Bose and Elizabeth's actions had scared off the planned attack on the fort—the raiders assuming that a guard-party of soldiers must have been on duty there.

Mrs. McLellan lived to a good old age, and would never give up that she did not kill or desperately wound an Indian and save all in the fort. During her entire life she held an unconquerable antipathy against Indians; still she treated them kindly. In passing through the town they always made her a call, and she never let one go away hungry, and made her conduct invariably kind to them. From policy she did not let them know her feelings. An Indian was never known to treat her otherwise than with kindness and respect, and she enjoined on every member of her family to treat the Indians kindly, for she knew the talk among the settlers was that the barbarities exercised toward the Bryants was heightened by a trifling insult received previous to the war, by a young Indian, from one of the females of the family. And as peace with the Indians was precarious, she kept an eye on the main chance.[46]

Recent Relationships
The Maine Indian Federal Recognition and Land Claims "Settlement" of 1980 and Supplement of 1991 (in both of which I was honored to be involved) soon were found to be only incomplete, temporary patchwork. Native sovereignty over various key matters was not clearly established, and some rights usually present in similar treaties with other Native American peoples were somehow omitted. Like many Indian treaties of the past, their shelf lives were short and souring.

Unlike the other four of the six Wabanaki peoples of Maine, the Abenaki and Pennacook peoples are *not* "Officially Recognized" and seem to suffer from the curse of the old truism that "History is a Winner's Tale." In their parts of the Dawnland, many more encroaching English colonists crowded them out early, and they then became affiliated with French bases in Canada. Still today, their "history" works against them in New England frontier folklore. Non-Natives too easily forget who invaded whom first, as they too easily remember Chief Polin as the last Native raider.

The descendants of the Presumpscot Wabanakis, like the descendants of other Abenaki-Pennacook Wabanaki peoples, surely must cynically notice that existing stewardship of the Presumpscot River *still allows* on paper but *does not enforce* the fish passageways that Chief Polin actually won—a goal for which he worked and died.

---

[1] This article is a compilation of Alvin Hamblen Morrison's lifelong work on the Wabanaki Peoples.

[2] *Wabanaki* (meaning "Dawn-Land-ers") is the collective name for those Northeastern Algonquian-language-family peoples of northern New England and Maritime Canada, specifically known as today's Micmac, Maliseet, Passamaquoddy, Penobscot, Abenaki, and Pennacook. All of these peoples were and are living in Maine, and each people had a number of locally named communities. When in doubt as to what name to use for any or all "Maine Indian" group(s), the one safe answer is always "Wabanaki." In the 1600s, the Wabanaki peoples appear to have consisted of four blocs: Micmac, Eastern-Etchemin, Western-Etchemin, and Abenaki-Pennacook, with fluid membership and fluid locations caused by natural disasters, diseases, warfare, English push, and French pull. Tactically regrouping and relocating was the Wabanaki peoples' inextinguishable strategy for collective survival in their Dawnland.

[3] Kendall, D. L. (1987). *Glaciers & granite: A guide to Maine's landscapes and geology.* Camden, ME: Down East Books, 93.

[4] Sullivan, J. (1795). *The history of the district of Maine.* Boston: I Thomas and E. T. Andrews. https://archive.org/details/historyofdistric00sull

[5] Eckstorm F. H. (1941, November). Place-names for the Penobscot Valley and the Maine Coast. *The University of Maine Bulletin, 44*(4), 159. Reprinted by the University of Maine in 1960.

[6] Ethnohistory combines the findings and theories of ethnology (cultural anthropology) with the methods of historiography (history writing), thereby mitigating the bias of the limited written records about the peoples *without history.* An analogy I like is that *ethnohistory* snowshoes beyond the end of the snowplowed pavement called *history, t*o quote Axtell, J. (1979, Winter). Ethnohistory: An historian's viewpoint. *Ethnohistory, 26(1), 4.* https://blogs.stockton.edu/hist4690/files/2012/06/James-Axtell-Ethnohistory-A-Historians-Viewpoint.pdf

> Practitioners have discovered the utility of maps, music, paintings, photography, folklore, oral tradition, ecology, site exploration, archaeological artifacts (especially trade goods), museum collections, enduring customs, language, and place-

names . . . They can bring to bear "special knowledge of the group, linguistic insights, and the understanding of cultural phenomena," which allow them to utilize the data more fully than the average historian (Lurie, N. O. [1961]. Ethnohistory: An ethnological point of view. *Ethnohistory 8*, 83.)

[7] Document 25 (1614). In Quinn, D. B., & Quinn, A. M. (Eds.). (1983). *The English New England voyages 1602-1608* (2nd series, No. 161). London: The Hakluyt Society; Document 50: The countrey of Mawooshen, discovered by the English in the yeere 1602. (1625). In Quinn, & Quinn, *New England voyages.* Although the full "Mawooshen Description" is in several modern publications, Quinn & Quinn is my favorite venue, because it appears in such detailed context with so very many other relevant contemporary documents. However, I must give warning: Although the Quinns are high among the foremost *historical* scholars of the Age of Discovery, when it comes to the *ethnohistory* of the Wabanaki peoples, they erred grievously in following the lead of Sturtevant & Trigger wherein the entire 1500s-1600s past of the Western Etchemins is wrongly added to the 1700s-present period of the Eastern Abenakis. See Sturtevant, W. C. & Trigger, B. T. (Eds.). (1978). *Handbook of North American Indians, Vol. 15: Northeast.* Washington, DC: Smithsonian Institution. Therefore, in their "Notes" about the documents of the 1500s-1600s, every time the Quinns say "Eastern Abenakis," they should have said "Western Etchemins." This means that most of Captain Waymouth's five Wabanaki captives from Muscongus Bay, and certainly paramount-sakamo Bashaba on the Penobscot River (who headed the Mawooshen confederacy), were really Western Etchemins. Relocations following Native trade wars, European-disease epidemics, English pushing, and French pulling, led the Etchemins to move eastward out of the area, into which came eastward the equally disrupted Abenaki

[8] Purchas, S. (1906). The description of the countrey of Mawooshen, Discovered by the English in the yeere 1602. In H*akluytus posthumus, Or, Purchas his pilgrimes: Contayning a history of the world in sea voyages and lande travels by Englishmen and others* (vol. 19 of 20). Glasgow: James MacLehose and Sons, 400-405.

[9] Hakluyt, R. (1599). *The principal navigations, voyages, traffiqves, and discoveries of the English nation...* London: G. Bishop, R. Newberie, and R. Baker. https://archive.org/details/principalnavigat1and2hakl/page/n7

[10] Purchas, *Purchas, his pilgrimes.*

[11] Purchas, Mawooshen description, 404-405.

[12] de Champlain, S. (1922). *Works* (Vol. 1 of 6: 1567-1635). H. P. Biggar (Ed.). Toronto: Champlain Society, 321. The University of Toronto Press published a reprint in 1971.

[13] Ibid., 327.

[14] Ibid., 329.

[15] Levett, C. (1624). *A voyage into New England, begun in 1623 and ended in 1624.* London: William Jones, 43. https://quod.lib.umich.edu/e/eebo2/A72554.0001.001?view=toc

[16] Smith, J. (1616). *The description of New England.* London: Humfrey Lownes. http://digitalcommons.unl.edu/cgi/viewcontent.cgi?article=1002&context=zeaamericanstudies

[17] Eckstorm, Place-names, 168-169.

[18] Levett, *A voyage*, 43.

[19] Forbes, C. S. (1894, January). The story of the Presumpscot. *Collections and Proceedings of the Maine Historical Society* (Quarterly, Pt. 1). Portland, ME: Brown Thurston Company, 361-386.

[20] Ibid., 371. Emphasis added.

[21] Kendall, *Glaciers & granite*, 93.

[22] Forbes, The story of the Presumpscot, 364.

[23] Ibid., 365.

[24] Odanak was/is the village/community of the "St. Francis Abenaki" famous for outliving Rogers' Rangers' Raid there on 4 October 1759. It is located in southern Quebec Province, Canada, near the mouth of the Saint François River, which flows northwest from Sherbrooke city, through Drummondville city, to Pierreville community, where it joins Lake St. Peter (*Lac St. Pierre*), which is a very large bulge in the big St. Lawrence River. (From the flat Vermont border 75 miles due north.)

Arsikontegok was the Native name of both river and village, a place-name derived from geographical characteristics, not from any name of the founders, as some have claimed. In some English treaties, Arosaguntacooks appear as delegates from St. Francis/Odanak.

Odanak became both an important French religious-political mission station and the rendezvous point for French and Indian raids on the English frontier settlements. Indian refugees moved to Odanak after suffering English attacks, famines, and diseases. Many refugees were temporary, however, and returned home whenever possible, at least seasonally—confusing English confiscation of "abandoned" lands.

Odanak's two major resident peoples were the Sokoki/Sokwaki/Squakeheag from the middle Connecticut River in northernmost Massachusetts, and the Abenaki from all across northern New England (ME, NH, VT). The Abenaki gave the name to the heteroband of "St. Francis Abenaki," and the language was of combined dialects. See Day, G. M. (1998). *In search of New England's native past: Selected essays by Gordon M. Day*, M. K. Foster & W. Cowan (Eds). Amherst: University of Massachusetts Press.

[25] Eckstorm, Place-names, 161.

[26] Trelawny, R. (1884). Trelawny papers. In *Collections of the Maine Historical Society* (2nd Series): *Documentary history of the State of Maine* (Vol. 3). J. P. Bater (Ed.). Portland, ME: Hoyt, Fogg, and Donham, 461.

[27] Willis, W. (1865). The history of Portland from its first settlement (Part 1). In *Collections of the Maine Historical Society* (Vol. 1). Portland, ME: Bailey & Noyes, 118. https://archive.org/details/historyofportlan1865will/page/n7

[28] According to William Willis, a year later (1658), when Massachusetts took over government of southern Maine, there were other "transfers" of land, and he specifically names them: "On the east side of Presumpscot River" four persons' families; and "On the west side of that river" three persons' families (Willis, History of Portland, 98). Willis did not include Francis Small's name in the list, because he was counting only settlers at the mouth of the river who had received their lands from English grantholders who had previously received *their* lands "directly" from the English Crown (Christian to Christian), with no consideration whatever about (Pagan) Indian possession as a potential issue. King's grants were the first and only "legality" early-on. This ethnocentric, racist, et cetera thinking was simply in-sync with the earliest Western European mindset at the dawn of the Age of Discovery—

namely, that God granted all lands to the Pope to distribute to Christian monarchs. The Papal Line of Demarcation (1493-1494) divided the entire nonChristian world between Spanish and Portuguese spheres of influence. Balboa's 1513 "discovery" (and claim for Spain) of the Pacific Ocean was the first proof of a "New World" between the western and eastern sides of the then-known Eurasian landmass (thereafter called the "Old World"). The existence of Native peoples in this New World (not being mentioned in *Genesis* and called "Indians" when Columbus thought in 1492 that he had landed off the coast of India) caused a theological and practical crisis that took time to ponder. Finally, a Papal Bull of 1537 pronounced the decision that Indians were "truly human." (Protestants had to make up their own minds.).

[29] Davis, S. (1825). Declaration of Sylvan Davis inhabitant of the town of Falmouth, in the Province of Maine, in New England, concerning the cruel, treacherous and barbarous management of a war against the English in the eastern parts of New England by the cruel Indians . . . *Massachusetts Historical Society Collection* 3rd ser., 101-112.

[30] Rowlandson, M. (1682). *A true history of the captivity and restoration of Mrs. Mary Rowlandson* (4th ed.). London: Joseph Poole. "The preface is thought to have been written by Increase Mather," n.1. https://www.csus.edu/Hum/Program%20Syllabi/Fall%202011%20Syllabi/Rowland son.pdf

[31] Swarton, H. (1981) A narrative of Hannah Swarton containing wonderful passages relating to her captivity and deliverance (as related by Cotton Mathers), in *Puritans among the Indians: Accounts of captivity and redemption, 1676-1724*. A. T. Vaughan & E. W. Clark (Eds.). Cambridge, MA: Belnap Press.

[32] Massachusetts Sabbath School Society (1837). *Hannah Swanton, the Casco Captive: or, the Catholic Religion in Canada, and its Influence on the Indians in Maine*. (1837). Boston: Author. https://archive.org/details/cihm_45552

[33] Willis, *The history of Portland*, 449.

[34] Official records about Polin seem limited to three named and one unnamed primary-source accounts in the Maine Historical Society's publications of archival manuscripts. Listed by date they are:

1736: *Maine Historical Society documentary history Baxter manuscripts, 11* (1908),172-173.

1739: *Maine Historical Society documentary history Baxter manuscripts 23* (1916), 257-262.

1749: *Maine Historical Society collections 4*, 145-167, especially 147.

1754: *Maine Historical Society documentary history Baxter manuscripts 24* (1916), 17.

[35] How can Pooran be the same person as Polin? Simply because some Algonquian-language families have different dialects; thus, a speaker of an "R" dialect would pronounce this chief's name differently than a speaker of an "L" dialect, and an English translator or secretary would write it down differently. Given that this statement was *about* Polin, not *by* him, that scenario seems like the simplest explanation of the difference.

[36] Grehe, D. L., & Morrison, A. H. (1996). Sanctions for slaughter: Peacetime violence on the Maine frontier 1749-1772. *Papers of the twenty-seventh Algonquin conference*. D. H. Pentland, (Ed.). University of Manitoba, Winnipeg, 105-116.

[37] Maine Historical Society (1754). *Baxter manuscripts*, 17.

[38] Smith, T. (1949 [1849]). *Journals of Rev. Thomas Smith & Rev. Samuel Deane*. W. Willis (Ed.). Portland, ME: Joseph S. Bailey. https://archive.org/details/journalsofrevtho00lcsmit/page/n8

[39] Ibid., 165.

[40] Ibid., 165-166.

[41] The *Last* Freedom Fighter? On the Presumpscot, yes. Among the Wabanakis, no. Although some Wabanakis joined the American Colonial forces to fight the British in the American Revolution (War #7), others stayed neutral, and a few even joined the British cause, if only for revenge against past American Colonists' taking away their homeland or hunting-fishing livelihoods. Bethel, Maine (then still called Sudbury, Canada) was raided, with a few Colonists killed or captured. In the War of 1812 (War #8) people properly feared that the same grudges might erupt again, but they seem not to have done so.

[42] Whittier, J. G. (1841). Funeral Tree of the Sokokis. In *The writings of John Greenleaf Whittier* (Vol. 1). J. G. Whittier (Ed.). New York: Houghton Mifflin. http://www.perseus.tufts.edu/hopper/text?doc=Perseus%3Atext% 3A2001.05.0312%3Achapter%3D3%3Asection%3Dc.3.7

[43] Pitt, W. (1777, November 18). *Quotegeek.* http://quotegeek.com/personalities/william-pitt-1st-earl-of-chat/6718/

[44] McLellan, H. D. (1903). *The history of Gorham, Maine.* Portland, ME: Smith & Sale Printers. Reprinted in 1992 in Camden, ME: Picton Press.

[45] Ibid.

[46] Ibid., 65. See also 62-64, 658-660.

Quakers Along the Presumpscot

Introduction

For thousands of years, the Wabanaki people thrived among the abundant resources of the Presumpscot River and its valley. They harvested fish from the river; captured birds and mammals from its fields; and cultivated crops, notably corn, on its banks. The fertile floodplains along the ancient river proved ideal for corn growth, and the abundant spring migrations of fish provided plentiful and easily obtained fertilizer.

After the conclusion of the early Indian wars, white settlers soon discovered the ready natural wealth offered by the river and its surrounds. From Lower Falls to Ammoncongin, Quaker families proliferated to become arguably the dominant English culture prior to the American Revolution. They were millwrights; land speculators; yeoman farmers; and, eventually, industrialists who created and expanded the growing and canning of corn into a nationwide industry from their small farms along the Presumpscot shore.

This is the story of how James Winslow made his way from Pilgrim, Massachusetts to the Presumpscot and employed the Quaker values of family loyalty, community networking, and honest industriousness to build a foundation that ultimately produced a new worldwide industry based on Presumpscot corn.

James Winslow in Massachusetts

Born in 1687, James Winslow was of high Pilgrim pedigree. Edward Winslow, one of the first signers of the Mayflower Compact and later Governor of Plymouth Colony, was his grandfather's brother. Like many of his generation, James' father Job migrated from greater Plymouth to settle new lands. This general urge stemmed, in part, from a desire to escape the stern judgment and harsh rules of the colony. He moved southeastward to a place that, although still part of Plymouth Colony, was closer to Roger Williams's more liberal Providence than to Plymouth.

Job Winslow built his home at Swansea, Massachusetts, in about 1666. He and his family soon understood that establishing themselves on the Massachusetts frontier exposed them to real danger. In June of 1675, the Indian leader Metacom, known by the English as "King Philip," launched a united assault on colonial towns throughout the region, beginning with Swansea. The home of Job Winslow and his wife Ruth was one of the first two burned in the horrific King Philip's War, which spread throughout New England for three years.[1] They survived and, a few years later, moved with their family to their final destination, the adjoining settlement of Freetown. Job became a selectman and a deputy to the General Court of Plymouth Colony and was Town Clerk.[2] He was a man of the established Puritan order who was active in starting a proper Congregationalist Church in Freetown—and decidedly not a Quaker.

In 1658, the General Court of Plymouth Colony required an oath of fidelity from all Colony citizens and defined certain classes of men who should not be admitted freemen. Among these were Quakers.[3] In 1660, Quaker Mary Dyer and three others were hanged on the Common for returning to Boston after their banishment. Whippings, fines, disfranchisement, and imprisonment continued for many years as punishments for Quakers and others who refused to pay tax for the support of an officially approved minister or to perform military service.[4]

James, Job Winslow's sixth son and eighth child, was born in Freetown and would become Old Falmouth's first Quaker. Quakerism was a powerful force in Freetown, perhaps from its founding, and Quakers formed a majority of its population by the early 1700s.[5] For 75 years after James' birth, Quakers were numerically the largest worshiping congregation in town, "embracing the men of first minds, most money, and best manners."[6] But nothing indicates that James joined the Quakers while still in Massachusetts.

Like his father and so many of his relations, James was an adventurer at heart, so he embarked for Maine (then still part of Massachusetts). Shortly after this move, various deeds list him as a "cordwainer," or "heelmaker." Given that he appears to have lived all his years until then in Freetown, we must assume that he learned and practiced the shoemaker's trade there.

James Winslow to Maine and Blackstrap

During Colonial times, the Massachusetts township that encompassed all of what is now Portland, South Portland, Cape Elizabeth, Westbrook, and

Falmouth was once "Falmouth on Casco Bay," to distinguish it from the Cape Cod town of the same name. The earliest settlers, mostly Englishmen from Massachusetts, had suffered mightily while trying to maintain a foothold, abandoning Old Falmouth when the French and Indians destroyed the township in 1690.

One of James' first cousins, known as "Doctor" Nathaniel Winslow (he may have been a veterinarian), arrived in Falmouth around 1717, as the township was under resettlement. He there served on the committee to lay out lots on Falmouth Neck, now the Portland peninsula.[7] The two cousins resided in Freetown from 1701 to 1705, when James was a teenager and Nathaniel was in his early twenties.[8] Nathaniel likely had a positive influence on James' decision to remove to Maine.

In 1728, the influx of new settlers began in earnest and included James Winslow, 41 years of age, along with his wife and seven children, ages one to nineteen. Immigrants settled mostly on the Neck and the north side of what is still Back Cove. The town was offering lots in the common (unimproved) lands within the eight-mile square that then comprised Falmouth. Upon payment of ten pounds, James received 104 acres, the standard for new settlers. Later that year, for reasons unknown, Nathaniel gifted to his cousin all his holdings in Falmouth, presumably at least another 104 acres.[9] James was now a land-wealthy man in a burgeoning new town.

Before 1728 ended, James "had a grant of land on Fall-cove brook, at Back Cove, to erect a mill on. . . ."[10] The privilege at Fall Brook for a corn mill was voted to him in 1729."[11] He didn't waste time: by the end of that year, he was living near his mill site, probably on what is now Ocean Avenue, adjacent to Fall Brook. His was one of just a few grist mills in or around Falmouth.

James became active in Falmouth town affairs. In 1730, the Proprietors of the Common and Undivided Lands of the Township of Falmouth selected him as one of their agents in defending a case pending at County Court.[12] The decision to select James the heelmaker to serve as their "defense attorney" demonstrates the standing of high respect they accorded him just two years after he arrived in his new community. This esteem was probably due in part to the fact that James sprang from the respected family of Edward Winslow and his son Josiah, two of Plymouth Colony's governors. Also, his cousin Nathaniel had risen to prominence in the town many years before.

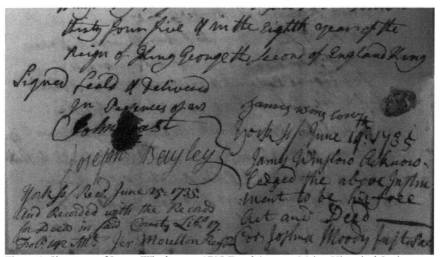

Figure 1: Signature of James Winslow on 1735 Deed (source: Maine Historical Society Collection 175, Book #T1, *Willis Papers*. p. 221)

In 1731 and 1732, James served on the Proprietors Committee (committee for laying out lands) in Falmouth. In this capacity, he would have had knowledge of the choicest land still available and an insider's opportunity to select the finest for his sons and others he knew. But some of these new land claims trespassed on earlier, seventeenth-century grants to old proprietors. An edict required that lands granted to the new proprietors be returned to their prior owners. Ironically, James Winslow signed as a witness to this document.[13] As a result, the edict forced James to abandon his mill (and, presumably, his home) at Back Cove sometime after 1732, the year of the eviction notice. Eminent Portland historian William Willis relates that, after leaving his grist mill privilege behind, James Winslow "removed . . . northerly to the Presumpscot River, near where its course is turned southerly by Blackstrap Hill."[14]

We have good reasons (see below) to conclude that James's home existed on the northeasterly side of the present-day Blackstrap Road in Falmouth, touching the southeasterly bank of the Presumpscot. He and his wife would there raise four boys and three girls. By this time, James owned at least 200 acres of land in the greater Town of Falmouth, most of it abutting the shores of the Presumpscot River.

Quakerism Ignited

Willis writes that James Winslow "was the first person who joined the Quakers in this town and carried all his family with him."[15] This conversion must have been no later than 1740, when the town's Congregationalist minister, Thomas Smith, organized a period of prayer and fasting "on account of the spread of Quakerism."[16] In July of 1742, Reverend Smith commented in his journal on the "many strange Quakers in town."[17] In 1743, the English Quaker minister Edmund Peckover visited Falmouth, where "a few Friends are settled."[18] One of those Friends was undoubtedly James Winslow.

When the first recorded Quaker meetings began in 1751, the eight participants in the Men's Monthly Meeting included James Winslow, his son Benjamin, and four men from Harpswell. Meetings alternated monthly among participants' homes in these distant towns. The challenge of doing so must have been extreme. These men, and those who joined them, demonstrated their passionate desire to grow a larger community of Friends from the few seeds they represented.

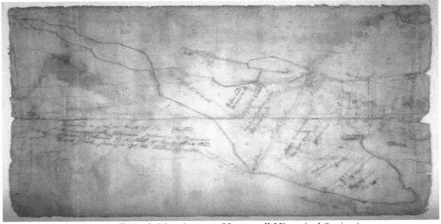

Figure 2: Early Harpswell Neck Map (source: Harpswell Historical Society)

At a 1752 Men's Monthly Meeting in Falmouth, James Winslow granted the Society of Friends a one-acre parcel of land near his home at Blackstrap on which they would build their first meetinghouse and establish their burying ground. No deed has yet appeared for this transaction, which may have been simply a "Friends agreement."

The final mention of James in the monthly meeting records is dated 1754, when he was 67 years old. Because he had earlier requested and received a "certificate to travel . . . westerly," it may be that he took his leave and headed away on a mission with his second wife Ruth to spread the Quaker "word."[19]

More on the Quakers at Blackstrap

Winslow's Quaker group erected the first meetinghouse in early Falmouth, probably the first in Maine, sometime around 1752 on the acre granted by James Winslow alongside the river, where they also established a burying ground. As of this writing, 53 low, unmarked fieldstone markers are visible on the site. Such markers were common in eighteenth-century Quaker communities, where modesty and equality were well-accepted values. In the same year, the town surveyed the road to James Winslow's. It later became known as Quaker Lane.

Figure 3: Quaker Cemetery Sign (source: Author)

In February 1768, the growing Quaker community, which included some of James' children, agreed to build a new meetinghouse with dimensions of 40 x 32 feet, "w[ith] one Teer of gallery [tier, or balcony] by subscription."[20] Twenty-six subscribers pledged 136 British pounds toward its construction. No images of this meetinghouse are available, but we may deduce clues to its appearance by examining another Quaker meetinghouse built in Dover, New Hampshire in 1768, which stands to this day. It is a two-story building of the same approximate dimensions, built by a community with connections to the Falmouth Friends.

Figure 4: Dover NH Meetinghouse (source: Silas Weeks, 2001, *New England Quaker Meetinghouses Past and Present*)

In 1771, the Court of General Sessions of the Peace, meeting in Falmouth, ordered a road survey to "bound out a Highway or Road from Falmouth to Bakerstown [now Poland] . . . in the most convenient and proper place for the benefit of the King's subjects according to the rules and directions of the law of this Province."[21] The Town Record shows that "Benjamin Winslow [son of James] . . . was much interested in said road."[22] Because it passed directly alongside Benjamin's home at Blackstrap, near the river, the improvement would undoubtedly enhance his travels into Falmouth.

The survey formalized a system of existing roads that now encompasses Allen Avenue easterly from Morrill's Corner to Allen's Corner, Washington Avenue Extension northerly, and Blackstrap Road to the Presumpscot River. Here, for the first time in the historical record, we see the name "Quaker Lane."[23] Several houses appear as landmarks on the survey, including those of Quakers Benjamin Winslow, Elijah Pope, and John Morrell.

In 2016, the owner of the house at 17 Blackstrap Road reported to this writer his belief that Benjamin's house lay directly across the street from his own, and that at least a portion of that house was moved across the street (probably in the mid-1800s) to become an attached barn. Portions of the barn interior, he said, are plastered. He heard that the Winslow building was a tavern. That claim, however, lacks corroboration.

James Winslow's will was proved (accepted as a valid legal document in a court of law) in 1773, the year he died.[24] Presumably, his remains lie with those of his family in the burying ground at Blackstrap, beneath the acre he deeded to the Society of Friends.

Previous to 1774, the Falmouth Quakers had to pay taxes for the support of the (Congregationalist) ministry. But, as historian Willis notes, ". . . at the town's annual meeting in that year, perceiving the injustice of compelling persons to contribute to the support of a mode of worship from which they derived no benefit and of which their consciences did not approve,"[25] citizens at the town meeting voted to exempt certain named individual Quakers, including eight Winslow men and several of their in-laws, from paying parish taxes in that year.

By a selectmen's count in 1777, 64 male Quakers over 16 years of age resided in Falmouth.[26] Projecting this number to include women and children, we can reasonably estimate that the town included 300 or more Quakers in total. Likely, most were still living near the Presumpscot River, as well as northerly on both sides of today's Blackstrap Road to Duck Pond (now Highland Lake). At least nine of these fine colonial homes still stand.

With the establishment of the Portland Friends Meeting in 1794 and changing demographics, the population of Friends at the Falmouth meeting dropped off. On March 24, 1842, the first of several discussions appear in monthly meeting records of the "dilapitated [sic] state of the meeting house and sheds."[27] Also, the burying ground was nearly at full capacity.

Years passed. On June 5, 1845, in the last meeting held at the old meetinghouse, a committee from the quarterly meeting recommended that "the proper place for the . . . Meeting house of Friends . . . is the county road leading from Pride's Bridge (so called) to Portland."[28] This spot, at what is now 1837 Forest Avenue, is the site of today's Portland meeting.

The one-acre Blackstrap lot that James Winslow had donated nearly a hundred years earlier sold for $2,300 and became "a place for the manufacture of gravestones and monuments."[29] Beams transported from the dismantled Blackstrap meetinghouse formed the structure of today's Riverton meetinghouse. Some of those beams, overloaded for years by attic storage, sagged and caused a ceiling collapse in the 1990s, necessitating replacement with a truss-roof system.[30]

Figure 5: Current Portland Friends Meetinghouse (source: Author)

Lambert's Tavern and Bridge

In 1790, a young, single Josiah Dow moved into a farmhouse "just beyond the covered bridge" on Quaker Lane and began to learn the tanner's trade while teaching in the winter.[31] His future son Neal Dow would become the mayor of Portland, a Civil War general, and the "Father of Prohibition" in the United States. In his 1898 *Reminiscences*, Neal Dow wrote:

> A few rods south, on the Portland side of the river, in full view of the home my father had chosen, stood at that time a Friends' meeting-house. Long ago it was taken down, but it survived until my day, and there, in my boyhood, I frequently attended with my parents the Friends' Quarterly Meetings.[32]

Although Josiah Dow spent only five or six years at the farm, he found a bride among the thriving Quaker community that surrounded him. Less than a mile to the west of where he resided, in a large house fully visible to him across the Presumpscot valley (the view to this house at 321 Falmouth Road, still standing, is now blocked by trees and the Hannaford Supermarket), lived the well-to-do Quaker Isaac Allen and his daughter Dorcas. Josiah and Dorcas married in 1796 at the Falmouth Quaker meetinghouse.

After Josiah moved with his wife to Portland, Zaccheus Lambert came to Falmouth from Bath and bought the farmstead where he had lived.

Lambert's Tavern, although located in the Falmouth Quaker heartland, was popular for thirty years among the hearty denizens of Portland and drovers on the Old County Road.[33]

> Said to be of poor appearance even when it was new . . . it had a room for locals and travelers and several rooms for overnight stage riders and the overflow from nearby taverns. It was well known for an unusual drink served in a tin cup that contained rum and a generous dollop of Blackstrap molasses and, for some, an added dollop of cream. Imbibers joked that no one knew whether the drink was named for Blackstrap Hill or the hill was named for the drink.[34]

Figure 6: Lambert's Tavern (source: Falmouth Historical Society)

Figure 7: Sketch of Lambert's Tavern (source: Falmouth Historical Society)

Figure 8: Lambert's Tavern Signature (source: Stagecoach/Tavern book at Falmouth Historical Society)

On 5 September 1813, the USS *Enterprise* sighted the HMS *Boxer* off Pemaquid Point and closed on the enemy brig. In a brief but fiery encounter recalled in Longfellow's poem *My Lost Youth*, British Commander Samuel Blyth and Lt. Burrows, Commander of the *Enterprise,* died within moments of each other. Their remains were interred with military honors in Portland's Eastern Cemetery. A court martial later determined that a number of British seamen had deserted their quarters during the action.[35]

In a newspaper article published just as the old Lambert's Tavern was about to be demolished, the grandson of tavern-owner Zaccheus Lambert recounted what he called the great event in the old tavern's history, and the one for which her name will be remembered. The sailors of the British warship Boxer, and the American warship Enterprise came out to the tavern the day after the fight off the harbor . . . and had their great carousal. American and English were all the same [that day]. It is doubtful if an Englishman could have told his own countryman from that of the enemy, the American, whom he had just been fighting. It was a historic day for the old inn, as well as for the residents of Portland.[36]

And this just across the road from the Quakers' sacred meetinghouse!

Zaccheus Lambert gave up the tavern business in the 1830s.[37] The farm buildings, which were torn down around 1901, were on what is now the site of a Central Maine Power Co. substation.[38]

Although the 1752 town survey shows the road later called Quaker Lane ending at the river, an ancient road or path probably continued across the river to what are now Gray and Poland.[39] People have mentioned a log bridge at the river crossing, as well as Indian massacres, but the first official confirmation of a bridge there is from the 1771 town survey, which shows "Winslow's Bridge."[40] A new bridge replaced that one in 1787, when the town reimbursed Benjamin, son of James Winslow, 180 pounds for its construction.[41] It later became Lambert's Bridge after the nearby tavern.

Figure 9: Lambert's Bridge (source: Falmouth Historical Society)

This bridge had an unusually long lifespan. When a covered bridge on this site burned down around 1910, a Portland newspaper made it front-page news with the headline "Famous Old Lambert Hill Bridge Burns. . . . [It] Marked Historic Spot of Indian Massacre." It called the bridge "the oldest bridge probably in the county and the second oldest in the state."[42] It had withstood the flood of 1896, which had wiped out many on the river, including at the Auburn Street crossing.[43] A concrete bridge replaced it after the fire.

The Winslows of Westbrook

In 1732, Dr. Nathaniel Winslow gifted land along the southeast shore of the Presumpscot at Ammoncongin Falls (now Cumberland Mills) to his cousin James, shortly before moving to Damariscotta. An 1836 survey suggests that Nathan Winslow (probably the great-grandson of James) inherited land at this spot, where he planned to build a complex of five saw and grist mills; nine boarding houses; a power canal; and three streets: Canal, Middle, and Winslow. The proposed development would have covered about 21 acres and stretched more than a quarter-mile downstream from the bridge that today carries Cumberland Street.[44] This plan never materialized.[45]

The first papermill at Ammoncongin was built on the northeast side of the river by Day and Lyon around 1845. Nine years later, S. D. Warren and a partner bought the mill. The business thrived, and, in 1860, Warren bought the Winslow heirs' land, which stretched from the present Warren Avenue to the river.[46]

Figure 10: Old Winslow-Boody House, c. 1900 (source: Michael Sanphy, *Westbrook Then and Now*)

Nathan Winslow was born on the family farm at 473 East Bridge Street, reputed to be the oldest house now standing in Westbrook. Ernest Rowe and another local author, John R. Lewis, opine that the original house on this property was built beside the Presumpscot River by James Winslow in 1728 and moved up in 1748 and attached to the rear of the later structure.[47] However, no one has located reliable corroborating evidence of an older house, so this account may be merely a local legend. At any rate, at least four generations of Winslows and their relations lived in this house until selling it in 1909.

Figure 11: Current Winslow-Boody House (source: Author)

From a historical standpoint, the home is not pristine, although two of the front windows still include operable in-wall pocket sliding wood shutters, and the old walk-in cooking fireplace still has its built-in brick oven. The house has several other fireplaces, probably original, surrounded by impressive vintage wood paneling. A finely crafted built-in corner cabinet in a front parlor is probably from the earliest period. Many interior doors and their hardware appear original, and ceiling beams are exposed in some rooms. Rowe relates:

> The first school in Westbrook was held in the . . .Winslow house . . . starting in 1794. . . . Off the kitchen there is a room with deep windows and a great fireplace where Quaker meetings were held. . . . The first school of which we have records was held in [this] room and its teacher, Robert Blair, also acted as a Quaker minister.[48]

Although they conducted it as a Quaker school, Blair and the Winslows welcomed any and all pupils from Saccarappa, Congin, and Rocky Hill, the principal villages nearby. When North School, Westbrook's first public school, opened around 1811, at the present corner of Bridge and Cumberland Streets, all students from the Winslow house school transferred there.[49]

When Jane Winslow, great-granddaughter of James, married Benjamin Boody in 1807, the house and its outbuildings became known as the Winslow/Boody Farm. An article from 1896, after their son Charles' death, states, "The Boody Farm contains two hundred acres of valuable and well-located land, including tillage, pasture, and woodland; and the late owner [Charles] improved the property to a considerable extent. . . . He was a citizen of the highest repute."[50] In 1909, someone outside the family purchased the Winslow homestead for the first time since its construction.

In 1937, Clara Newhall Fogg wrote charmingly of her visit to the farm. At that time, the house sat on 125 acres of fertile farmland. She wrote that from the entrance porch near the well sweep, she could see "the winding Presumpscot and sweeping stretches of woodland,"[51] which the owners later subdivided for new homesites in the 1960s.

The present owners know an odd outbuilding that stands on the property as "the canning shed." Although the Winslows were involved in developing the corn-canning industry in the United States, actual links to this building's involvement in that history remain obscure.

In 1868, a huge landslide occurred on a steep bank of the Presumpscot behind the property, causing its name: the "Boody Slide." In the course of a few hours, approximately 30 acres of level forestland and 800,000 cubic yards of soil tumbled into the river, changing the course of its channel. At the Warren mill, the water below the dam rose three feet, as the ground trembled. Workers who feared that a tidal wave had swept upstream tasted the water for salt. Detecting none, they headed downriver, where they found large fissures in the riverbank soil that were continuing to widen. The rising water stopped just below the grates in the mill boilers, but the height of it caused the mill to stop operation until the river cut itself a new channel, allowing the water level to normalize.[52]

James Winslow's Legacy
James and Elizabeth Winslow had four sons, all born in Freetown, Massachusetts. In 1739, after eleven years in Maine, the land-rich James gifted each of his three adult sons 30 acres at different locations along the Presumpscot River.[53] One of them, second son Job, died at age 25 of unknown causes, leaving a wife, three young daughters, and an impressive property inventory for someone of his age.

Also in 1739, James' first son Nathan helped Joseph Conant build the first house in what is now Westbrook, northeast of Saccarappa Falls.[54] Later, Nathan, perhaps working with his sixty-one-year-old father, built "the family manse," at 473 East Bridge Street, where he probably lived out his life.

Third son Benjamin was early at Blackstrap, where he likely lived across Quaker Lane from his father. He had extensive land holdings and, in 1762, obtained from Samuel and Francis Waldo the rights to a mill at Presumpscot Lower Falls. According to the deed, it contained "a one-quarter share of a saw [mill right] in Presumpscot Mills called the middle saw."[55]

Figure 12: Presumpscot Lower Falls (source: Falmouth Historical Society)

In 1752, youngest son, also James, ventured with his wife to Broad Bay (now Waldoboro), where their first child was born. Indian troubles drove him back to Falmouth; there he honed wheelwright skills. In 1760, Silvester Gardiner hired him to help build dams on Cobbosseecontee Stream. He never returned to live in Falmouth.[56]

Samuel, son of Benjamin, probably inherited his father's mill rights. He owned a 200-acre parcel and built a large house in 1762 that still stands at the top of Summit Street Hill, Portland's highest elevation. With the land newly cleared, its windows would have commanded a panoramic view of the curving Presumpscot River from Quaker Lane perhaps all the way downstream to Lower Falls.

According to historian Willis, Nathan's son, also Nathan, was a "large land speculator."[57] He was also the last Clerk of the Falmouth Proprietors, formed in 1732 to grant parcels in the common lands of what had been

Old Falmouth. One can only imagine the competitive advantage that Nathan and the family gained by having him so positioned within the Proprietorship.

The family continued to prosper. Its involvement in the early development of food canning is well documented. When Captain Richard Bagnall returned to Plymouth in 1779 from Major General John Sullivan's expedition against the Six Nations, he brought several ears of Indian corn from the upper Susquehanna River country. The Susquehanna corn, so much sweeter and more succulent than plain Indian corn, spread rapidly among the northern seaboard settlements. Maine, blessed with a short but warm growing season and nutritious soil properties, produced exceptionally good sweet corn for commercial canning.[58]

Isaac Winslow, great-grandson of James, obtained food-canning patents in France (to remedy the sailors' ailment scurvy), retired from whaling, and returned to the family home in Westbrook. In 1839, he first began experimenting "on the family farm" with canning corn, some of which came from his brother-in-law Caleb Jones, a Quaker who owned extensive farmlands along what is now Riverside Street in Portland. Isaac filed for a canning patent in 1852 and invented a corn knife in 1853. Winslow Packing Co. received large Civil War contracts with Union Army. When he died in 1862, his canning business went to his nephew John Winslow Jones, son of Caleb.[59]

"King" John's company, "Winslow's World Renowned Green Corn," built the largest food-canning factory in the world in 1870, near the present Forest Avenue bridge over the Presumpscot. It was 235 feet long and 3.5 stories high and processed meat, corn, and other vegetables. During this era of business prosperity, Jones gave the name "Riverton" to the vicinity.[60]

This huge factory burned to the ground five years later, and the Riverton Trolley Park and casino emerged years later on the same land. After his business failed, other Maine companies like Burnham & Morrill used many of John W. Jones' techniques to grow to prominence.[61]

Isaac's brother Nathan had a store at Federal and Middle Streets in Portland. He also had a stove foundry in Portland and, in 1820, an early patent for a cooking woodstove in the US. By the 1840s, he had a tinsmithery-stove shop on Front Street (later Commercial St.) in Portland, where he hand-made corn cans for brother Isaac.[62] Nathan and Isaac benefited greatly from the support of family and successful members of the greater Quaker community.[63]

Figure 13: John Winslow Jones (source: Maine Historical Society, *Maine Memory Network* Item 16951)

Figure 14: Canning Factory (source: Maine Historical Society, *Maine Memory Network* Item 16948)

These innovative Winslow brothers were generous contributors to the abolitionist cause. In 1832, William Lloyd Garrison, editor of the abolition-ist newspaper *The Liberator* spoke in Portland. He continued the evening with other guests at Nathan Winslow's home and later described his host as "one of the most thoroughgoing friends of the abolition cause in our land" and "one of the object[s] of marked attentions from the colored citizens." Nathan had subscribed to the *Liberator* from its first number and took it to the day of his death in 1861, more than once preventing its suspension by his liberal assistance.[64]

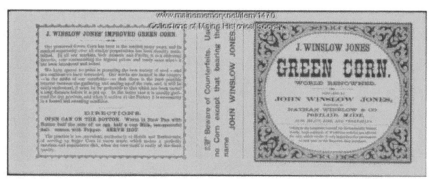

Figure 15: John Winslow Jones' Canned Corn Label (source: Maine Historical Society, *Maine Memory Network* Item 1470)

Figure 16: John Winslow Jones' tools, used to prepare corn for canning, likely at Westbrook, c. 1858 (source: Maine Historical Society, *Maine Memory Network* Item 6959)

In 1865, Portland historian William Willis wrote:

The Society [of Friends] has not increased in size here of late years and may be considered declining, the vacant places occasioned by death not being supplied by accessions of new members. The number of adult members in 1864 did not exceed nineteen. . . . The number that usually attend meeting does not exceed twelve, more often less. They pursue the still and quiet way which their religion

93

dictates and their conduct appears to be influenced by the pure principles of that religion which suffers long and is kind. If the society does not increase in numbers it may with truth be said of it that it does not degenerate in its character.[65]

After struggling with low numbers over many subsequent decades, the Portland Friends began to rebuild their number in the late-twentieth century and are now a thriving community. Now happily ensconced in their century-plus meeting house on outer Forest Avenue, the society comprises over one hundred members, with every meeting drawing scores of worshipers. Quaker meetings now exist in twenty Maine locations. The spread of Quakerism throughout Maine can be traced directly back to its founding family, the Winslows of Quaker Lane on the Presumpscot.

---

[1] Savage, J. (1862). *A genealogical dictionary of the first settlers of New England.* (Vol. 4). Boston: Little, Brown and Company, 600-601.

[2] Holton, D. P. (1877). *Winslow memorial.* (Vol. 1). New York: Author, 80.

[3] Usher, R. G. (1918). *The Pilgrims and their history.* New York: The McMillan Company, 262.

[4] Lowry, A. G. (1940, August 14). *Quakers and their meeting house at Apponegansett.* Paper presented at a meeting of the Old Dartmouth Historical Society, New Bedford, MA, 5.

[5] Phillips, A. S. (1946). *The Phillips history of Fall River.* (Fascicle I). Falls River, MA: Dover Press, 4.

[6] Hurd, H. (1883). *History of Bristol County.* Philadelphia: J. W. Lewis & Co., 297.

[7] Willis, W. (1865). *The History of Portland.* Portland: Maine Historical Society, 858.

[8] Holt, *Winslow memorial*, 88.

[9] York County Maine Registry of Deeds. (1728). *York deeds.* (Vol. 13). Alfred, ME: Author, Folios 197, 198.

[10] Willis, *History of Portland*, 405, f. 2.

[11] Ibid., 451.

[12] Falmouth Proprietors, *Proprietors Book of Records,* at Cumberland County Registry of Deeds (1730).

[13] Willis, W. (1865). *William Willis papers*. (Maine Historical Society Collection 175, Vol. 20), 1.

[14] Willis, *History of Portland*, 405, f. 2.

[15] Ibid., 858.

[16] Ibid., 404, f. 4.

[17] Smith, T., & Deane, S. (1849). *Journals of the Rev. Thomas Smith and the Rev. Samuel Deane. W. Willis (*Ed.*)*. Portland, ME: J. S. Bailey,110.

[18] Friends Historical Society. (1932). *Journal of the Friends Historical Society* (Vol. 1). London: Friends Historical Society, 103-104.

[19] Falmouth Society of Friends (1842, March 24). *Monthly meeting records,* (Vol. 42). Falmouth and Portland, ME: Author, 3. (Maine Historical Society, Portland, Brown Library Collection #820).

[20] Ibid., 34.

[21] Highway Survey Committee. (1771). *Report to the Cumberland County Court of General Sessions of the Peace*. Portland, ME: Cumberland County Registry of Deeds.

[22] Town of Falmouth. (1752). *Falmouth Town records*. Falmouth ME: Author.

[23] Ibid., 202.

[24] Holton, *Winslow memorial.*

[25] Willis, *History of Portland*, 406.

[26] Smith & Deane, *Journals*, 94, f. 1.

[27] Falmouth Society of Friends (1842, March 24). *Monthly meeting records* (Vol. 42).

[28] Falmouth Society of Friends. (1845, June 5). *Quarterly meeting records* (Vol. 155), 462.

[29] Willis, *History of Portland*, 409.

[30] Personal conversation with Andrew Grannell, archivist for Portland Friends Meeting (2016).

[31] Dow, N. (1898). *The reminiscences of Neal Dow, Recollections of eighty years.* Portland, ME: The Evening Express Publishing Company, 13-14. https://archive.org/details/reminiscencesofn00down

[32] Ibid., 14.

[33] Famous Lambert Tavern soon to be torn down (1901, June 30). *Portland Sunday Telegram* (reference created from a partial copy found at the Falmouth Historical Society).

[34] Falmouth Historical Society. (2009). *Images of America: Falmouth*. Portsmouth, NH: Acadia Publishing, 62.

[35] Lohnes, B. J. (1970). *British naval operations in Maine, 1814*, 17-333. (Paper written for a seminar in military and naval history taught by Robert G. Albion, University of Maine at Orono).

[36] Famous Lambert Tavern.

[37] Ibid.

[38] Lambert's Tavern: Memories the old inn left behind (2003, February). *Falmouth History, 4*(1), 1, 3, & 4 (reference created from a partial copy found at the Falmouth Historical Society).

[39] Town of Falmouth, *Falmouth Town Records.*

[40] Highway Survey Committee, *Report*.

[41] Wallace, C. (1976). *E Pluribus Unum*. Falmouth, ME: Falmouth Bicentennial Commission, 41.

[42] Famous old Lambert Hill Bridge burns. . . . [It] marked historic spot of Indian massacre (reference created from a partial copy found at the Falmouth Historical Society).

[43] Goold, N. (1898, July 27). Portland—old and new, no. 21, The Pride's Bridge and others. *The Portland Transcript*.

[44] Beard, T. A. (1836, November). *Plan of the mill sites on the Congin Falls surveyed and planned for N. Winslow* (surveyor's map located at the Portland Engineering Office).

[45] S. D. Warren Company. (1954). *A history of S. D. Warren Company, 1854-1954*. Westbrook, ME: Author, 8.

[46] Ibid., 9.

[47] Lewis, John R. (c. 1966). *An Early History of Pride's Corner*. Westbrook, ME: Men's Club of the Pride's Corner Congregational Church, 21.

[48] Rowe, E. (1952). *Highlights of Westbrook history*. Westbrook, ME: Westbrook Women's Club, 171.

[49] Ibid., 100.

[50] Biographical Review Publishing Company. (1896). *Biographical review of Cumberland County*. Boston: Author, 156.

[51] Quoted in Maine Writers Research Club. (1937). *Historic churches and homes of Maine*. Portland, ME: Falmouth Book House, 100.

[52] S. D. Warren Company, *History*, 26, 27.

[53] York County Maine Registry of Deeds. (1739, May 17). *York deeds*. (Vol. 21). Alfred, ME: Author, 94-95.

[54] Chapman, L. B. (1896). First occupancy by Europeans of Saccarappa Falls on the Presumpscot River, now Westbrook. *In Collections and proceedings of the Maine Historical Society* (Second Series, Vol. 10). Portland: Maine Historical Society, 290.

[55] Cumberland County Maine Registry of Deeds. (1762, November 4). *Cumberland deeds* (Book 2). Portland, ME: Author, 247.

[56] Hanson, J. W. (1852). *History of Gardiner, Pittston and West Gardiner*. Gardiner, ME: William Palmer, 63.

[57] Willis, *History of Portland*, 858.

[58] May, E. C. (1937). *The canning clan*. New York: The MacMillan Company, 15.

[59] Bibber, J. K. (2008). Nearly all in the family. *Maine History, 28*(4), 186-208. https://www.mainehistory.org/publications.shtml

[60] *Winslow, world renowned green corn scrapbook* (Maine Historical Society Collection #1789).

[61] Ibid.

[62] May, *The canning clan*, 14-15.

[63] Bibber, Nearly all in the family, 186-208.

[64] Garrison, W. P. & Garrison, F. J. (1885). *William Lloyd Garrison 1805-1879: The story of his life told by his children* (Vol. 1). New York: The Century Company, 289.

[65] Willis, *History of Portland*, 409.

Postcards from the River: Picturing the Presumpscot in the Early-Twentieth Century

G.W. Morris, "Looking up the Beautiful Presumpscot River at Riverton," ca. 1907

Views of the Presumpscot River—stretching through Standish, Windham, Gorham, Westbrook, Portland, Falmouth, and outlying areas of Cumberland County, Maine—were a popular subject of picture postcards in the early-twentieth century. These postcard views, the bulk of them published between 1904 and the 1940s, help modern viewers to understand the many historic uses of the river—agricultural, industrial, and recreational—as well as the value that residents, visitors, and postcard publishers alike all placed on the picturesque scenic views to enjoy along its winding path. In his 1894 lecture to the Maine Historical Society, "The Story of the Presumpscot," Charles S. Forbes noted the continuing appeal of the Presumpscot River throughout the centuries:

It is rich in historic interest and the scenery along its course is charming and picturesque. Here it flows with rippling current over rugged rocks, and there its course is through wide intervales, dotted with stately elms. For several miles along the Saccarappa, the quiet beauty of the scene gives no hint of the power of the river as it tumbles down the falls.[1]

As one traveled the river, the views often shifted from pastoral to industrial; to this end, postcards of it generally fall into three categories: recreational, including views of the Riverton Trolley Park in Portland, Maine, built on the banks of the Presumpscot in 1896; industrial views of mills and dams on the river, including producers of paper and silk; and general scenic views that demonstrate the role of the river in agriculture as well as in manufacturing interests dependent upon power generated by falls and dams. This chapter addresses each of these categories in turn and includes a variety of postcard illustrations.

Tens of millions of postcards were available during the Golden Age of the Postcard in the United States between 1907 and 1915. Although picture postcards existed in the United States since their debut at the Chicago World's Fair in 1893, two significant Postal Acts, one in 1901 and the other in 1907, allowed private publishers to create cards called Post Cards—previously only the purview of the United States Postal Service—and to print these postcards with a divided back, the left side for messages, the right side for the address and stamp (one-cent for delivery in North America, and two-cents for abroad). This "Divided Back Era" marks the Golden Age of the Postcard, when millions of Americans used the small illustrated cards as a popular form of communication and correspondence.

Although we most often associate postcards today with tourism and souvenirs, in the early-twentieth century, these missives were vital forms of communication between friends, families, and business associates in an era before telephone use was widespread. Mail delivery occurred twice a day, and, as Fred Bassett explains:

> Postcards were so ubiquitous that a person could not visit any sizable town, without seeing them in almost every store window—either for sale, or for the sheer delight of sharing a view. In turn, postcard publishers endeavored not only to sell cards embracing a variety of subjects, but also tried to provide for the public a postcard of charm and originality, often superbly colored and even embossed.[2]

The selection of postcards of the Presumpscot River sold throughout southern Maine in the early decades of the twentieth century and featured in this chapter include colorful views created by local Maine postcard publishers, such as the Hugh C. Leighton Company, as well as images produced by national firms, such as the Detroit Photographic Company. During the Golden Age of the Postcard, Mainers were as likely to send these views within the state as vacationers were to send them home to other states. Postcards of the river, like many other historic views, allow modern viewers to trace change and continuity along this twenty-five-mile landscape over time. In many respects, these visual documents also allow us to see that which no longer exists.

Many of the most popular recreational and scenic postcard views of the Presumpscot River feature the forty-acre Riverton Trolley Park, built by the Portland Railroad Company on the banks of the river in 1896. The popular park was previously the home of the Deering Factory from 1870 to 1875, one of the largest canning companies extant in America at the time, which produced canned corn until it was destroyed by fire.[3] Decades later, the once-productive industrial environment that made use of the river's power transformed into a popular recreational destination for locals and rusticators alike. Visitors to the Riverton Trolley Park would hop on a trolley (the Breezer) at Monument Square in downtown Portland; pay five cents for a thirty-minute ride to the outskirts of the city; and get off at the intersection of Riverside Street and Forest Avenue, where they would be greeted by a variety of attractions, including an outdoor amphitheater (with seating for 2,500), a casino, a dance hall, and a small zoo.[4]

The Presumpscot River was a central feature of the park's landscape. As the *Board of Trade Journal* reported in 1904:

> At Riverton the grounds rise from the river bank in natural terraces, covered with neatly kept greensward, bordered by groves. . . . A natural terrace, surmounted by a grand stairway, leads from the Casino to a level playground of some half dozen acres. . . . Upon the rustic stage are produced the cleverest and cleanest of Vaudeville shows, with weekly changes of programme.[5]

The park offered something for all ages and abilities. Visitors could rent canoes at the boathouse to paddle along the Presumpscot River (as pictured in the postcard from 1910, and in many others), picnic on the lawns or in the woods, play croquet, or listen to an outdoor concert.[6] Children could visit the petting zoo or ride the popular carousel, while their parents dined and danced inside the casino designed by well-known Portland architect John Calvin Stevens.

The Hugh C. Leighton Company, "Portland, Me. Boating on the Presumpscot River, Riverton Park," 1910

C.S. Woolworth and Co., "Casino at Riverton Park, Portland, ME," ca. 1905

Inside the casino were card rooms, smoking rooms, lounges, and a large restaurant.[7] The park was open during the daytime and in the evenings, and rarer postcard views, like the one below, feature couples enjoying the romance of the Presumpscot River under the light of a full moon, a pleasure boat floating in the distance. The rustic landings and gazebos on this postcard were popular features in many of Maine's turn-of-the-century trolley parks.

Chisholm Brothers, "Moonlight on Presumpscot River, Riverton Park, ME," ca. 1917

The Riverton trolley park closed in 1920, in many ways the victim (along with the trolley itself as a popular form of transportation) of a new era of leisure and tourism ushered in by the ubiquity of the automobile. Riverton sold and ran as an amusement park and automobile destination until 1929. The casino building met its end in 1933, and only scattered ruins of the once-vibrant trolley park remain on the land bordering the river, which is once again forested. The dozens of postcards that feature the Riverton Trolley Park depict a landscape unrecognizable to twenty-first century viewers. Portland Trails, a nonprofit urban land trust, currently manages and maintains the former trolley park site, which is now popular with hikers and dog-walkers.

The Riverton Trolley Park was such a popular and well-known destination in the first decades of the twentieth century that the name of the park often appears as a geographic reference on other more pastoral and agricultural postcard views of the Presumpscot River from the same era. For instance, this 1904 postcard by the Detroit Photographic Company pictures the calm river in the foreground, surrounded by lush trees and flanked by farmland and grazing cows.[8]

Detroit Photographic Company, "Up the Presumpscot River, from Riverton Park, Portland, ME," 1904

Even though the bustling trolley park is nowhere in sight, the publishers chose to title the postcard view, "Up the Presumpscot River, from Riverton Park, Portland, ME," thus allowing the sender and receiver to better locate and contextualize the view.

For hundreds of years, farmers have cultivated the land along the Presumpscot River for hay and other crops and have used the riverbank areas as pastures for cattle.

Another early postcard by the local Hugh C. Leighton Company also frames the scene as "near Riverton Park" and features a herd of cows in the foreground, with the Presumpscot River behind them, directly alluding to the rural traditions so important to understanding the past and present uses of the river. These pastoral views particularly appealed to vacationers who flocked to Maine in the early years of the twentieth century, seeking an escape from rapidly industrializing cities up and down the East Coast.

The Hugh C. Leighton Company, "Presumpscot River, near Riverton Park, Portland, Maine," ca. 1905

These postcards, like other contemporary Maine scenic images by artists, photographers, and illustrators, "perpetuated the region's distinct sense of place, composed of seemingly timeless natural landscapes and more traditional ways of life, to a regional and national audience."[9] As evidenced by the sheer number of unique postcard views that exist of it, the Presumpscot River was very much a part of Southern Maine's distinct sense of place during this era.

Finally, a third category of postcard views make visible the growing industrial landscape that sprung up alongside the banks of the Presumpscot River in the nineteenth and twentieth centuries. Although the modern viewer may find sending postcards of mills and industrial landscapes strange, a century ago, these factory views were quite popular with postcard publishers in Maine throughout the early decades of the twentieth century, as they often helped to showcase a local town or city's growing fortunes and major landmarks. People who lived in southern Maine sent the cards to friends and family members in outlying areas, and tourists bought them while visiting towns through which the river flows. Just as the Presumpscot River featured prominently in dozens of scenic and pastoral postcard landscapes, it was also central in a series of industrial postcard landscapes from the same era.

The bulk of the extant postcards that highlight the Presumpscot River are comprised of scenes from mills located in Westbrook and largely clustered around the falls at Saccarappa. Although early postcards from the first decade of the twentieth century show the gradual growth and development of a variety of paper, cotton, and silk mills along the river, later postcards from the 1940s feature birds-eye views of Westbrook that showcase a well-developed industrial city situated around the river. As we move through time, the river begins to lose its prominence as a feature on postcards. Eventually, as we move into the 1930s and 1940s, the industrial and urban landscapes of the Westbrook mill complexes become the focal point, and the river fades to the background.

In 1874, James Haskell founded The Haskell Silk Company along the banks of the Presumpscot River. Like many manufacturers before him, Haskell developed his mill around the Saccarappa Falls, initially converting buildings on Bridge Street that had once housed cotton mills. The production of silk was an attractive endeavor for Haskell, due to the increasing demand for silk thread to use in new sewing machines following the Civil War.[10] As business grew and expanded, Haskell constructed a new mill farther up the river in 1901-1902. The new brick mill, featured on the next postcard, ran by electricity and included a separate facility for dying silk.

A silk mill was an unusual sight in Maine and New England, so the novelty of the enterprise, coupled with the new, modern mill building, likely contributed to its prominence on postcards from the early 1900s. An alternate postcard view of the Presumpscot River at Westbrook from the same era also features the Haskell Silk Mill, and, downriver, a smokestack from the S.D. Warren Papermill, one of Maine's oldest papermills, established in 1854.

As Jeffrey L. Meikle explains:

There were as many postcard views of factories and manufacturing as of agriculture, mining, and shipping. Factory tours remained a staple of corporate publicity, and a postcard may occasionally have served as a souvenir of such a visit. More often, however, travelers drove past on a highway, looking down a valley or across a river at an industrial site, enjoying the experience of the sublime familiar to tourists at the Grand Canyon or Yosemite.[11]

106

Publisher Unknown, "Presumpscot River & Silk Mill, Westbrook, Me.," ca. 1907

The Hugh C. Leighton Company, "Presumpscot River at Westbrook, Me," ca. 1907

In northern New England, mills often sprung up in relatively pastoral areas along rivers—towns and cities growing up around them—as evidenced in these postcards. They were, for a time, tourist attractions on par with Maine's more rugged natural landscapes, especially when set against attractive natural backdrops.

Tichnor Quality Views, "Birdseye View of Westbrook, Maine," ca. 1940

Although the Golden Age of the Postcard as an important means of correspondence and communication faded with World War I, both residents and tourists continued to send thousands of postcards throughout the twentieth century. The Presumpscot River routinely appeared on postcards of the towns through which it flows, especially Westbrook. The 1940s birds-eye view featured above showcases a busy urban landscape—industrial, commercial, and residential—all set against the backdrop of the river. Unlike the earlier images of nascent mills and factories where the river dominated the postcard, these later views focus primarily on the buildings. Although this postcard, like the others throughout this chapter, is based on a photograph, the illustrative nature of the image allows the viewer to imagine the multiple negative impacts these mills had on the Presumpscot River—including man-made dams preventing the natural migration of fish, and heavy pollution from industrial byproducts, to name but two. If we begin to imagine new postcards of the Presumpscot River for the twenty-first century, perhaps they will once again feature the river as a site of agriculture, recreation, and leisure in balance with industry, and as an important habitat for the wildlife and people who reside along, and beneath, its shores.

---

[1] Forbes, C. S. (1894). The Story of the Presumpscot. *Collections and Proceedings of the Maine Historical Society* (2nd Series, Vol. 5). Portland: ME: Historical Society, 362.

[2] Bassett, F. (2016). Wish you were here! The story of the Golden Age of Picture Postcards in the United States. *New York State Library*. http://www.nysl.nysed.gov/msscfa/qc16510ess.htm

[3] Maine Historical Society (ca. 1870). Deering Factory, Portland, ca. 1870. *Maine Historical Society, Maine Memory Network*. https://www.mainememory.net/artifact/16948

[4] Tatnall, A. (1988). Trolley parks around Portland. *Maine Historical Society, Maine Memory Network*. https://www.mainememory.net/sitebuilder/site/1988/page/3243/display?use_mmn=1

[5] Portland Board of Trade (1904, July). Portland, Maine, The reception city for Eastern tourists. *Board of Trade Journal, 17*(3), 104-105.

[6] Tatnall, Trolley parks around Portland.

[7] Brechlin, E. (2004). *Bygone coastal Maine: A Postcard Tour from Kittery to Camden.* Camden, ME: Downeast Books, 51.

[8] The Detroit Publishing Company quickly distinguished itself in the burgeoning postcard industry by introducing the photochrom color reproduction process to American consumers. Invented in Switzerland, the photochrom process allowed publishers to mass-produce colored lithographs from black and white photographic negatives that were transferred directly onto the printing plates. Most cards featured between six and fifteen different ink colors—resulting in lush color views of popular landscapes and landmarks in an era before the mass production of color photographs was possible. By the early decades of the 1900s, the Detroit Publishing Company was one of the leading American publishers of postcards and scenic views, producing between 10,000 and 30,000 unique views over the life of the company. The firm showcased a great variety of Maine scenic images that the company produced and sold over nearly four decades. Such images were not only meant to entice viewers to Maine but, when transformed into color postcards,

became mementoes of tourists' vacations to the state—the views that visitors came to associate with Maine in this era. Library of Congress (n.d.). *Detroit Publishing Company: Background and scope of collection.* http://www.loc.gov/pictures/collection/det/background.html

[9] Bischof, L. (2017). A Region Apart: Representations of Maine and Northern New England in Personal Film, 1920-1940. In M. McNamara & K. Sheldon, *Amateur Movie Making: Aesthetics of the Everyday in New England Film, 1915-1960.* Bloomington: Indiana University Press, 48-70.

[10] Field, J., Senechal, M., & Shaw, M. (2007). *American silk, 1830-1930: Entrepreneurs and artifacts.* Lubbock, TX: Tech University Press, 93.

[11] Meikle, J. L. (2015). *Postcard America: Curt Teich and the imaging of a nation, 1931-1950.* Austin: University of Texas Press, 233.

Maine's Gunpowder Mills[1]

The beginnings

The most important gunpowder mill in Maine in the nineteenth century was commonly called the "Gambo Powder Mill," because it was located at Gambo Falls on the Presumpscot River. The first powder mill buildings were erected on the Gorham side of the river, but, after being in operation for about ten years, extensive developments took place on the Windham side of the river. Facts substantiate the importance of the "Gambo Mill": it was the first commercial powder mill built in Maine and operated longer than any other Maine mill; it was the largest mill of its kind in Maine and among the largest in the nation for many years. Also, good record is available of its business from 1872 to 1905.

Some authors have claimed that the Gambo Powder Mills commenced in 1818, notably Hugh McLellan[2] and Samuel Dole.[3] However, no clear evidence supports their statements that Fowler and Laflin bought the land at Gambo Falls in 1817, erected powder mills, and started producing gunpowder the following year. A search of deeds in the Cumberland County Registry of Deeds does not show the transaction to which McLellan refers.[4] A search of various records in Southwick, Massachusetts, reveal that Edmund Fowler was a taxpayer active in the civic and church affairs of Southwick until 1824. According to the same records, Lester Laflin would have been 16 years of age in 1817, not old enough to engage in land transactions.[5] Arthur Van Gelder and Hugo Schlatter state that the first powder mill in Maine of which we know anything was established by a Mr. Whipple of Lowell, Massachusetts, in 1824 in Cumberland County with capital of $7000.00.[6] It was first known as the Gorham Powder Company (locally as the Gambo Powder Mills).[7] Although Mr. Whipple did *not* establish the powder mill, the year 1824 is probably correct.

First deed

The Cumberland County Registry of Deeds in Portland, Maine, records the sale of twenty-five acres of land with the water right and mill privileges at

Gambo Falls to William Fowler (brother of Edmund Fowler) of South-wick, Massachusetts, from Oliver Pierce of Otisfield (Maine) for $1000 on December 23, 1823.[8] Thus, it appears that Edmund Fowler and Lester Laflin started manufacturing gunpowder at Gambo Falls in 1824. Laflin's family in Southwick had been making gunpowder since before the Revolutionary War.[9]

Information is lacking on the size of the original operations at Gambo Falls. The *Portland Advertiser* for years contained a section that gave the prices of many commodities under "Prices Current." Gunpowder from Fowler & Laflin's Mill was listed in 1826 at $4.00 for a 25-pound cask,[10] which dropped to $3.25 in 1828[11] and matched the price in Chelmsford, Massachusetts.

Melancholy events

The first record of an explosion took place in the summer of 1826, re-counting the memory of Mr. George Goold in Samuel T. Dole's handwritten record book. A worker, Mr. Bills, struck a spark with his tool and subsequently had his hands severely burned when he used them to protect his face.[12]

In 1827, five people, including Fowler, Laflin, and foreman Matthew McCulley, died in a boating accident. The *Portland Advertiser* recorded the details on June 29, 1827. Mr. Laflin had recently married, and his wife was left "deranged in consequence of this melancholy event."[13]

At the time of the drownings, Edmund Fowler owned 2/5 or 40% of the powder mills and Lester Laflin owned 1/5 or 20%. Their widows, Olive and Huldah, respectively, acquired their husbands' shares. Edmund Fowler's younger brother, William Fowler (born 1795), owned the remaining 2/5 or 40%. William moved to Portland after March 1827 (when he was in Southwick) and before September 1828 (when he was a "merchant" in Portland). It seems highly probable that he came after the tragedy of June 1827 and remained manager of the mills for several years. Joseph M. Forward of Southwick started acquiring the mills in February of 1831 and continued to do so for eighteen months. William Fowler was definitely living in Portland in May 1832 when he sold his 2/5 share to Joseph Forward for $1500.[14]

The Fowler and Laflin Company (sometimes called the Cumberland Powder Manufactory) was struck with another major disaster on July 19, 1828, when an explosion killed seven men. The accident took place in the "pounding mill." Thus, we know that the method of incorporating the three ingredients—saltpeter, sulfur, and charcoal—to make gunpowder was accomplished by the oldest of means: mortars and pestles. Although wheel mills were invented about 1820, they did not have wide use at the time of this accident. We also know that the pestles, sometimes called "stampers," were made of copper and usually weighed between 30 and 38 pounds each.[15]

Figure 1: Saccarappa and Cumberland Mills Birdseye (source: Maine Historical Society, photo by Robert Sanford)

Rev. William Gragg, a minister in Windham, recorded the following in his journal for Sunday, July 20, 1828:

> After divine service in the afternoon I attended the funeral of Mr. Oliver Dole's infant child; from this house of mourning I went directly to attend the funeral of a young Mr. Mains, whose death was caused by the explosion at Gambo powder factory.[16]

Evidently, the damaged mill underwent repair, because advertisements and/or wholesale prices appeared from time to time in the *Daily Courier* during the following three years. In August 1831, Jewett & Read offered for sale, "rice, sugar, etc., 4000 lbs. Patent Shot assorted, 50 casks Gorham Powder."[17]

THE WHIPPLE YEARS

Commencing in June 1832, Oliver M. Whipple of Lowell, Massachusetts, started purchasing land and the "powder manufacturing establishment" in

Gorham from the Fowler and Laflin heirs, plus land and water rights on the Windham side of Gambo Falls.[18]

Oliver M. Whipple was born in Weathersfield, Vermont, in 1794. He went to Lowell, Massachusetts, in October 1818 after having spent about three years in Southwick learning the powder manufacturing trade. He soon entered into a partnership with Moses Hale and William Tileston for the purpose of making powder in Lowell.[19] Eventually, he bought out the other partners and carried on the business alone until 1855. In addition to making gunpowder, he was involved with many other business enterprises, served as a Lowell alderman six years, and was a member of the Massachusetts Legislature four years[20]

Whipple made extensive repairs on the existing mills at Gambo and, during the next nine years, purchased additional land and water rights in Gorham, Windham, and Standish in order to expand his operations. The expansion included erecting new powder mills on the Windham side of the Presumpscot River in about 1833-1834.

Oliver Whipple never resided in Maine; rather, he appointed his brother, Lucius Whipple (born 1799) as agent or superintendent of the Gambo Mills, commencing in January 1833. After Lucius died in 1847, Oliver Whipple appointed another brother, James (born 1801). According to local records, Lucius Whipple was one of the three selectmen in Windham from 1839 to 1845, with the exception of 1842.[21]

Dole wrote, "He [Lucius] died in the prime of life and was succeeded as agent by his brother James, a man of good capacity and genial nature, but who lacked the executive ability of his brother."[22]

According to the Portland City Death Records, Lucius Whipple died in March of 1847 as a result of "an accident." The day of death is not on the record, and I have not found any newspaper accounts that mention the death or the nature of the accident. The date of death on his granite tombstone in Portland's Evergreen Cemetery is 1848. I believe that the discrepancy of one year between the Death Record and the tombstone may have resulted from the stone not being set and inscribed until some years after his death.

During the Whipple years of ownership, a destructive flood in the spring of 1843 occurred when Sebago Lake overflowed into the Presumpscot River. The flood carried away most of the bridges spanning the river and also did considerable damage to the powder mills.[23] In addition, five separate explosions that resulted in the loss of lives occurred. The first took place on November 17, 1835, killing Charles Humphrey. The next was on September 2, 1847. On Thursday, July 19, 1849, a workman named Hatch accidently created a spark while driving a nail and died soon after of his wounds.[24] On October 1, 1850, two buildings and a dry-house worker named Leander White (of Sebago) were blown up.[25] The final explosion took place almost a year later, in September 1851. The mixing mill blew up, "killing one hand, a Mr. Bickford, who had been over 30 years in Mr. Whipple's employment. Loss of property is trifling."[26] Thomas Bickford is buried in the Leavitt Cemetery by the River Road in Windham. His inscription states: "Thomas Bickford Killed by the Explosion of a Powder mill Sept. 24, 1851, AEt. 47 Yrs."

Business in the 1850s

The manufacture of powder from the 1830s on was a sizable business. The old mills were rebuilt and new mills added. The Russian government was engaged in the Crimean War from 1853 to 1856 and proved to be a profitable customer.[27]

Sometime during Whipple's ownership, wheel mills replaced pounding or stamping mills for incorporating ingredients. The first wheel mills at Gambo used smooth stone wheels, the broken remains of which are still visible on the Gorham side of the river.

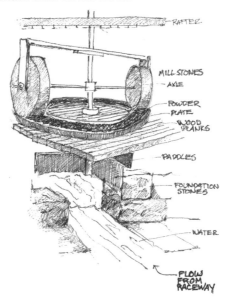

Figure 2: Powder Mill Cross Section (source: Michael Shaughnessy)

115

Figure 3: Stone Wheel (source: Robert Sanford)

G. G. NEWHALL YEARS

In poor health in 1854-1855, Oliver Whipple started selling his various mill properties to others; some went to his brother James, but he sold the Gambo Mills for $10,000 on January 20, 1855, to G. G. Newhall and Company. Gilbert G. Newhall had as associates: Francis Cox and William H. Jackson, all of Salem, Massachusetts. Newhall and Company acquired several parcels of land, including some with water rights, in the following eighteen months.[28]

The new owners had only been operating the gunpowder mills for about ten months when a terrible explosion took place on October 12, 1855, killing seven men, equal to the fatalities of July 9, 1828.[29] The next day, Oliver Whipple's son, George Oliver Whipple (whose name sometimes appears as Oliver George Whipple), died from the explosion. James, Oliver's brother, who had been the superintendent or agent for his absentee brother-owner, was also killed.[30] Apparently, the new owner had retained James as an employee, but in what position is uncertain.

The Newhall Company put into effect more stringent safety regulations and posted copies in all parts of the premises. According to verbal accounts, every new employee had to read the regulations to the superintendent before being hired.

Cumberland and Oxford Canal

The Cumberland and Oxford Canal was built to connect the inland farms and communities with Portland and its harbor. It opened in June of 1830 and closed in 1871, after railroads started running in the region it served. The powder mills owned its own boat for many years and, by some accounts, sailed it down the canal to Portland; if weather conditions were favorable, it sometimes went nonstop to Boston Harbor with a load of gunpowder.[31] An Act of the Massachusetts Legislature in 1816 regulated the "storage, safe-keeping, and transportation of Gunpowder in the town of Boston . . . no ship or other vessel, on board of which Gunpowder shall be laden, shall lay at any wharf in the town of Boston, nor within two hundred yairds [sic] of any wharf in said town."[32] This and subsequent acts resulted in the storage of all large quantities of gunpowder on a retired navy vessel that served as a "floating magazine" anchored in a secluded and protected area in Boston's outer harbor. Licensed sellers could come by small boats to the magazine to remove small amounts necessary for trade permitted by regulations.

Besides their own boat, the Gambo Powder Mills made extensive use of the other canal freight boats to receive raw materials and to ship finished powder. The following canal toll rates were published in 1862:

Powder	5 cents per mile per ton
Charcoal	100 bushel 3 cents per mile
Saltpeter	3 cents per mile per ton
Brimstone	4 cents per mile per ton

Repairs, Expansion, Explosions

After the devastating explosion of October 12, the company repaired the damages then expanded drastically in the next three or four years, erecting new mill buildings and replacing older machinery and equipment with new, improved models. Under Newhall ownership, several houses went up, including a large boarding house for single workmen and at least two duplex houses for employees with families.[33] The Newhalls also altered and improved the brick house at the corner of Gambo and River Roads for the owner or superintendent of the mills and built a large stable for the company's horses. All of the housing developments were on the Windham side of the river on Gambo Road.

Explosions continued to plague the company, however. The next one took place on the morning of May 6, 1856, resulting in the death of one workman.[34] On August 4, 1856, another explosion killed three men.[35] The kernelling mill blew up on Saturday afternoon, January 15, 1859, killing workman David R. Jones.[36] It was customary for all mills at that time to be in operation six days a week and a minimum of ten hours per day.

Name Change

Figure 4: Oriental Powder Company Image (source: Windham Historical Society, photo by Robert Sanford)

After being in operation for approximately four years, G. G. Newhall and Company decided to change the name of the firm to the Oriental Powder Company and become incorporated by the legislature in February 1859. The Act of Incorporation contains several interesting facts. First, another member, Watson Newhall, joined the firm. Second, it was authorized to manufacture "dye stuffs and chemicals" in addition to gunpowder at Gambo Falls, although whether the company ever produced dyes or chemicals is unknown. Third, the capital stock would be at least $200,000 but not over $500,000: a very sizeable capitalization for a pre-Civil War firm.[37]

Keg Mill Fire

"Keg Mills, at the foot of Sebago Pond, in Windham," a supplier of kegs to the Oriental Powder Company, was destroyed by fire on October 24, 1859.[38] A factory producing staves and shooks for barrels and kegs was located on the powder mill property, on the Gorham side of the river. I have been unable to find when this operation started or ceased. Presumably, the owners of the gunpowder mills operated it, but it also could have been run independently or as some kind of subsidiary.

THE CIVIL WAR YEARS

A comparison of the industrial census ending in June 1, 1850, with the census ending June 1, 1860, reveals that the gunpowder operation grew many times over within a decade.[39] The start of the Civil War in 1861 presaged big business for the company. Less than one month after the outbreak of war, however, an extensive flood damaged the Presumpscot region. "Heavy rains the last days of April and the 5th and 6th of May" caus[ed] the "Pond" to be 10-15 feet higher than ever before.[40] "The dam at the foot of Little Sebago Pond gave way on May 7, 1861."[41] A reporter for the *Eastern Argus* wrote "and the Cumberland and Oxford Canal is nearly ruined for a long distance—besides great damage to Gorham Powder Mils."[42]

In addition to dealing with natural disasters like the flood, the Oriental Powder Company continued to cope with explosions, such as one on July 9, 1861, that killed Charles Carmichael.[43] The most severe explosion at the Gambo Mills that had no fatalities took place on May 2, 1862. Accounts of it appeared in the *Lewiston Falls Journal* and the *Oxford Democrat* in addition to the Portland papers. The *Eastern Argus* gave this account:

> The first explosion took place in the glazing mill, on the Windham side. This was immediately followed by an explosion of a mill on the Gorham side of the river. Then followed . . . almost simultaneously, two more mills on the Gorham side and four more on the Wind-

ham side, making eight mills in all, containing about 200 barrels of powder. It is impossible to account for the cause of the explosion .... Fortunately, not a person was injured. About five minutes before the explosion, the hands had left the mills to go to supper. ... The concussion shook the houses in Gorham violently, rattling crockery, but doing no damage.[44]

It is possible that workers hadn't completed all repairs to buildings and machinery when another explosion shook the Powder Company on July 7, 1862, killing three workmen. The *Portland Daily Advertiser* recorded that disaster:

At about 8 o'clock yesterday morning, two of the Gambo Company's powder mills . . . blew up. August Little of Windham was instantly killed. Albert Glidden of Effingham, N.H., and Mark Varney of Windham who was shockingly mutilated have since died. In one of the mills, there happened to be nobody at the time of the explosion. There was a loss of about 25 tons of powder. Cause of the explosion unknown.[45]

The *Eastern Argus*, in an account several days later, was more specific about the explosion: "The wheel mills blew up. . . . The workmen were removing the charges from the mill at the time."[46] Many years later, in "Sketches of Windham History," the *Narragansett Sun* included a list of families. Hiram and Susan Varney had twelve children. Their ninth child, "Mark S. [was] killed by an explosion of the powder mills at Gambo (now Newhall)."[47]

Another explosion on November 14, 1863, resulted in the last mill fatality, Haggart Freeman, during the Civil War period. Some accidents occurred during the transportation of gunpowder but, fortunately, not all of these ended in explosions.

The Civil War brought huge contracts for military gunpowder for the North. The government specified that all powder for the military should be shipped in heavy oak barrels that contained 100 pounds each of the finished product.[48] Production increased rapidly to over 2,500,000 pounds of powder per year.[49] It has been estimated that approximately 25% of all powder used by the Union forces in the Civil War was produced at Gorham-Windham.[50] The powder produced by the Oriental Powder Company was known for its excellent quality and met military specifications of 75% potassium nitrate, 15% charcoal, and 10% sulfur.[51]

120

In the 1850s, it was commonly recognized that a serious problem existed when firing a cannon, so-called large guns of five inches and larger bore (inside diameter). When the big guns were charged with typical "cannon-powder," tremendous pressure built up so rapidly that it burst the cannon instead of propelling the projectile with great velocity and distance.

About 1859-60, Captain Thomas J. Rodman of the U.S. Army Ordnance Corps began a series of experiments at Frankford Arsenal in Philadelphia dealing with the size of the gunpowder grains on rate of combustion, gun pressure, and projectile velocity. He soon concluded that the small grains of "Cannon-Powder" burned so rapidly that they were consumed before the shot had time to move but a little in the gun; consequently, an enormous pressure was exerted on the gun, without a corresponding velocity to the shot. The conclusion arrived at was that the proper size for the fifteen-inch gun was a granulation between six-tenths and nine-tenths of an inch, which is known as "Mammoth Powder." The charge for the fifteen-inch gun was, at that time, from thirty to fifty pounds of powder, but with the improvements made since then [to about 1876], the service charge has been increased to one hundred, and even to one hundred and fifty pounds, in experimental firing.[52]

General Rodman (having been promoted from Captain) developed "Perforated Cake Powder, consisting of masses the size of the bore of the gun, perforated with holes of different sizes and numbers, [known as] Rodman s Hexagonal Cake-Cartridges,"[53] made for the big guns in various sizes from 5 inch to 15 inch.

Rodman's "Cakes" were formed by the grains of black powder being pressed into shape on specially designed dies or molds and were produced by the Oriental Powder Company and other suppliers in addition to rifle powder and other military powder. The Cake Cartridges burned more slowly than the loose granular form of black powder, thus building up pressure more gradually and maintaining a steady pressure on the projectile. The more effective propelling action resulted from the increased surface area of the powder as the combustion progressed so the maximum rate of release of energy took place only after the shot had started to move up the barrel of the cannon.

The end of the Civil War in April 1865 was a time of mixed emotions for most gunpowder manufacturers. Happily, they would lose no more relatives and friends to war in this highly patriotic state (Gorham, which had a population of 3250 in 1860, provided approximately 700 men for the

Union Army and Navy.)[54] According to Van Gelder and Schlatter, "In the year immediately following the war, the powder business, in common with other industries, suffered a profound depression which eventually culminated in the panic of 1873."[55] Military powder remained a glut on the market for many years. There were reports of the Army and Navy having difficulty with some cannon powder during the Spanish-American War in 1898. The problem was with old powder left over from the Civil War, which had been stored in government ammunition depots or magazines for thirty-three years. An increasing demand for blasting powder was finding widespread use in coal mines as well as other mines; granite, marble, and limestone quarries; clearing farmland; and helping prepare roadbeds for railroads.

The war over, in 1867 the Maine Legislature granted the Oriental Powder Company broad manufacturing rights in materials additional to gunpowder and granted the right to increase the capital stock to one million dollars.[56]

Explosions, 1869-1871

On a Saturday morning, February 20, 1869, an explosion at the mills resulted in the death of Charles Charls from Prussia (although one account had it as Russia). Various reports spelled his last name as Charlo, Charlow, and Shailes. An explosion of the corning mill and three hundred pounds of powder was reported by the *Eastern Argus* on February 22, 1869.[57] On July 2, 1869, another explosion killed worker Moses Hawkes. The next took place on the morning of August 2, 1870, injuring James Jordan of Raymond and Clinton B. Hooper of Windham.[58] Mr. Jordan, sometimes identified as Frank Jordan, eventually died of his injuries. Mr. Hooper lived another 38 years but was permanently blinded.

Another explosion resulting in a fatality rattled the Gorham-Windham area on November 15, 1871, killing worker John Densmore (Dinsmore). This was yet another instance of an explosion getting little to no attention in the press.

Canal Closes, Railroad Opens

1871 was an important year for transportation in the region. It marked the end of the Cumberland and Oxford Canal, opened in 1830. At its peak of operations, approximately 150 boats were using it. Many private boats plied the waters of the canal besides the C & O Canal Association's boats. The demise of the canal was caused by the arrival of the railroads, which were faster, ran in all seasons, and could go from one community to another no matter how far removed from water.[59] In the case of Windham, the railroad to serve the Gambo Falls area was the Portland and Ogdensburg railroad. Newell Station was accompanying the depot. Beers' 1871 map of Gambo Falls shows both the C & O Canal and the P & O Railroad.[60]

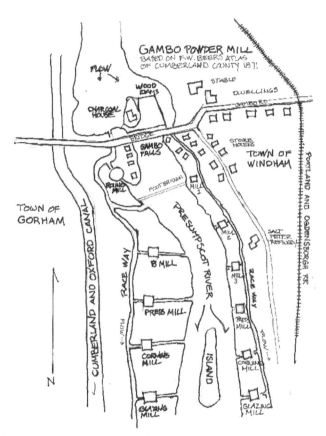

Figure 5: Gambo Powder Mill Complex (source: Michael Shaughnessy, based on Beers, *Atlas of Cumberland County, Maine*)

On January 10, 1872, the Portland and Ogdensburg Railroad purchased the Oriental Powder Company "for $1.00 and other valuable considerations": a parcel of land in Windham "about 5,000 feet long and six rods wide across the land and tenements of the Oriental Powder Company."[61]

THE 1870s

Many gunpowder mills had been suffering financially since the Civil War ended in 1865. Some reworked their surplus military powder for which there was no market into blasting powder for mining and related activities. Depression conditions grew steadily worse in 1871. By 1872, many Maine businesses were failing. The Oriental Powder Company had been operating at a loss; it then suspended business and ultimately went through bankruptcy in 1872.[62]

The Maine legislature act incorporating a new company for the Mills was approved by the House of Representatives on February 13, 1872. The Senate approved the act on February 14, 1872.[63] In 1872, the newly reconstituted company decided to take out insurance on the lives of its workmen. How much coverage each man had is not clear.

Another unknown is where the Powder Mills obtained their machinery from 1824 to 1876. From then on, Elden Gammon made some of their machinery. The *Lewiston Journal* described the "Fairy-Glen" mill wheel and site adjacent to Main Street in Gorham (behind where the old Sunoco station stood). The wheel, the undershot type, was 26 feet in diameter and 2 ½ feet wide on the water surface. It was erected in 1866.[64]

After the Portland and Ogdensburg Railroad reached Newhall in 1871, the Oriental Powder Mills continued to use horses extensively in its operations. The *Portland Transcript* in December 1876, reported that "in the gale of Saturday a barn belonging to the Oriental Powder Co. at Gambo was blown down and a huge quantity of hay destroyed."[65] The last of the company's stables on the Windham side of the river remained standing until the 1970s.

The Powder Mills occasionally had disagreements with other companies that used the water of the Presumpscot River for power. The most violent disagreement broke out in January 1877, between the S. D. Warren Company in Cumberland Mills, Westbrook, and the Oriental Powder Mills, and had to be settled by the courts.[66]

The Mills and Their Products

Several Maine newspapers ran articles in the first four months of 1877 describing the size of the Oriental Powder Mills. Some also pointed out the range of its products: gunpowder dust for fireworks, rifle powder, blasting powder, and military powder in many grain sizes and shapes for a variety of cannon sizes.[67]

Russia, a Customer

The Russo-Turkish War broke out early in 1877, when Russia intervened to prevent the Bulgarians from being massacred by the Turks. Russia again started purchasing large quantities of military powder from Gambo, as it had in the 1850s Crimean War. The Hayden Anderson *Scrapbook* contains a news item dated April 2, 1877, regarding the shipping of ammunition, and the following handwritten note: "This bark has 3600 hundred cases of powder of which 2100 were ours. 157500 lbs. for the Russian Government."[68]

Saltpeter Tax

In 1877-1878, Congress planned to substantially increase the tax on saltpeter, which the United States had to import because it had no large-scale supply. India, a colony of Great Britain, had supplied the United States and most European countries for years. All saltpeter left India through Calcutta, the closest major port to the saltpeter fields or mines. Incidentally, the opening of the Suez Canal in 1869 greatly expedited the importing of saltpeter by American powder manufacturers.[69]

New Explosives

At this time, the United States and Europe were producing new types of explosives. In 1878, Professor Hayes, State Assayer for Massachusetts, gave a paper on "The Three Classes of Explosive Agents Now in Use." He described how nitroglycerine was first prepared by the chemist Ascanio Sobrero in 1847 and remained a laboratory curiosity for about sixteen years. He also noted how much safer dynamite was to handle and use than nitroglycerine for blasting purposes:

> Gunpowder is still the best explosive for blasting operations of certain kinds, especially in mining coal and soft ores. But for the sudden disruptive force, so necessary in breaking hard rock, it has been almost replaced by explosives of a different class.[70]

It was clear in 1878 that the use of the "new" explosives for blasting would steadily increase, and the use of black gunpowder would decrease.

Another article entitled "Wholesale Powder Trade" describes the vast gunpowder storage and distribution facilities in the Chicago area. DuPont, Laflin & Rand, Hazard Powder, American Powder, and Oriental Powder Company all had magazines near Brighton, Illinois.[71]

Gunpowder Test at Naval Academy

Anderson's *Scrapbook* contains a brief item regarding a trial of Oriental gunpowder at the U.S. Naval Academy:

Mssrs. W. P. Whiting & Co. are also Baltimore agents for the cele-brated Oriental gunpowder; the well-known reputation of this brand having been thoroughly tried is fully appreciated at the NAVAL ACADEMY, Annapolis, where it has been severely tested, as well as by sporting men throughout the country.[72]

Another Fatal Explosion

After operating almost eight years without a fatal explosion at Gambo, the record was broken on October 27, 1879, when Sumner Stokes of Gray and Clinton Mayberry of Windham were injured, Mr. Stokes dying soon after.[73]

Sale of Mills and Reorganization

At a meeting of the directors in Boston on December 22, 1879, four directors resigned and four new directors, all from New York City, were elected. Five days later, more resignations and appointees occurred. Mr. Arthur Williams became president at $5,000 per year. The new directors held strong connections to other powder mills and related industries.[74]

A special meeting of stockholders was held on January 6, 1880, at the Falmouth Hotel in Portland, to amend the company's "Bye-Laws."[75] This meeting revealed the new major owners after the temporary cessation of manufacturing operations about December 8, 1879. From January 1880 on, three powder companies, Hazard, Laflin & Rand, and E. I. DuPont de Nemours & Company were in firm control of the Oriental Powder Mills.[76]

THE 1880s

Oriental Buys North Buckfield Mills

On August 30, 1880, at a meeting of the directors of Oriental Powder Mills held in New York City, Mr. E. H. Marble of Paris Hill, Maine, reportedly proposed to sell his powder mill (at North Buckfield) for $5000 and take payment in blasting powder at $2.50 per keg.[77] At a subsequent directors' meeting on October 27, 1880, records show that "Mr. Williams [President of OPM] reported verbally that the 'Marble Mills', at Paris Hill, Me. were purchased Sept. 11, 1880, for Forty-five hundred dollars payable in powder at $2.85 for A and $2.50 for B blasting *delivered*."[78] This sale ended the gunpowder mills at North Buckfield. No evidence shows that the mill produced any powder after the autumn of 1877. Apparently, after the sale, the machinery was removed to Gorham-Windham and the buildings were left to decay. Gunpowder had been made in the North Buckfield-Sumner area for approximately 35 years, starting at Basin Falls in 1842.

A Variety of Gunpowder

Oriental Powder Mills produced a wide variety of gunpowder according to grain size, trade name, and container size (up to 6.25 lb. canisters and kegs up to 25 lbs.). The powder was advertised for birds, sporting, breech-loading, and cotton fuse.[79]

Another Explosion Fatality

Explosions continued at the Gambo Mills under the new management. One on January 30, 1884, killed Reuben E. Kenney, a workman from Gorham, throwing him 150 feet onto the ice from the kernelling ("corning") mill. He survived for only about an hour after the accident, reporting that there was something wrong with the "cake" he had been working on.[80] Mr. Kenny was the first workman killed in which newspaper accounts mention the existence of insurance paid for by the company.

Sporting Powder

In April 1885, Oriental Powder Mills began selling a new brand of powder known as "Wing Shot" for sportsmen and hunters. Sporting powder, so-called, was becoming an increasingly important component of the business of most gunpowder manufacturers.[81]

Explosions Get More News Coverage

Another devastating explosion rocked the area on March 11, 1886, killing Clarence Clay, 33 years of age, according to information on his tombstone in Sapling Hill Cemetery in Gorham, having been born on February 2, 1853. Henry (Harry) Hooper was severely injured in the same explosion and died Saturday, March 13, 1886.[82] Henry Hooper's father was Clinton B. Hooper, who was blinded in the explosion of August 2, 1870.[83] Coverage of these two 1886 explosions extended all the way to Boston newspapers.

Oriental Purchases Warren Machinery

On July 25, 1887, the Warren Powder Mills blew up. No repairs followed. The owner, Elbridge Wason of Boston, died on August 21, 1887, according to the *Rockland Courier-Gazette.*[84] The same paper reported in November that "the Warren Powder Mills have been sold to the Oriental Powder Co. at South Windham and men are here taking the machinery apart and getting ready for the removal of same to that place, requiring 30 [freight] cars."[85] Oriental Powder Mills purchased only the machinery. Mrs. Wason sold the water privilege, land, and buildings to people in Warren.

Continuing Explosions

Another devastating explosion at Gambo occurred on the morning of November 5, 1888, and was audible as far away as Portland. Two workmen, Edward C. Williams (who had worked at the Warren powder mills) and Walter Childs, were mortally wounded. A kernelling mill and three wheel-mill buildings were destroyed.[86]

Four weeks later, at 9:00 a.m. on December 3, 1888, another explosion destroyed the Oriental Powder's last remaining kernelling mill, which was on the opposite side of the river from the previous explosion. William Bamblett, an Englishman from Westfield, Massachusetts, was badly injured and died a few minutes after. "In spite of this, however, there are lots of people who can be hired for $2.50 per day to risk their lives in the powder mills at Gambo."[87]

The *Portland Daily Advertiser* described the manner in which people observed the shock waves of these two explosions:

A somewhat peculiar circumstance connected with the late explosion of the Gambo Powder-mills has been noted by a number of people. This is a difference in the perception of the concussion. I noticed it myself having been in the same place both times, and spoke of it at the Club, when it appeared that all of the members who had heard the shocks had observed the same thing. This was that the first explosion some weeks ago, [Nov. 5] seemed beneath us while that on last Monday [Dec. 3] appeared overhead. I remember this particularly because at the time of the first explosion the remark was made that somebody was unduly vigorous in shutting doors downstairs, while Monday it was said that probably Mr. R. had let his piano lid drop upstairs. The report of the disaster in the *Advertiser* stated that the last mill to explode was across the river from the one that went up the first time. I presume that this fact bearing upon the geological formation Gambo, with which I am not sufficiently familiar to state positively, explains the difference.[88]

On April 22, 1890, another destructive explosion injured three men on the Windham side of the Presumpscot River. This explosion was the result of a forest fire that had been raging in Windham. Windows rattled in Portland. The new pulverizer building and six others were lost.[89]

Edna Leavitt, the daughter of one of the injured men, William Hooper Leavitt, married Professor Louis B. Woodard, my predecessor at Gorham State Teachers College. Mrs. Woodard told me that her father worked for Oriental Powder Mills for at least twenty years, where he was in charge of repairing machinery. They lived in a white two-story house that was the closest house to the mills in Windham. She remembered some explosions that broke the glass in every window. She also recounted that her father had to wear shoes with wooden pegs in them instead of nails to avoid striking a spark, and that no one was ever allowed to smoke in the mill or on the grounds. Her father retired from the Powder Mills in 1895, and the family moved to Gorham, where he did carpentry, building at least one house, and worked at the tannery. Regarding the explosion of April 22, 1890, she said:

> My father was thrown into the river. He was hit by a piece of metal and at that time he was wearing a breast pocket watch. The piece of metal hit the watch and broke it. The doctor said had he not had this watch in his pocket, he probably would have been killed. I remember my father was in bed a long time. My brother and I had to be very quiet. My father was seriously hurt but eventually he recovered and went back to work at the mill until sometime in 1895 when he retired.[90]

THE 1900s

Hydraulic Press Mill

A notable explosion on February 7, 1901, took out the new hydraulic press mill described as the "very latest improved machinery for pressing gunpowder into cakes." It was also interesting that the "plates," which were about a quarter of an inch thick and two feet square, were made of aluminum. This is the first time that aluminum was mentioned in relation to Maine powder mills of which I am aware. All of the older presses reportedly used copper sheets about two feet square and about half the thickness of the aluminum plates. This hydraulic press mill was on the Gorham side of the Presumpscot River, deduced from a paragraph from the company office describing how to get to the explosion site. Later in the same article, the *Portland Evening Express* noted, "The power was water supplied from the old canal . . ." After the Cumberland and Oxford Canal ceased operations in 1871, the Oriental Powder Company augmented the water in the Company's raceways by diverting water from the Canal when and where needed by means of connectors or gates under small bridges in the old towpath of the Canal.[91]

Figure 6: *Springtime Crooked River* (David Little, 2004, oil on canvas, 18" x 18")

Final Fatal Explosion

The last fatal explosion at the Oriental Powder Mills took place on March 4, 1904, and involved one workman being killed and another seriously injured. The *Westbrook Chronicle and Gazette* described it and also carried an obituary of Mr. Shaw.[92]

The *Westbrook Chronicle and Gazette* continued to publish frequent, brief news items concerning the Gambo Powder Mills, noting on April 1, 1904, that "the Oriental Powder company is removing the powder from their magazines in Portland out to Newhall."[93]

Two weeks later, the newspaper contained a brief report on James Freeman's recovery. "Mr. James Freeman, who was injured in the powder mill explosion, was calling on friends Wednesday. His nurse has returned to the Eye and Ear Infirmary in Portland."[94]

One month later, the *Westbrook Chronicle & Gazette* reported on the explosion of one of the Oriental Powder wheel mills on May 27, providing the first account known to my knowledge that mentions the possible presence of nitroglycerine on the premises: "Reports say that there are large quantities of nitro-glycerine stored in the village near the powder mills and grave fears are entertained as to the result if fire should come in contact with the building where it is stored."[95]

Charcoal Shortage

In November, the *Westbrook Chronicle & Gazette* reported: "On account of a shortage of charcoal, some employees of the Oriental Powder Co. are having a [forced]vacation while waiting for that commodity."[96] The mills could no longer produce all the needed charcoal on their premises. Possibly the supply of alder and willow within convenient transporting distance had become depleted. Some mills used maple for making charcoal when alder or willow was unavailable, but all powder makers claimed that maple charcoal was not as satisfactory an ingredient as the other two kinds of wood.

New Year Rumors

The first issue of the *Westbrook Chronicle & Gazette* for 1905 contained a general news item concerning the mill closing, plus an added item under "Newhall News." They follow respectively:

The Oriental Powder mills at Gambo, North Windham, which have been in operation very many years, shut down Saturday night [Dec.

131

31] for good. The machinery will be sent west. It is rumored that the valuable water power so long used by the Oriental Powder Co. at Gambo has been acquired by the S. D. Warren Co. of this city... Howard Smith, Superintendent of Oriental Powder Co., and his employees are cleaning up the mills which will be closing up this week, probably for an indefinite period.[97]

Winding Down

Some activity continued at the mills. The *Westbrook Chronicle* & *Gazette* reported, under "Newhall News" on February 3, 1905, that "Superintendent Howard Smith, book-keeper Willard, Mr. Howard Mayberry, and perhaps others are yet in the employ of the Oriental Powder Co. we are informed."[98] On August 23, 1905, the stockholders acted on a December 7, 1904, resolution of the Board of Directors in which they unanimously voted to sell the company to Laflin and Rand Powder Co. for $878,023.36, the "book value" of the company as of November 1, 1904. It was further voted after winding up all of Oriental Powder Mills' business that they "apply to the Supreme Judicial Court of the State of Maine in and for the County of Cumberland for a decree of dissolution."[99] The Eastern Dynamite Co. acquired the Oriental Mills' site in South Windham and started construction of the large wood-flour mills. Wood flour is primarily "used as an absorbent for the packing of dynamite."[100] In 1907, a concrete dam raised the height of the Presumpscot River, completely flooding the old wooden dam upstream that the Powder Mills had used for so many years. The Eastern Dynamite Company, with abundant water power and plenty of trees for making wood flour, started production in 1907 and continued until shortly after World War II.

As we have seen, for approximately 125 years, the industrial activity of the Gambo Falls area was very closely linked to the explosives industry.

Remaining evidence of powder mills

What evidence besides newspaper accounts, deeds on file, maps, and census listings exists that there was a large gunpowder manufacturing establishment on the Presumpscot River at Gambo Falls in Gorham and Windham? I have found the following kinds of evidence. Other people may know of additional evidence.

1. Stone foundations. The Gorham side has a wide variety of foundations: the older ones are made of fieldstones; the more

modern ones are cut granite blocks. Only in three of ten structures now visible was a small amount of brick along with the stone.

The Windham side also has foundations of fieldstone and cut granite, although they are fewer in number because of continued industrial activity on the Gorham side. In the early 1970s, there were at least 18 mill buildings, not including boarding houses and stables, on the Windham side of the river. The powder mills were succeeded on the Windham side by the Eastern Dynamite Company flour mills in 1907 and were later acquired by the E.I. DuPont Company, which operated them for almost forty years, to be in turn followed by other types of industries. The electric power-generating station owned by S. D. Warren Co. (now Sappi) has also altered raceways, etc. on the Windham side. The only concrete foundation for a relatively small building, undoubtedly a magazine, was located on the Windham side.

Figure 7: Round Mill Foundation at Gambo (source: Robert Sanford)

Figure 8: Square Mill Foundation at Gambo (source: Robert Sanford)

2. Remnants of the old dams, made primarily of wood with some stone, are still in existence, submerged under several feet of water due to the construction of the present dam in 1907, with modern improvements raising the height of the river several feet. The old wooden dams were located north of the present highway bridge. The principal dam was of unusual shape. Starting from the charcoal house island, it ran easterly toward the Windham shore, then southerly under the bridge, then more easterly to the "old stone mill." A small dam and bridge connected the island to the Gambo road on the Gorham side. The dams were all visible, right to their bottom parts submerged in the silt of the river, when S. D. Warren Co. in 1979 held the water back upstream to make extensive repairs on the 1907 dam at Gambo Falls.

3. Raceways were constructed on both sides of the river. Much of the raceway on the Windham side has been obliterated over the years. Some parts of the old Gorham raceways were dug in soil

and walled up with granite blocks, like cobblestone paving blocks, to function as retaining walls. This older raceway received its water from a culvert or conduit that crossed under Gambo Road. The gatehouse to control the flow was on the north side of the road. On the Gorham side, a shorter raceway blasted out of solid ledge ran parallel to the river for several hundred feet.[101]

4. When the water in the river is very low, there is revealed on the south side of the charcoal house island, facing the highway, a well-built cut granite foundation that was part of the foundation for the bridge to the mainland and anchored the wooden dam, which prevented water from eroding the island around the north end of the dam. At low water, the remains of the old dam are visible, as well as wooden piers that helped to support the bridge. The gatehouse in item three above was located to the west of the pier supports.

5. Downstream some distance below the present electric power-generating plant, at very low water, one can see the two small islands on opposite sides of the river that supported piers for one of the footbridges that connected the millworks. These islands were built by constructing a wooden crib and then filling it with rocks. Some of the crib work still remained in the mid-1970s.

6. The remains of the old Cumberland and Oxford Canal are visible in many places on the Gorham side, where it bordered the Powder Mills' property for several thousand feet. The Canal ceased operations in 1871, about the time that financial panic was gripping the gunpowder industry, and the Mills of Gambo sold in 1872. Starting at about the mid-1870s and in the 1880s, Gambo Mills expanded considerably, which created a demand for more water for power. The logical source would be water from the defunct C&O Canal. In ten places, the old towpath was breached and some type of gate installed to control the flow of water into the Powder Mills' raceways. Bridges were built at each of these cuts in the towpath, so that people, prob-

ably employees, could still use the path, which was elevated and had a slight grade and good drainage. None of these intersections of the towpath appears in Beers' Atlas of 1871, which supports my belief that they were constructed later in the decade. I have been informed by several area residents that the towpath and bridges were in good condition for walking and bicycling until about 1930.

7. Many broken stone mill wheels were left on the Gorham side. Some of these are just a few feet from the river; others are many yards from the river, closer to the old towpath. Most likely, these broke as a result of the explosions in the wheel mills in the earlier years of operation, before cast-iron wheels came into use. The wheels were usually about five or five-and-a-half feet in diameter. The rolling surface was extremely smooth. Each of the pair of matched stones in each wheel mill weighed approximately three tons.

8. The powder mills, from the time the Newhalls acquired them until they ceased operations in 1905, were quite self-sufficient and could make repairs expeditiously. They always had one or two carpenters and a head millwright with an assistant on the payroll. The "old stone mill" on the Windham side served as a carpenter shop and foundry for many years. A number of wooden pattern machine parts are still in existence, all of them stamped O.P.M. Ralph Willis owned several of them at this writing (1998).

9. When the mills closed, farmers in the area bought their wooden wheelbarrows (inside dimension 5 feet long, 2 feet wide, 14 inches deep), which were made without any iron or steel to avoid striking a spark. All metal used was copper or copper-alloy. The wheels were covered with cotton felt to avoid sparking. Ralph Willis and Walter Stevens own wheelbarrows.

10. Various containers are still in existence. The wooden kegs came in three sizes, 25 lb., 12 ½ lb., and 6 ¼ lb. They were usually closed by a wooden knob with three or four threads on it, or

by a bung. Eventually, all blasting powder was put up in metal drums that held 25 pounds. Sporting powder for hunters was usually sold in one pound or half-pound cans or flasks. If the can was made of steel, the opening would be of a zinc or lead alloy to avoid sparking. I have not seen any of the 100-pound-capacity oak barrels with the manufacturer's label or name, used for military powder during the Civil War.

11. Mrs. Louis B. Woodward gave me a small wooden display cabinet of the type distributed to hardware stores and powder agencies by the Oriental Powder Mills so that their different types of powder could be exhibited to potential buyers.

12. All employees of all powder mills were *not* allowed to wear boots or shoes with metal nails. Wooden pegs served as substitutes. Some of these are still in existence, owned by Ralph Willis (verified in 1988).

13. In Maine, containers of finished powder were usually stored in wooden sheds about 16 by 18 feet. Frequently windowless, some would have one small window resembling a basement window in the back of the structure. These magazines were scattered at considerable distances from each other in the woods so that if an explosion occurred in one building, they would not lose everything. I have heard from several sources that Oriental Powder Mills had brick or concrete magazines on both the Gorham and Windham sides of the river, but I have never seen one. Supposedly, some of these were underground.

14. Several buildings on Gambo Road in Windham specifically relate to the Powder Mills. The Newell family purchased the brick house at the corner of Gambo and River Roads when G. G. Newhall and Co. acquired the Powder Mills (1855). For years it was called the "Superintendent's House." The DuPont Company owned it for quite a few years. The late Bertha Verge's mother bought the house from the DuPonts in the spring of 1910. It was in the Verge family about 65 years. The large house on the north side of Gambo Road, nearer to the

river, was supposedly a rooming and boarding house for the single men employed by the Oriental powder Mills. On the south side of Gambo Road were two "duplex" millhouses. These were demolished in the summer of 1975. On the north side of Gambo Road, back about 250 feet from the road and overlooking the river, was a large stable used by the Mills to house their horses and store hay. In a bad state of repair, the stable was finally destroyed in the 1970s.

Figure 9: Gambo Powder Mill Outside View (source: Michael Shaughnessy)

15. The Powder Mills did not have a steam whistle; someone would ring a bell on the Windham side to regulate the activities of workers. According to verbal reports handed down genera-

tionally, the bell was rung to wake workers in the morning, again to start the day at 7:00 a.m., to announce the start and finish of the lunch period (probably 30 minutes), and to end the workday at 5:30 or 6:00 p.m.. In summer, it sounded a curfew at about dusk. It also served as an alarm bell for fires in the area.

16. The Newhall Railroad Station on the south side of Gambo Road, built about 1871-1872 when the Portland and Ogdensburg Railroad reached the area, has undergone a metamorphosis and is now a private home. The railroad tracks nearby are in the approximately 5000 feet of right of way conveyed by the Oriental Powder Mills to the Railroad for "one dollar and other . . . considerations."[102]

17. The tombstone of Thomas Bickford, who was killed in the explosion of September 22, 1851, has the inscription, "killed by the explosion of a Powder mill." The grave is in the Leavitt Cemetery in Windham.

18. The Windham Historical Society has a rifle that the Powder Mills used to test some of their rifle powder.

19. The Windham Historical Society also has an Oriental Powder Mills advertising poster that shows a number of different views of the establishment, including the President's Office, a powder wagon, and their canal boat.

20. Some receipts for the sale of gunpowder are still in existence. In 1988, Ralph Willis had two of these that his grandfather received when he purchased blasting powder from the Oriental Powder Company.

21. A variety of records of the Oriental Powder Mills, including minutes of the Directors, the Executive Committee, and the Stockholders from 1872 to 1906, are available in the Hagley Library in Greenville, Delaware.

22. Several late-nineteenth-century advertising brochures or booklets still exist.

23. Etchings drawn by artists in different time periods depict the Oriental Powder Mills. One is in the Collections of the Library of Congress; the same one appears in Lossing's book (1878). Below the lower left corner is, "Engd by J. A. J. Wilcox," while below the right corner is "W. H. Brett & Co." Some etchings show smoke rising from a train in the woods; these must have been drawn after 1871 when the trains were running into Newhall.

---

[1] This chapter is condensed from Whitten, M. (2006 [1990]). *The gunpowder mills of Maine.* Enfield, NH: Enfield Publication & Distribution Company.

[2] McLellan, H. D. (1903). *History of Gorham, Maine.* Portland, ME: Smith & Sale, 273-274.
https://babel.hathitrust.org/cgi/pt?id=coo1.ark:/13960/t3417jj4k;view=1up;seq=9

[3] Dole, S. T. (1916). *Windham in the past.* F. H. Dole (Ed.). Auburn, ME: Merrill & Webber Co., 227-228.
https://babel.hathitrust.org/cgi/pt?id=loc.ark:/13960/t5r78gr41;view=1up;seq=9

[4] Cumberland County Registry of Deeds, Book 389, p. 528.

[5] Davis, M. G. (1951). *Historical facts and stories about Southwick. The Laflins in gunpowder business,* 204-211.Typscript on file at Southwick (MA) Public Library. Fowler, C. C. (1950); *The history of the Fowlers.* Batavia, NY: Miller-Mac Printing Co.

[6] Van Gelder, A. P., & Schlatter, H. (1927). *History of the explosives industries in America.* New York: Columbia University Press.

[7] Ibid., 105.

[8] Cumberland County Registry of Deeds, Book 96, p 519.

[9] Encyclopedia Dubuque. (2018). Laflin and Rand Powder Company. http://www.encyclopediadubuque.org/index.php?title=LAFLIN_AND_RAND_PO WDER_COMPANY

[10] Prices current (1826, November 24). *Portland Advertiser*.

[11] Prices current. (1828, June 30). *Portland Advertiser*.

[12] Dole, S. T. (1894). *Handwritten record book*. Coll. 110, 2/16. Collection of the Maine Historical Society. 1916. I

[13] *Portland Advertiser* (1827, June 29).

[14] Cumberland County Registry of Deeds, Book 129, 313, 402. J. M. Forward did not keep the Fowler & Laflin Powder Co. but promptly sold it to Oliver Whipple. Whitten, *Gunpowder mills*, Appendix I, 248.

[15] Van Gelder & Schlatter, *History of explosives*, 75.

[16] Gragg, W. (1828). *Scrapbook*, Vol. 3, p. 120. Collections of the Maine Historical Society.

[17] *Daily Courier* (1831, August 27).

[18] Courier-Citizen Company (1897). *Illustrated history of Lowell and vicinity*. Lowell, MA: Author, 147.

[19] Ibid.

[20] Lowell Historical Society (1913, April 19). *Lowell Historical Society Contributions*, 1.

[21] Smith, T. L. (1873). *History of the Town of Windham, Maine*. Portland: Hoyt & Fogg, 68. https://archive.org/stream/ historyoftowofw00smit/historyoftownofw00smit_djvu.txt

[22] Dole, S. T. (1895, December 19). Gambo, old and new. Paper delivered to the Maine Historical Society, Portland, Maine. (pp. 255-262). In Willis, W. (Ed.). *Collections and proceedings of the Maine Historical Society* (Second Series, Vol. VIII), 259.

[23] Dole, *Windham*, 282.

[24] Powder Mill blown up (1849, July 19). *Eastern Argus*.

[25] Powder Mills blow up (1850, October 1). *Portland Daily Advertiser*.

[26] *Oxford Democrat* (1851, October 3). Thomas Bickford could not have worked for Oliver Whipple for 30 years at Gambo, because Whipple didn't start to acquire the property until June 1832. Thus, Bickford's maximum time working for Whipple at Gambo would have been 19 years. Possibly, Bickford worked at Whipple's gunpowder establishment in Lowell before coming to Gorham-Windham.

[27] Gambo Powder Mills. *Tour historical Gorham script from May 25, 1986.* http://www.gorham.k12.me.us/~jgauley/gorham_tour/ files/tour_1986.html

[28] Dole, *Windham in the past*, 228.

[29] Frightful accident in Gorham (1855, October 13). *Eastern Argus*.

[30] Dole, *Windham in the past*, 228.

[31] *Portland Sunday Telegram.* (February 2, 1936). Portland, Maine

[32] State Library of Massachusetts. (1816, June 18). *Chap. 0026: An act regulating the storage, safe-keeping, and transportation of gunpowder, in the town of Boston.* Boston: Secretary of the Commonwealth. https://archives.lib.state.ma.us/bitstream/handle/2452/109649/ 1816acts0026.txt? sequence=1&isAllowed=y

[33] Dole, *Windham in the past*, 229.

[34] *Portland Daily Advertiser* (1856, May 8).

[35] Explosion of powder mills at Gorham and fatal results (1856, August 5). *Eastern Argus*.

[36] *Eastern Argus* (1959, January 17).

[37] Maine Secretary of State (1859). *Acts and resolves of the Thirty-Eight Legislature of the State of Maine.* Augusta: Sprague, Owen, & Nash, Printers to the State, 239.

[38] Keg mill burnt (1859, October 27). *Daily Advertiser*.

[39] United States Census (1850-1860). Census schedules for agriculture, industry, and social statistics [Maine]. http://catalog.crl.edu/search/Y?SEARCH=Agricultural%2C%20industrial%2C%20and%20social%20census%2C%20Maine&searchscope=1

[40] Dole, S. T. (n.d.). *Scrapbook*. Vol. 3, Maine Historical Society.

[41] Smith, T. L. (1873). *History of the town of Windham, Maine*. Portland: Hoyt & Fogg, 78-79. https://archive.org/details/historyoftownofw00smit/page/n5

[42] *Eastern Argus*. (1861, May 9).

[43] Dole, Gambo old and new, 262.

[44] Powder mill explosion (1862, May 3). *Eastern Argus*.

[45] Powder mill explosion (1862, July 8). *Portland Daily Advertiser*.

[46] *Eastern Argus* (July 12, 1862).

[47] Sketches of Windham history (1898, April 21). *Narragansett Sun*.

[48] Wescott, D. C., & Whitten, M. M. (2000-2019). Civil War gunpowder making at Gambo. *Maine Memory Network*. https://www.mainememory.net/sitebuilder/site/2484/page/3975/display?use_mmn=1

[49] Wescott, D. C., & Whitten, M. M. (2000-2019). Gunpowder for the Civil War – The Oriental Powder Mills of Gorham-Windham. *Maine Memory Network*. https://www.mainememory.net/sitebuilder/site/2482/page/3973/display?use_mmn=1;popup=1

[50] Ibid.

[51] Van Gelder & Schlatter, *History of Explosives*, 115-116.

[52] Lossing, B. J. (1878). *History of American industries and arts*. Philadelphia, PA: Porter & Coates, 241.

[53] Ibid., 242.

[54] McLellan, H. D. (1903). History of the Civil War of 1861-1865, and the Soldiers' Monument (pp. 340-355). In *McLellan, History of Gorham*.

[55] Van Gelder & Schlatter, *History of explosives*, 126.

[56] Maine Secretary of State (1867). *Acts and Resolves passed by the Forty-Sixth Legislature of the State of Maine*. Augusta: Stevens and Sayward.

[57] *Eastern Argus* (1869, February 22).

[58] Explosion of a powder mill at Gorham (1870, August 3). *Eastern Argus*.

[59] Pal, H. (2018). It happened in Windham: The Big Ditch. *Keep Me Current*. http://news.keepmecurrent.com/it-happened-in-windham-the-big-ditch/

[60] Beers, F. W. (1871). *Atlas of Cumberland County, Maine*. New York: F. W. Beers & Co.

[61] Cumberland County Registry of Deeds, Book 389, 528.

[62] Ibid., 395.

[63] Maine Secretary of State (1872). *Acts and Resolves passed by the Forty-Ninth Legislature of the State of Maine*. Augusta: Stevens and Sayward.

[64] *Lewiston Evening Journal* (1918, July 8). Illustrated Magazine Section.

[65] *Portland Transcript* (1876, December 23).

[66] *The Paper Trade Journal* (1877, February 3), 37.

[67] *Oriental Powder Mills*, Portland, Maine (1867). https://www.mainememory.net/media/pdf/98545.pdf

[68] Anderson, H. L. V. (1877). Handwritten entry *Scrapbook*, 3.

[69] Anderson, H. L. V. (1878). A petition to Congress. *Scrapbook*, 18.

[70] Hayes, S. D. (1878, April 1). The three classes of explosive agents now in use (Paper Abstract). *Boston Commercial Bulletin*.

[71] Anderson, H. L. V. (1877). Wholesale powder trade. *Scrapbook*.

[72] Anderson, H. L. V. (1879, September 15). News item, paper unknown. *Scrapbook*.

[73] Fearful explosion. A Gambo Powder Mill blown up (1879, October 28). *Portland Advertiser*.

[74] DuPont Co. (1880, August 30). Oriental Powder Mills, II/1, Vol. 1405. *Oriental Powder Mills*. Courtesy of Hagley Museum and Library.

[75] The complete record of the meeting is in Whitten, *Gunpowder mills*.

[76] DuPont Co. (1880, January 6). *Oriental Powder Mills*, II/1, Vol. 1408. Courtesy of Hagley Museum and Library.

[77] DuPont Co. (1880, August 30). *Oriental Powder Mills*, II/1, Vol. 1405. Courtesy of Hagley Museum and Library.

[78] DuPont Co. (1880, October 27). *Oriental Powder Mills*, II//1 Vol. 1405. Courtesy of Hagley Museum and Library.

[79] *Havre de Grace Republican* (1882, September 29).

[80] *Eastern Argus* (1884, January 31).

[81] *American Field* (1885, May 9); *American Field* (1885, June 20).

[82] Fearful Explosion. Two mills at the Oriental Powder Company at Windham have blown up (1886, March 12). *Eastern Argus*; A powder mill explosion (1886, March 13). *Eastern Argus*; *Boston Globe* (1886, March 12); An earthquakelike shock. Powder mills near Portland blow up (1886, March 12). *Boston Herald*.

[83] *Eastern Argus* (1870, August 3).

[84] *Rockland Courier-Gazette*, (1887, August 23).

[85] *Rockland Courier-Gazette*, (1887, November 29).

[86] With lightning swiftness (1888, November 6). *Eastern Argus*.

[87] Powder mill explosion (1888, December 3). *Portland Press*.

[88] *Portland Daily Advertiser* (1888, December 5).

[89] Three mills exploded (1890, April 23). *Eastern Argus*; Anderson, H. L. V. (1890). *Scrapbook*.

[90] Woodward, Edna (October 8, 1973). Personal Communication.

[91] *Portland Evening Express* (1901, February 7).

[92] Explosion at Oriental Powder Mills. Two workmen seriously injured and Mill Number Two dismantled. (1904, March 25). *Westbrook Chronicle & Gazette*.

[93] *Westbrook Chronicle and Gazette* (1904, April 1).

[94] *Westbrook Chronicle and Gazette* (1904, April 15).

[95] South Windham news (1904, June 1). *Westbrook Chronicle & Gazette*.

[96] *Westbrook Chronicle & Gazette* (1904, November 8).

[97] Powder Mill at Gambo closed (1905, January 6). *Westbrook Chronicle & Gazette*.

[98] Newhall news (1905, February 3). *Westbrook Chronicle & Gazette*.

[99] DuPont Co. (1905, August 23). *Oriental Powder Mills*, II/1, Vol. 1405. Courtesy of Hagley Museum and Library.

[100] South Windham news (1905, September 22). *Westbrook Chronicle & Gazette*.

[101] Beers, *Atlas*. Only the last raceway does not appear in Beer.

[102] Cumberland County Registry of Deeds, Book 389, 528.

Chapter 7

The River in Literature—Presumsca:
Getting into the Flow

The Presumpscot (source: Author)

> "River gravel. In the beginning, that."
> —Seamus Heaney, *The Spirit Level*

Introduction

Consider the river for a long, moving moment.

Imagine the flood waters of Biblical time set down among us now filled with the contemporary life of baby eels, alewives in their spring runs, and clouds of black flies, a Maine special. Even the Native American name for the river, Presumpsca, links this moment's flow to an earlier time and the earlier human experience of its 25.8-mile watery path from Sebago Lake toward the sea, finding a soft outlet in Casco Bay and eventually sloshing in around the pilings of Portland's piers. You can consider the river as it considers you, from its centuries of being.

Rivers give us pause, because they cannot wait. Because they mix eternity and the moment into a potent cocktail. Because we can't wait to drink from them, to dip our toes in, to float along, to probe the depths and survey what's hidden, almost visible. The Presumpsca belongs to past time but gives us a vocabulary for naming what we see *here*, *now*, for the kind of intimate feeling that a sense of place can grant. If a river has a language of its own, maybe it can help articulate both knowledge and compassion, such that the words help us to care. Stewardship is the pure gold baby of a love that looks forward and back.

Flow & Pause, Sensation & Sense

Visiting the Presumpscot today, in early spring, is an adventure in traction—and losing it. An excess of rain makes the trail at the Oat Nuts Park access point in Portland a place of wet mystery. Just behind the suburban, straightened-out cul de sac of a grid-like neighborhood street so like any other that you could easily get lost but for the large boat parked in the usual spot for a car . . . the trailhead map presents a friendly face. *This is where you are*, it says, and *this is where you should go next*. And, finally, *this is where you are destined to go, down here to the water's edge. This ripple not visible on the map, this liquid reveal of life beneath.* That's where we're headed.

If you're traveling in a pair, one of you can hike to higher ground, sighting the riverbank from above the tangle of tree edge. One of you can indulge in the "plop" and "suck" your sneakers make before pulling out of your own footsteps in the center of the trail. Both of you must take the handy, brief boardwalk by the bent-over pine tree that makes a right angle of itself, facing back where you came from. Deceptive rushing sounds come in from your right, where a small stream courses down the banks in the inevitable lowering toward water-level. This is the not-river. Your aim is the real current you can just begin to hear below. The terrain is hilly and lovely and complicated . . .

Newsworthy?

Not the least of this river's complications are the occasional reports of dam debates, drownings, accidents, enormous snakes, and hidden bodies. I include a few recent headlines not to distract us from the main business of tracking down to the river itself, but to acknowledge the "literature of the river" in the news media of the twenty-first century, our moment of still-consumable sensationalism.

"Giant Snake Loose in Maine: Wessie the Python"[1]
[*Time Magazine*, August 20, 2016]
"Snake Skin Found in Maine Belongs to Anaconda"[2]
[*Boston Globe*, August 30, 2016]

These two make a great pair; witness the divergence in species name that suggests the possibility of a hoax. Or faulty journalism. We're invited to consider the reaches between species of snake but also the reaches between local legends. Wessie and Loch Ness Nessie might be distant cousins. Except that police officers saw Wessie eating a beaver on the banks of the river and "her" discarded skin later appeared along the banks. Lest we think our skins innocent: this one went off to a biologist at the University of Texas at Tyler who confirmed the translucent evidence. Anaconda. Without a doubt. Juvenile green anaconda, ten feet long at shed time. Can deliver a painful bite but not a deadly one.

We're also invited to remember the classic distinctions between the news and literature—and to wonder if the distinction still holds. William Carlos Williams wrote in 1955 of the search for meaning in a diminished (Robert Frost's adjective) world:

It is difficult
to get the news from poems
Yet men die miserably every day
for lack
of what is found there.

"Do not turn away," Williams insists, in the penultimate lines of this long poem "Asphodel, That Greeny Flower."[3] Do not turn away from the need that we have, as deep as our bone depth, for something beyond what the news can give us. I've always been troubled by the vagueness of Williams's word "there," at the end of these lines. Men die for lack (now there's a fresh appraisal) of what's found in the news? In poems? Either way, our heads are turning back and forth between these directions. And men are dying, how miserable that is, from an absence of meaning in the world. The news, like these Wessie headlines, scares us but doesn't include the sentiment we expect of literature; poems can offer us profound insight but only if we can access it. *The Washington Post, Time Magazine,* and *CNN* all picked up the story.

I cannot resist another, to return us to the meandering river:

"As Triathletes Swim in Presumpscot River, Many Eyes Will Be On Snake Watch"

On September 7, 2016, the *Portland Press Herald* reported some trepidation among athletes and supporters of the Major League race. No wonder, with several snake sightings in the area and the finding of that miraculous shed skin, the chrysalis of one life season, the gossamer wrapper of truth. What is the meaning of a snakeskin but as a placeholder? This is the place, *here*. An empty case but a certain cipher, a fact of serpentine presence. Don't we often describe the river itself as 'snaking' around a bend? Perhaps they are elementally related, snake and river, closer cousins than Wessie and Nessie. Perhaps in every river there is a snake. Perhaps there's nothing wrong with using a cliched phrase that still moves us toward the smell of danger. Toward that decentering in the pit of your stomach that you feel in seeing the dissolving, impossible movements of a snake slithering, all coil and boil, *sans* elbows and shoulders. *Sans* everything but sheer pulsing movement. Cauldron of trouble. But a comment from one of the swimmers appeared to put things in perspective: "With 180 people in the water, Wessie will be going the other way."[4] Go, Wessie, go.

It's hard to look away.

Humans are rubbernecking creatures when it comes to danger and mystery. That's exactly where we want to look. Right into the twisting gyre. And when the scene is shrouded a bit, we might crane ourselves a little further to look again. And gasp. Nothing beats a good local story. Nothing beats a police statement that admits defeat. Even the liquidity of a local river can hide a body:

"Maine State Police Divers Searching Presumpscot River in Westbrook"[5]

This headline from July 17, 2017, startles us back into the present. It seems there's a young man missing, and that his fiancé had received a tip about looking for him in the river. Whatever relation she had with the Presumpscot before, she must hear its name differently now. River of triathletes, river of murderers. Carrier of the dead. Styx an ancient cousin. One deeper reason to fear rivers: for what they almost conceal. For how they mythically contain opposing shores of life and death, a skilled boatman able to ferry the passage. On one side, bodies. On the other, souls. No good resting place for a discarded snake skin, unless we imagine Wessie crossed over, slipped her new-skinned body for spirit.

It's not ethically right to mix such headlines. Whatever became of the real anaconda, whose fate was looking grim by media reports in late October pointing to the unsurvivable winter temperatures coming to Maine—and whatever became of Sebastian Kelley, the thirty-year-old man somehow caught up in a predicament of large proportions; their stories are joined only by place in this one way, this one riverine thread. I chronicle the human story in short form, hoping the climax hasn't happened yet, that it didn't already happen long before the good name of the Presumpscot was dragged in.

But there are more:

"Teen Swimming with Friends Drowns in Presumpscot River"[6] [*Bangor Daily News*, September 11, 2011]

"Westbrook Police Identify Man Who Drowned in the Presumpscot River"[7] [*Bangor Daily News*, August 26, 2014]

"Emergency Crews Recover Body of Missing Kayaker from Presumpscot River"[8] [WCSH News, 6 June 3, 2016]

Perhaps these headlines alone are enough to convey whole stories about the allure and danger of moving water. They shock us out of absent-minded estimations of current, temperature, debris, rocks, on the streambed. The *locus amoenus*, the pleasant place, turns dark in the shadow of such typesetting. Beyond stark fact, with its hush of permanency, what do we know of these persons or their grip on lives that ended? Add them up and the individual fates create an unarguable statistic. One river. Three lives.

Men die miserably for lack of what is found there. Where? If the newspaper column lacks in poetry what it gives us, in spades, in head-turning 'fact,' what should we read? Where should we look?

Mill Brook Preserve

Let's look here. Another end of another residential road. I took lots of pictures so that I could better evade the mosquitoes by not pausing to take wonderfully descriptive notes on site. Map and chart will have to do. The visual record reminds the mind, piques the senses again, and I want to return there now, as Wordsworth would (apologies for the grand comparison meant to invoke the literary aspects of reimagined rivers) to his Lake District, to his River Wye. One thing I've been learning about the Presumpscot is how much one relies upon comparisons to write about it—indeed, to write about anything, perhaps. This to that, that to this, just as the early explorers of the new continent turned back to the countryside of England in order to marvel at the flora and fauna of a wild new world for which they had no express language. But they had eyes to see. Look.

Parking at 847 Methodist Rd., one designated spot up from the sheriff's house in Westbrook, adds a religious-legal feeling to walking this access route to the Presumpscot. As the only living body in the early summer air, I was nearly taken hostage by blood-smelling insects despite the obvious wrongness of this assault. Hat strapped on, atomizer of worthless lavender oil in my right hand, I navigated the generous mown path behind the sheriff's house to the tree line and then descended through hardwoods on a crumbling path well marked with blue slashes on the trunks, just above eye level. Another thing I've been learning about the Presumpscot is how embedded it is in the suburban landscape, evidenced here not only by the back-of-duplexes views from above its banks but also by the demonstrable care its supporters give it. All those blue slashes say *yes, you're still on the trail, this way please, keep going up if you want out*. Because down is always the way to the river. Down to the bed, the water level. To where the air is cool and damp and despite the stinging, biting insects of early summer in Maine, you want to get there. *This way. Down here is where you want to be. You can leave your hat on.*

A cavalcade of images. Flip book of snapshots. Cool crisper drawer of sensory impressions. Seriously. The river is already doing the work of inspiration. I take stock of another bit of poetic wisdom from Seamus Heaney in telling some of the Presumpscot's story in this personal, associative, wandering way. "To be marvellously yourself like the river water," a line from his book *Electric Light,* seems like an invitation to the water-loving essayist.[9]

Maps charm us with their certainties: this dotted line corresponds to 'Trail,' this blue line denotes 'Mill Brook.' A lighter line marks 'Tributaries' and lighter still, 'Contours.' Preserve boundaries and the three trailheads raise the area into near-relief, framing the fish-viewing pond as central attraction. Yet the watershed ranges beyond the grid as the water flowing through the riverbanks undoes any notion of containment, visual or otherwise.

And rivers have a long history of bursting their boundaries, natural and human-engineered. The Presumpscot's own Cumberland and Oxford Canal, opened for business in 1830 but unused by 1872, offers a close-hand example of boundaries failing in a larger sense: the coming of the railroad obliterated the usefulness of the four-mile-an-hour passage of raw materials and finished goods along the twenty miles of canal studded with twenty-seven locks to negotiate the 265 ft. elevation between Sebago Lake and the outlet of Portland. All these numbers were blurred by the locomotive.

Some of the following 'facts' are taken from Kent Ryden's musings on "an ongoing effort to dominate water" in *Landscape with Figures: Nature & Culture in New England*.[10] In a chapter titled "Redesigning the River: Nature, Technology, and the Cumberland and Oxford Canal," he looks to the famous literary exemplars of Mark Twain's *Life on the Mississippi* and John McPhee's *The Control of Nature* to see the loggerheads between rivers and engineers, or between culture's control and nature's waywardness. A canal reroutes and regularizes nature's way.

Siding with nature while maintaining a grasp on the necessities of in-dustrial progress (Thoreau would say "so called progress," as he does of the suddenness of telegraph and railroad and even dinner parties, in *Walden*, in 1854), Ryden describes the look of the abandoned canal bed in or around the millennium: "The canal is dry, the water in the landscape confined not within its sculpted sides but within the shaggy rough banks of the Pre-sumpscot." Now, the water is "no longer held hostage"[11] or made to flow through a tunnel eighteen feet wide at the bottom and thirty-two feet wide at the top. But when in use, the C&O Canal regularized space and short-ened travel time between two points; viewed in light of the larger discourse on nineteenth-century attitudes toward nature and the human place in it, the canal may have symbolized a complicated sense of divine right to improve a God-given landscape. Whether the river or the canal is preemi-nent in the nineteenth-century view may be hard to answer from a twenty-first-century perspective. But surely we know which one was there first, which was preexisting. We've always known it. "In the Beginning, river water." Closing with a tribute to the long-forgotten Irish laborers who worked in dangerous conditions to build the canal (and the gunpowder mills at Gambo Falls in Gorham, which claimed more than forty lives during its tenure), Ryden compassionately re-orients his focus on the figures in the landscape who had intimate knowledge of its muddy, frozen pockets and the real weight of lumber cut from its forests. These bodies don't show up on any map, within any boundaries, or on any key.

And so even as we reach for the details of history to ground ourselves, to balance the rash of new headlines, we're dealing in bodies again. Sub-merged, washed, moved. Today, says Ryden, standing firmly on the ground in Audubon sanctuary land near Portland's East End, today the old canal landscape is "a human sanctuary as much as a wildlife sanctuary."[12] Today we can wonder about the shorthand of symbols on a map and their abbreviated correspondences. Cardinal directions do not shift from the compass rose pointing "N" in its reassuring fashion. But the river raises a lot of questions. You can count on it.

~ ~ ~

I take a selfie. This is the selfie-loving, meme-propagating, viral universe we live in. To document my journey, to map my body onto this wide mown path when I'm halfway down it, I take a headshot. Green grass and green leaves and green air, and I'm thinking again of Williams' obsession with "that greeny flower" asphodel. But a flower inventory comes later. Trust me.

In the picture: wide-brimmed ripstop fabric hat, side-angled view of the better side of my nose, guide-yellow backpack straps overlaid on fleece. A tree trunk sprouting directly out of my head. Well, out of my hat. The darkest shadows fold inside that hat brim, over my ears, where my hair is tucked back and out of the way. Tucked back in the distant background, beech and oak trees live their way into a foggy luminescence not possible in real air. The absolute backstop of the image bleaches out apocalyptically, more blast than blessed, this light offstage. My expression says *let's go, I'm ready, I'm armed. I can drop this fleece and this pack if I need to, but just don't try to take my hat.* My selfie doesn't behave well enough for inclusion on the staid area map, though I'm headed for the fish-viewing pool right in the center. It doesn't resolve into the stick-figure symbol of a hiker with a hiking stick and bent back, just as the Presumpscot doesn't resolve into a non-modulated line of blue ink. Topographical elevation is met with concentric circles nested tightest at the steepest peaks. What documents the flat-paper rush of river water or gurgle or spray?

Not long after my selfie moment I'm at water level, trying to shed whatever skin of stimulae still trails me from the parking area, the map kiosk, the block letters of the sheriff's SUV impressed in my retinas. It's not hard. The wet smell of water and moss works like a super conductor to help funnel my footsteps and my friable thoughts toward what matters. As I'm thinking about skins, still, I see the pattern of low ripple on the river's surface much like a topographical map or the wrinkles on a bedsheet. If I were a physicist (gasping laugh expected here), maybe I'd know something about why the ripple lengthens between the bigger rocks, fidgets and worms into an opaque surface of glare in the center. Standing on the rough and shaggy banks of the Presumpscot in 2017, I know why those adjectives made sense in 2000, as some of what I'm standing on is likely even rougher and shaggier. Where the water cuts away the land on the far side I see a sandy lip and then above it, hanging over it greenly, a foot-high rounded bank lined with moss. On the near side, peering down the steep terrain of loose pine needles (one million million Pick Up Sticks, a game not for the faint of heart), I defy gravity as no physicist would, for a second or two, looking from one brown, downed leaf to its neighbor leaf, hopscotching with my eyes. But this promotes a kind of vertigo, given the 95% humidity, so I choose a more pedestrian route to hone in on the prize.

Because it's a gift, right? What I came for. The payoff. I want to admire the promise of dark pockets in the shadowed edges of the large rocks, imagining the tiny fish that might rest there. The plush pocket of depth and dark alone is a gift, all by itself. A damp full lap of not-quite-drinkable rightness. Old memories of playing in the 'gulley' behind a family home in Freeport well up; evidently one thing rivers do especially well is to invite comparisons to one's own estuarine experiences. Rivers make (new) memories, and in the recalling of earlier moments they have a hand in characterizing the past. In that gulley, the gulley of my mother's childhood and her father's before her, and so on, back to about 1830, downed trees served as magical footbridges. Here, a couple of fallen trunks tip their barkless selves all the way across but at such an angled pitch only a fleet-foot red squirrel might consider them safe passage. In this one walk, I know something more about the considerations of red squirrels, too, as I startled the fur off one near its personal pinecone pile, near its little throne of foodstuffs at the base of a tree. Hat brim down and motivated to elude the mosquitoes, I must have been a locomotive to Mr. Red, a young one still deserving of the title, as I never saw but the after-image of red wavering an inch above the dead leaves. I was the machine in his garden. That's the thing about walking in the woods, even in the slightly compromised, suburban woods of this river preserve. You become acutely aware of what you have almost seen. There is an anterior world. The Transcendentalists were not wrong. The flash of insight may be only a flash, but the potency of it makes a pleasant buzz in your brain or the seat of your soul.

The Poetry of the Presumpscot: Then

Is it time to take a break? Take up the 'literary' again? Get cozy with the past flashes of some sentimental writers?

I'm game.

I looked, and I found them, lifted their lines from the crypt-like database containers of respected libraries, to see how they shine in the light of twenty-first-century day. Library exploration is not much like preserve exploration except that you do feel occasionally mired in the wilderness of broken-off search results, the impoverishment of relevant full-text hits. Part of the story of the literature of the Presumpscot is that there is hardly any literature of the Presumpscot. The Penobscot, the Androscoggin, the Kennebec, the Allagash, the St. John, the Saco show up in Google and specialized databases; even Merrymeeting Bay has its own beautiful book *Confluence*, with text by Franklin Burroughs, Professor Emeritus of Bowdoin College, and photographs by Heather Perry. But the Presumpscot? Well, we're working on it.

To get a handle on the more well-known nineteenth-century players, we could start earlier, with Samuel Deane, b. 1733, whose "Pitchwood Hill" is collected in a thick volume called *The Poets of Maine*, published by his alma mater Harvard in 1760, and first published in the *Cumberland Gazette* March 5, 1795. The poem was later collected in *The Poets of Maine*, an anthology compiled by George Bancroft Griffith, published in 1888 in Portland, Maine.

In this celebration of the local landscape for the natural features affording poetic inspiration, the few relevant lines abuse syntax a bit to craft the perfect rhyme:

> Down the eastern slope below,
> See the grand PRESUMPSCOT flow!
> Noble river, broad and deep,
> Majestic, slow his waters creep![13]

"Noble," "grand," "majestic" . . . these adjectives give high praise to the local river. The block-ends of the line breaks, however, undermine 'flow' by making the movement nearly stop. This is one hemmed-in big river. It presses up against the rough banks, perhaps, but it's not given much momentum or scrutiny.

Deane's poem picks up in liveliness as it continues, reaching for the majesty of mythic comparison to show us the greatness of the river. While the Presumpscot moves by the logic of gravity, the poet's mind climbs further into the fevered ether of myth to imagine whimsical river nymphs and gods convening for nights of sport. As the river winds "his serpentine way / From Sebacook to the sea":

> Fancy, on the verdant banks,
> Views the fairies' midnight pranks.
> Naiads, Tritons, here may seem
> To wanton o'er the limpid stream.[14]

Just as the mythical Eden was protected from the howling wilderness by such a band of water, the speaker finds himself safely separate from the dark, forested lands on the other side of the "moving flood" by the river itself. The woods are dark and unplumbed, "hideous" as they were in the days of Indian presence there; now the deep shadows cover the haunts of wild animals. Deane follows the biblical line quite closely, offering in 1795 an early literary account of the Gorham area that claims special status for this familiar stretch of water near his home.

But soon the poem shifts its gaze away from the mythic proportions to the ultra-local fact of the nearby dam. The falls create a roaring sound that is magnified by the juggernaut of industry, and most interesting here is the way Deane allows for the earthly qualities of his river while maintaining his status as onlooker. See here how he describes the tremendous, unnatural noise of the dam at Saccarappa Falls (much contested over the years and in 2016 under a proposal to be removed by 2020) as so usual to citizens that they no longer hear it:

> Saccarappy's falling stream
> Does like distant thunder seem;
> Grinds the soil from either side,
> Foaming down a hoary tide.
> Though it needed nothing more,
> To complete the wild uproar;
> Various mills erected there,
> With clatt'ring din torment the air.
> But the village planted round,
> Scarcely hears the deaf'ning sound.
> Habit heeds not constant screams,
> Eternal noise like quiet seems.[15]

Strong language prevents any misunderstanding of the evil of the mills. Posing a question to the reader about the "clangor" that assaults the ears with "uncouth" sounds and then naming Saccarappy Dam and the working mills along the river as the offenders, the poet emphasizes his point that this part of the river is anti-Eden. It's a new kind of "hideous" wilderness, human-made. Like the locomotive passing through the New England forests, supplanting even the system of canals, the dam is a visible and audible reminder of our disconnection to nature: Leo Marx's "paradox" of the machine in the garden.

One way out of the trap, real or poetic, is to climb back up again, above the scene, so as to look down on the pastoral views of grazing sheep and the free-flowing river. Pitchwood Hill, "Sacred height!" becomes an accessible Parnassus where the muses may visit pilgrim seekers and help them become so virtuous as to one day summit a "happier Hill." From its water-level sensory description of the dam to its gazing into eternity, this poem travels farther than the 25.8 miles of the Presumpscot. The river-as-vehicle prompts quiet contemplation as much as revivification of actual scenery, leading to a gratifying, moral end. Almost to transubstantiation. Why write poems at all, about rivers or hills or otherwise, unless the purpose is to get closer to immortality? We could say that Deane crosses over his river, in poetic rapture, in a long literary tradition of crossing over rivers to achieve some unknown but better shore.

Henry Wadsworth Longfellow missed the Presumpscot, though he did, famously, chronicle the river-based story of Hiawatha, "On the shores of Gitche Gumee, / Of the shining Big-Sea-Water."[16] Literary associations with waterways often include themes of heroic travel, transformation, restoration. The very rhythmic pounding of Longfellow's end-stopped lines, pair after pair after pair, created a drumbeat of inevitability in the listener's ear, at a time when poetry was as much listened to, around the hearth in the evenings, as it was read by individuals in the solitary poses that we understand manifested more substantially in the second half of the nineteenth century with the advent of the dime novel and more affordable, mass production of the nation's literature. It gives us pause, today, to picture a family gathered by the fire to listen to a patriarchal voice read the latest installment of Dickens's *Great Expectations* when we operate under the cultural realities of separate Netflix subscriptions streaming in separate earbuds in separate rooms of family houses.

Longfellow's poem "To The River Charles," however, trades on a signal feature of the river that we see writers probing along more local banks: the river-as-spiritual-guide and comforter. In sum: the far side of Longfellow's river is sunshine and light; the side closest to him is dark with memories of lost loved ones. But the river has a way of winding through past and present such that it gives a positive outlook toward the future—the poet ends in gratefulness for the memories given back to him, though the persons can never be returned. The river's connection to a transcendent peace of connections beyond the immediate frame continues to captivate (see Appendix 1).

Thoreau missed it, though he wrote movingly of the Penobscot in *Into the Maine Woods*. And John Muir, a latter-day voice for rivers and impassioned foe of dams, seems to have come close to the Presumpscot, very close, without putting pen to paper. On October 20, 1898, he came southeast to Portland from the White Mountains: "His train came down the Saco River valley along a scenic stretch of Sebago Lake, to South Windham, a borough of the east bank of the Presumpscot River, two stops before Portland."[17] We have the fact of proximity.

John Greenleaf Whittier came close to direct mention of the Presumpscot River and was certainly writing about the immediate environs in his long rhyming romances about Indian battles and virtues. Although the river named in his poem "Funeral Tree of the Sokokis" is the Saco, this poem set on the shores of "Sebago's lonely lake" appears to commemorate Chief Polin. (In a footnote to Whittier's poem in Griswold's *The Poets and Poetry of America*, we learn that Polin was killed at Windham on Sebago Lake in the spring of 1756, he who "claimed all the lands on both sides of the Presumpscot River to its mouth at Casco, as his own."[18] In a note of our own, it's worth mentioning that Griswold's anthology survived sixteen editions, a sign of poetry's popularity in the nineteenth century.) Territorial conflicts over land appear not only in historical studies. A companionable book from 1899, innocuously titled *Stories from Maine*, recalls stories of an attack by "savages" at the cove at Presumpscot River, while the settlers are cutting hay.[19] One hundred and fifty years after the fact, the tale is still chilling.

In Whittier's poem, springtime has arrived with fresh grasses, but the frosts still linger in the shady spots. Spring's renewal proves no balm to the fact of Polin's wrongful murder over territorial conflict:

Her tokens of renewing care
Hath Nature scattered everywhere,
In bud and flower, and warmer air.
But in their hour of bitterness,
What reck the broken Sokokis,
Beside their slaughtered chief, of this?[20]

The compression of syntax makes for halting travel through these lines, which is perhaps effective in conveying the tribe's grief. Whittier's scene shows us the immediate aftermath; the "turf's red stain is yet undried" and the "death-shot echoes" have barely faded.[21] Hunters from the Sokokis tribe maintain stoic appearance as they bury their chief between the snaking root-arms of the lone beech tree on the shore. Grave digging is a rough business, contending with the massive tree to make a space beneath it: "They heave the stubborn trunk aside, / The firm roots from the earth divide,-- / The rent beneath yawns dark and wide."[22] Once their chief has been laid in the earth, however, the laying on of symbolic garments softens into ritual. He is arrayed in "tasselled garbs of skins" and "girded with his wampum-braid."[23] The silver cross, marker of Polin's contact with tribes beyond his own, is buried with him, and we are given a last glimpse of his mortal body, his "scarred and naked breast."[24] While aspects of the elegy may turn toward stereotypes of native people's stoic countenances and warrior-strength, the tribesmen's contest with the "beechen-tree," a lone, last member of its tribe, standing tall amidst pines, firs, birch all succumbed to "fire and the axe," embodies a depth of struggle full of feeling. "Rent" and "reck" are not so far apart, in the end. This is a rent that cannot be reckoned, only marked and mourned. The poem's significance in the present moment may lie in its refusal to absolve the distance between wounding and thought. Elsewhere Whittier employs rivers as sites of transport or confirmation of faith, where God's angels can share the messages of love from those still walking an earthly shore, but here grief is buried deep (see Appendix 2).

A poem from 1885, close to Muir's time in Maine, by Caroline Dana Howe, shows us how the river looks to a woman poet. The lyricism is lighter, the wildlife more specifically noted, but the sentimental impulse, a dominant strain in nineteenth-century poetry regardless of the author's gender, is still strong. Howe's poem, "In the Elm Tree," uses the fluid song of a robin as muse-note for a moving elegy.

Fairies are still present, one-hundred years later—this time in the guise of the robin's "fairy realm" nest safely tucked away in the tree. Listening to the robin's song occasions a remembrance of childhood's perfect innocence, set in this natural place:

That song!
The fields grow green again
Where sunbeams gleam and quiver,

> We hear the falling of soft rain
> Along Presumpscot river.
> The robins sing beside the brook
> Where buttercups lean over.
> Blue violets hide in every nook,
> And bees hum through the clover.[25]

This view is better than a hazy nostalgia, as the former world has been fully recreated, complete with climatological conditions of filtered sunlight and delicate rain showers—it's magical to have both at once. The riverbanks feature generous buttery yellow blooms and the more secretive, blue petal-faces of shy violets that enjoy shade. The poem's soundtrack is the buzzing of bees, not the roar of the mill dam, and the whole scene swells with health and life.

And then we see our Eve: "Here young Helen's white feet stood / Amid the ripples shining."[26] But by the final line of the poem, a general reference to "tired feet" eclipses nostalgia to reach a grounded, saddened awareness of the losses on life's path:

> For disappointments come with years,
> And bitter pains and losses;
> Our laughter hath a sound of tears,
> Our wayside marks are crosses![27]

For this poet, birdsong occasions a reverie of beauty, which occasions a confrontation with the white-footed Helen. But as with other Helens of literary note, this one too has a tragic cast. The toll of mortality soon sounds, mixed into birdsong and river spray:

> Yet with that song we hear the showers
> Along Presumpscot River,
> And see the broad fields, rich with flowers,
> Where sunbeams gleam and quiver.[28]

We had Helen, and we lost her. We saw her again briefly, as a lovely vision in a kind of Eden. In the finality of her absence, the river remains. And it is good.

As with the Deane poem ascending to the height of the muses and a satisfactory glance ahead, this poem too allows that the pained memory of lost beauty can be generative when set in the lap of nature. Helen's "gleaming" feet walk the golden streets of heaven now, where she is "Grown fair beyond our dreaming."[29] And so we almost see her again. The focus on her feet confers saintliness. Conferring a "blessing" on the one who remem-

161

bers, this vision perfectly captures a kind of Keatsian melancholy, though Keats's "Ode to a Nightingale," also dwelling in the memories provoked by birdsong, was first published in 1819. The Romantics' hold on American verse makers was as strong as the natural landscape surrounding them.

Jumping forward a few years, over the banks of one century and into the next, Maine's many rivers receive mention in a book that celebrates the state's natural landscape. Although the "Presumpscot of Sebago" is only briefly mentioned in the opening long poem simply titled "Maine," George Arthur Cleveland's 1915 *Maine in Verse and Story* continues to witness nature's divine origin and character in local Maine *terra firma* and its waterways.

Cleveland's color palette for the state appears to be predominantly comprised of blues and greens, and the majesty of natural forms like trees and rivers is still sacred:

> In plume of fern, in drape of shrub and trees,
> From pines on high waved ever to the breeze,
> Her altars stand in every grandeured mont,
> Her baptistries in every lake's pure font.[30]

The names of the rivers themselves are poetic, vowels and consonants tumbling about on the page and in the mouth. They tell "wond'rous stories," retaining the agency of their early names from indigenous people who knew the rivers as more than facts of geology. The rivers of Maine have origin and trajectory, bounties of fish and flood, and, as one poet suggests, stories to tell:

> The alien Saco comes from 'Hampshire's snowy peaks,
> Presumpscot of Sebago, and the Songo speaks,
> The Androscoggin's mighty circled drain flows out,
> Umbagog, Rangeleys, Parmacheenee's realms of trout.
> The Kennebec, its rushing gorge bound floods begin,
> Where Moosehead's sluice ways spill, or bar the waters in.
> Penobscot, Oh Penobscot, what can thy waters tell?[31]

We should consider these names for a moment in comparison. The Presumpscot is more familiar than the "alien" Saco, which has a distant source. The nearby Songo river "speaks," which seems a more definite offering of a wondrous story than may be possible from the mighty Androscoggin, here, or the other rivers named in the poem for their quantity of fish or flood waters. However we parse these lines, they point to the river itself as a locus of knowledge, a near-sacred keeper of secret wisdom. As difficult to translate as birdsong, the river's song tempts and haunts us with an audible glimpse of something delightful as often as something darker. Maine rivers are hallowed tributaries where great schools of fish run rapids and ardently return to run them again, where aquatic life is so thick that "thy legioned feeders kiss."[32]

The Poetry of the Presumpscot: Now

Today, the literature of the Presumpscot includes a long-running but now out of print literary journal, *The Presumpscot Review*, from the University of Maine at Orono, a short list of 'hits' from nineteenth-century poetry chronicles, and a more current presence in web text.

A recent blog project, *The Presumpscot: River of Rough Places*, by Emma Deans, offers a refreshing leap into the twenty-first century, complete with hypertext and high resolution images. The river is luminous at 480 x 1600 pixels, glowing on the computer screen. We meet the young author as she crafts this piece for her SALT certificate, the prestigious documentary journalism program in Portland, Maine. Formerly a student at Gorham High School, Deans shows the local knowledge of a river-lover augmented with historical and personal research. In paddling the length of the river, she learns how fragmented it is, due to those rough places and dams requiring portages. In some places the river runs clear and startlingly beautiful; in others, it's home to discarded items from people's lives. Ultimately, Deans realizes that "this is not just a story about coming home; it's a story about finding home." She learns a great deal about herself and her ethical responsibilities in the world:

> It's about sacrifice and compromise, understanding that the world is bigger than one's own self and one's own interests. That the effects of one fish or rock or dam or house along a river are not isolated or insular . . . in order to create healthy communities filled with people who care about where they live there needs to be connection. There needs to be hope.[33]

As we think more about ways in which texts can become multi-modal and accessible in the cloud to a vast readership, one result of writing the river in such a platform is that the Presumpscot thus gains a virtual space of its own. Combined with the robust website of The Friends of the Presumpscot River, which shares links to newspaper articles, scientific information, details about guided walks and paddling events, as well as fundraising goals,[34] Deans' work gives a rich and vital home to the river appropriate for the current moment.

Whether *River of Rough Places* constitutes 'literature' is a good question, given its informational structure and content. As a thorough and well-written blog, it offers a rich example of ways in which writing about the river might find starting points of personal interest and a sense of history. Given the emphasis on personal connection with the place, the blog genre may open up to include aspects of the literary—care with diction, concern with narrative arc, an impetus toward arresting images created in prose as well as the artful photographs. This work seems a case in point for how our definition of the literary must continue to change even as the river continues to flow and be modified into the future. The literary river today exists in books, magazines, journals, poems, websites. Running through it all is the old allure: the river transports our senses. The nineteenth century's sentimental desire to align the river's beauty and strength with our own—which magnifies our human potential—may have disappeared, but the romantic tendency remains.

A second strong example of how the Presumpscot appears in poetry now may be found in another work by a young writer. In 2015, a poetry contest hosted by The Telling Room, a nonprofit writing center in Portland, asked high school students to submit poems and prose pieces that fit the theme "Bodies of Water." Out of the many carefully crafted entries, jurors chose one poem: "The Presumpscot Baptism of a Jewish Girl," by Lizzy Lemieux.

There are many reasons why jurors might choose this poem—confident and fresh figurative language, precise imagery, insight. It's the story of girls on the edge, literally and imaginatively, looking over and jumping into the river and soon into adult bodies and adult responsibilities. In August, these twelve-year-olds are "skinny" and "still children," able to swim without bragging about it but still clutching a bit of wild bravado. And it's a scene that summons bravery, as the river welcomes them with a host of carnage-like items submerged but identifiable:

> Rusting leather-seated wheelchairs,
> Slatted red-handled, silver-wired shopping carts,
> Old-fashioned, newly made, ten-speed racing bikes,
> And children's tennis shoes with tongues like dogs.
> The Presumpscot boiled like tomato soup,
> Frothing with all these things we swam with.[35]

This is a picture of the Presumpscot we haven't seen yet, not even in Emma Deans' blog. Holder of refuse, keeper of unwanted goods, the river performs its familiar trick of concealing and revealing at the same time. The machine is undeniably in the garden, if we can read the tossed-out junk as evidence of human industry and still read the urban riverscape as a pastoral place. Depth complicates surface.

For the children, the plunges of August are a kind of contest that symbolizes a larger confrontation and the sheer will of youth: "We fought with the placid river / Sometimes we won and we drew / The Presumpscot into our mouths."[36] By September, they are sitting on the banks watching the departing geese, "hollering" up to them the call and response songs of campfires, thrilling in the mutual noise they create. The seasonal turn presages another turning: the big sisters come home and present a picture of the inevitable. One of the sisters returns, "Hanging off a boy like a playground tire swing."[37] This is occasion for concern and wonderment, for looking back to the river for answers. The closing lines echo a pair of earlier lines and extend into a keen listening:

> Then we listened to the water
> Hitting flesh on flesh, hand to skin,
> Listened to who we would be
> When we resurfaced.[38]

Contact with the river water reminds the girls of their bodies, of the facts of having a body, and serves as a conduit, intimating some essence of the future and identity. From the city's unofficial dump to playground/waterpark to oracle, the river has transformative powers, different selves. From foe to confidante, the river shape-shifts, conferring a fluid sense of self-awareness on the teetering girls.

Packing Up

Rather than rest here, on the brink, with the girls of the contemporary poem and the image of the Presumpscot tarnished though prophetic, I'd like to return to a mid-century picture of the Maine landscape to look again at the literature of the river more broadly. Henry Beston's *White Pine and Blue Water: A Maine Reader*, from 1950, offers again a perspective of Maine's natural landforms washed in pure colors.[39] It contains very early works, from 1613, 1622, and 1689, including Longfellow's "My Lost Youth," a meditative and strange poem, on Portland and "Deering's Woods." Poems by Edwin Arlington Robinson, Harriet Beecher Stowe, James Russell

Lowell, Joshua Chamberlain, Elizabeth Coatsworth, Thoreau, Robert Peter Tristram Coffin, Sarah Orne Jewett, Celia Thaxter, E.B. White, Elisabeth Ogilvie, Ruth Moore, Elinor Graham, and others fill its pages.

One lesser known figure, Rosalind Richards, contributes a portion from her book, *A Northern Countryside* (1916) to the *Maine Reader*. While Richards's "River," capital 'R,' is the Kennebec, a select passage grants a view of the Maine landscape as an amalgamation of working and wild areas interrupted suddenly and miraculously by flowing water. She covers the farms, woods, and poor soil with prose that appreciates beauty in botanical diversity and in the various forms of water that grace an inland swath, creating and sustaining life. For the sheer pleasure of reading about her thrill with the "secret places" awaiting discovery, and for the refreshing example of published prose by a woman at this time, I quote a passage at length:

> If the first impression of our country is its uniformity, the second and amazing one is its surprises, its secret places. The long ridges alternate themselves suddenly into sharp slopes and steep cup-shaped valleys, covered with sweet-fern and juniper. The wooded hills are often full of hidden cliffs (rich gardens in themselves, they are so deep in ferns and moss), and quick brooks run through them, so that you are never long without the talk of one to keep you company. There are rocky glens, where you meet cold, sweet air, the ceaseless comforting of a waterfall, and moss on moss, to velvet depths of green.
>
> The ridges rise and slope again with general likeness, but two of them open amazingly to disclose the wide blue surface of our great River. We are rich in rivers, and never have to journey far to reach one, but I never can get quite used to the surprise of coming among the hills, on this broad strong full-running stream.[40]

Indeed, we are rich in rivers. They are our secret places and, increasingly, our known places. And yet we can never get quite used to the surprise of their generosity. Even where the water thins to a modest depth, in the early 1900s, when Richards was writing, the Maine rivers enjoyed fewer dams and more fish, which would create better habitat for wildlife and the immediate riverine ecosystem. And though a term like 'ecosystem' didn't appear in our vocabulary until decades later (coined in 1930; distinguished in 1935), reading Richards, we can imagine her awareness of the life sustained by the diversity of landscape forms. Those "quick brooks" that "talk" still attract and hold human interest. May these places—and the Presumpscot River at the heart of this meandering chapter—persist in some measure of purity, with "broad strong full-running stream."

Envoi

Any chapter on the river must return to the river itself. So I did.

I took a left turn and a right turn, to find myself at a specific address:

Mallison Falls Hydroelectric Project

SD Warren Company

FERC Project No. 2932

The map near the bridge had all the aesthetic attributes one might look for: directional key in the top corner, balanced proportions of river sections, the bridge clearly marked near the various curbs and halts and abutments linked to the falls. No fires, swimming, firearms, alcoholic beverages, or controlled substances are allowed. Power lines bisect the clouds in narrowing parallels toward an unseeable horizon. Broad leaves of sumac gone rusty, blown thistles with tufted crowns, a long-ago-cut zone of grass bent with stale footprints and the underside of sunshine. Here is the modern day Asphodel, maybe, from William Carlos Williams' affecting poem. Again I'm ankle deep in tropes of surface and depth, machine and garden, public signage and hidden insight, poetry and prose. The headline news of the heart's secrets. To be absolutely current, this time I record a brief video of the falls. I can listen to the murmur, just under the pitch of roar, as I run an editorial eye over earlier writing in this chapter, listening for the ways the audioscape offers hints of continuance, even transcendence. Seamus Heaney says, "In the beginning, river gravel." Presumpsca says, "In the future, that." The literature of the river has a long history and runs through the present moment still headed toward the ocean. To be rich in rivers is to embrace their complexity, the myriad connections they offer us in the still-more-than-human world of the early-twenty-first century.

APPENDIX 1

Henry Wadsworth Longfellow's poem, collected in his *Ballads and Other Poems*, 1842

To the River Charles

River! that in silence windest
   Through the meadows, bright and free,
Till at length thy rest thou findest
   In the bosom of the sea!

Four long years of mingled feeling,
   Half in rest, and half in strife,
I have seen thy waters stealing
   Onward, like the stream of life.

Thou hast taught me, Silent River!
   Many a lesson, deep and long;
Thou hast been a generous giver;
   I can give thee but a song.

Oft in sadness and in illness,
   I have watched thy current glide,
Till the beauty of its stillness
   Overflowed me, like a tide.

And in better hours and brighter,
   When I saw thy waters gleam,
I have felt my heart beat lighter,
   And leap onward with thy stream.

Not for this alone I love thee,
   Nor because thy waves of blue
From celestial seas above thee
   Take their own celestial hue.

Where yon shadowy woodlands hide thee,
  And thy waters disappear,
Friends I love have dwelt beside thee,
  And have made thy margin dear.

More than this;--thy name reminds me
  Of three friends, all true and tried;
And that name, like magic, binds me
  Closer, closer to thy side.

Friends my soul with joy remembers!
  How like quivering flames they start,
When I fan the living embers
  On the hearth-stone of my heart!

'T is for this, thou Silent River!
  That my spirit leans to thee;
Thou hast been a generous giver,
  Take this idle song from me.

APPENDIX 2

John Greenleaf Whittier (1807–1892). *The Poetical Works in Four Volumes.*
1892.

"The River Path"

[Set in Pleasant Valley, Amesbury, MA, overlooking the Merrimac River.]

No bird-song floated down the hill,
The tangled bank below was still;
No rustle from the birchen stem,
No ripple from the water's hem.
The dusk of twilight round us grew,   *5*
We felt the falling of the dew;
For, from us, ere the day was done,
The wooded hills shut out the sun.
But on the river's farther side
We saw the hill-tops glorified,—   *10*
A tender glow, exceeding fair,
A dream of day without its glare.
With us the damp, the chill, the gloom:
With them the sunset's rosy bloom;
While dark, through willowy vistas seen,   *15*
The river rolled in shade between.
From out the darkness where we trod,
We gazed upon those hills of God,
Whose light seemed not of moon or sun.
We spake not, but our thought was one.   *20*
We paused, as if from that bright shore
Beckoned our dear ones gone before;
And stilled our beating hearts to hear
The voices lost to mortal ear!
Sudden our pathway turned from night;   *25*
The hills swung open to the light;
Through their green gates the sunshine showed,
A long, slant splendor downward flowed.

Down glade and glen and bank it rolled;
It bridged the shaded stream with gold;   *30*
And, borne on piers of mist, allied
The shadowy with the sunlit side!
"So," prayed we, "when our feet draw near
The river dark, with mortal fear,
"And the night cometh chill with dew,   *35*
O Father! let Thy light break through!
"So let the hills of doubt divide,
So bridge with faith the sunless tide!
"So let the eyes that fail on earth
On Thy eternal hills look forth;   *40*
"And in Thy beckoning angels know
The dear ones whom we loved below!"

---

[1] Zorthian, J. (2016, August 20). Giant snake loose in Maine: Wessie the python. *Time Magazine*. http://time.com/4461569/python-loose-maine-10-feet/

[2] Annear, S. (2016, August 30). Snake skin found in Maine belongs to anaconda. *Boston Globe*. https://www.bostonglobe.com/metro/2016/08/30/snake-skin-found-maine-belongs-anaconda/qf9d3p1L6SZFNt3qS7tI2L/story.html

[3] Williams, W. C. (1955). *Journey to love*. New York: Random House.

[4] Hoey, D. (2016, September 7). As triathletes swim in Presumpscot River, many eyes will be on snake watch. *Portland Press Herald*. https://www.pressherald.com/2016/09/07/triathletes-to-swim-in-river-where-wessie-lurks/

[5] Evans, C. & Costa, C. (2017, July 17). Maine State Police divers searching Presumpscot River in Westbrook. *News Center Maine*. https://www.newscentermaine.com/article/news/local/maine-state-police-divers-searching-presumpscot-river-in-westbrook/97-456997944

[6] Associated Press (2011, September 11). Teen swimming with friends drowns in Presumpscot River. *Bangor Daily News*. https://bangordailynews.com/2011/09/11/news/portland/teen-swimming-with-friends-drowns-in-presumpscot-river/

[7] Brogan, B. (2014, August 26). Westbrook police identify man who drowned in the Presumpscot River. *Bangor Daily News*. https://bangordailynews.com/2014/08/26/news/portland/westbrook-police-identify-man-who-drowned-in-presumpscot-river-on-thursday/

[8] Gagne, J. (2016, June 3). Emergency crews recover body of missing kayaker from Presumpscot River. *WCSH News*. https://www.newscentermaine.com/article/news/local/emergency-crews-recover-body-of-missing-kayaker-from-presumpscot-river/97-229011129

[9] Heaney, S. (2001). *Electric Light*. New York: Farrar, Straus, and Giroux, 1.1.

[10] Ryden, K. C. (2001). *Landscape with figures: Nature & culture in New England*. Iowa City: University of Iowa Press, 166.

[11] Ibid., 167.

[12] Ibid., 198.

[13] Deane, S. (1888 [1760]). Pitchwood Hill. In G. B. Griffith (Comp.). *The poets of Maine: A collection of specimen poems from over four hundred verse-makers of the Pine-tree state, with biographical sketches.* (pp. 3-6, lines 83-86). Portland, ME: Elwell, Pickard & Company. https://babel.hathitrust.org/cgi/pt?id=hvd.hnmhl4;view=1up;seq=7

[14] Ibid., lines 87-92.

[15] Ibid., lines 105-116.

[16] Longfellow, H. W. (1855). *The song of Hiawatha*. London: David Bogue. https://archive.org/details/ songhiawathathe00longrich/page/n3

[17] Huber, J. P. (2006). *A wanderer all my days: John Muir in New England*. Sheffield, VT: Green Frigate Books, 149.

[18] Whittier, J. G., Funeral tree of the Sokokis. In R. W. Griswold (1842). *The poets and poetry of America* (lines 1 & 26). Philadelphia: Carey and Hart, 401. https://en.wikisource.org/wiki/Funeral_Tree_of_the_Sokokis

[19] Swett, S. M. (1899). *Stories of Maine*. New York: American Book Company, 117. https://archive.org/details/ storiesofmaine00swet/page/n8

[20] Whittier, Funeral tree, lines 25-30.

[21] Ibid., line 31.

[22] Ibid., lines 43-45.

[23] Ibid., lines 47, 48.

[24] Ibid., line 51.

[25] Howe, C. D. (1885). *Ashes for flame & other short poems*. Portland, ME: Loring, Short, and Harmon, lines 9-16.

[26] Ibid., lines 19-20

[27] Ibid., lines 24-28.

[28] Ibid., lines 29-32.

[29] Ibid., line 36.

[30] Cleveland, G. A. (Ed.). (1915). *Maine in verse and story*. Boston: R. and G. Badger, lines 123-126.

[31] Ibid., lines 133-139.

[32] Ibid., line 141.

[33] Deans, E. (2013). *The Presumpscot: River of rough places*. http://www.presumpscot.com/

[34] Friends of the Presumpscot River (2019). https://www.presumpscotriver.org/

[35] Lemieux, L. (2015, May). The Presumpscot baptism of a Jewish girl. *Maine. The Magazine*, lines 4-9. www.themainemag.com/people/2729-the-telling-room-young-writers-contest/

[36] Ibid., lines 19-21.

[37] Ibid., lines 32.

[38] Ibid., lines 33-36.

[39] Beston, H. (1950). *White pine and blue water: A Maine reader*. New York: Farrar, Straus. https://www.nwcbooks.com/get/ebook.php?id=SImO6ha8aUMC

[40] Richardson, R. (1916). Quoted in Ibid., 134-135.

Works Consulted

Brooks, L. & Brooks, C. (2010). The reciprocity principle and traditional ecological knowledge: Understanding the significance of indigenous protest on the Presumpscot. *International Journal of Critical Indigenous Studies, 3*(2), 11-28, Print. https://www.researchgate.net/publication/269874990_ The_Reciprocity_Principle_and_Traditional_Ecological_Knowledge_Understandin g_the_Significance_of_Indigenous_Protest_on_the_Presumpscot_River

Burroughs, F. (2006). *Confluence: Merrymeeting Bay*. Gardiner, Maine: Tilbury House.

Conforti, J. A. (2005). *Creating Portland: History and place in northern New England*. Durham: University of New Hampshire Press.

Norton, M. B. & Baker, E. W. (2007). "The names of the rivers": A new look at an old document. *New England Quarterly, 80*(3), 459-487. https://www.jstor.org/stable/20474557?seq=1#page_scan_tab_contents

Senier, S. (Ed.). (2014). *Dawnland voices: An anthology of indigenous writing from New England*. Lincoln: University of Nebraska, 2014.

Whittier, J. G. (1849). *Leaves from Margaret Smith's journal in the Province of Massachusetts Bay. 1678-9*. Boston: Ticknor, Reed, and Fields. https://archive.org/details/leavesfrommarga00whitgoog/page/n15

Cascade, Current and Pool : For the Vanquished Falls of the Presumpscot River,
(Michael Shaughnessy, 2011, Hay and Twine, Dimensions Variable)

175

Chapter 8   Firooza Pavri & Timothy Lynch

The Changing Landscape of Maine's Presumpscot Watershed[1]

Introduction

The lower Presumpscot River flows from Lake Sebago, through Cumberland County, and into Casco Bay. Its floodplain and estuary provide evidence of early settlement activity by Native American farming and fishing communities and European trading outposts.[2] The name Presumpscot translates from the Abenaki language as "ledges in channel," or often alternatively as "many falls," which is in keeping with early descriptions of the river.[3] Falling 270 feet over 26 miles, the Presumpscot River has driven the economic engine of southern Maine since the erection of its first dam in 1735. Over its settlement history, researchers have recorded its use as a pristine fish hatchery and a chemical waste dump; a means of Native American travel and a way to float lumber down to Portland; a tranquil, rippling swimming spot and a ferocious, destructive force.[4] It is as important today as it was during its early settlement. It is also the site of many firsts in riverine development for the state. It hosts the first dam, mill, and hydroelectric dam ever built in the state, and it saw a legislative victory as early as 1735 that ensured the passage of fish despite dam activity.[5]

Before the construction of its numerous dams, the river was a spawning ground for several species of ocean and landlocked fish, such as eastern Brook Trout (*Salvelinus fontinalis*), Blueback Herring (*Alosa aestivalis*), Atlantic Sturgeon (*Acipenser oxyrinchus*), Striped Bass (*Morone saxatilis*), Alewives (*Alosa pseudoharengus*), and more.[6] The Abenaki used land around present-day Cumberland Mills as corn planting grounds, and rotting fish from the abundant Presumpscot served as a fertilizer. The river was also a transportation link between Sebago Lake and the Abenaki over-winter settlement on the Casco Bay island of Mackworth.[7]

Flowing through Maine's most populated and economically diverse county—comprising nearly a quarter of the state's total population—the communities of Standish, Windham, Gorham, Westbrook, Falmouth, and

176

Portland adjoin the banks of the Presumpscot, and have all depended on its waters and resources since their establishment (see Figure 1). Industries crucial to Maine's historic development and growth, including the paper and pulp industry, fisheries, and hydropower, have also benefited from the Presumpscot's resources. The river is the largest source of freshwater flowing into Casco Bay and, as such, provides a rich environment for the dependent estuarine ecosystem.[8] The recent expansion of population and development in southern Maine, however, raises important concerns for land-use change across the region, especially for the health of the Presumpscot and its adjoining floodplain.

Figure 1. *Riverwalk 4* (Caren-Marie Michel, 2007, 6" x 12", acrylic on canvas, private collection. Photo by Jay York Photography)

In recent years, numerous studies have highlighted threats to the sustainability of freshwater resources from increased demand, intensive agriculture, the expansion of development, and changes in global climate regimes.[9] One report cites the Presumpscot, including Lake Sebago, as among the most vulnerable watersheds of the northeastern United States to development pressures. The Presumpscot basin is also on this list, due to rapid recent urban expansion and the large numbers of people across southern Maine dependent on its surface waters for domestic and industrial freshwater needs.[10] Moreover, scientists expect future development pressures to intensify the threats to water quality across the basin. Given the vital role that freshwater plays in meeting ecosystem and human needs, scientists have urgently called for the careful monitoring, management, and protection of such source-water-supply regions to ensure their sustainability.[11] Studies have particularly focused on the adjacent one-mile buffer along rivers, as land-use activities within these buffer zones can directly influence the health of a river.

Riparian buffers, with their restrictions on development, have long since provided a means to manage and protect rivers from the stressors of agriculture, urban development, or other land-use conversions. Within the state of Maine, the Mandatory Shoreland Zoning Act (MSZA) of 1971 requires a 250-foot buffer around all ponds over 10 acres, salt marshes, tidal zones, and rivers with drainage basins over 25 square miles (64.75 square kilometers).[12] Municipalities adopt local land-use ordinances that are consistent with the legislation, and plans require approval from the Commissioner and Board of Environmental Protection. Development activity is closely regulated within the buffer zone to protect and conserve unique ecosystems and control and prevent water pollution.[13] Buffers provide ecosystem services including habitat, food, and migration corridors for wildlife and are able to link patches of forests or wetlands that agricultural expansion or urban development may have fragmented.[14] These corridor connectors also augment the probability of plant and animal species survival.[15] Studies indicate that the effectiveness of riparian buffers in pollution abatement has to do with not only the width of the buffer itself but also soil type, hydrology, and biochemistry considerations. Collectively, these conditions aid in mitigating nutrient overload, stabilizing river banks, and minimizing erosion and flood damage[16] As Gregory, Swanson, McKee, and Cummins point out, their ecosystem contributions, then, far exceed their relative sizes when compared to other landscape features.[17]

The River and a History of Land Use
Agriculture was the predominant form of land use around the Presumpscot floodplain by Native American Abenaki groups, who found fertile locations upstream from the Presumpscot's estuary.[18] Documents suggest that early European settlement activity across the larger region started in the 1650s, with the clearing of forests and the use of the river as a transport route into the interior.[19] Abundant pines were a high-value commodity ideal for ship masts, and early Europeans developed this resource to meet local and foreign markets. Shipyards found a home at the mouth of the Presumpscot and provided ready employment for Portland residents during the 1700 and 1800s.

Industrial uses of the river dominated from the 1700s through the present day, with evidence of saw, grist, and paper and pulp mills during the 1700s.[20] Mills were the driving force behind development during that early period. Tanneries for leather, textile mills for cloth, foundries and brickyards for building, and ice for preservation all thrived along the Presumpscot. By 1867, six of the current eight dams on the Presumpscot appeared in records by name and actively powered paper, wool, and textile mills and iron works.[21] In 1880, the S. D. Warren mill at Westbrook was possibly the "largest paper mill in the world."[22] Even as the river provided the resources necessary to sustain a thriving economy, overuse and wanton discharge of pollutants from tanning agents to sawdust and chemicals were resulting in its destruction.

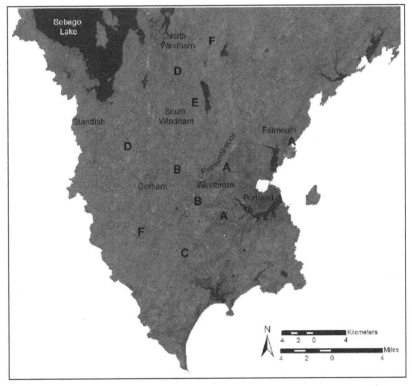

Figure 2. Presumpscot River Watershed, Landsat Thematic Mapper Composite Bands 3, 4, 5 (source: Pavri, F. & Lynch, T. [2011]. Assessing land use and riparian buffers along Maine's Presumpscot watershed using Landsat Thematic Mapper. *Northeastern Geographer* 3, 22-34)

The continued industrial use of the river well into the twentieth century left it polluted and channelized, and its water flow restricted in its lower reaches.[23] Clearly, it was far from the swift-flowing river with many falls that its name suggested.[24] Reports in the 1970s even went as far as to suggest that fumes from the Presumpscot may have caused "paint to peel from nearby homes,"[25] while others described the river from Westbrook to its mouth in Casco Bay as an "industrial sewer."[26] The Presumpscot River estuary and Casco Bay were akin to the country's most polluted harbors toward the end of the twentieth century, and the river made the Maine Department of Environmental Protection's (ME DEP) "List of Impaired Waterbodies" due to high levels of total suspended solids and low dissolved oxygen.[27]

The river currently has eight dams, seven of which are owned by South African Pulp and Paper Incorporated (SAPPI), which acquired the 1854-founded S. D. Warren Co. in 1995 to launch its North American presence. In 1995, Sappi filed for renewal of its five hydroelectric dams on the Presumpscot, under Federal Energy Regulatory Commission (FERC) guidelines, but protested the requirement to file water-quality certifications with the ME DEP as well. This disagreement eventually resulted in an important 2006 U.S. Supreme Court decision that upheld states' rights in the *S. D. Warren Co. v. Maine Board of Environmental Protection* ruling,[28] which stated that "operators of hydroelectric dams must meet a state's water quality requirements in order to qualify for a federal license."[29] In 2003, FERC granted renewal for each of Sappi's dams but required it to install fish passages at dam sites and allow minimum water flows to mitigate low dissolved oxygen levels.[30] The case proved to be a significant victory for environmental groups not only associated with the Presumpscot but also with rivers nationwide.

Efforts to reverse the river's health began as early as the 1960s, in response to legislation and public outcry. In that early period, the S. D. Warren Co. constructed settling lagoons and treatment plants to partially mitigate wastes from its Westbrook papermill.[31] Municipal sewage-treatment plants for all communities adjoining the river were in place by the 1970s and significantly aided the repair of the river ecosystem.[32] In 1992, the Maine Department of Inland Fisheries and Wildlife established a salmon and trout fishery just below Sebago Lake. With combined efforts spurred on by the Clean Water Act and the eventual closing of many mills, the health of the river steadily improved.[33] The Sappi mill in Westbrook, a primary pollution source for the lower river, ceased its pulping activities in 1999, leading to the removal of the Smelt Hill dam near the Presumpscot estuary and reopening seven miles of potential habitat to the *Alosa sapidissima* (American shad), *Salmo salar* (Atlantic salmon), and *Alosa pseudoharengus* (alewives) among other species.[34] The ME DEP subsequently delisted the main stem of the Presumpscot below the Sacarappa Dam in Westbrook from the impaired listings for the state and considered the dam removal a major success for the health of the river.[35] The most recent 2016 Integrated Water Quality Report by the Maine Department of Environmental Protection indicates further improvements in water quality, including reductions in bacterial concentrations at key locations near Westbrook.[36]

Despite these positive developments, vigilance around urban and agricultural non-point sources of pollution is always a continual and ongoing effort. Efforts by local government agencies and strong local grassroots organizations continue to work toward a sustainable and thriving Presumpscot by monitoring water quality, expanding land for preservation, and engaging in community-education projects. The chief concerns today still remain non-point pollution sources, the fragmentation of the riparian buffer, and the rapid expansion of impervious surfaces due to development activities along the lower Presumpscot.

A Look from Above

A visual assessment of a Landsat image of the region (Figure 2) indicates a landscape interspersed with urban and rural land uses. Urban land uses (A on Figure 2) are closer toward the coast along the lower reaches of the Presumpscot, particularly around the cities of Westbrook, Falmouth, and Portland. Sections of Westbrook's central business district directly abut the banks of the river. The larger region—including Portland, Maine's largest city—is typified by medium- and high-density residential housing, industrial activities, and large commercial outlets. Road networks linking towns observe linear patterns of residential and industrial development, especially between Westbrook and Portland suburbs (B on Figure 2) and along Interstate-95 (C on Figure 2), which runs from south to north, west of the city of Portland. Residential expansion has taken place along major roads connecting towns like Gorham, South Windham, and Falmouth, which serve as bedroom communities to Portland.

Outside Portland, rural land uses—including open agricultural fields, pastures, tree cover, and smaller villages—dominate the landscape. These areas also display characteristic geometric field patterns southeast of Standish and south of the town of North Windham (D on Figure 2). Upstream and northeast from South Windham, the Presumpscot winds through agricultural fields interspersed with tree-covered private land (E on Figure 2). Development activities are evident along highways, and utility lines cutting through forested sections are also clearly visible on the image composite (F on Figure 2).

In compliance with the Clean Water Act, many states have enacted laws to regulate land use within riparian and other shoreland zones. A case in point is Maine's Mandatory Shoreland Zoning Act, which requires a 250-foot (76-meter) zone along major rivers, where all development activities are closely monitored and require a permitting process.[37] Buffers also allow the assessment of general land-use trends and identify potential contaminants from nearby sources that might reach the river.

A previous study using Landsat imagery reveals a non-contiguous, fragmented riparian buffer of tree cover along the Presumpscot River from Lake Sebago to the town of South Windham.[38] As the river meanders south and east of South Windham, urban and agricultural activities extend all the way to almost the river's edge, with limited room for a buffer. The total land area contained within buffer zones, although small, belies the buffers' significant biological and ecological services. Although the pattern across buffers along the river indicates a greater proportion of green space closest to the river, urban- and developed-land categories gain in proportion along the outer edges of the buffer.[39] Exceptions do occur where towns meet the river's edge, as in Westbrook. Potential non-point pollution threats from impervious-surface runoff to the Presumpscot from the zone contiguous to the river will have a significant impact on its health. Agricultural non-point pollution sources upstream through overland flow or seepage into the water table would also make the river vulnerable to heightened nitrogen and phosphorous loading, erosion, and sedimentation. Urban runoff contributions of suspended and dissolved solids; toxic organics; trace metals; and salt, sand, and hydrocarbons off roadways are chief pollutants downstream.[40] Studies indicate that even narrow buffers can significantly slow and help mitigate some of these pollutants.[41] The expansion of impervious surfaces with urban and suburban development, as is the case with this part of southern Maine along the lower Presumpscot, will no doubt exacerbate these issues.

Conclusions

Here we trace a history of use for the Presumpscot River and use satellite data to examine dominant land-use activities that influence the health of this ecosystem. Industrial uses of the river have abated from their height during the twentieth century due to stricter regulation and the region's changing economy; however, threats from non-point pollution sources and the expansion of impervious surfaces along development corridors remain issues of concern. The sustained pressure from development activities poses significant challenges to the river's health. Building protections for fragile ecosystems, buffers in this case, have helped to mitigate some stressors to river systems. Over time, Maine's MSZA has worked toward controlling land-use activities and preserving much of the green space in the immediate buffer along the river. Such efforts often work in tandem with other laws to ensure further compliance and meet a state's broad environmental and habitat-protection objectives. For example, the Maine Natural Resources Protection Act regulates the alteration of streams, rivers, ponds, etc. and consequently targets similar land features as the MSZA.[42] As with the Presumpscot, landscape changes can have far-reaching consequences for ecosystems and human populations. Systematic assessments using satellite data now provide us with the ability to monitor land-management needs and model longer term impacts from specific land-use activities. Local municipalities, planning boards, and the Maine Department of Environmental Protection benefit from using now ubiquitous satellite data when monitoring and regulating development activity along riparian zones and lake boundaries. Such data can strengthen our understanding of how landscapes change and the efficacy of regulatory efforts and can contribute to our knowledge of human impacts on and modifications of the environment.

[1] This paper is an adaptation of an earlier publication that appeared in the *Northeastern Geographer*. Submitted for re-publication with permission.

[2] Blake, B. (1975). *Presumpscot: A profile of estuarine pollution and recovery*. Portland, ME: Center for Research and Advanced Study, University of Maine at Portland-Gorham and the Allagash Environmental Institute; Bourque, B. J. (2001). *Twelve thousand years: American Indians in Maine*. Lincoln: University of Nebraska Press.

[3] Bright, W. (2004). *Native American placenames of the United States*. Norman: University of Oklahoma Press.

[4] Butler, B., & Ricardi, C. (1994). *Guide to the Presumpscot River: Its history ecology and recreational uses*. A. MacDonald (Ed.). Portland, ME: Presumpscot River Watch.

[5] Casco Bay Estuary Project. (2003). *A Plan for the future of the Presumpscot River*. https://www.cascobayestuary.org/wp-ontent/uploads/2014/07/2003_prmp_intro.pdf

[6] Butler & Ricardi, *Guide to the Presumpscot River*.

[7] Ibid.

[8] Casco Bay Estuary Project. (1996). *Casco Bay plan*. Portland, ME: Author.

[9] Mimikou, M., Blatas, E., Varanaou, E., & Pantazis, K. (2000). Regional impacts of climate change on water resources quantity and quality indicators. *Journal of Hydrology 234*(1-2), 95-109. https://doi: 10.1016/S0022-1694(00)00244-4; Vörösmarty, C. J., Green, P., Salisbury, J., & Lammers, R. B. (2000). Global water resources: Vulnerability from climate change and population growth. *Science 289*(5477), 284-288. https://doi: 10.1126/science.289.5477.284; Alcamo, J., Flörke, M., & Märker, M. (2007). Future long-term changes in global water resources driven by socio-economic and climatic change. *Hydrological Sciences Journal 52*(2), 247-275. https://doi.org/10.1623/hysj.52.2.247.

[10] Barnes, M. C., Todd, A. H., Lilja, R. W., & Barton, P. K. (2009). *Forests, water and people: Drinking water supply and forest lands in the Northeast and Midwest United States.* (Technical Report No. NA-FR-01-08). Newtown, PA: United States Department of Agriculture, Forest Service. https://www.fs.usda.gov/naspf/sites/default/files/forests_water_people_watersupply.pdf

[11] Kundzewicz, Z. W. et al. (2007). Freshwater resources and their management. In M. L. Parry, O. F. Canziani, J. P. Palutikof, P. J. van der Linden, & C. E. Hanson (Eds.), *Climate change 2007: Impacts, adaptation and vulnerability. Contribution of working group II to the fourth assessment report of the Intergovernmental Panel on Climate Change* (pp. 173-210). Cambridge, UK: Cambridge University Press https://www.ipcc.ch/pdf/assessment-report/ar4/wg2/ar4-wg2-chapter3.pdf; Barnes, Todd, Lilja, & Barton, *Forests, water and people.*

[12] Maine Legislation - Maine Revised Statutes (2017). *Waters and navigation: Mandatory shoreland zoning.* http://www.mainelegislature.org/legis/statutes/38/title38sec435.html

[13] Maine Department of Environmental Protection. (2008, Spring). *Maine shoreland zoning: A handbook for shoreland owners* (Pub. No. DEPLW0674-D08). https://www.maine.gov/dep/land/slz/citizenguide.pdf

[14] Cox, J. E. (1996). Management goals and functional boundaries of riparian forested wetlands. In G. Mulamoottil, B. G. Warner, & E. A. McBean (Eds.), *Wetlands: Environmental gradients, boundaries, and buffers* (pp. 153-163). Boca Raton, FL: CRC, Lewis Publishers.

[15] Harker, D., Libby, G., Harker, K., Evans, S., & Evans, M. (1993). *Landscape restoration handbook.* Boca Raton, FL: Lewis Publishers.

[16] Mayer, P. M., Reynolds, S. K., Jr., Canfield, T. J., & McCutchen, M. D. (2005). *Riparian buffer width, vegetative cover, and nitrogen removal effectiveness: A review of current science and regulations.* Cincinnati, OH: Office of Research and Development, U.S. Environmental Protection Agency. https://cfpub.epa.gov/si/si_public_record_report.cfm?dirEntryId=140503

[17] Gregory, S. V., Swanson, F. J., McKee, W. A., & Cummins, K. W. (1991). An ecosystem perspective of riparian zones. *BioScience 41*(8), 540-5551. https://doi.org/10.2307/1311607 http://oregonstate.edu/instruction/fw580/pdf/1.%20Riparian%20Zones.pdf

[18] Casco Bay Estuary Project, *Plan.*

[19] Blake, *Presumpscot: A profile;* Bourque, *Twelve thousand years.*

[20] Eves, J. H. (1992). "Shrunk to a comparative rivulet": Deforestation, stream flow, and rural milling in 19th-century Maine. *Technology and Culture 33*(1), 38-65. https:// doi: 10.2307/3105808

[21] Goodale, S. L. Ed. (1868). Abstract of returns from the agricultural societies of Maine. *Twelfth annual report of the Secretary of the Maine Board of Agriculture 1867.* Augusta, ME: Stevens & Sayward, Printers to the State, 101-103.

[22] Warren, S. D. (1973). Warren and Westbrook: How it all began. *Warren's Standard*, 1-2. (The *Standard* was put out by S. D. Warren employees. Copies are available at the Maine Historical Society).

[23] Maine Department of Environmental Protection. (1999, December). *Biomonitoring retrospective of the Presumpscot River* (Maine DEPLW1999-26). https://www.maine.gov/dep/water/monitoring/ biomonitoring/retro/pt1ch1pref.pdf

[24] Blake, *Presumpscot: A profile.*

[25] Lewis, L. (2008, October 12) Nothing to love about that dirty water. *Lewiston Sun Journal*, C9. http://www.sunjournal.com/nothing-love-dirty-water/

[26] Blake, *Presumpscot: A profile, 5.*

[27] Casco Bay Estuary Project (2005, April). *Final habitat restoration inventory summary report for the lower Presumpscot River watershed: Vol. 1.* Prepared by Northern Ecological Associates, Inc. https://www.cascobayestuary.org/wp-content/uploads/2014/08/2005_nea_habitat_inventory_ presumpscot_volume1.pdf; Maine Department of Environmental Protection. (2008). *Integrated water quality monitoring and assessment report* (Maine DEP 2008 305(b) Report and 303(d) List: DEPLW0895). https://www.epa.gov/sites/production/files/2018-03/documents/2016-me-integrated-rpt.pdf

[28] Environmental News Service. (2006, May 15). *U.S. Supreme Court upholds states' right to regulate dams* http://www.ens-newswire.com/ens/may2006/2006-05-15-03.html

[29] Greenhouse, L. (2006, May 16). Justices uphold state rules in decision on dam licenses. *New York Times*, A18.

[30] Environmental News Service, *U.S. Supreme Court.*

[31] Blake, *Presumpscot: A profile.*

[32] Blake, *Presumpscot: A profile;* Greater Portland Council of Governments. (1993). *Presumpscot River watershed management plan: Phase I, inventory and analysis.* Portland, ME: Author.

[33] Maine Department of Environmental Protection. *Integrated water quality.*

[34] Ibid.; Casco Bay Estuary Project, *Plan.*

[35] Maine Department of Environmental Protection. *Integrated water quality.*

[36] Maine Department of Environmental Protection (2016). *Integrated water quality monitoring and assessment report.* https://www.maine.gov/dep/water/monitoring/305b/2016/28-Feb-2018_2016-ME-IntegratedRptLIST.pdf

[37] Maine Department of Environmental Protection, *Maine shoreland zoning.*

[38] Pavri, F. & Lynch, T. (2011). Assessing land use and riparian buffers along Maine's Presumpscot watershed using Landsat Thematic Mapper. *Northeastern Geographer 3*, 22-34.

[39] Ibid.

[40] Casco Bay Estuary Project, *Plan.*

[41] Mayer, et al., *Riparian buffer.*

[42] Maine Department of Environmental Protection, *Maine shoreland zoning.*

Fishes of the Presumpscot River:
To the Sea and Back

Most people might consider marine and freshwater environments as distinct ecosystems, each with its own defining assemblage of flora and fauna that create an appearance of two separate places: the ocean and the lake. In Casco Bay and the Gulf of Maine, the coastal biota is often characterized by the gulls and cormorants and the marine megafauna, including whales, sharks, and turtles; by the staples of seafood cuisine, such as cod, halibut, lobster, and oysters; or by the rocky shoreline dominated by seaweeds and barnacles. Inland, an expansive system of freshwater rivers and lakes takes on an entirely different identity, mostly associated with recreational access. In these freshwater bodies, swimming among our pondweeds, cattails, and water lilies, are the calling loons; the highly praised sportfish of trouts, basses, and pikes; and their prey, the minnows, crayfishes, and insects.

Of course, we know that marine and freshwater systems are connected—the river runs to the sea. Runoff from rain falling on mountains, fields, and parking lots, satiates our ponds, lakes, and water tables. This water makes its way slowly underground or more rapidly above ground by trickling, rushing, and even falling toward the main-stem rivers of Maine's many watersheds. These primary rivers, such as the Presumpscot, flush out to sea an abundance of fresh water, each with its own unique chemical signature: a record of the geology, wildlife, and human life it passed along the way.

Is the connection between Maine's freshwater systems and the Atlantic Ocean simply unidirectional, running from the river to the sea? Indeed, the answer is "no." The diadromous fishes of the Presumpscot River and Maine, which migrate from our freshwater systems to the open ocean—including lampreys, sturgeons, salmons, herrings, eels, and others—also run back. The following chapter aims to briefly contextualize and appreciate the rarity and complexity of diadromous life and to introduce and describe the historic and current fishes of the Presumpscot River.

Introduction to Diadromous Fishes

Approximately 65,000 species of vertebrate animals exist on Earth: 6,000 mammals, 10,000 birds, 10,000 reptiles, 7,000 amphibians, and 32,000 fishes.[1] Indeed, fishes are without a doubt the most speciose vertebrate group on the planet. Intuitively, this fact may seem obvious—Earth is roughly 70% water, so it follows that most vertebrates would be aquatic. The numbers are not so obvious, however. Oceans make up approximately 98% of all water on the planet. Of the 2% that is freshwater, nearly all of it is uninhabitable groundwater, permafrost, or glaciers; only 0.02% of Earth's water is habitable freshwater lakes and rivers.[2] Considering just how small a fraction of Earth's water is available for freshwater life, it is an astonishing fact that roughly half of the 32,000 fish species on Earth reside in freshwater.[3]

Diadromous fishes are neither freshwater nor marine, or, perhaps, they are both. They are the unassigned. To this day, consensus on why diadromy evolved remains elusive. Evolutionary thought has produced multiple hypotheses for how these migratory species evolved and can be generalized into a single evolutionary framework: diadromous fishes represent lineages in transition.[4] That is, resident freshwater or marine fishes began to "wander" into the other habitat, hunting for food or seeking refuge from predation. Over evolutionary time, this behavior became innate and led to the appearance of diadromy in the lineages of fishes we find them in today. It is thought that diadromy eventually leads to speciation and diversification in the newly invaded habitat. Indeed, this may be a useful framework for thinking about the evolution of diadromy, but more recent scientific inquiries using evolutionary-modeling techniques have generally failed to explain diadromous fishes as representing a transitional evolutionary state, suggesting that diadromy may just as likely be an evolutionary dead end. The most likely scenario may be that diadromous migrations have evolved for different reasons in different fish lineages and have no universal explanation.[5]

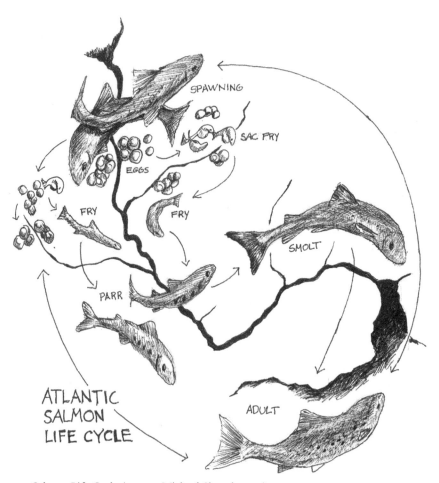

Salmon Life Cycle (source: Michael Shaughnessy)

The world holds roughly 250 species of diadromous fishes,[6] less than 1% of all fish species on Earth. Perhaps their rarity underscores the physiologically challenging nature of migration between freshwater and seawater; maybe it reflects relatively limited habitat space, given that a path between freshwater and seawater is necessary; maybe still, diadromy, compared to residing solely in freshwater or seawater, simply does not confer a substantial benefit to the migrating fish. Irrespective of a universal evolutionary explanation for how or why these fishes evolved, one point remains clear: diadromy is a special way of life on this planet and, so, should be cherished where present.

Patterns of Fish Movement and Migration

The commonly accepted reason for why fishes migrate is simple to embrace: it is a strategy to take advantage of ideal nursery habitats for juvenile development and productive feeding grounds for adult growth. Many marine mammals and fishes (such as whales, cods, and tunas) migrate between latitudes as temperatures change across seasons. These "oceanadromous" migrations are typically synchronized with developmental and reproductive cycles. Freshwater fishes regularly make "potadromous" migrations, moving up and down streams or between tributaries and larger freshwater bodies. Potadromous movement is common within Sebago Lake and the Presumpscot River. These freshwater fishes seek the benefits of the higher water quality and lower risk of predation in the streams and the more abundant food resources and opportunities for growth in lakes or main-stem rivers. The Presumpscot River meets the tide below Presumpscot Falls in Falmouth and forms a small estuary that reaches beyond Mackworth Island. Estuaries, the intertidal zones that many invertebrates and fishes call home, are typically rich with food resources and are thus feeding grounds for many diadromous and marine fishes. Numerous estuarine invertebrates and fishes move throughout the estuary with daily or tidal rhythm.

Perhaps the most remarkable fish migrations are those made by diadromous fishes, which migrate from the small streams and ponds at the far inland reaches of a freshwater system out to the open ocean, potentially thousands of miles away. The two types of diadromous fishes, "anadromous" and "catadromous," are defined by the direction of their migrations. Anadromous fishes—lampreys, sturgeons, salmons, and herrings—hatch in freshwater; migrate out to sea as larvae or juveniles; then return home, often to their natal streams, to spawn as adults. Catadromous fishes, primarily eels, exhibit the opposite strategy, hatching in the open ocean and migrating as larvae and juveniles into freshwater systems to grow into adulthood before migrating back out to sea to spawn.

For nearly a century, researchers had little evidence for where pre-spawning adult American Eel migrated to once they exited freshwater systems. They believed that all American and European Eels spawned in the Sargasso Sea, southwest of Bermuda, but direct evidence of this theory remained elusive—unbelievably, no one had ever observed an adult American Eel in the ocean. Only in the past few years have researchers discovered the precise location in the Sargasso Sea where eels spawn and the route they take to get there.[7]

Living in Freshwater and Seawater

Most vertebrate animals, including most fishes, regulate their water content and internal electrolytes (minerals such as sodium and chloride). We humans do so by drinking water and eating salty foods; our intestines and kidneys absorb the water and salt we need, and the rest passes as waste. Humans and fishes alike maintain an internal water and salt content resembling roughly one-third the concentration of seawater, not as dilute as a river yet not as salty as the ocean.

Fishes living in either freshwater or saltwater have a constant challenge to maintain a healthy water and salt balance.[8] In freshwater, fish gills are not just for breathing dissolved oxygen. They are lined with a single layer of cells that separates blood from the outside water. In freshwater fishes, this cell layer is highly adapted to extract salts from the incredibly low concentrations present in freshwater surroundings, moving salts into the blood so that fishes can maintain healthy concentrations of internal electrolytes. Freshwater fishes do not appreciably drink but still passively absorb water like sponges and urinate large volumes of water to maintain appropriate water balance.

When an Alewife or American Shad out-migrating from the Presumpscot River enters seawater just off the Eastern Promenade in Portland, it undergoes a truly remarkable physiological transformation to avoid lethal dehydration in the ocean. The fish entering seawater begins to drink in much larger quantities than when it was in the river, now filling its gut with saltwater. The cells that line the esophagus and intestine of this fish transform to produce an intricate and coordinated process to enable the absorption of water. At the frontward regions of the gut, esophageal and intestinal cells desalinate the ingested saltwater, moving large amounts of sodium and chloride into the blood. After desalination, the fish's body more easily absorbs water into the hind regions of the gut. The gills of the fish also transform to facilitate survival in the ocean. As a fish enters seawater just downstream of Presumpscot Falls, the gill cells at the blood-seawater barrier now completely reorganize to secrete salts—the large quantities of sodium and chloride absorbed in the gut—back out into the ocean.

Surviving in freshwater or seawater requires fundamentally different physiological strategies. It is difficult to even imagine a human analogy to the challenge of entering seawater and this phenomenal transformation that diadromous fishes exemplify—consider the hypothetical, for example, of feeling dehydrated and thirsty but having only saltwater to drink. Such a scenario would quickly be fatal to any human. This ability by diadromous fishes to move between salinities is unique even among fishes. In fact, 95-98% of all fishes on Earth can survive in only freshwater or seawater, but not both. The ~250 species of diadromous fishes, however, are among the ~1,500 species (3-5% of fishes) called "euryhaline" fishes, which can survive in a large range of salinity, from freshwater to seawater.

Initiation of Migration and Homing

All anadromous fishes begin life in freshwater, but whether they migrate out to sea depends on internal (genetic) or external (environmental or ecological) factors. Many of Maine's anadromous fishes exhibit "facultative anadromy," in that migration to sea is not necessary for survival. Consider the numerous instances of landlocked Atlantic Salmon, Alewives, and Brook Trout that can live fully freshwater lives. When a path to the sea is available to them, individuals or larger runs may migrate into the estuary or ocean to feed and grow into maturity, or they may not. Less common are fishes that exhibit "obligate anadromy" and are genetically programmed to migrate to sea, losing the ability to survive in freshwater. American Shad serve as an example. Young-of-year juvenile American Shad appear to lose the ability to maintain salt and water balance in freshwater and must migrate downstream to the sea to survive into adulthood.[9]

A migrating fish uses a variety of clues, cues, and senses to navigate to the sea and find its way back again.[10] The downstream migration to the ocean is perhaps the easier of the two journeys. Even larval fishes that have a limited ability to swim can be passively carried downstream with the flow. Juvenile and adult fishes capable of orientation and swimming can discern the direction of the current using a hydrological sensory system along the sides of their bodies called the "lateral line" and orient themselves to actively swim downstream to the sea.

Once mature and seeking to return, a more mysterious and fascinating physiological process of navigation and homing takes place. After one or several years in the open ocean, many anadromous fishes (most famously the salmons) return to spawn in the same rivers and tributaries from which they hatched years before. These fishes seem to draw on many navigational clues to find their way home. Out at sea, they pilot themselves using cues from the geomagnetic field, position of the sun, and ocean currents. Closer to their natal estuary, they way-find by following familiar odors.

Streams and rivers have distinct chemical signatures that fishes appear able to perceive and distinguish among using odor receptors in specialized sensory tissue in their nostrils called "olfactory rosettes" for their rose-like shape. Juvenile fishes may imprint on the chemical signatures of their natal waterways before and during out-migration and then use an innate homing sense to find and follow these odors back to their natal tributaries. Laboratory studies show that migrating adult salmons can distinguish and even prefer the unique odors of their larval and juvenile rearing conditions.[11] Recent research suggests that ocean acidification, an outcome expected to worsen as the oceans continue to absorb the CO_2 emitted by humans, may impair the chemosensory ability of marine fish to perceive and home on chemical signals.[12]

Unlike anadromous herrings and salmons, which imprint on natal streams as larvae and juveniles and generally return to their freshwater origins to spawn, Sea Lampreys seem to be an exception to this rule of anadromous life. Although they do tend to return to the general coastal regions from where they out-migrated, they seem to select individual rivers based on contemporaneous factors that indicate suitability for spawning success.[13] Young Sea Lampreys live as larvae in freshwater for many years before out-migrating as juveniles but, unlike other anadromous fishes, do not imprint on the chemical composition of a river. Instead, pre-spawning adults sense and follow chemical signals released upstream by larvae. These signals may serve as assurance that a suitable spawning habitat lies upstream and also increase the likelihood of a single Sea Lamprey finding a mate that would have followed the same chemical signals upstream to spawn.

The Ecological Importance of Diadromy

The freshwater systems from which anadromous fishes out-migrate are often relatively nutrient poor compared to the nutrient-rich ocean. Once grown into adult form, anadromous fishes can derive more than 95% of their biomass from sea nutrients.[14] Thus, runs of these adults back into Maine's freshwater streams, rivers, and lakes bring with them an abundance of marine-derived nutrients—nitrogen, phosphorous, and fatty acids—that they deposit in the form of gametes (eggs and sperm), bodily waste, and carcasses in cases of post-spawning mortality. The characteristically short duration and large volume of anadromous runs result in nutrient loading events in rivers and streams that can have important and lasting ecological outcomes manifested generally as increases in biological productivity both within and above the water.

In Maine and New England rivers that host anadromous Sea Lamprey, for instance, the Spring upstream migration of adults and resulting deposition of carcasses provide much-needed nutrients at a critical seasonal period when biological demand is increasing in nutrient-poor freshwater habitats.[15] The ecological impact of anadromous runs extends beyond the water as well. Streams that host runs of Pacific salmons tend to have larger groups of breeding birds and even larger than expected trees compared to streams that do not host anadromous runs.[16] After the famous 2012 removal of the Elwha Dam—the largest dam removal in U. S. history—on the Elwha River (which runs from Olympic National Park in Washington), a rapid recolonization by anadromous Chinook Salmon resulted in a detectable rise in marine-derived nutrients in birds along the riverbanks upstream of the dam site.[17]

The return of adult fishes is governed by one of two genetically determined post-spawning outcomes. Some anadromous fishes, such as Sea Lamprey and many of the Pacific salmons, are "semelparous": genetically programed to die after spawning. Post-spawning mortality is the primary vector for marine-derived nutrients to enter freshwater systems.[18] Most of the other anadromous fishes of Maine, however, including herrings and Atlantic Salmon, are "iteroparous," making multiple trips upstream to spawn in a lifetime. Contributions of marine-derived nutrients by East Coast iteroparous fishes like herring are apparently less robust and more site specific across populations than the *en masse* biomass loading by semelparous Sea Lamprey or the Pacific salmons.[19] Still, post-spawning mortality in iteroparous fishes can be as high as 40%, so they can still contribute large amounts of marine-derived nutrients to host ecosystems.

The Historical Demise and Recent Re-emergence of Diadromous Fishes

Diadromous fishes have been victims of urbanization and industrialization in both the Presumpscot River and the world over. Where a river meets the sea is not just a throughway for migrating fishes; these locations were also strategic points for colonial and pre-industrial economies. People first used rivers as convenient means to move goods from inland agriculture and lumber production to a port for shipping; later, rivers provided abundant sources of power and coolant for mills. This is especially true of the Presumpscot River—likely, no river or watershed in Maine has been more industrialized or urbanized.

River damming, for industry or otherwise, has been the demise of the diadromous fishes of Casco Bay, which need a clear path between their freshwater nurseries and marine food resources. In the year 1600, all the lakes, streams, and rivers that feed into Casco Bay were accessible to an abundance of native diadromous fishes. With the construction of a main-stem dam on the Presumpscot River in 1762, access for these diadromous fishes to their stream and riverine nursery habitats was reduced by 50%, and access to their lake nursery habitat (Sebago Lake) was reduced by 97%. In Maine at large, mill dam construction between 1634 and 1850 reduced the amount of lake habitat for Maine's diadromous fishes by more than 95%.[20]

Maine, specifically, is an important host of diadromous fishes. For instance, wild Atlantic Salmon runs historically existed in vast numbers and in every watershed north of the Hudson River in New York, including in the Presumpscot River. Today, however, only a few rivers in Downeast Maine serve as the last hosts of wild Atlantic Salmon runs in the United States.[21]

Maine is also home to the vast majority of wild and migratory Brook Trout in the United States.[22] Known as "sea-run Brook Trout" or, more colloquially, "salters," these migratory fish are a major focus of trout conservation efforts and fishermen alike; in fact, their rumored whereabouts even inspired the locations of many exclusive fishing lodges in the 1800s.[23]

The Penobscot River Restoration Project in Maine is an interesting case study on the return of anadromous fishes following dam removal or the construction of fishways. In 2012 and 2013, two lower dams on the Penobscot, the Great Works Dam and the Veazie Dam, were removed. In the years since, early reports have shown increased ecological connectivity across the former dam sites, and anadromous fishes like Alewife and American Shad have begun to return and recolonize.[24] A few years earlier, on a tributary to the Penobscot River, a 2009 dam removal led to the rapid recolonization of miles of previously unavailable nursery habitats by anadromous Sea Lamprey and an increase in the number of upstream migrating adults from approximately 50 to 250 within two years.[25]

The Presumpscot River was once home to large runs of Alewife, American Shad, and Atlantic Salmon; however, rapid colonization of the Portland area and construction of numerous dams within the Presumpscot watershed between 1600 and 1850 led to the absence of anadromous runs on the Presumpscot by 1900.[26] In recent decades, major milestones for river restoration have paved the way for returns of anadromous fishes to the Presumpscot River. In 2002, the removal of the head-of-tide Smelt Hill Dam, which had been out of operation for decades, provided natural access to the river. Updates in the 2000s to the fishway at the outlet to Highland Lake has led runs of Alewife on the Mill Brook in Westbrook to reach nearly 50,000 annually. In 2013, fish passage was restored at the Cumberland Mills Dam, upstream of where Mill Brook diverts from the main stem of the Presumpscot River. As recently as 2018, 50,000 Alewife and 55 American Shad passed Cumberland Mills Dam and swam through downtown Westbrook, which is a rapid increase from 2015, when only 3,000 Alewife and no American Shad passed that dam.[27] Estimations suggest that a restored Presumpscot River could support an anadromous run of up to 800,000 fishes of various species.

Closing Remarks on Diadromy

Diadromy, running to the sea and back, is certainly a special way of life on this planet. On the one hand, these fishes are wild in ways we cannot imagine. They are in touch with the forces and currents of the Earth, the smell of the rivers, and the salty taste of the ocean. They are compelled to move by instinct, physiology, and ecology. On the other hand, diadromous fishes have urbanized alongside us humans. Whereas they used to gain elevation by navigating long stretches of cascading waters, they now pass upstream in short but intense bouts of elevation gain using stair-like fishways we call "ladders" or even elevator-like "fish lifts." Their environment, too, is warming, incorporating CO_2, and cycling through various bouts of pollution. So, like us, they seek out pristine and natural spaces in a world otherwise dominated by human influence. Although their way of life, like ours, is managed by the principles and policies of our legislative bodies and regulatory agencies, diadromous fishes have no voice. It is difficult to interpret their preferences and needs, which is why we inevitably end up modifying fishways and reconstructing nursery habitats. The only form of feedback we can gather on whether we, acting as stewards of this precious way of life, are doing right by these migratory fishes is whether they return home once they leave to sea. With the recent and continuing restoration efforts on the Presumpscot River and elsewhere, it appears that our diadromous fishes will run back, by the tens and hundreds of thousands and more each year.

Historical and Current Fishes of the Presumpscot River

This section characterizes the diversity of the historical and current fishes of the Presumpscot River based on historical records, more recent assessments, and guides.[28] The most recent assessment of the Presumpscot River, conducted via electrofishing in 2006 and 2007, identified a total of 28 fish species in the mainstem river and its three primary tributaries. Of these 28 species, American Eel, Common Shiner, Smallmouth Bass, and White Sucker made up nearly 70% of the total number of fishes collected. Following these species in abundance were Pumpkinseed, Yellow Perch, Fallfish, Largemouth Bass, Alewife, Golden Shiner, and Striped Bass, then the remaining 16 less abundant species. Although this section will provide a general introduction to the physical characteristics, ecology, and history of Presumpscot River fishes, it should not be considered a complete and accurate record of the river's past and present fishes.

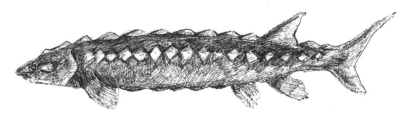

SHORTNOSE STURGEON

Acipenseridae

Shortnose Sturgeon (*Acipenser brevirostrum*)[29]

Sturgeon species are among the most primitive fishes in American waterways. As such, they retain many characteristics of ancient fish lineages, such as sharks and rays. Though they are classified as bony fishes (Osteichthys), they still have cartilaginous skeletons. Other primitive characteristics of sturgeon are their asymmetric ("heterocercal") tail and a corkscrew-shaped segment of the lower intestine known as the "spiral valve." Sturgeon species are characterized by their bony plates or "scutes" that run down the length of the body in five rows. The Shortnose Sturgeon can reach a maximum length of 4.5 feet, but adults are more commonly 3-4 feet long and up to 25 pounds. Their size is dwarfed by the other Maine sturgeon, the Atlantic Sturgeon (*Acipenser oxyrhynchus*), which can reach a maximum size of 14 feet and weigh up to 600 pounds. Shortnose Sturgeon are a long-lived fish with an average lifespan of 30 years, although records show some female sturgeon living over 60 years. Contrary to its name, one cannot always differentiate Shortnose Sturgeon from Atlantic Sturgeon by "nose" size but, rather, by a wider mouth relative to body size and the absence of a row of scutes near the base of the anal fin.

Shortnose Sturgeon are bottom-feeders, eating crustaceans, invertebrates, and shelled mollusks that they locate in the substrate using four sensory barbels around the mouth. They are anadromous and usually migrate upriver in Fall, staying in the river until they spawn in late Spring. Not all members of a population spawn each year, making their movements difficult to predict. Experts attribute population declines to overfishing and habitat degradation caused by dams, resulting in Shortnose Sturgeon appearing on the Endangered Species List in 1967.[30]

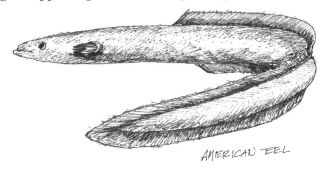

AMERICAN EEL

Anguillidae
American Eel (*Anguilla rostrata*)

The American Eel is easily identified by its long snake-like body—the only other species in Maine freshwaters that resembles eel is the Sea Lamprey, which is easily distinguished from the American Eel by its lack of pectoral fins or a true jaw. In adult American Eel, the dorsal, anal, and tail fins are fused into a long, single fin that runs across its posterior. American Eel is the only catadromous fish on the Presumpscot River, living as adults in the river before migrating out to sea to spawn.

Remarkably, after hatching in the Sargasso Sea, larval American Eels are carried along ocean currents toward North and South American coasts.

In taxonomy, true eels (including European and American eels) are actually defined by their larval form, *leptocephali*, meaning "clear head," which looks little like their parents. Larval eels have a compressed, translucent body that resembles a clear willow leaf more than a fish. Many months after hatching, still at sea and still transparent, larval eels take their snake-like form (the life-stage referred to as "glass eel") and begin to actively swim toward coastal rivers. A large commercial fishery exists for glass eels entering Maine rivers, as Maine remains the only state without limits on harvesting glass eels, which can sell for over $2,000 per pound at market.[31] American Eels can spend more than a decade in freshwater rivers and become very large (females may reach anywhere from 3 to 6 feet, whereas males tend to be smaller) before out migrating back to the Sargasso Sea to spawn. The long body of adult American Eels is particularly vulnerable to injury leading to death as they pass downstream through the turbines of hydropower dams.

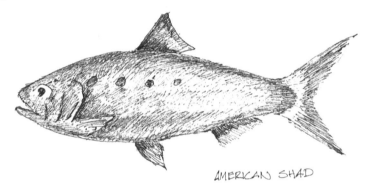

AMERICAN SHAD

Clupeidae
American Shad (*Alosa sapidissima*)

American Shad, like other local herring species, are deep bodied and covered in large silvery scales, giving them an iridescent blue sheen. Sharp, saw-like scales are present on its belly. American Shad are very fragile, exhibiting loss of equilibrium (the ability to stay upright) and scale loss after stress from handling or an arduous migration. American Shad are well known for their impressive migrations throughout major East Coast rivers, swimming hundreds of miles each spring to reach natal spawning grounds. Large females, ranging in size of up to 2 feet or more, can produce more than 500,000 eggs in a single spawning run before making their way back to the ocean. Like the Pacific salmons, the southern populations of American Shad are generally only capable of spawning once before dying.[32]

American Shad spend the majority of their lives in the ocean, where their diets are almost entirely comprised of plankton and occasionally small crustaceans and fishes. The ability for such large fish to feed on only small organisms is attributable to long, hair-like structures in their mouths called gill rakers, keratinous extensions of the gills that many fish use to guide food into the esophagus. The feeding behavior of adult American Shad during their spawning migration remains somewhat mysterious, though they may arrest feeding on their upstream migration to spawning grounds and resume feeding on their way back to sea. Despite their dubious feeding behavior, American Shad fishing during their upstream migration is very popular. They have all the makings of a great gamefish—the musculature required for long migrations makes for a strong fight that often includes jumping. American Shad are excellent for eating as well, so long as diners take care to avoid swallowing up to 1,000 bones present in an adult fish.

American Shad were of great importance to New Englanders in the past. In addition to widely consuming them, they were so numerous that farmers used their bodies to fertilize crops. The Presumpscot River is known to have had historic American Shad runs, although no records of run size seem to exist.[33] American Shad were abundant in Casco Bay as recently as the late-1800s, with reported yearly landings at over 200,000 pounds. In Maine at large, landings of American Shad decreased considerably from well over a million pounds in 1900.[34] By 1960, the only reported commercial landings of American Shad in Maine were from Casco Bay, totaling just 300 pounds. Like many other anadromous runs, the enormous declines in American Shad abundance in Maine is almost entirely the result of nursery habitat loss from dam construction.

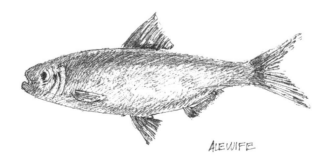

ALEWIFE

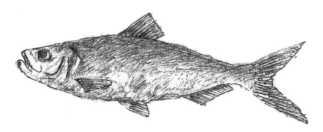

BLUEBACK HERRING

Alewife (Alosa pseudoharengus) and Blueback Herring (Alosa aestivalis)

Alewife and Blueback Herring, collectively known as "river herring," are closely related to each other and to American Shad. Like American Shad, river herring, too, make an impressive spawning migration in spring. Unlike American Shad, however, they can also live fully freshwater existences in landlocked lakes. River herring are difficult to distinguish from American Shad, especially in juvenile form. Adults, on the other hand, are more easily distinguishable, as river herring, at 6-7 inches long, are almost always smaller than migrating American Shad. River herring also have a single spot on the shoulder, just behind the gill flap. This large spot is present in American Shad and is usually accompanied by several smaller ones in a line along the side of the body. Almost no traits are completely reliable when trying to distinguish between the two species of river herrings. Stock and run assessments are, therefore, challenging and often lead to the collective assessment of "river herring." In general, Blueback Herring has a narrower body shape with a blue-tinted back that fades to silver on the sides, whereas the backs of Alewife are more likely to be dark gray or black. The primary trait to identify preserved specimens is the darker coloration of the body cavity present in Blueback Herring, although, again, this feature is not always reliable.

The river herring migration is ecologically important for introducing nutrients to riverine environments. A substantial amount of the organic carbon uptake by freshwater predators like the black basses is from oceanic sources linked to the spawning migrations of anadromous herring and is partly due to the fact that less than 1% of the eggs laid during spawning (in the hundreds of thousands per spawning adult) actually make it to the ocean. In addition, researchers link the death and subsequent decomposition of the fish that do not survive spawning migrations to an increase in overall microbial and invertebrate life.[35]

In addition to their impressive spawning migrations, both landlocked and anadromous river herring are known for their daily vertical migration, when they travel up and down the water column following the movement patterns of their preferred prey, zooplankton. Due to these small-scale migrations, river herring often feed near the surface during sunset.

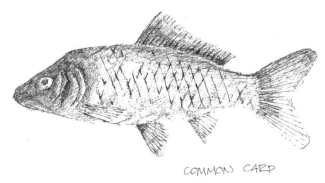

COMMON CARP

Cyprinidae
Common Carp (*Cyprinus carpio*)

The Common Carp is an introduced species to all of the United States, brought to North America from Eurasia during the nineteenth century as a food fish and still widely aquacultured for that reason. Common Carp flesh is high in fat, giving it a favorable taste and texture. Most carps are large, long-lived fishes—the Maine state record for a carp exceeds 16 pounds. Adult Common Carp have several distinct characteristics that set them apart from other freshwater fishes. They have a stocky build with a single dorsal fin and deeply forked tail fin and are covered in large circular scales. They also have a pair of sensory barbels in the corner of the mouth. The coloration of Common Carp is typically a dark brown at the top of the body that fades to white toward the belly, and several of the fins have a red coloration. Other varieties of Common Carp, such as the Mirror Carp, have an irregular pattern of even larger scales.

Common Carp prefer warm, slow-moving areas of rivers, lakes, and ponds, although they are tolerant of a wide range of environmental conditions. They spawn in densely vegetated areas when water temperatures reach 60 °F. The Department of Inland Fisheries and Wildlife considers these fish detrimental to Maine's freshwater ecosystems, as they can cause widespread habitat destruction.[36] Their large size and appetite for benthic plants and insects can uproot vegetation and disturb sediment, leading to decreased water clarity and quality in areas they inhabit. Recent assessments of fish diversity in the Presumpscot River did not find Common Carp,[37] although common sampling techniques such as electrofishing are not particularly effective at locating this species. In polluted waterways, carp are bioaccumulators of mercury at levels significantly higher than other fishes.[38]

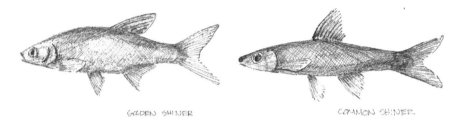

GOLDEN SHINER   COMMON SHINER

Golden Shiner (Notemigonus crysoleucas) and Common Shiner (Luxilus cornutus)

People frequently encounter two species of shiners, the Golden Shiner and Common Shiner, in the Presumpscot River. Although they are members of different genera, they are very similar in appearance. Both shiner species are native to large portions of the eastern United States, including Maine, and are most known for their use as baitfish. The use of Golden Shiner in angling has led to their introduction in most of the United States and Canada. Shiners have large silvery scales along the sides of the body that darken into a golden hue as they mature. They also exhibit countershading, with the top of the body being distinctly darker than the silvery underside. This coloration pattern is an important camouflage technique used by many fish species, making them more difficult to see when potential predators view them from above or below. In the wild, Golden Shiners only grow to a maximum length of 3-4 inches, whereas Common Shiners can be larger at 5-7 inches. Aquacultured individuals can grow even larger, sometimes up to 12 inches. Golden Shiners are deeper bodied, with a lateral line that has a sharp downward curve. Common Shiners are narrower, with a much less curved lateral line. One of the most useful characteristics for differentiating between the two species is an area lacking scales on the underside of Golden Shiners.

Both Shiners species share similar habitats and life histories. They prefer weedy ponds, although they also appear in the slower moving portions of rivers. Shiners, like most members of the minnow family, are important forage fishes for larger predators, such as trouts, pikes, and smelts. Shiners are omnivorous, with algae and plant material making up a greater proportion of the diet of Golden Shiner than Common Shiner. Otherwise, both species feed on a similar variety of zooplankton, insects, and even small fishes.

BRIDLE SHINER

Bridle Shiner (Notropis bifrenatus)

Unlike other shiners of the Presumpscot River, Bridle Shiners do not serve as bait. It is important to be able to identify this species, as Maine Fish and Game has listed it as a species of "special concern" due to population decline in recent decades.[39] Bridle Shiners are very small minnows, usually less than 2 inches in length. They have a single dark band that runs down the length of the body, with a distinct dark spot just before the tail fin. Juveniles of other minnow species may exhibit some of these traits, but they do not have the large, clearly outlined scales that this species exhibits. Bridle Shiners are schooling fish that often inhabit heavily vegetated, slow-moving waters on the outskirts of ponds and streams. Despite their small size, these shiners are almost exclusively predatory, mainly feeding on zooplankton and insects. Bridle Shiners are short-lived fish, rarely surviving past their second year.

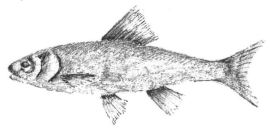

FALLFISH

Fallfish (Semotilus corporalis)

205

Fallfish are the largest native minnow species in the eastern United States, with maximum lengths reaching up to 15 inches. They are members of the chub family characterized by their elongated bodies, blunt noses, and small barbel in the corner of the mouth. Adult Fallfish exhibit countershading, with the dark brown back color much less pronounced on the lower half of the fish. They have a dark outline around many of their scales. Unlike most other Cyprinid species in the Presumpscot River, Fallfish prefer fast-moving waters, like the stretch of the Presumpscot below Eel Weir Dam. Anglers often catch these fish when targeting trout, due to the overlapping habitats. Most anglers don't mind, however, as the large size of Fallfish and their propensity for fast-moving waters mean that they can put up a strong fight.

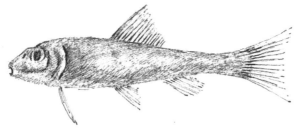

WHITE SUCKER

Catostomidae
White Sucker (*Catostomus commersonii*)

Nearly all of the over 70 Catostomid species, colloquially referred to as "suckers," reside in North America (with the exception of a single species in China). This group is closely related to carps and minnows and are similar in appearance. Some shared characteristics include a symmetrical tail fin; large, round scales; and no true teeth in the mouth. Like carps, suckers have pharyngeal teeth, structures near the gills that crush prey. Adult coloration is quite distinct, with dark brown flanks and a white or cream-colored belly. Suckers are distinguishable from their relatives by the round head with a mouth positioned more toward the underside, lending to their bottom-feeding habits. Their diet is comprised mainly of mollusks and invertebrates in river substrate. White Suckers are crepuscular, meaning they are most active around sunrise and sunset.

White Suckers live in a range of water types throughout their lives. Juveniles prefer to stay in shallow, slow-moving waters. Adults frequent more swift, turbid water. Though not usually the target of anglers, White Suckers are relatively long fish with a delicate white flesh perfectly suited for eating.

These fish can reach lengths exceeding 16 inches and live for more than 15 years.

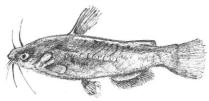

BROWN BULLHEAD

Ictaluridae
Brown Bullhead (*Ameiurus nebulosus*)

Brown Bullhead, more commonly called "Hornpout," are the only native species of catfishes in Maine freshwaters,[40] so they are difficult to misidentify. They are stocky fish with four pairs of sensory barbels and are notorious for a sharp spine located directly in front of the pectoral fins. Brown Bullhead are omnivorous and, like most catfish, are primarily nocturnal feeders. They typically inhabit heavily vegetated ponds and slow-moving areas of streams, where they feed on a wide variety of mollusks, insects, crustaceans, fishes, and even some plant material. They can "taste" the substrate using their long sensory whiskers to locate buried prey. Brown Bullhead spawn throughout spring when females build nests under rocks and inside logs. Males exhibit protective behavior over their young, scooping the eggs into their mouths when threatened.

These are some of the most resilient fish in riverine ecosystems, capable of dealing with relatively high levels of pollution. In addition, Brown Bullhead survive a large range of temperatures; some studies show that they are capable of tolerating water temperatures exceeding 96°F.[41] They also have several adaptations that allow them to survive in environments with little dissolved oxygen, including the ability to gulp air into their swim bladder, using it like a primitive lung; they can also absorb oxygen directly through their skin, like many amphibian species.[42]

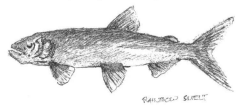

RAINBOW SMELT

Osmeridae
Rainbow Smelt (*Osmerus mordax*)

Rainbow Smelt are closely related to salmons and trouts. They are one of only two smelt species to inhabit western Atlantic waters. The other species, Capelin, is not known to enter freshwater. Adult Rainbow Smelt are commonly 7-9 inches and weigh up to 3 ounces, although some have reached over 12 inches. Rainbow Smelt are slender fish with large silvery scales that give them an iridescent sheen. The mouth is large relative to their size and has a protruding lower jaw and many rows of teeth present even on the tongue and roof of the mouth. Oddly, the distinct odor of Rainbow Smelt can aid in identification—freshly caught smelt smell like cucumbers.

Rainbow Smelt are a native anadromous species, although they can be landlocked, as the transition to seawater is not necessary to complete their life cycle. The Gulf of Maine population of Rainbow Smelt spends warmer months of the year near shore before starting their upstream spawning migrations in mid-March. Rainbow Smelt are relatively poor swimmers when compared to other anadromous fishes and are generally incapable of passing even small impediments. For this reason, fish passage for species like Atlantic Salmon and American Shad is usually unsuccessful in passing Rainbow Smelt.[43] These fish spawn in fast-moving areas of the river, where fertilized eggs attach to the riverine substrate. Soon after hatching, the current carries them into estuaries to live out the first year of life.[44] It is truly impressive that only days after hatching, Rainbow Smelt can survive the transition from freshwater to saltwater. Estuary temperatures can fall below freezing in the winter, as ice starts to form in seawater at 28.5 °F. To combat the cooler temperatures, Rainbow Smelt produce glycerol, an alcohol that acts as an anti-freeze, to prevent their blood from freezing in these conditions.[45] Filling an important ecological role in the food web, they are voracious predators of smaller fishes yet also a key forage fish for larger species, including Atlantic Salmon, Bluefish, and Striped Bass. A 1973 study shows an increase in landlocked Atlantic Salmon populations after the introduction of Rainbow Smelt to the Great Lakes.[46]

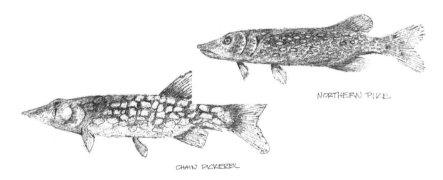

NORTHERN PIKE

CHAIN PICKEREL

Esocidae

Northern Pike (*Esox lucius*) and Chain Pickerel (*Esox niger*)

Northern Pike and Chain Pickerel are members of the same genus; thus, they closely resemble each other in both appearance and life history. They are easy to identify among other fishes by their characteristic pointed heads, with numerous rows of sharp, pin-like teeth and their tube-shaped bodies with dorsal and anal fins located directly across from each other. This body style is known as sagittiform, which means "arrow-like" in Latin. Their characteristic shape gives them the advantage of short, precise bursts of speed. This benefit, combined with teeth perfectly suited for grasping prey, make Northern Pike and Chain Pickerel formidable ambush hunters. These predatory fishes stay nearly motionless just above the substrate or under the cover of vegetation, waiting for unassuming prey to swim by. In addition to eating other fishes, Northern Pike will also eat birds and even small mammals. Both species lay their eggs in vegetation in early spring. Once eggs hatch, juveniles use a specialized organ on the head to adhere themselves to vegetation for the first couple of weeks. At this stage, their diet is primarily small aquatic invertebrates. The Northern Pike is a fast grower, generally reaching over 6 inches by the end of the first summer.

Northern Pike and Chain Pickerel can be difficult to tell apart due to their similar body shape and coloration pattern. A keen eye, however, can differentiate the two by the black teardrop mark just below the eye as well as the fully scaled gill cover present only in Chain Pickerel. In general, Northern Pike attain larger sizes than Chain Pickerel, from 15 inches to over 3 feet. The Maine record pike weighed in at over 30 pounds, making it one of the largest freshwater fishes caught in the state (bested only by Lake Trout and Atlantic Salmon). In contrast, the typical Chain Pickerel does not exceed 2 feet. Northern Pike have the widest native range of any freshwater fish species in the northern hemisphere. They are native to much of Asia, Europe, and North America, though this native range does not include Maine. Northern Pike are a recently introduced population, first seen in the state in the 1970s.[47] Northern Pike and Chain Pickerel are excellent warm-water gamefish for their fight and willingness to take a variety of lures. They do have the tendency to get hooks and lures caught in their mouths, so flattening the barb on one's hooks is necessary for catch and release angling.

ATLANTIC SALMON

Salmonidae
Atlantic Salmon (*Salmo salar*)

Atlantic Salmon are among the most iconic fishes worldwide. Once abundant in many rivers in the northeastern United States and Canada, populations of Atlantic Salmon have substantially declined in the last few centuries. Currently, only eight rivers in the United States, all of which are in Maine, support wild migratory Atlantic Salmon.[48] The population specific to the Gulf of Maine has been listed under the Endangered Species Act since 2000.

Anadromous Atlantic Salmon have a complicated life history. After hatching in freshwater, they usually remain there for 1-3 years as yolk-sac "fry" and then "parr." Some Canadian populations of Atlantic Salmon can spend up to eight years in freshwater before out-migrating to the sea. Once parr reach a certain size threshold (around 12 cm) they undergo a months-long transformation from February to May into downstream-running "smolts" that are physiologically pre-adapted for life in seawater. Atlantic Salmon can spend up to 13 years in the ocean, although they are typically ready to spawn within 1-4 years of life at sea. Unlike the Pacific salmon species, which die after spawning, Atlantic Salmon will spawn several times throughout life.

As juveniles in freshwater, the parr stage, they do not resemble adults. Parr are shorter and wider bodied than adults, with a pale brown coloration. Their bodies have short, dusky, vertical bands, or parr marks, with red spots interspersed between them. This coloration pattern acts as camouflage in their freshwater environment. As juveniles prepare to migrate into seawater, their bodies transform into the smolt stage and become more elongated. Parr marks fade, a silvery blue color develops across their bodies, and the edges of their fins darken. Once smolt out-migrate to marine environments, they become "post-smolts" for the first year and adults thereafter. Although development between the post-smolt and adult stages is less pronounced than that of the parr-smolt transformation, the onset of adulthood is an important distinction with regard to aquaculture; this period is characterized by rapid growth and development of the iconic pink flesh, which is due to the incorporation of pigments from an increased adult diet of marine shrimp and krill. During upstream spawning migrations, the coloration of adult Atlantic Salmon darkens—a feature especially pronounced in males, which develop a striking red and blue pattern with large, black x-shaped spots. The lower jaw of males becomes distinctly hooked, a "kype" structure present in many salmons. We do not fully understand the purpose of the kype, although studies associate its size with reproductive success and hierarchical position.[49]

Sebago Lake is home to a specific population of Atlantic Salmon with an exclusively freshwater lifecycle. Before the mid-nineteenth century, landlocked Atlantic Salmon appeared to exist in only four bodies of water in Maine; since then, they have been widely stocked throughout inland waters. Research suggests several reasons for how these landlocked Atlantic Salmon populations originated, including isolation after glacial recession, river damming, or simply changes in migratory behavior. Landlocked Atlantic Salmon first appeared in the 1700s, around the time that the first dams went up on the Presumpscot River.

Interestingly, although these landlocked populations still undergo the morphological and physiological changes of the parr-smolt transformation that occur in anadromous strains, Sebago Lake salmon have evolved away from their anadromous counterparts and are less capable of coping with seawater life.[50] Adult landlocked Atlantic Salmon are smaller but still retain the physical characteristics of the sea-run populations. Slight physical and genetic differences between landlocked and anadromous Atlantic Salmon have led to the historic and controversial classification of Maine's landlocked Atlantic Salmon as a distinct subspecies: *Salmo salar sebago*. A renowned biological history and strong body make landlocked Atlantic Salmon revered sportfish throughout Maine, with the *Salmo* genus name referring to their propensity to jump once hooked.

BROWN TROUT

Brown Trout (Salmo trutta)

Brown Trout are close relatives of Atlantic Salmon and look very similar, differing mostly by the pattern of spots on the face and body, as well as the tail fin shape, which is more forked in salmon. Brown Trout always have 3 or more spots on their cheeks, whereas Atlantic Salmon usually have less than 2. In addition, the red spots randomly distributed across the flanks of Brown Trout are mostly relegated to the lateral line in Atlantic Salmon.[51] Brown Trout were introduced to the U.S. from Europe in the mid-1800s. The particular strain most frequent in our waters may come from a population in Germany. Another prized sportfish, Brown Trout, too, were once heavily stocked all across Maine waters. This practice was mostly discontinued during the mid-twentieth century, although some limited stocking still occurs in a manner that limits the impact on native salmons like Brook Trout and Atlantic Salmon. Adult Brown Trout are usually 8-10 inches, but older specimens may be as long as 15 inches, and sea-run populations can grow to even larger sizes. Brown Trout are primarily insectivorous as juveniles, although their diet shifts to include more fish as they age.

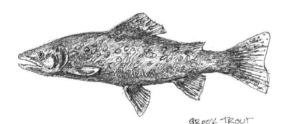

BROOK TROUT

Brook Trout (Salvelinus fontinalis)

Brook Trout are native salmonids, abundant in the coastal regions of Maine and regularly stocked as sport fish. Relatively short-lived when compared to other trout and salmon species in Maine, Brook Trout typically live for 3-4 years and reach 10-14 inches, although members of the same age group can vary in length by as much as a foot. Brook Trout are members of the *Salvelinus* genus, which includes Lake Trout and Arctic Char. All have a distinct white line on the leading edge of their ventral fins. Despite sharing a similar body shape to other salmonids, the distinct coloration pattern of Brook Trout makes them difficult to misidentify. Their sides are covered with yellow spots interspersed with blue-haloed red marks; a series of wavy, worm-like lines is present along the back and dorsal fin. Males of the species have a longer snout and a flat belly. Both sexes develop a striking orange color on the lower portion of their sides during spawning season.

Brook Trout prefer fast-moving, highly oxygenated streams, where they feed on a variety of insects, invertebrates, and small fishes. They are easily out-competed for food, making them highly susceptible to the impacts of invasive fishes like the Black Crappie. Brook Trout do not undergo a parr-smolt transformation like many other salmonid species, yet they can still acclimate to and survive in seawater. "Sea-run Brook Trout" or "salters" migrate to sea frequently in search of food. The increase in food availability, especially during winter, gives these populations an advantage over individuals that stay in freshwater.

BANDED KILLFISH

Cyprinodontidae
Banded Killifish (*Fundulus diaphanus*)

Banded Killifish are part of a large group of minnow-like fishes with a variety of lifestyles. Some killifish species are fully marine, some are estuarine, and others reside entirely in freshwater. The root word "kill" is a rarer term for a creek or a tidal river, which is an apt description for the preferred habitat of most killifish. The only truly freshwater species of killifishes in the northeastern United States is the Banded Killifish. Despite this designation, even these fish can still tolerate a wide range of salinities and may on rare occasion occupy the brackish waters at the mouth of the Presumpscot River. As killifish are so small, their preferred habitat is in shallow, slow-moving areas of rivers and ponds. These fish especially gravitate toward clear waters with dense vegetation and sandy substrate.

213

Banded Killifish are slender and only a few inches long, closely resembling a minnow. Despite the resemblance, the presence of true teeth in the mouth of killifish sets these two groups apart. Banded Killifish have a dull olive coloration on the top of their bodies that fades to white along the belly. This coloration changes during spawning seasons, when males develop a vibrant blue coloration near their tail fins. Banded Killifish have 10 to 15 silvery vertical stripes running along the length of the body. They are carnivorous, with a diet entirely made up of aquatic insects and crustaceans. Banded Killifish are a renowned schooling fish, and have been the subject of several studies looking into the dynamics of shoal size. When the chance of predation is apparent, killifish tend to incorporate into larger schools than when conditions are more favorable and predation decreases.[52]

FOURSPINE STICKLEBACK

Gasterosteidae
Fourspine Stickleback (*Apeltes quadracus*)

Sticklebacks are an interesting group of small fishes in estuarine and riverine environments throughout Maine. They are most closely related to pipefishes and seahorses. Unlike most other more recently evolved fishes, sticklebacks are scaleless. The name "stickleback" derives from the sharp scutes on the top and bottom of their bodies. These spines, which they use defensively against predation, will occasionally lodge the stickleback in the esophagi of fishes that try to eat them.

The Fourspine Stickleback is the smallest species of the family, reaching a maximum size of around 2.5 inches. They typically have 4 to 5 spines along the back, though some rarely have up to 7. Fourspine Sticklebacks are primarily an estuarine species, with a preferred habitat of salt marshes. Despite this preference, they occasionally enter freshwater and reside in regions of streams and lakes connected to the ocean.[53] Fourspine Sticklebacks are nest brooders; males build these nests out of the substrate and glue it together using mucus secretions produced in the kidneys. After spawning, the male chases the female away and protects the eggs until hatching.[54] These solitary fish live their lives close to the substrate and rarely swim in open water. Being so small, Fourspine Sticklebacks primarily feed on microscopic invertebrates like worms and diatoms. In addition, they exhibit a symbiotic relationship with some killifish species, feeding on external parasitic worms.[55]

Moronidae

The *Morone* genus, which encompasses Striped Bass and White Perch, is sometimes known as the "white basses." As the name suggests, both fishes have a relatively light coloration with silvery scales. As open-water fishes, they exhibit countershading, with a darker coloration on the back fading to a light silver on the sides. They have a very similar body shape to *Micropterus*, the genus of "black basses"; however, the two groups are difficult to confuse. The light silver coloration is usually more than enough to differentiate these two groups of basses.

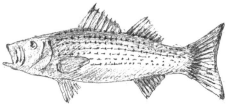

STRIPED BASS

Striped Bass (Morone saxatilis)

Striped Bass, affectionately called "Stripers," are one of the best sportfishes in New England, known for their size and strength. They are a primary target of surf casters, who use a wide variety of live and artificial baits. Striped Bass are large, long-lived fish, capable of surviving more than 30 years and reaching lengths of more than 4 feet in that time. The largest example of a Striped Bass caught in Maine was 68 pounds, although they can be even larger. Like the Atlantic Salmon, Striped Bass are anadromous, returning from the sea to natal streams during spawning migrations in the spring, coinciding with the migrations of their prey, river herrings and shad, on which they feed as they head inland. As juveniles, Striped Bass primarily feed on zooplankton and small invertebrates.

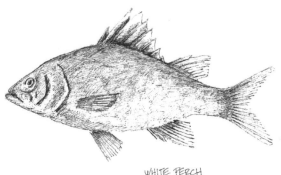

WHITE PERCH

White Perch (Morone Americana)

White Perch share many characteristics with Striped Bass, although they differ in their smaller size, more compressed body, lack of horizontal stripes, and connected (but still deeply notched) dorsal fins. The size of White Perch is highly variable, depending on environmental factors such as temperature and overall population size. Adults can range anywhere from 5-12 inches and usually weigh about a half pound. Although White Perch prefer a habitat that connects to the ocean, they live in landlocked bodies of water in Maine as well. Small temperature variations in the water can drastically affect the survivability of offspring. For this reason, White Perch spawn several times throughout late Spring and early Summer. Eggs are adhesive and stick to the substrate where they are deposited. These fish are very prolific, often becoming a primary species in bodies of water where they are introduced, placing increased competition pressure on other sportfishes such as trouts and salmons.[56]

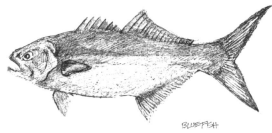

BLUEFISH

Pomatomidae

Bluefish (*Pomatomus saltatrix*)

Bluefish avoid freshwater but inhabit the mouth of the Presumpscot River and throughout Casco Bay during summer months. They are identifiable by their small scales, deeply forked caudal fin, and dark blue-to-silver countershading. They are notorious for their single row of extremely sharp

216

teeth and are predatory schooling fish with nearly global distribution. Researchers have extensively studied their migrations, showing that their movement toward river mouths coincides with the spawning migrations of anadromous fishes like herrings and smelt. They are well known for their voracious near-shore attacks on large schools of forage fishes and can even injure humans who swim too close to one of these feeding frenzies. Their aggressive feeding behavior drives small forage fish like anchovies to the water's surface, where seabirds can also feed on them. Research links the timing of this feeding to the reproductive success of some tern species.[57] Bluefish are popular gamefish, especially with surf-casters, as they are swift and powerful. High in fatty acids, its dark flesh spoils quickly, so it is best eaten fresh.

YELLOW PERCH

Percidae
Yellow Perch (*Perca flavescens*)

Yellow Perch are common gamefish that actively feed throughout the winter, making them excellent ice-fishing targets. Yellow Perch can reach a length of over 12 inches and commonly weigh about a pound, although they can be upwards of 2 pounds. These are relatively long-lived fish that can survive for over a decade under the right conditions. Yellow Perch are elongated, with two dorsal fins and a deeply forked tail fin. Their coloration is usually yellow or golden, giving them their name, though a blue color morph also exists. They have 6-9 darker vertical bands running down the length of the body. Spawning occurs in Spring near the shoreline, during which time male specimens exhibit a vivid orange color in their pelvic and anal fins. Females lay strings of eggs wound together in a gelatinous mass that become wrapped around vegetation, rocks, and other snags in the substrate of the shallows. A single egg mass can be up to 8 feet long and may be fertilized by dozens of males. The gelatinous nature of the egg clusters makes them widely inedible to predatory fishes and serves to increase offspring survival.[58] Yellow Perch are carnivorous, feeding on invertebrates and other fish, including smaller members of their own species.

SMALLMOUTH BASS

Centrarchidae
Smallmouth Bass (*Mictorpterus dolomieu*)

Smallmouth and Largemouth basses are members of the black bass genus *Micropterus*. Neither species is native to Maine; both were introduced after the Civil War, with Smallmouth Bass first in 1869, and Largemouth following shortly after, in the early 1900s.[59] Both species are among the most sought-after gamefish in Maine, and the Department of Inland Fisheries and Wildlife manages them so that they generally do not impact other important gamefish, like landlocked Atlantic Salmon and Brook Trout.[60]

Smallmouth Bass, as the name implies, are identifiable by how far the mouth edge reaches across the face; it rarely fully passes the pupil of their dark red eye, whereas the mouth of Largemouth Bass usually reaches beyond the eye. Smallmouth Bass also have several dark brown horizontal bands across the face, in contrast to the single horizontal band in Largemouth Bass. Pound for pound, they put up one of the strongest fights of all the freshwater gamefish when caught on light tackle.

Spawning occurs in early Spring, when water temperatures exceed 50°F. Once laid, the male watches over the eggs, obsessively fanning them with his pectoral fins to keep them sufficiently oxygenated. During this period, the male rarely leaves the nest to feed. One study shows a 3% reduction in lean mass in these fish over the period of parental care, and, because spawning occurs after over-wintering with minimal feeding, mortality rates in males can be very high in their first spawning season.[61]

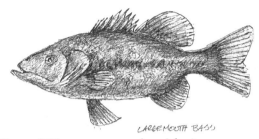

LARGEMOUTH BASS

Largemouth Bass (Micropterus salmoides)

Largemouth Bass generally attain larger sizes than Smallmouth Bass. Although they may not fight as hard on rod and reel as their smaller counterparts, they are still a coveted gamefish. The average size of an adult Largemouth Bass is 12-15 inches, and the Maine state record is over 11 pounds. These bass present an olive-green body with a dark horizontal stripe down the midline of the body, which fades as they age. They prefer relatively shallow, heavily vegetated bodies of water and are rare at depths greater than 20 feet. Like other members of the bass and sunfish family (Centrarchid), Largemouth Bass build nests to spawn. Their nests are among the largest of the Centrarchids, reaching more than 3 feet in diameter. Spawning occurs in late Spring once water temperature exceeds 60 °F. Juveniles feed on invertebrates but become primarily piscivorous as they grow. Adult Largemouth Bass are voracious predators that will strike at small mammals, birds, and frogs in addition to other fishes. Juvenile Largemouth Bass have a diet of insects and invertebrates similar to that of the Pumpkinseed; however, their body shape as juveniles is similar to that of adults, which evolved to feed primarily on fish. Consequently, Largemouth Bass are less successful in feeding at the early stages, although once grown into adult form, they have little trouble finding prey.[62]

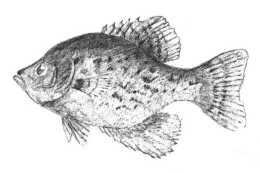

BLACK CRAPPIE

Black Crappie (Pomoxis nigromaculatus)

Black Crappie is a member of the Centrarchidae family, along with the black basses and sunfishes. They have deep, compressed bodies and irregular silvery coloration marked with dark brown and black spots. Individuals range from 6 to 12 inches, although larger examples are not uncommon. Crappies closely resemble black basses and sunfishes and can be difficult to differentiate. Counting the number of fin spines is a common way to accurately identify Crappies. Fin spines are like fin rays but much harder and often sharper. The first few rays of Crappies' dorsal fins are actually more like spines, solid and sharp. Crappies have less than 8 dorsal spines, whereas other Centrarchids typically have more than 10. In addition to counting spines, Crappies have dorsal and anal fins of similar length and a slightly upturned mouth. Schools of Black Crappie usually reside in slow-moving waters with dense cover, though larger fish can be solitary. They spawn from late spring to early summer and, like other Centrarchids, are nest brooders. Black Crappie nests are small at 5-8 inches and are built by males into sandy substrate.

Despite Black Crappie being native to much of the United States and parts of Canada, it is an introduced species in Maine. These fish are currently classified as invasive due to their ability to outcompete other native gamefishes like landlocked Atlantic Salmon and Brook Trout. The first record of these fish in Maine is from Virginia Lake in the early 1920s. By 1952, they had spread to Sebago Lake and the Presumpscot River. Anglers revere Black Crappies for their fight, and they make for excellent panfish due to their large size and flavor. As an invasive species, there are currently no regulations on catch size or daily creel in the state of Maine.

PUMPKINSEED FISH

Pumpkinseed (Lepomis gibbosus)

Pumpkinseed, also known as "kivver," is a member of the common sunfish genus *Lepomis* and is often among the first fish any new angler will encounter. Due to their propensity to take just about any bait and their small size, usually under a pound, some anglers consider these fish to be a nuisance. Ecologically, however, they serve the important role of a forage fish for predatory species such as Atlantic Salmon, Brook Trout, and Rainbow Smelt. Pumpkinseeds are famed for their striking coloration, with blue and orange stripes stretching across the cheek. The flanks of this deep-bodied fish are an olive color with alternating light and dark vertical bands and an orange belly. They have a bright red, crescent-shaped spot at the posterior edge of the gill cover, which can help to distinguish Pumpkinseed from Bluegill (another common sunfish). Pumpkinseeds are most active during the day, primarily feeding on insects, mollusks, and crustaceans. At night, they stay near the bottom of the water column and seek shelter under rocks, fallen trees, and aquatic vegetation. Males congregate in late Spring to early Summer to build nests and wait for females to arrive. Once females lay their eggs, they leave the nests, and males become territorial and defend their offspring against predation.

The Future of Fishes on the Presumpscot River

Like the diadromous fishes of the Presumpscot River, the river itself is a body in transition. While this chapter has aimed to serve as an introduction to the biology of migratory fishes and to characterize many prominent fish species of the Presumpscot River, this chapter has not thoroughly provided a population-level sketch of the assemblage of fishes on the river. Indeed, the mosaic of species on the river differs mile by mile and month by month. For instance, the salmonids enjoying the swift current of the river

221

just below Eel Weir Dam are much less abundant in the lower and slower reaches of the river, and Mill Brook hosts a much greater density of fishes in June than during the rest of the year due to the large run of Alewives up to Highland Lake. The continuing restoration of fish passage on the Presumpscot River will undoubtably lead to greater ecological connectivity throughout the river. Of particular importance is the most recent decision to remove the Saccarappa Dam in Westbrook and establish anadromous fish passage to above Saccarappa Falls by the Springtime runs in 2021. This will introduce many more miles of potential nursery habitat in the main stem and tributaries of the river to the increasing annual runs of herrings and shad and could potentially lead to the restoration of runs of other anadromous fishes as well.

For centuries, the fishes of the Presumpscot River have endured changes to the world around them. Even throughout the partitioning, depopulation, and pollution of the river, the Presumpscot River fishes have persisted still. Now, after decades of a renewed sense of stewardship among the communities along the river, the Presumpscot River is cleaner and more connected than it has been at any time post-industrialization. These restoration efforts on the Presumpscot River have not occurred in isolation but as a part of a larger trend on rivers worldwide to reconsider our human influence on these aquatic ecosystems, which has led to the removal of small and large impediments on rural and urban rivers world-wide. In effect, some kind of a worldwide experiment is occurring on the impacts of river restoration and the re-establishment of aquatic ecological connectivity. The more immediate results of this experiment appear to show that these restoration efforts have the expected impact on the assemblage of fishes, as evidenced by the increased runs of Alewives and American Shad on the Presumpscot River. How these anadromous runs and the rest of the Presumpscot River fishes will respond long-term to the improved and expanded habitat is yet to be seen but will be likely watched closely by members of this community and river communities all over the world.

---

[1] Mora, C., Tittensor, D. P., Adl, S., Simpson, A. G. B., & Worm, B. (2011, September 8). How many species are there on Earth and in the ocean? *PLOS Biology.* https://doi.org/10.1371/ journal.pbio.1001127

[2] Dawson, M. N. (2012). Species richness, habitable volume, and species densities in freshwater, the sea, and on land. *Frontiers of Biogeography, 4*(3), 105-116. https://doi.org/10.21425/ F5FBG12675

[3] Carrete Vega, G., & Wiens, J. J. (2012). Why are there so few fish in the sea? *Proceedings of the Royal Society B: Biological Sciences 279*(1737), 2323-2329. https://doi.org/10.1098/ rspb.2012.0075

[4] Gross, M. R. (1987). Evolution of diadromy in fishes. In M. Dadswell, R. Klauda, C. Moffitt, & R. Sanders (Eds.). *Common strategies of anadromous and catadromous fishes* (pp. 14-24). Bethesda, MD: American Fisheries Society Symposium 1; Dodson, J. J., Laroche, J., & Lecomte, F. (2009). Contrasting evolutionary pathways of anadromy in euteleostean fishes. *American Fisheries Society Symposium, 69*(485), 63-77. https://pdfs.semanticscholar.org/ b781/ 4bec36e62bb2acdc8fa8e57ce1721129398d.pdf; Tsukamoto, K., Miller, M. J., Kotake, A., Aoyama, J., & Uchida, K. (2009). The origin of fish migration: The random escapement hypothesis. *American Fisheries Society Symposium, 69*(485), 45-61. https://www.researchgate.net/publication/313511464_The_origin_of_ fish_migration_the_random_escapement_hypothesis

[5] McDowall, R. M. (1997). The evolution of diadromy in fishes (revisited) and its place in phylogenetic analysis. *Reviews in Fish Biology and Fisheries, 7*(4), 443-462.

[6] Milton, D. A. (2009). Living in two worlds: Diadromous fishes, and factors affecting population connectivity between tropical rivers and coasts. In I. Nagelkerken (Ed.). *Ecological connectivity among tropical coastal ecosystems* (pp. 325-355). New York: Springer, Dordrecht, Heidelberg. https://www.researchgate.net/publication/227220555_Living_in_Two_Worlds_ Diadromous_Fishs_and_Factors_Affecting_Population_Connectivity_Between_ Tropical_Rivers_and_Coasts

[7] Righton, D., et al. (2016). Empirical observations of the spawning migration of European eels: The long and dangerous road to the Sargasso Sea. *Science Advances 2*(10). https://doi: 10.1126/scidv.1501694; Béguer-Pon, M., Castonguay, M., Shan, S., Benchetrit, J., & Dodson, J. J. (2015). Direct observations of American eels migrating across the continental shelf to the Sargasso Sea. *Nature Communications, 6.* https://doi.org/10.1038/ncomms9705

[8] McCormick, S. D., Farrell, A. P., & Brauner, C. J. (Eds.). (2013). *Fish physiology: Euryhaline fishes* (Vol. 32, 1st ed.). Oxford, UK: Elsever (Academic Press).

[9] Zydlewski, J., & Wilkie, M. P. (2012). Freshwater to seawater transitions in migratory fishes. In *Fish Physiology* (pp. 253-326). https://doi.org/10.1016/B978-0-12-396951-4.00006-2 (Abstract).

[10] McKeown, B. A. (1984). *Fish migration*. New York: Routledge.

[11] Hasler, A. D., & Scholz, A. T. (2012). *Olfactory imprinting and homing in salmon: Investigations into the mechanism of the imprinting process*. New York: Springer-Verlag.

[12] Munday, P. L., Dixson, D. L., Donelson, J. M. Jones, G. P., Pratchett, M. S., Devitsina, G. V. & Døving, K. B. (2009). Ocean acidification impairs olfactory discrimination and homing ability of a marine fish. *Proceedings of the National Academy of Sciences, 106*(6), 1848-1852. https://doi.org/10.1073/pnas.0809996106; Williams, C. R., et al. (2018). Elevated CO2 impairs olfactory-mediated neural and behavioral responses and gene expression in ocean-phase coho salmon (*Oncorhynchus kisutch*). *Global Change Biology*, 25(3), 963-977. https://doi.org/10.1111/gcb.14532 (Abstract).

[13] Waldman, J., Grunway, C., & Wirgin, I. (2008). Sea lamprey *Petromyzon marinus*: An exception to the rule of homing in anadromous fishes. *Biology Letters,* 4(6), 659-662. https://doi: 10.1098/rsbl.2008.0341. https://www.researchgate.net/publication/23180977_Sea_lamprey_Petromyzon_ marinus_An_exception_to_the_rule_of_homing_in_anadromous_fishes

[14] Groot, C., &, Margolis, L., (Eds.). (1991). *Pacific salmon life histories*. Vancouver: University of British Columbia Press. http://citeseerx.ist.psu.edu/viewdoc/download? https://doi=10.1.1.456.4017&rep=rep1&type=pdf

[15] Nislow, K. H., & Kynard, B. E. (2009). The role of anadromous sea lamprey in nutrient and material transport between marine and freshwater environments. *American Fisheries Society Symposium, 69*(485), 485-494. https://naldc.nal.usda.gov/download/39954/PDF

[16] Willson, M. F., Gende, S. M., & Bisson, P. A. (2004). Anadromous fishes as ecological links between ocean, fresh water, and land. In G. A. Polis, M. E. Power, & G. R. Huxel (Eds.). *Food webs at the landscape level* (pp. 284-300). Chicago: University of Chicago Press, 284-300.

[17] Tonra, C. M., Sager-Fradkin, K., Morley, S. A., Duda, J. J., & Marra, P. P. (2015, December). The rapid return of marine-derived nutrients to a freshwater food web following dam removal. *Biological Conservation, 192*, 130-134. https://doi.org/10.1016/j.biocon.2015.09.009 (Abstract).

[18] Flecker, A. S., McIntyre, P. B., Moore, J. W., Anderson, J. T., Taylor, B. W., & Hall, R. O., Jr. (2010). Migratory fishes as material and process subsidies in riverine ecosystems. *American Fisheries Society Symposium, 73*(2), 559-592. http://www.dartmouth.edu/ ~btaylor/index/ Publications_files/flecker_ etal_2010_AFSS_migrator-fishes.pdf

[19] MacAvoy, S. E., Garman, G. C., & Macko, S. A. (2009). Anadromous fish as marine nutrient vectors. *Fishery Bulletin, 107*(2), 165-174. http://aquaticcommons.org/8799/1/ macavoy_Fish_Bull_2009.pdf

[20] Hall, C. J., Jordaan, A., & Frisk, M. G. (2011). The historic influence of dams on diadromous fish habitat with a focus on river herring and hydrologic longitudinal connectivity. *Landscape Ecology, 26*(1), 95-107. https://doi: 10.1007/s10980-010-9539-1.

[21] National Research Council. (2002). *Genetic status of Atlantic salmon in Maine: Interim report from the Committee on Atlantic Salmon in Maine.* Washington: National Academies Press. https://www.ncbi.nlm.nih.gov/ books/NBK223890/

[22] Conservation Strategy/Habitat Work Group Eastern Brook Trout Joint Venture (2011). *Conserving the eastern brook trout: Action strategies.* http://www.fishhabitat.org/files/ uploads/EBTJV_Conservation_Strategy-Nov2011.pdf

[23] Trout Unlimited (2015). *State of the trout: A report on the status and trends of native trout in the United States.* Arlington, VA: Trout Unlimited.

[24] Watson, J. M., Coghlan, S. M., Jr., Zydlewski, J., Haayes, D. B., & Kiraly, I. A. (2018). Dam removal and fish passage improvement influence fish assemblages in the Penobscot River, Maine. *Transactions of the American Fisheries Society, 147*(3), 525-540. https://doi.org/10.1002/tafs.10053 (Abstract).

[25] Hogg, R., Coghlan, S. M., Jr., & Zydlewski, J. (2013). Anadromous sea lampreys recolonize a Maine coastal river tributary after dam removal. *Transactions of the American Fisheries Society, 142*(5), 1381-1394. https://doi.org/10.1080/00028487.2013.811103 (Abstract).

[26] MacDonald, A., Butler, B., & Ricardi, C. (1994). *The Presumpscot River watch guide to the Presumpscot River, its history, ecology, and recreational uses.* Portland, ME: Presumpscot River Watch. https://www.cascobayestuary.org/ wp-content/uploads/2018/03/PRW-Guide-to-the-Presumpscot-River-1994.pdf

[27] Gray, M. (2018, January 16). Fish passage efforts result in big herring run in Presumpscot. *Portland Press Herald.* https://www.pressherald.com/2019/01/16/ fish-passage-efforts-result-in-big-herring-run-in-presumpscot/

[28] Kendall, W. C. (2010 [1914]). *The fishes of Maine.* Whitefish, MT: Kessinger Publishing; Maine Department of Inland Fisheries and Wildlife (2002). *Fishes of Maine.* Augusta: Author. https://www1.maine.gov/ifw/docs/fishesofmaine.pdf; Bigelow, H. B., & Schroeder, W. C. (1953). *Fishes of the Gulf of Maine.* Washington, DC: U.S. Government Printing Office. http://www.gma.org/fogm/; Everhart, W. H. (1966). *Fishes of Maine.* Augusta: Maine Department of Inland Fisheries and Game; Yoder, C. O., Hersha, L. E., & Rankin, E. T. (2008). *Fish assemblage and habitat assessment of the Presumpscot River, MBI technical report.* [Report MBI/2008-12-6 submitted to the Casco Bay Estuary Partnership]. Portland: University of Southern Maine, Muskie School of Public Service, Casco Bay Estuary Partnership. https://digitalcommons.usm.maine.edu/cgi/viewcontent.cgi? article=1113& context=cbep-publications; McDonald, Butler, & Ricardi, *Watch guide*; La Monte, F. (1945). *North American game fishes.* New York: Doubleday And Company.

[29] All fish illustrations in this section were drawn by Michael Shaughnessy.

[30] Shortnose Sturgeon Status Review Team (SSRT) (2010, November 1). *A biological assessment of shortnose sturgeon (Acipenser brevirostrum)* (Report to the National Marine Fisheries Service, Northeast Regional Office, National Oceanic and Atmospheric Association), 417 pp. https://repository.library.noaa.gov/ view/noaa/17811

[31] State of Maine Department of Marine Resources (2016). *The Maine eel and elver fishery factsheet.* https://www.maine.gov/dmr/science-research/species/eel-elver/factsheet.html

[32] Walburg, C. H., & Nichols, P. R. (1967). *Biology and management of the American shad and status of the fisheries, Atlantic coast of the United States, 1960.* Washington, DC: U.S. Department of the Interior, Fish and Wildlife Service.

[33] Taylor, C. C. (1951). *A survey of former shad streams in Maine.* Washington: U.S. Department of the Interior, Fish and Wildlife Service.

[34] Walburg & Nichols, *American shad.*

[35] Garman, G. C., & Macko, S. A. (1998). Contribution of marine-derived organic matter to an Atlantic coast, freshwater, tidal stream by anadromous clupeid fishes. *Journal of the North American Benthological Society, 17*(3), 277-285. https://doi: 10.2307/1468331

[36] Lucas, J. (2002). *Minor sportfish management plan.* Augusta: Maine Department of Inland Fisheries and Game. https://www.maine.gov/ifw/docs/strategic-management-plans/minorsportfish.pdf

[37] Yoder, Hersha, & Rankin, *Fish Assemblage*, 142.

[38] Carrasco, L., Benjamin, L., Benito, J., Bayona, J. M., & Diez, S. (2011). Methyl-mercury levels and bioaccumulation in the aquatic food web of a highly mercury-contaminated reservoir. *Environment international, 37*(7), 1213-1218. https://doi.org/10.1016/ j.envint.2011.05.004 (Abstract).

[39] Maine Department of Inland Fisheries and Wildlife (2015). *State wildlife action plan.* Augusta: Author. https://www.maine.gov/ifw/docs/2015%20ME%20 WAP%20Element%204_DRAFT.pdf

[40] Vaux, P. D. (2005). *Freshwater biodiversity in Maine.* Augusta: Maine Depart-ment of Environmental Protection. https://www1.maine.gov/dacf/mnap/about/ publications/aquatic/contents.pdf

[41] Brett, J. R. (1944). *Some lethal temperature relations of Algonquin Park fishes.* Toronto: University of Toronto Press. http://www.harkness.ca/PDFs/ OFRL%20Publications/Journal63.pdf

[42] Guth, R. (2011). *Ameiurus nebulosus* (brown catfish). *University of Michigan Museum of Zoology.* https://animaldiversity.org/accounts/Ameiurus_nebulosus/

[43] Landsman, S., & van den Heuvel, M. (2017). *Fish passage requirements for rainbow smelt (Osmerus mordax) and gaspereau (Alewife alosa pseudoharengus and blueback herring A. aestivalis) at fishways and culverts* (Canadian Technical Report of Fisheries and Aquatic Sciences 3210).

[44] Buckley, J. (1989). *Species profiles: Life histories and environmental require-ments of coastal fishes and invertebrates (North Atlantic): rainbow smelt.* Washington: U.S. Fish and Wildlife Service. https://apps.dtic.mil/dtic/tr/fulltext/u2/a214305.pdf

[45] Raymond, J. A. (1995). Glycerol synthesis in the rainbow smelt *Osmerus mordax.* *Journal of Experimental Biology 198,* 2569-2573. http://jeb.biologists.org/content/jexbio/198/12/2569.full.pdf

[46] Christie, W. J. (1974). Changes in the fish species composition of the Great Lakes. *Journal of the Fisheries Board of Canada, 31*(5), 827-854. https://doi.org/10.1139/f74 (Abstract).

[47] Brautigam, F. & Lucas, J. (2008). *Northern pike assessment.* Augusta: Maine Department of Inland Fisheries & Wildlife. https://www1.maine.gov/ifw/docs/strategic-management-plans/northernpike.pdf

[48] WWF 2001. *The status of wild Atlantic salmon: A river by river assessment.* Washington, Oslo, Copenhagen: Author.

[49] Haugland, T., Figenschou, L., Rudolfsen, G., & Folstad, I. (2011). Is the adipose fin and the lower jaw (kype) related to social dominance in male Arctic charr *Salvelinus alpinus?* *Journal of Fish Biology, 79*(4), 1076-1083. https://doi: 10.1111/j.1095-8649.2011.03087. https://www.researchgate.net/publication/51689320_Is_the_adipose_fin_and_ lower_jaw_kype_related_to_social_dominance_in_male_Arctic_charr_Salvelinus_alpinus

[50] McCormick, S. D., Regish, A. M. Björnsson, B. T., & Bernier, N. J. (2019). The evolutionary consequences for seawater performance and its hormonal control when anadromous Atlantic salmon become landlocked. *Scientific Reports, 9*(1), 10 pp. https://doi.org/10.1038/s41598-018-37608. https://www.nature.com/articles/s41598-018-37608-1.pdf

[51] Miller, D. J. & Ringler, N. H. (1996). *Atlantic salmon in New York.* SUNY College of Environmental Studies and Forestry. https://www.esf.edu/pubprog/brochure/ salmon/salmon.htm

[52] Hoare, D. J., Godin, J-G. J., Couzin, I., & Krause, J. (2004). Context-dependent group size choice in fish. *Animal Behaviour, 67*(1), 155-164. https://doi: 10.1016/j.anbehav.2003.04.004. https://www.researchgate.net/publication/222564679_Context-dependent_group_size_choice_in_fish

[53] Baker, J. A., Dewey, J. E., & Foster, S. A. (2010). Variation in reproductive traits of female fourspine stickleback (*Apeltes quadracus*) in Nova Scotia, Canada. *Copeia, 2010*(3), 437-442.

[54] Reisman, H. M. (1963). Reproductive behavior of *Apeltes quadracus*, including some comparisons with other gasterosteid fishes. *Copeia, 1963*(1), 191-192.

[55] Tyler, A. V. (1963). A cleaning symbiosis between the rainwater fish, *Lucania parva* and the stickleback, *Apeltes quadracus*. *Chesapeake Science, 4*(2), 105-106. https://doi: 10.2307/1350830.

[56] Smith, M. R. (2002). *White perch management plan.* Augusta: Maine Department of Inland Fisheries and Wildlife. https://www1.maine.gov/ifw/docs/strategic-management-plans/whiteperch.pdf

[57] Safina, C., & Burger, J. (1985). Common tern foraging: Seasonal trends in prey fish densities and competition with bluefish. *Ecology, 66*(5), 1457-1463. https://doi.org/10.2307/1938008 (Abstract).

[58] Newsome, G. E., & Tompkins, J. (1985). Yellow perch egg masses deter predators. *Canadian Journal of Zoology, 63*(12), 2882-2884. https://doi.org/10.1139/z85-430 (Abstract).

[59] Everhart, *Fishes of Maine.*

[60] Jordan, R. M. (2001). *Black bass management plan.* Augusta: Maine Department of Inland Fisheries and Game. https://www.maine.gov/ifw/docs/strategic-management-plans/blackbass.pdf

[61] Wiegmann, D. D., & Baylis, J. R. (1995). Male body size and paternal behaviour in smallmouth bass, *Micropterus dolomieui* (Pisces: Centrarchidae). *Animal Behaviour, 50*(6),1543-1555. https://doi: 10.1016/0003-3472(95)80010-7; Gillooly, J. F., & Baylis, J. R. (1999). Reproductive success and the energetic cost of parental care in male smallmouth bass. *Journal of Fish Biology, 54*(3), 573-584. https://doi: 10.1111/j.1095-8649.1999.tb00636.x

[62] Werner, E. E., & Gilliam, J. F. (1984). The ontogenetic niche and species interactions in size-structured populations. *Annual review of ecology and systematics, 15*(1), 393-425. http://doi.org/10.1146/annurev.es. 15.110184.002141 (Abstract).

Frothy Green Snail (Anne Alexander, 2014, H 5 x W 8 x L 13, Ceramics)

Taking Back Our River:
The Story of the Friends of the Presumpscot River

The Beginning: Stone & Webster and Virgin Pulp Substitute De-
Inking Plant Project

When Friends of the Presumpscot River (FOPR) came into being in 1992, Windham, Maine, was a town of approximately 12,000 people.[1] By then, town officials had seriously begun looking into developing a larger industrial or business tax base to lessen the property tax burden on single-family homeowners. Windham's proximity to Portland, the largest city in Maine, made it an ideal suburban bedroom community. It had always had a summer population, who came for the seven lakes in and around the town, but the increase in population from a sleepy farming community in the 1970s to an expanding suburb in the early 1990s brought cries from citizens about an unfair tax burden on homeowners. With an ever-increasing budget for schools and municipal services, Windham's location, far from interstate transportation corridors, put it at a disadvantage for attracting industry. The town did have one advantage, however: abundant land for large industries needing space for expansion. Town officials decided to investigate having an industrial park on two large parcels of vacant land in South Windham that were historically agricultural and residential. In 1989-1990, a large industry considered one of these locations, but the project fell through due to various difficulties. Even with this setback, the town approved an overlay zone that would allow industrial development on 150 acres of previous farmland.

When the town council made this overlay zone public, landowners near the parcel made known their disagreement with the establishment of industry in their backyards and went to council meetings en masse to protest these changes to their neighborhood.

Another company proposed a new project, a sludge-processing plant in the Gambo area of South Windham, and citizens rallied against building this facility in a residential neighborhood. Although designated as an industrial area, this landlocked parcel, which bordered the Presumpscot

River, was only accessible by a dead-end, rural road. The Windham Planning Board held one meeting, on October 28, 1991, to discuss the proposal. As a *Portland Press Herald* article stated:

>...about 80 people attended a Windham Planning Board meeting to hear representatives from Comtex Inc. of Topsham discuss a proposal to build a sludge-processing facility on Gambo Road. . . . Sludge would be churned in an enclosed building in six large vats 30 feet in diameter and then piled in another enclosed area to compost.

Residents were worried about the site's proximity to the underlying aquifer and the odor that the plant would generate.

Figure 1: *Boulder Falls* (Andy Curran, 2012, 18" x 18", acrylic)

This facility also fell through, but the neighbors had set up relationships that would allow them to organize quickly. The nature of the previous industrial proposals, specifically ones that involved possible pollution of the river, had made them realize the need for vigilance to protect their homes and quality of life. When Stone & Webster and Virgin Pulp Substitute (VPS)—the VPS partners—approached the Town of Windham in the early fall of 1991 about building a paper de-inking/recycling facility at the end of Gambo Road in the Newhall area of South Windham, local residents were already in touch with each other and awakened the formerly uninvolved citizenry. The Town of Windham and the Windham Economic Development Corporation (WEDC), a town-formed entity that allowed it to negotiate with developers, aggressively courted the VPS partners to build in the newly formed Gambo Development District.

When people became aware of the project and the proposed one-million-gallon-per-day wastewater-treatment facility adjacent to the de-inking plant, protestors started attending meetings, canoe paddles and signs in hand, to vocalize their concerns. The Gambo area is a historic settlement containing a number of the oldest homes in Windham, and, at the beginning of the citizen protests, many of the descendants of the original settlers were part of the opposition. The proposal to the planning board described the plant as consisting of four buildings: one of 6,000 square feet, two of 37,000 square feet each, and a boiler house of 5,000 square feet. The smokestack would measure ninety-feet high, and the estimated maximum number of tractor-trailer trips during daylight hours would be one every seven minutes. Gambo Road was basically an old dirt road built to accommodate horses and wagons. Although now paved, the prospect of large trucks using this country road panicked neighbors and spurred them into action.

Portland Water District (PWD) owned the land targeted for the project and would also build an essential wastewater-treatment plant that workers at the de-inking plant would operate. PWD's charter did not allow it to sell the property to commercial interests, but it could sell to the WEDC, which represented the town. The town was banking on these combined projects to stimulate more industry, which would ostensibly produce enough tax dollars to offset increasing residential property taxes.

Neighbors gathered at the homes of residents near the Gambo site to discuss concerns such as traffic through this historically residential neighborhood; water quality; the transportation of chemicals on local roads;

debris around the industrial facility; and, most of all, the effects of 750,000 gallons per day of effluent from the proposed wastewater-treatment plant on the river, which would add unwanted nutrients such as nitrogen and phosphorus into the river, depleting oxygen. Within weeks, FOPR had a name (we abbreviated it as FOPR but some people pushing the de-inking plant called it FOP, having the connotation of ridiculousness); a board of directors; a loose membership structure; and a phone tree. Members were also searching for an attorney to represent us before the planning board. A group that had successfully opposed a coal-fired plant in Bucksport recommended their attorney, Martha Gaythwaite, who was reluctant to take up our case, because she was in favor of recycling and thought that this was a green project. After Martha saw the tape of a town council meeting in which the council chair essentially told the citizens in attendance who opposed the project to sit down, put our hands in our laps, and be quiet, she decided to represent FOPR as a matter of conscience. One councilor told us to do our homework, which was the best advice we ever got, because, from then on, we were always prepared and had facts to back up our comments.

Several more meetings took place in various Gambo neighborhood homes and at the Windham/Gorham Rod and Gun Club to form strategies to combat the town's advocacy for the plant and the VPS partners' public relations effort to convince citizens that this industry would be good for Windham. Sixty to seventy-five people attended most meetings and were willing to do whatever was necessary to stop this project. On March 1, 1992, a large band of concerned citizens officially became FOPR and shortly thereafter filed nonprofit paperwork with the state. Because of the urgency to set up this group as a formal organization—important for fundraising and any legal work—members borrowed a basic bylaws template from a private-road association to serve as a structural outline.

During house-to-house canvassing, FOPR advocates relayed our environmental concerns with the de-inking plant and explained the impacts that we believed it would have on the river. Most of the time, we were shaking in our boots when we had to canvass, but we knew that this tried-and-true political campaign method would put recognizable faces to the fight. It also gave us the opportunity to talk neighbor to neighbor instead of appearing to be the NIMBY (Not in My Backyard) faction that the opposition made us out to be.

Talking with the Maine Department of Environmental Protection (MDEP) and other organizations, however, was like learning an exotic new language. We had to understand all the acronyms that the regulators used and be able to speak intelligently about what certain terms meant to the health of the river and the surrounding shorelands: BODs (biological oxygen demands), SAG points (the place in the stream where the oxygen levels are at their lowest due to the discharge of pollution), TMDLs (total maximum daily loads), river classification criteria, and the toxicity of the chemicals that the de-inking plant would use. On and on, we educated ourselves until we were able to show why this proposed development and attendant wastewater-treatment plant would be harmful.

In order to pay for Martha, the mailings, and the ads, members organized bean suppers at the Windham Rod and Gun Club, which donated both the space and supplies to the cause. We also had a huge yard sale (in searing 90-degree heat), held a raffle, put on pancake breakfasts, and went door to do for support and donations. The developers and the town officials periodically posted press releases or called press conferences to answer questions; rebut information that FOPR published in letters to the editor in local papers; or put out other comments that they wanted to communicate as part of their information campaign to influence citizens on a referendum vote that would take place in June to decide the Tax Increment Financing (TIF), the key funding component of the de-inking project.

The FOPR membership that was available during regular business hours needed to be nimble and able to gather quickly to counteract these statements. We made and posted signs all over town—sometimes with Sandy Cort pulling her van onto the side of the road, and me jumping out of the backseat to stick a sign in the road shoulder. Once, after a drive-by sign-napping incident by disgruntled opponents, we found the uprooted signs on our president's lawn. When we spray painted SAVE OUR RIVER on giant half-circle pieces of wood, the grass and trees around Sandy's house were blue for weeks. We wrote weekly newsletters on a typewriter, with cut-and-paste lettering for large print or pictures, as no one in the group had a computer or copying equipment. A couple of businesses donated use of their copiers, and we actually damaged one belonging to a member's business from overuse.

Our members seemed to be everywhere. If the VPS partners' representatives were having a press conference, FOPR members would somehow hear about it and show up to tell our side of the story. One longtime

Windham resident, a Windham Historical Society member, would arrive in her wide-brim straw hat and pass out cookies and drinks as we gathered across from the developers' news conference. Other tactics ranged from taking out half-page ads in local papers to writing letters to the editor on a seemingly daily basis. To counter the developers' statements that these small country roads could easily handle the increase in truck traffic, FOPR hired a well-respected traffic engineer, who demonstrated that making the roads usable for those size trucks would likely require taking down one or two houses on the main access road to widen the approach.

The homeowners who were part of FOPR would only give up their homes if the town took them by eminent domain. This topic caused a huge stir among the council, as no one was willing to invoke that law, especially when one home belonged to an elderly couple who had lived there for most of their lives.

Prior to the June referendum, we placed several signs at Windham's rotary on Route 302, where political signs abound during any election season. Windham's town manager, who was backed by the WEDC and other factions in town, ordered them removed. To us, this was another sign of how spiteful and nasty the fight had become. Our lawyer saw the sign removal as "an apparent violation of [the 'Friends'] civil rights," and the ACLU offered to help. In letters to the editor and other public venues, those who opposed us used terms like "insane, crazy, zealots"; "NIMBY"; and "BANANAS" (Build Absolutely Nothing Anywhere Near Anybody), throwing such pejoratives at us like stones. We used publicity as part of our strategy, and the larger newspapers and television stations in the area were fair in their coverage of the issues. On the other hand, the small, local weekly, the *Courier Free Press*, had one reporter who published articles in nearly every issue under the guise of reporting that were thinly veiled attacks on FOPR and cheerleading pieces for the developers of the project and the town's position. Never written as editorials or opinion pieces, they criticized everything FOPR did, even saying in one article that the reporter would gladly take our president with her if she ever needed help in a street fight in New York. Some Council members, the local press, and the WEDC frequently criticized FOPR for having hired a lawyer, even though 15 to 20 "suits" for the developers would show up at press conferences and public meetings to tout the benefits of TIF and the project.

TIF would allow the town to hold aside taxes from the project to pay for roads and infrastructure improvements at the site, instead of those funds adding to Windham's tax base and decreasing state aid to schools and municipal services, since state funding is partially based on a town's ability to fund its own services. As a rule, with a higher tax base, the town should need less state funding. Windham had never used this type of funding mechanism before, and citizens widely saw it as corporate welfare, a perception that FOPR used to convince people that this project was a bad idea.

Our *coup de grâce* came when we produced and mailed a brochure to every household in Windham, urging people to defeat the TIF proposal. It arrived on Monday afternoon, June 8, 1992, just one day before the election, leaving no opportunity for our opponents to counter it. VPS partners' officials threatened to file a Slapp Suit (Strategic Law Suit Against Public Participation) against the FOPR's board of directors, saying that we misled the public in our statements. Imagine how scary this prospect was to us—volunteers who were just acting on our convictions that this project was completely wrong for the chosen site. Even though we'd used newspaper quotes by their own representatives to show that defeat of the TIF would force the company to leave Windham, many of us feared losing our homes and facing unaffordable legal costs. Because of the intimidation from the VPS partners' representatives, the MCLU (Maine Civil Liberties Union) offered to represent us if they sued. They finally backed away from their threats.

From a small neighborhood start in late January 1992 until the election in June, FOPR grew into an organization with considerable strength. The variety of personalities involved in forming FOPR, our desire to preserve the Presumpscot, and the derision and disrespect we received from our adversaries forged our group character. We developed the ability to zone in on the essential elements of a problem and figure out a solution, using the talents that each of us brought to the organization. We had lifelong Windham residents and newcomers who had moved there for the quality of life, politically active people and folks who had never spoken out about town affairs in their lives. One member grew up on the Presumpscot but had moved to Alaska. He sent donations to help our struggles and is still a member today. Very few members own land along the river, so the effort wasn't initiated by a select few to preserve their own properties. Instead, we had a sense of neighborhood, of working together to protect a precious resource and a community. As an example of FOPR's unifying diversity, the Windham Rod and Gun Club donated meeting space for many years, and people who valued Maine's outdoor traditions but would never hunt or fish joined with locals who had been doing both for generations.

Such a variety of people and talents! Will Plumley, a board member who worked in marketing, offered invaluable skills in getting our message out, especially through the whole-town mailing; Judy Waltz had a medical background and was accustomed to conducting research on health issues associated with chemicals in the de-inking process; we had multi-generation Windhamites who had close ties to lots of folks; and several of us were available during business hours to attend the news conferences and interviews. Many days, Sandy, Judy, and I would sit at Judy's, trying to figure out how to accomplish what we needed to do or doing whatever tasks had to be finished. Volunteers all, we gave tremendous amounts of time and energy to this work. With the exception of hiring a very good attorney to lead us through the most complicated legal matters, this was truly a labor of love and being a part of something bigger than ourselves. It was the time when FOPR formed its roots of bottom-up activism, can-do spirit, and multitasking, working on several fronts at once.

On one such front, the town had delegated site review to the state, which was one reason why the developers chose Windham: according to the state's review, the Windham Planning Board could decide if the environmental impacts of the plant would meet the town's codes. Consequently, we had to convince other towns to request that the Maine Department of Environmental Protection (MDEP) take over the review of this project from the Windham Planning Board. These bordering towns had the right to make this request, because the river is a shared resource, and new discharge from the wastewater-treatment facility could have regional implications. Planning boards in neighboring communities requested MDEP intervention in order to trigger a provision in the state's site-review plan that would force the MDEP to intervene. The Gorham City Council voted 7-0 to ask the MDEP to review the project, and the Westbrook City Council joined Gorham (7-0).

Another strategy was to raise awareness in the press about how much pollution this river could take, even though we had no real scientific proof that the treatment plant's discharges would harm the river at the time. This was a case of listening to our hearts, living near and using the river, and seeing changes over the years. *We knew what was happening to this river in our guts.* The lower Presumpscot wasn't meeting its "C" classification, the lowest state water-quality standard, due to S.D. Warren's discharge, so we stressed the point that another discharge would tip that segment of the river even further over the edge of non-compliance with the state's water-quality laws, as well as endanger the water quality in the segment below the new treatment plant.

One MDEP water-quality scientist referred to the segment below Westbrook's S.D. Warren paper mill as "the dirtiest little section of river in the state." In May, the MDEP informed Windham officials that it could not issue a permit for the wastewater-treatment plant under the current condition of the Presumpscot. The river couldn't tolerate any additional waste load. It couldn't even attain a C classification in the segment from the Saccarappa Dam in downtown Westbrook to the estuary. The MDEP gave the town two choices: it could update the water quality data from 1980 to demonstrate that the river could take additional loading of wastewater, or it could try to convince other dischargers downriver to give up some of their present allocation. No entity downstream was willing to do so; therefore, PWD asked the MDEP if it could conduct an abbreviated study to prove that the river was capable of handling additional effluent. The agency said that it would consider a shorter study after it had reviewed the methodology used by any consultant firm that Windham chose to do the study, but other events made this point moot as the weeks progressed.

As three FOPR board members sat in the Westbrook City Chambers, successfully petitioning the planning board to request state (MDEP) overview of the VSP partners' de-inking project, the TIF vote was taking place in Windham. On June 9, 1992, we saw the TIF defeated: 1892 against /1442 in favor, with 37% of registered voters participating.

To celebrate our victory, on a rainy 46-degree day, we decorated a large, donated flatbed truck to look like the river—with canoes, fishermen, and swimmers—for Windham's Fourth of July parade. In a way, the float and our participation in the parade may have seemed like we were thumbing our noses at the people who had been so vicious in their attacks on us and our motives, but this display really was only to let everyone know that we were still around and would continue working for the Presumpscot. We were highlighting the joys of using the river and celebrating the protection that we'd won. Although strong feelings of disrespect and condemnation of our actions still existed among some local officials and the WEDC, our organization would continue to bring focus to the river's problems and prove that we were not just a one-issue group of NIMBYs.

After the TIF defeat, FOPR asked the town council to dismantle the TIF District in the Gambo area, but great disagreement remained as to what the vote actually meant, and the council was divided on what action to take. Several councilors believed that Windham's "silent majority" hadn't spoken in the election, but 37% was an above-average turnout, especially during a June election. Even today, it isn't unusual for only 14-24% of Windham's registered voters to come out during any June election. The intent of the ballot question was clear: people were voting on whether or not to approve the TIF and the creation of the industrial overlay district. Several councilors tried to make the issue about voter intent, but others said that the vote was a response to the ballot question . . . period. The town finally dismantled the district in late September 1992.

Not Yet Done

FOPR's original board of directors had member support and decided to continue. We still had work to do to protect this valuable resource, and our next actions would prove all the doubters wrong; we were not a one-issue organization. Members organized a watershed survey and received training in proper methods of data collection from Scott Williams, a leader in volunteer training. We then set out in teams to ask landowners' permission to access their properties in order to document pollution sources and eroding riverbanks that were causing sediment to cloud up the river. The teams located places along the river where people had dumped trash and noted many eroded streambanks. Articles from that local paper still questioned our every move. A local reporter interviewed us about the watershed survey and seemed to be insinuating that we were not collaborating with other groups in this endeavor. We turned over our findings of problem areas on town property to the Windham Conservation Commission. Those on private property were not as easily remedied, and we were unsuccessful in fixing any of those areas.

In 1992-1994, the MDEP initiated a modeling study of the lower river, due to its historically poor water quality. FOPR volunteers helped gather study data. The results upheld our observation of changes and proved our assumption that the Presumpscot could not take more of a waste load from any source. Data that Presumpscot River Watch had collected for several years confirmed where the river wasn't meeting classification criteria, which was very helpful in showing its vulnerability.

Protecting the Upper Presumpscot: River Reclassification

In July of 1993, FOPR members spoke with area legislators and David Courtemanch at the MDEP about a bill to upgrade a section of the Presumpscot River (from Dundee Dam to Little's Island, above Little Falls Dam) from Class B to Class A. It wasn't within the customary cycle for river reclassification through the MDEP, but MDEP advised us that anyone could put in a reclassification bill. Naturally, FOPR took on this task, not knowing what the process would entail but sure that something had to be done. Our connections and members' talents again came into play. One member's father had been a state senator and knew the ins and outs of the legislative process, which helped us to figure out how to proceed. Senator Don Esty of Westbrook submitted the bill title (the first step in the legislative process to move a bill forward) to the Legislative Council, which he chaired. Maine has a two-year legislative cycle: the first year is to hear all bills; the second year is a short session, with only emergency bills on the docket. This Legislative Council decides which bills the legislature will hear in the emergency session. FOPR needed lawmakers to hear this bill before another threat to the river came up, because changing the classification meant that the MDEP could not license any further discharges for this river segment.

Working together, the Majority Leader, Senator Esty, and Representative Ann Larrivee from Gorham co-sponsored our bill, as both towns border the Presumpscot and had supported greater state oversight of the de-inking proposal. The legislative Natural Resources Committee heard FOPR's reclassification bill, LD 1737, on Feb 3, 1994.

Proponents and Opponents Abound

None of us had even *been at* a legislative committee hearing before we took on this mission, to say nothing about *initiating* our own bill. In our usual grassroots manner, FOPR organized testimony, enlarged photos of the beautiful parts of the river to counteract the negative image of the Presumpscot in legislators' minds, and cajoled varied interests to testify in favor of upgrading its classification.

People unfamiliar with the upper parts of the Presumpscot pictured it as basically a sewer, a conduit for waste discharge that had no hope of restoration. We had to show them what we saw: the beautiful falls, clear waters, and lovely sections that we were trying to protect from more pollution.

Figure 2: *River Evening* (Andy Curran, 2014, 9" x 11", acrylic)

The people who spoke before the Natural Resources Committee in favor of upgrading represented the Presumpscot River Watch, Windham/Gorham Rod and Gun Club, Sportsman's Alliance of Maine, Gorham Land Trust, and Saco River Salmon Club. The legislators were impressed by the number of citizens from Windham, Gorham, and the other towns along the river who gave up their time, many leaving work for the day, to speak before the committee.

We again, however, received extensive criticism from officials of the Town of Windham, and a number of councilors rebuffed our efforts to educate them about the bill, believing that we were not truly trying to be collaborative. Consequently, we encountered a fight at the hearing before the Natural Resources Committee. Many people who had pushed for the de-inking plant were still smarting over the defeat of a project that they had considered a win-win situation for Windham. Part of the strong lobbying and reclassification objections by Windham officials centered on their concern about being able to continue the Windham School District's discharge into the Pleasant River, (a tributary of the Presumpscot and a source of extra pollutants in the river) due to its cost. Windham Town Council members vilified FOPR.

Natural Resources Committee members, however, were appalled at the thought of Windham wanting to reserve the Presumpscot as a receiving water for its waste instead of trying to solve the wastewater problems of a quickly developing North Windham. In fact, Representative Cole of Harpswell was insistent that the record be clear on Windham officials' reasons for not wanting to upgrade the entire segment. His thoughts are typical of the reaction we often received when people heard officials' protests over preserving the Presumpscot:

> Many Windham citizens and citizens of Gorham on the other side of the river supported that proposal. My comments pertain to the reasons why the Town Council and the Chamber of Commerce and the Economic Development Corporation of Windham opposed the proposal. They were afraid that in 15 or 20 years . . . the pace of development in North Windham would threaten the quality of the groundwater upon which that section of Windham depends for drinking water, that they would have to build a sewage treatment plant, which would need to discharge into the river. In other words, they are fouling their own nest and at some point it will be so foul that it will have to begin to foul up the Presumpscot River. Now, the solution to their problem is to regulate development in that area so they do not end up contaminating their own drinking water. Because the Representative from Gorham agreed to this compromise, I did not carry this any further, but I wanted to put this statement on the Record in hopes that it might prove useful to some future legislature the fact that the Town of Windham has a very poor reason for opposing this upgrading of this vital recreational resource to Class A status.

At this time, Windham had a population of nearly 13,000 people but only a small sewage-treatment plant in South Windham that it shared with Gorham. This plant serviced approximately 50-75 households and was 20 years old. Much debate had taken place over the years about the need for public sewers in the town—especially with accelerated commercial development in North Windham, and a large sand and gravel aquifer under all this development—but sentiments prevailed that new sewer lines would increase growth and change the "rural character" of Windham. Town leaders, including Windham Town Council and Chamber of Commerce members, spoke of the necessity to reserve the Presumpscot as a dumping ground for future town needs, if and when the town decided to build a public sewer system.

Any public hearing for a bill is followed by a workshop so that committee members can talk before they vote and make a recommendation to the full legislature. After much discussion and debate in the workshop session, the committee gave FOPR and our supporters the chance to consider a compromise devised by supporting legislators who attended the meeting that would give us a partial victory. As we talked, we sensed that we'd be much better off making a concession that would protect a portion of the river and trying to upgrade the rest of the river in the future. We accepted the change, upgrading only the segment from Dundee Dam to the confluence of the Pleasant River for the time being, keeping the segment from the Pleasant River to Little Falls for the next year, when MDEP could include it in the list of river segments that it would recommend for an upgrade. The bill then went to the full legislature for a vote.

Modeling Studies, Water Quality, and Assimilative Capacity

In order to better understand the Presumpscot's current condition and assimilative capacity, MDEP began a river-modeling study from the Gambo impoundment to the estuary. "Friends" volunteers did field work sampling water temperature, salinity, and dissolved oxygen at the Smelt Hill dam site on the lower river. During the battle for the de-inking plant, the Town of Windham, and the Portland Water District had commissioned a limited-scope study to determine if the river could take a wastewater-treatment plant in the segment between Gambo dam and Little Falls dam. One didn't need to be a scientist to realize how little additional discharge would push this segmented river over the edge, with the dams so close together, the sediment in the watershed, and all the changes happening to the land around its tributaries. There were competing modeling studies and much conflict over the data on the river's water quality and assimilative capacity. Results of the final large-scope MDEP study showed that the instincts of the people living around the river were correct and validated all that we had argued before the town in our de-inking fight and the struggle to protect the Presumpscot from any more assaults with our upgrade petition. This river, controlled by the dam owners and located in one of the fastest growing areas of southern Maine, had reached its limits.

Another Citizen Effort to Upgrade the Presumpscot

Although we didn't succeed in reclassifying the complete river segment that we targeted in 1994, we again worked through Maine's reclassification process to protect the section of the Presumpscot (from the confluence of the Pleasant River to Little's Island) that had remained Class B. In 1998, we asked the MDEP to upgrade this segment. The same issue of the discharge from the Windham schools located on the Route 202 and Windham Center Road campus into the Pleasant River cropped up again.

Such discharge into a small, beautiful, and productive river would never receive a license under today's standards; back then, however, Windham hadn't implemented an alternative solution. When planning for a new high school presented a reasonable opportunity to rethink and improve upon the discharge situation by changing from the small treatment plant that served the school system, Windham did not consider removing the discharge by sending its wastewater to a treatment plant such as the Portland Water District plant, where the town had a reserved allowance. The old system was very outdated, but the plans for the new school didn't change the discharge location. With the MDEP's input, FOPR again reached a compromise, and the MDEP inserted restrictive language into the reclassification bill that prevented new discharge in the targeted segment. Although the reclassification wasn't to Class A, it basically made the river a B+ and kept the town from building new treatment facilities from the confluence of the Pleasant River to Saccarappa Dam.

The school continued to discharge into the Pleasant River, but the old system was replaced by an updated model when Windham built the new high school. The other licensed discharges in this river segment—the treatment plant from the Maine Correctional Center in south Windham and the small package plant serving South Windham and the Little Falls section of Gorham—have been removed and piped to a larger full-treatment facility in Westbrook.

Next Steps for FOPR

Concurrently with Presumpscot River reclassification efforts, FOPR developed partnerships with regional and statewide coalitions to address issues that affected all of Maine's rivers. This collaboration continued as an all-volunteer effort of all involved parties, as the majority of our original board members were still involved in FOPR projects. We lost our first president, but another board member quickly stepped into the position and expanded the other officers' roles to spread the work around and avoid burn out. With help from the rest of the board and strong membership support, Sandy Cort and I became heavily involved with the Coalition for a Dioxin Free Maine, which was working to pass legislation to eliminate dioxin discharges into Maine's rivers from its paper industry.

The largest discharger into the Presumpscot, Sappi (South African Pulp and Paper, owners of the S.D. Warren mill in Westbrook), was still using the bleaching process during its pulping operation, and FOPR members knew that we had to become involved. The lower Presumpscot suffered from low dissolved oxygen and considerable concentrations of dioxin in fish tested from the area.

This time was difficult for campaign workers. Paper industry leaders, from mills to suppliers and loggers, pressured workers and threatened that changes would jeopardize jobs. The disinformation campaign whipped up hostility and anger in papermill employees. High-paying industrial jobs don't come along every day in Maine, and some families had worked there for several generations. At the SD Warren (now Sappi) mill in Westbrook, and throughout the city, the mill was known as "Mother Warren." The large corporations that owned the mills, such as Verso, South African Pulp and Paper (SAPPI) or Sappi North America, and others, had already cut the number of workers by thousands. With this attending fear and resentment, the hearing before the legislative committee that would vote on the new bill was very tense.

Studies show that mills can cut or eliminate dioxin through changes in processing methods, but that would require large investments by owners. Moreover, emerging studies show endocrine or hormone disruptor effects from dioxin *in utero*. We reached no compromise with these owners, who were unwilling to make such long-term investments into Maine's mills. Both Sandy and I testified at the public hearing, which was held in an auditorium to accommodate the crowds. We left to jeers and name calling from workers who had been bused in by their employers. The Maine legislature passed a dioxin-testing bill, with fish sampling as a requirement. Moreover, fish above and below the outfalls of the mills must meet the same standards, as set forth in the bill. The testing methods and results are still controversial.

During this time, we also formed the Presumpscot River Watershed Alliance to bring together groups working on Presumpscot issues, including representatives from the towns along the river and local legislators. We explored the need for a statewide river organization to promote policy changes that would protect Maine's rivers. This work reached fruition in the alliance of state groups to form Maine Rivers in 1998, under the umbrella of the Natural Resources Council of Maine. FOPR also began to discuss the upcoming relicensing of the five mid-river dams on the Presumpscot.

River Clean-Ups

In 2002, FOPR formed a partnership with Raft Maine, a coalition of Maine rafting companies, to initiate clean-up days along several sections of the Presumpscot. These events occurred in conjunction with National River Clean-Up Week in May and included various area schools, with students from Windham, Westbrook, and Portland. One year, we also had volunteer help from several staff people at the Patagonia store in Freeport. Generally, we had 30-70 children from fourth grade through middle school in rubber rafts donated by the rafting companies and staffed by volunteer rafting guides and a couple of FOPR members. The initial classes from King Middle School in Portland and Westbrook's middle school were studying the environment, and the Presumpscot itself, so a day on the river was a perfect hands-on activity. We formed a great rapport with the teachers in Westbrook and Portland, who were very supportive of FOPR's efforts to educate people about the Presumpscot. The fourth graders were challenged by the length of the paddles and were not as enthusiastic as the older groups. Some years, the river would be very high with the spring runoff; one year, we had to cancel due to dangerously high water, but most years we hauled a huge amount of trash and debris from each segment that we paddled.

Access to the Presumpscot is pretty much nonexistent due to the dams, so we had to find creative ways to launch these large rubber rafts. Lots of legwork was necessary to locate places to "put in" safely, park buses, and load the students. We managed with help from the recreation departments in Westbrook, Windham, and Falmouth, which also generously hauled off the trash that we picked out of the river.

While we were in the middle of our many battles with Sappi, these clean-ups served dual purposes. We collected trash—tires, computers, plastic chairs, paper, bottles, and cans—and also showed off the river to people who weren't aware of this resource in their own backyards. Many

King Middle School students had never been in a boat before and had no exposure to a river environment. It was amazing to see children from many national backgrounds slogging through the shallow waters, vying for who could pick up the most trash.

In addition to clean-ups, we went into schools and talked about the history of the Presumpscot, its environmental problems, and how students could help the river by becoming involved in groups like FOPR or talking with their parents and local officials.

Next, FOPR's Biggest and Longest Challenge . . .

In 1996, FOPR became aware that Sappi, dba SD Warren, had petitioned the Federal Energy Regulatory Commission to relicense five dams on the Presumpscot in one single proceeding. The licenses for these hydropower dams were expiring within a few years of each other, and the company wanted to do the required studies and filings for new licenses at one time. As FOPR researched the impacts of dams on the river's ecology, its wildlife, and the surrounding communities, we knew that we had to take bold and decisive action for change. Thus, began an effort to restore the entire function and perception of the Presumpscot that would take us to the present day and into the future with unimaginable and enormous challenges, victories, and rewards for the river.

Wescott Falls on the eel weir bypass. (source: Michael Shaughnessy)

Figure 3: *Temporal Beauty* (Andy Curran, 2016, 9x12, acrylic)

---

[1] This article is a reminiscence piece by a former president of Friends of the Presumpscot River.

Taking Back Our River: An Historic Opportunity

Introduction
In the mid-1990s, Friends of the Presumpscot River (FOPR) received what would be the most significant opportunity for sea-run fisheries restoration on the Presumpscot River since the first dams were erected in the 1700s. Nine dams spanned the river's 25-mile length, eight of them hydropower dams. The Federal Power Act (FPA) mandates that every 30 to 50 years, dams that produce hydroelectric power must undergo relicensing by the Federal Energy Regulatory Commission (FERC), the agency created by the Federal Power Act for that purpose.[1] According to the Hydro Power Reform Coalition,

"before 1986, dam licenses issued by FERC primarily considered a river's power-generation potential in issuing licenses, often without regard to the project's environmental impacts. The 1986 amendments to the Federal Power Act required FERC, when deciding whether to issue a license, to consider not only the power-generation potential of a river but also to give equal consideration to other values, such as energy conservation, protection of fish and wildlife, recreational opportunities, and preservation of general environmental qualities . . .
- Restoring more natural river flows below hydro dams,
- Minimizing the fluctuations of reservoir levels,
- Providing fish with safe passage around dams
- Restoring habitat for river wildlife,
- Maintaining appropriate water quality—such as temperature and oxygen levels—in the river,
- Protecting riverside lands from erosion, and
- Enhancing recreational opportunities.[2]

The Coalition continues: "Section 18 of the Federal Power Act states that FERC 'shall require the construction, maintenance, and operation by a licensee at its own expenses of such . . . fishways as may be prescribed by the Secretary of the Interior or the Secretary of Commerce, as appropriate.'"[3]

By the mid-1990s, S. D. Warren/South African Pulp and Paper (SDW/Sappi) owned and operated six of the eight hydropower dams on the river: Eel Weir (at the head of the river at Sebago Lake); Dundee (the largest dam on the river); Gambo; Little Falls; Mallison Falls; and Saccarappa (in downtown Westbrook), and one non-hydropower dam at the SDW/Sappi mill at Cumberland Mills in Westbrook. Central Maine Power (CMP) owned the Great Falls Dam, between the Eel Weir and Dundee dams, and the Smelt Hill Dam at the head of tide. The licenses that existed for five of SDW/Sappi's hydro projects (Dundee, Gambo, Little Falls, Mallison Falls, and Saccarappa) were issued between Oct 31, 1979, and September 1981.[4] SDW/Sappi requested that FERC consider those five dams in a single relicensing process. FERC's approval[5] of that request would prove to be of enormous benefit to state and federal fisheries agencies and nonprofits like FOPR. It meant that FERC would consider the five projects in a larger geographic scope than a project-by-project review, allowing the examination of the cumulative impacts of the dams and the cumulative restorative measures that it could order on new licenses. The expiration date of the dam licenses would now all be on January 26, 2001.[6]

FOPR members saw this relicensing as a once-in-a-lifetime opportunity to restore native anadromous fisheries. What we didn't understand at the beginning was how much time and effort we would expend to participate in the relicensing process. FOPR is comprised of citizens from the communities surrounding the Presumpscot River. Although members' efforts to upgrade the water quality of parts of the river directly through the legislature and through the Maine Department of Environmental Protection had seasoned us and taught us how to make our case on a larger stage, we had no expertise in participating in an intensive, highly legalistic federal process or running a "campaign" to win support from fisheries agencies or the public. When one local river advocate learned of FOPR's desire to restore anadromous fisheries to the river, he commented to the effect, "The Presumpscot, why bother?" Our group began research into the Federal Power Act and the relicensing process; we also had to determine how we could best participate in this highly regulatory process and what position we would take on the relicensing.

Two events occurred early in the process that made the restoration of the Presumpscot River a very real possibility. In October 1996, a flood significantly damaged the powerhouse and turbines of CMP's Smelt Hill

Dam and put the fish ladders out of operation, making it economically unfeasible to repair the dam. Early discussions began about removing it. In 1999, the Maine Department of Environmental Protection (MDEP), the U.S. Army Corp of Engineers (USACE), the Maine Department of Marine Resources (MDMR), and the Coastal Conservation Association-Maine (CCA Maine) announced an initial agreement with the owner to remove the Smelt Hill Dam, creating the possibility of opening the lower river to migratory fish.[7] The second event that occurred was the closing of SDW/Sappi's pulp mill. The river below the SDW/Sappi mill to the ocean was not meeting the minimum standards of its "C" state river classification (the lowest possible).[8] The company was faced with meeting new EPA regulations to its wastewater discharge by 2001; in 1999, under threat to its license to discharge unless it agreed to significant and expensive process improvements, the mill chose to close its pulping operations.[9] This decision would greatly improve the water quality of the lower river for migrating fish.

At the beginning of the relicensing process, three of FOPR's board members wrote letters and information requests to FERC. Then, in 1998, through our association with a new river advocacy group called Maine Rivers, FOPR reached out to Steve Brooke, who was the coordinator of the Kennebec Coalition in the Edwards Dam removal effort on the Kennebec River in Augusta, Maine—a highly publicized first dam removal ordered by FERC over the objections of the dam's owners. Steve was employed by American Rivers (AR), a national river advocacy organization, and would assist us in forming a partnership with AR that would last during the FERC process. He also introduced us to Ron Kreisman, the lead attorney of the Kennebec Coalition during the Edwards Dam removal and our now longtime attorney. In partnership with American Rivers, we began participating in a contentious and complicated set of regulatory proceedings that took years. Steve Brooke was an invaluable mentor early in this journey.

FOPR board members also began gathering information on how much this advocacy could cost and determined the need to assemble a legal team and a project coordinator. We began a long, in-depth discussion on the pros and cons of dam removal, how it related to the projects on the Presumpscot, and what position we would take. Dam removal wasn't common in Maine or nationally at that time. As an organization, we had to decide whether to advocate for the removal of the five dams, the installation of fish passages at all the dams, or some combination of both. We decided to work toward removal of the three smallest dams, which produced minimal power, and to place mechanical fish passages on the two larger dams. We reached these conclusions by researching how dams impact water quality and fisheries. We looked at land use and ownership along the impoundments, the distance between each dam for habitats for various fish species, and how such factors would change if dam removal occurred.

As part of the relicensing process, FERC required SDW/Sappi to perform various studies, which included a survey of the river's fish species and fisheries habitats, archeological sites, water quality, the economic value of generated power, recreational opportunities, river sediments, river flows, eel passage, and possible endangered plants and animals in the project area.[10] SDW/Sappi applied for new licenses for the five projects on January 22, 1999, and proposed that it operate the dams as it had been, with only minimal changes: that it re-water the original river channel or bypass sections at three dams, assist in the passage of American eel, and provide some recreational enhancements. The company did not propose anything related to anadromous fish-passage options or water-quality improvements.[11] Friends of the Presumpscot River filed as interveners in the process on June 18, 1999.[12]

Environmental Impact Statement

The relicensing process is not only governed by the Federal Power Act but also by the National Environmental Protection Act (NEPA), which required FERC to decide whether it would conduct an Environmental Impact Statement (EIS) or an Environmental Assessment (EA), statements on the environmental impacts of proposed actions and decisions.[13] An EIS, a far more comprehensive assessment, is necessary if significant federal action is proposed. On July 23, 1999, FERC issued a Scoping Document (SD) and held two scoping meetings associated with Presumpscot River projects on August 25 & 26 in Windham, Maine. FOPR work incredibly hard with outreach to members of the communities around the river and we turned out over 100 people to a public hearing in conjunction with the scoping meetings. Those in attendance spoke, urging FERC to perform a full EIS evaluation, as the dams and any decisions about them would have significant environmental impacts. FERC decided to perform an EIS; revised Scoping Document 1; and issued Scoping Document 2, which identified issues to address in the Environmental Impact Statement.[14] This first victory was significant, as FERC would now perform a far more comprehensive evaluation.

The issues that FERC would address in its EIS included water use and quality, aquatic and terrestrial resources, land use and aesthetic and recreational resources, and cultural resources. FERC would consider not only fish passages with dams in place but dam removal as well. Two significant challenges to addressing these multiple issues were the "baseline" used by SDW/Sappi and state and federal regulatory agencies, and the public perception that the current condition of the Presumpscot, with the dams in place, was the natural state of the river. Few people thought that this river could support sea-run fish or knew that it had once had excellent fish-spawning habitats and included 12 named falls. We would have to disprove many incorrect assumptions.

Building Capacity, a Team, and Agency and Public Support

FOPR/AR approached the Education Foundation of America (EFA) for a joint multiyear grant.[15] As part of the application process, foundation board members traveled to Maine, where FOPR board members and Steve Brooke of AR took them on a bus tour of the river and its dam sites. One EFA board member was looking for a "long shot," a grant project that had very little chance of winning. When the EFA awarded us the grant, AR and FOPR we were off and running and would be an effective advocacy team throughout the long FERC process and later court challenges.

Ron Kreisman was FOPR's attorney and strategist; Dusti Faucher, then FOPR president, became our campaign coordinator; and Margaret Bowman, an attorney with American Rivers, rounded out our team. Our attorney quickly reviewed our completed work and felt that we had positioned ourselves well in the FERC proceedings to advocate for dam removal. He advised undertaking a major effort to balance the information in the record that SDW/Sappi had provided, gain support from fisheries agencies, and expand public calls for dam removal. Throughout 1999, FOPR, AR, the U.S. Fish and Wildlife Service (USFWS), the Maine Department of Inland Fisheries and Wildlife (MDIF&W), the Maine Department of Marine Resources (MDMR), and the Maine Atlantic Salmon Commission (MASC) asked FERC for additional studies and information from SWD/Sappi.

We had several lines of advocacy that we could have pursued but only had resources to concentrate heavily on fisheries. Throughout the relicensing process, our group addressed water quality, land use, and recreational use issues as well, but our major focus was on anadromous fisheries restoration, which we thought would bring about the most benefit for the river and the animals living along and beneath it. Given that most of the dams on the Presumpscot had been in place for two centuries, state and federal fisheries agencies initially couldn't envision robust anadromous fisheries on the river. At a meeting, one biologist from Maine Department of Inland Fisheries and Wildlife completely opposed the idea of restoring Atlantic salmon, alewife, and American shad to the river. His experience with the present river conditions told him that the habitat could only support warmer water species, such as small-mouth bass and pickerel, because the impoundments behind the dams had created a "lake-like" habitat, and the substrate (river bottom) appeared to be just a clay base.

The FERC relicensing story wouldn't be complete without mentioning the extensive work that took place on two fronts and the importance of finding funding sources for that work. The three-year grant from the EFA was our base funding, but we also had to locate new financial sources. Board members initially conducted grant-funding research and proposal writing, jobs later taken on by the campaign coordinator. As a new and unproven group, a sustained effort was necessary to show funders that we could competently accomplish the work ahead. FOPR quickly developed a reputation for reliability. We focused our funding efforts on two fronts. The "inside" front was all the legal and scientific work we did to support our case before FERC and with state and federal resource agencies. The "outside" front was building support for our position from the people who lived in the communities along the river, including critical work with the media to bring our story to watershed residents and the state of Maine.

As the work of preparing major legal filings and engaging with consultants and resource agencies was underway, FOPR's campaign coordinator and other board members were also conducting the "outside" campaign of swaying public opinion. With funding from various foundations and donors, and donations of services from supporters and community businesses, FOPR was able to produce outreach materials that members used when speaking to audiences in surrounding communities. The Davis Foundation, a local resource, gave FOPR a $10,000 grant, a significant sum for a group that in its early years had a small annual budget.[16] The grant funded our effort, and, with graphic-design support from FOPR supporter Jack Barrett, we produced a detailed map of the river and a narrative of its history and fisheries. We gave the poster-size, two-sided maps to schools, libraries, and individuals in the river's communities. The River Network's newsletter featured our map outreach effort to showcase how maps can tell a river's story.[17]

Our next outreach endeavor was a video to flesh out our call for dam removal and fish passages. The video production company, Catama Productions of South Portland, facilitated a helicopter flyover video, which showed each dam and how it changed the river above it. One FOPR member wrote the narration, others were interviewed and a local person studying voice narration donated the voiceover. Catama and its owner Carlos Cuellar donated all its services and, with campaign coordinator Dusti Faucher, edited the video into a priceless resource to make our case.[18]

As part of our outreach, we also wrote multiple "Letters to the Editor" in all the local papers. As a result, the *Portland Press Herald* assigned a reporter and photographer to undertake a canoe trip of the river's entire length. The articles and photographs highlighted the Presumpscot as a wonderful resource but also showed how segmented it was by dams and difficult to portage.[19]

On the legal front, January 2000 began a very intensive period of research, strategizing, and preparation by FOPR/AR for major filings to FERC. Our legal advisor, campaign coordinator, and board member team decided that we needed to provide missing information in the FERC record. We hired qualified consultants, including an energy economist, a fisheries biologist, and an environmental assessment firm that would look at the substrate in the impoundments behind the dams up for relicensing. SDW/Sappi's position to FERC was that without conclusive documentation that American shad and river herring had once been present in the river, fish passage for these species was not warranted. The company argued that insufficient evidence existed to determine the exact historic range of these species and that fish passage would therefore constitute an enhancement, not a restoration, of the species to their historic range.[20] We needed to document the historic presence of these fish species, their past range, and whether fish passage had been ordered and constructed in the past. We also had to explore fish-passage engineering issues.

Steve Brooke suggested to FOPR the positive impact of developing a river-management plan to help guide future decisions by FERC, governmental agencies, and non-profit associations. In 2000, FOPR advocated for, and fully participated in, a more-than-year-long collaborative effort with the Casco Bay Estuary Partnership (CBEP) to formulate *A Plan for the Future of the Presumpscot River* (the Presumpscot River Management Plan).[21] The planning group consisted of representatives from FOPR; the Maine Department of Environmental Protection (MEDEP); the U.S. Department of Environmental Protection (USEPA); U.S. Fish and Wildlife Service (USFWS); Maine Department of Inland Fisheries and Wildlife (MDIF&W); the Maine Department of Marine Resources (MDMR); the University of Maine; Friends of Casco Bay; Cumberland County Soil and Water Conservation District (CCSWD); Portland Water District (PWD); SDW/Sappi; the City of Westbrook; the City of Portland; and the towns of Falmouth, Gorham, and Windham. Will Plumley, a longtime FOPR board member, served as chair. As part of this process, Maine's three fisheries agencies—the Maine Department of Marine Resources, the Maine Department of Inland Fisheries and Wildlife and the Maine Atlantic Salmon Commission (MASC)—prepared a "Draft Fishery Management Plan for the Presumpscot River Drainage," which was invaluable in convincing federal and state fisheries agencies to urge FERC to consider fish passage and dam removal in its EIS process and decisions.[22] The process required a lot of sharing of expertise, patience, persistence, and compromise. Through it, FOPR built trust with other stakeholders that would continue through the relicensing process.

Presumpscot Named One of the "Most Endangered Rivers"
In April 2000, American Rivers named the Presumpscot one of its "Most Endangered Rivers," based on the impacts that the many dams had on salmon, shad, river herring, and other fish and wildlife species that could no longer thrive in the dam-clogged river.[23] The dams, built to power mills and factories of a bygone era, continued to block migrating fish and degrade the river's overall health. Over the past three centuries, as many as 17 dams and many small mills had turned the river into a series of polluted impoundments.[24] AR highlighted the fact that three of SDW/Sappi's smaller dams up for relicensing, which FOPR was advocating for removal, produced less than 3.5 megawatts (MWs) of electricity combined. AR also pointed out that with many of the dams' licenses up for renewal, communi-

ties had an unprecedented opportunity to restore the river's health. This announcement, and a press conference at Riverbank Park in Westbrook, brought the Presumpscot local, state, and national attention.

Major FOPR/AR Filing

On December 4, 2000, FERC issued a notice that the Presumpscot River's hydro projects were ready for environmental analysis (REA) and solicited comments, recommendations, terms, and conditions to consider in the analysis.[25] With support from the Friends of Sebago Lake (FOSL), FOPR/AR conducted supplemental historical research and submitted a major filing to FERC on February 2, 2001. Attorneys Margaret Bowman and Ronald Kreisman coordinated with the authors of the studies that our groups had commissioned and wrote the filing, which stated that for two centuries, two major forces combined to decimate the river and its fisheries: dams and pollution. Both degraded the river's water quality and barred up the river for anadromous fish species. FOPR/AR further argued in our filing that SDW/Sappi's position of no fish passage set forth in its license renewal applications did not balance hydro power generation with fisheries restoration.[26]

The company's suggested measures to mitigate the effects of its five dams were (a) re-watering small bypass reaches[27] at three of the five dams, and (b) proposing minimal measures to assist in the passage of the American eel.[28] Our filing advocated that FERC (a) deny a new license for the Saccarappa Dam, with SDW/Sappi removing that dam contingent upon the removal of the flood- damaged CMP Smelt Hill Dam and the installation of fish passage for or removal of the Cumberland Mills Dam, both between Saccarappa and the sea; (b) deny new licenses for the Mallison Falls and Little Falls dams, with SDW/Sappi removing those dams; and (c) relicensing the Gambo and Dundee dams, with the installation of effective fishways. Removal of Mallison Falls and Little Falls and fish passage at Gambo and Dundee were conditional on Smelt Hill Dam removal and either fish passage or dam removal at Cumberland Mills. If FERC rejected (a) dam removal at Saccarappa, and (b) dam removal at Mallison and Little Falls, FOPR/AR advocated fish passage for the 5 dams (Saccarappa, Mallison Falls, Little Falls, Gambo and Dundee) contingent on the removal of CMP's Smelt Hill Dam and the installation of a fishway or dam removal at the Cumberland Mills Dam.[29]

Economic Value Analysis of Five Hydropower Projects, January 2001
One of the three studies FOPR/AR commissioned was to determine the
economic value of the five hydropower dams that FERC was considering
during the relicensing process. Our groups also felt that we needed an
independent analysis of the value of the hydro power, especially of the
smaller hydro projects, so we engaged Dr. Richard Parker of Red Oak
Research Services of Camden to evaluate the economic value of Sappi's
five hydropower projects. His work indicated that six of SDW/Sappi's
hydroelectric stations were collectively minor contributors to the mill's
power supply, together accounting for only about one-tenth of the total
power generation at the SDW/Sappi Westbrook complex. The six hydropower projects, of which five were up for relicensing, provided total
capacity of about 9 megawatts; the mill-owned multi-fuel biomass facility
had 65 MW of electrical capacity. SDW/Sappi indicated to FERC that it
did not intend to upgrade or add capacity to the hydro projects, that
extending the life of the projects was the only economic consideration.[30]
The generation capacity of the five dams up for relicensing were: Dundee
2.4 MW; Gambo 1.9 MW; Little Falls 1.0 MW; Mallison Falls 0.8 MW; and
Saccarappa 1.35 MW, for a total of 7.45 MW. According to Dr. Parker's
report, the five hydro projects up for relicensing had, at that time, a total
annual value to SDW/Sappi likely between $666,000 and $785,000, with
more than half of that annual value coming from the Dundee hydro project
alone. The combined value of Little Falls and Mallison Falls was, then, less
than $50,000 and quite possibly zero. Dr. Parker asserted that SDW/Sappi
generated sufficient power with its two larger hydro projects and biomass
power to meet its demand.[31] With Dr. Parker's evaluation, FOPR/AR felt
even more strongly that the balance lay with dam removal and the restoration of an anadromous fishery. The ecological damage by these small
projects that did not produce a significant amount of hydro power was too
great.

Fisheries Study of the Presumpscot: Past, Present, and Potential
Dr. Michael Dadswell, professor of biology at Acadia University in
Wolfville, Nova Scotia, issued the report *Fisheries Resources: Past, Present and
Potential: The Presumpscot River, Maine in Comments, Recommendations, Terms and
Conditions by American Rivers and Friends of the Presumpscot River*, which listed at
least 27 species of fish (freshwater and anadromous) known to occur in the

Presumpscot. Anadromous species included blueback herring, alewife, American shad, and Atlantic salmon. Sturgeon and striped bass were present in the lower river. He also noted the presence of American eel and reported that populations of Atlantic salmon, American shad, and smelt, once abundant, were now extinct or reduced to incidental fish below the Smelt Hill Dam at tidewater.[32]

Dr. Dadswell's analysis considered the potential of the Presumpscot River in view of the intended removal of the Smelt Hill Dam and with dam removal or fish-passage installation at the Cumberland Mills Dam. He detailed a highly managed (by MDIF&W) cold-water salmonid sport fishery in the Eel Weir by-pass in the upper river reach that consisted of hatchery-raised brook trout, landlocked salmon, and brown trout. His assessment of the Eel Weir by-pass fisheries highlighted how a high-quality catch-and-release fishing opportunity near an urban area could work in other parts of the river with dam removal. He also contended that the Presumpscot was once home to anadromous species and could provide suitable habitats once again if the dams were gone or the fish had access to tributaries and areas where they would thrive.

The report pointed out that the impoundments behind the dams and the small amount of free-flowing sections of the river had warmwater and seasonal cold-water fisheries comprised of largemouth bass, chain pickerel, yellow perch, smallmouth bass, brown bullhead, sunfish, brook trout, landlocked salmon, and brown trout. The habitat in the impoundments was less than optimal for these species. Dr. Dadswell stated that brook trout were more abundant than SDW/Sappi's fisheries report had stated. He thought that a brown-trout fishery would be highly successful with lower temperatures, higher summer flows, and larger numbers of suitable habitat created by dam removal and some stocking efforts.

Anadromous fish species that historically inhabited the river included blueback river herring, alewife, shad, and Atlantic salmon. The American eel, a catadromous fish, were and still are present in the river. Successful runs of alewives moved up the Mill Brook into Highland Lake, but the 1996 flood damage to the fishway at the Smelt Hill Dam restricted them. Removal of that dam and a fish passage or dam removal at Cumberland Mills could restore the river herring, alewife, and shad fisheries and enhance the eel fishery. Dr. Dadswell provided not only information on the current fishery of the river but also the historic record of what fish species the river had supported in the past. He gave a view of what was possible with dam removal. This report gave us invaluable information for FERC and a very good assessment of the river's past, present, and potential fishery for our future efforts.

Survey and Analysis of River Substrate

FOPR/AR also hired Northern Ecological Associates (NEA) of Portland to conduct a survey and analysis of the substrate of the impoundments behind the Saccarappa, Mallison, and Little Falls dams.[33] This work was to look at the composition of the river bottom to establish possible fish-spawning habitats in those reaches.

The Saccarappa impoundment is five miles long, and NEA defined multiple transects to sample. The middle section of the Saccarappa impoundment, below the confluence of the Little River, showed fine sediment, silt, and clay, with organic debris and fine sand in the center of the river. Above the Little River confluence were fine sediments; organic debris; and coarse sand, gravel, and small pebbles in the river's center. The upper portion of the impoundment had fine sediments grading to sand, gravel, cobble, and boulders toward the center. The lower impoundment showed fine sediments of clay, silt, and sand on the banks, with gravel and pebbles present in 35% to 45% of the river's center. NEA concluded that sand was the dominant substrate, but the river also had a significant amount of gravel and pebble substrate in the deeper water for fish spawning.

The Mallison Falls impoundment is a half-mile long, with the study defining two transects. The substrate samples were a composition of primarily pebbles, cobble, coarse gravel, and sand.

The Little Falls impoundment of 1.7 miles had three transects. Samples showed that the substrate in the lower impoundment, near the Rt. 202 bridge, was fine sediments (silt and clay), with the right-side bottom having fist-sized cobble. The middle of the impoundment also showed silt, clay, and sand but with small and large pebbles also present in areas. The upper impoundment, closer to the Gambo Dam, showed predominately small and large pebbles, and the right bank had larger stones and a rock ledge. The substrate study refuted Sappi's claim of very little habitat in the impoundments by clearly documenting the rock, cobble, and gravel necessary for spawning fish. The substrate study provided valuable information that anadromous fish-spawning habitats existed. Our task was to open the river to these anadromous fish.

Little Falls Dam (source: Michael Shaughnessy)

Ron Kreisman filed supplemental information on July 5, 2001,[34] on be-half of FOPR/AR, FOSL, and the Maine Council of the Atlantic Salmon Federation (the non-governmental organizations—NGOs) to counter a SDW/Sappi filing of April 18, 2001, (S. D. Warren's *Response to Agencies' and Non-Governmental Organizations' Terms and Conditions Filings*), which we felt contained incorrect information[35] Our NGO filing included additional information from Dr. Dadswell of the impact on fisheries from relicensing the five hydro projects, NEA's response to SDW/Sappi's incorrect infor-mation on the substrate, and Dr. Parker's economic analysis of the projects.

The NGO filing also responded to a claim that SDW/Sappi made that the request for the removal of certain dams or the installation of fishways was "untimely" and relied on flawed analyses. Moreover, the company stated that the economic valuation of its hydro dams, conducted by FOPR consultant Dr. Parker, that demonstrated the minor significance of Sac-carappa, Mallison Falls, and Little Falls contained errors or grossly under-valued the projects. In the NGO filing, we stated that FOPR had advocated for dam removal or fishway installation in the June 1999 motion to intervene. The filing also outlined that prior to 1999, the Maine Department of Environmental Protection determined that the Presumpscot River from SDW/Sappi's papermill to the ocean did not attain a class C designation, the lowest river water-quality classification, due almost entirely to the mill's wastewater discharge.[36] SDW/Sappi's closure of its pulp mill caused dramatic improvements in water quality to approximately one third of the river, and the upcoming removal of the Smelt Hill Dam would make this section accessible for fish. It was indeed timely for FERC to consider dam removal as part of fisheries restoration in the relicensing proceeding.

NEA's substrate analysis had revealed significant areas of salmonid habitat in the original riverbed. Contrary to SDW/Sappi's assertion, salmonid habitat in the Saccarappa, Little Falls, and Mallison impoundments exceeded that in many of Maine's Atlantic salmon rivers and was still more than adequate to support Atlantic salmon. Dr. Dadswell's potential production rates for Atlantic salmon were entirely justified in light of the historical experience on many similar Atlantic rivers in the last 30-40 years, the likely term of any new license.

The DEIS and FEIS Process

Earlier efforts by FOPR had convinced FERC to conduct the in-depth Environmental Impact Statement versus a lesser evaluation in an Environmental Assessment. In September 2001, FERC issued its Draft Environmental Impact Statement (DEIS), an analysis intended to give equal consideration to hydropower energy, the protection of fisheries and wildlife, and cultural and recreation opportunities.

The DEIS analyzed the effects of dam removal on fisheries resources (assuming removal of the Smelt Hill Dam and either removal of the Cumberland Mills Dam or installation of a fish ladder there) and concluded that the benefits would be marginal. FERC did make the following draft recommendations for flow management of the dams:[37]
- operate the hydro projects in run-of-the-river mode as it was doing
- monitor the head ponds, with no drawdowns between May and June
- notify state fisheries agencies before planned drawdowns
- provide provisions for seasonal minimum flows to the bypassed reaches at Dundee, Gambo, and Mallison Falls.

The DEIS also called for the design and installation of eel passages at all dams and a plan to assess the timing of shutdowns to protect outgoing migrant adult eels It also required the design and installation of upstream and downstream fish passages for shad and river herring at each dam in a phased approach. To enhance recreational opportunities, it called for improving portage around the dams, enhancing angler access to the bypassed reaches, conducting a recreational use study with a final plan for boating access. It also recommended that SWD/Sappi protect the Cumberland Oxford Canal and other historic areas.[38] FOPR/AR were disappointed in FERC's DEIS but determined to reassert our position. It was time to make another filing.

FOPR/AR's response to the DEIS focused on the information in the statement and FERC's staff recommendations related to restoring native migratory and residential fish species to the Presumpscot and the dramatic environmental impacts caused to these species by the operation of the five Sappi dams that were the subjects of this relicensing. Our groups chose not to modify our recommendations, terms, and conditions and instead reasserted those contained in our February 2, 2001, filing with FERC, which proposed alternative sets of recommendations, terms, and conditions, from the most preferred to the least preferred, to correct the imbalance of almost total hydro use to increased public benefit. The most preferred alternative was to deny a new license for the Saccarappa project, contingent upon dam removal of the Smelt Hill Dam and fish passage or dam removal at the Cumberland Dam; to immediately deny new licenses for Mallison Falls and Little Falls; to install effective fishways at the Gambo and Dundee projects once one or more species of anadromous fish reestablished themselves in the waters below the dams; and to immediately install and implement upstream and downstream passages at these two projects for American eels. To the extent that FERC was not prepared to order removal of the Saccarappa, Mallison Falls and Little Falls dams. FOPR/AR advocated that it order the installation of fishways that would be capable of moving American shad, Atlantic salmon, blueback herring, and American eel over the dams (after the removal of Smelt Hill Dam and installation of fish passage or dam removal at the Cumberland Mills Dam).

The DEIS contained discussion on each of these alternatives, but FERC chose FOPR/AR's least-favored approach to fisheries restoration: the installation of fishways at all five dams. We also thought that FERC's recommendation of phased fishway construction was ambiguous and open-ended and left opportunities for delays. FOPR/AR believed that FERC staff failed to evaluate and quantify with equal depth of analysis and level of critique the economic benefits of fisheries restoration through dam removal in comparison to the minor value of the hydro power produced at the three small projects. With the research work of our consultants (Dadswell, Parker, & NEA), we believed that our position on dam removal would provide more habitat and that larger numbers of fish would pass with the dams removed versus through multiple fishways. We also thought that the economic benefits that would accrue from multiple dam removals and a very attractive fisheries resource adjoining the largest and most populous city in the state would be far greater than the economic value of the power generated.

In July 2002, FERC released its Final Environmental Impact Statement (FEIS), which recommended measures that were basically more detailed versions of those in the DEIS and included suggestions for the improvement of portages and angler access and the protection of archaeological sites.[39] Section 18 of the Federal Power Act required FERC to order the hydro project owner to construct, operate, and maintain fishways as prescribed by the secretary of the Department of Interior and the USFWS.[40] In February 2002, the USFWS filed their final fishway prescriptions for the projects in the FEIS. The fishway prescriptions laid out the design and phased installation of upstream and downstream fish passages for American shad and river herring.[41] This approach would depend on removal of the Smelt Hill Dam and dam removal or fish passage at the Cumberland Mills Dam.

A parallel state process was also moving forward at the MDEP. Under section 401 of the Clean Water Act (CWA), dam license applicants must obtain state certification that any discharge from a project would comply with CWA provisions.[42] This MDEP 401 Water Quality Certification would, when issued in conjunction with the FERC licenses, result in a long legal challenge by Sappi.

In September 2002, FOPR/AR and the Friends of Sebago Lake made another filing to FERC. *Supplemental Historical Records Related to the Anadromous Fisheries of the Presumpscot River and Sebago Lake* looked at the historic records of the river's fisheries, including the past range of Atlantic salmon, American shad, and river herring in the Presumpscot River drainage.[43] Journalist Douglas Watts was the primary researcher for this effort, and most of the materials that he cites in the study/report are available at the Maine State Library; the Maine State Law Library in Augusta, Maine; and the Massachusetts Archives. Historic documents demonstrate that prior to construction of the mill dams, the Presumpscot River watershed and

Sebago Lake hosted large numbers of seasonal migratory fish that were important food sources for both Native Americans and early Europe settlers. Watts found no documents that stated or suggest that the natural falls on the Presumpscot River prevented American shad, river herring, and Atlantic salmon from reaching Sebago Lake as SDW/Sappi had claimed.

Records in the Massachusetts Archives document an August 10, 1739, meeting in Boston between Governor Belcher and Chief Polin, a Native American sachem of the peoples of the Presumpscot River. Polin traveled to Boston to discuss several concerns of his people, including the impact of mill dams on the Presumpscot River's migratory fish populations. At this meeting, Polin stated that Col. Westbrook had promised two years earlier (1736-1737) to provide passage for fish at his dam at Presumpscot Falls, the first falls on the Presumpscot River. The meeting transcript reads as follows:

Indian   I have to Say Something Concerning the River, which I belong too, it is barred over in Sundry places.

Govr'   What River is itt

Indian   itt is Pesumscott, which is Barr'd up, and the fish is thereby Barr'd up, which is Our food, and then laid downe an otter skin desires only that a place may be left open in the Dams that so the fish may come up in the Propper Seasons of the year.[44]

A petition filed in October 30, 1781, by the towns of Gorham, Windham, Pearsontown (Standish), Bridgton, and Harrison cite the need for fish passages at the dams on the lower Presumpscot River to allow American shad, alewife, and Atlantic salmon access to those portions of the river in these towns, which are all located above the existing SDW/Sappi dam at Saccarappa Falls in Westbrook. Bridgton and Harrison are at the tip of Long Lake, part of the upper Sebago Lake watershed, and are approximately 60 miles above the head of the Presumpscot. Standish is above all SDW/Sappi dams except the Eel Weir Dam at the outlet of Sebago Lake.

A report of the Dam Viewing Committee, which was appointed by the Massachusetts Great and General Court in 1777, stated that the owners of all mill dams on the Presumpscot River at that time (specified as Presumpscot Falls in Falmouth, Ammoncongin and Saccarappa Falls in Westbrook, and Mallison Falls in Windham) agreed to provide passage for migratory fish at these dams when the committee requested them to do so.[45] Moreover, none of the dam owners claimed that the river's natural falls prevented migratory fish from ascending the Presumpscot River or its tributaries.

Massachusetts laws of 1785, 1789, and 1794 required fish passages at all existing and future Presumpscot River mill dams and specifically cite the need and benefit for migratory fish to have access to the entire Presumpscot River drainage.[46] No records that we have seen show or suggest that dam owners challenged the laws on the basis that the Presumpscot's natural falls prevented migratory fish from ascending the river or its tributaries. This historical research demonstrated that the Presumpscot River did support a robust anadromous fishery, that the many falls on the river did not impede fish moving up river, and that dams did impact this fishery. Our effort in the FERC process was, indeed, to restore a fishery devastated by the building of dams and not an introduction of certain fish species. The fall of 2002 saw the removal of the Smelt Hill Dam at the head of tide in Falmouth. We had supported this effort, and this was a monumental action to restore the Presumpscot River fisheries. Several board members watched the breaching and removal. It was awe inspiring to see the river flow unencumbered over Presumpscot Falls, falls that had been hidden beneath one dam or another for over 250 years.

Issuance of Maine Water Quality Certification

In April 2003, the commissioner of the MDEP issued the 401 water-quality certification—necessary to allow FERC to issue licenses—that endorsed the findings of our historical fisheries research that anadromous fish had been present throughout the river. This certification required SDW/Sappi to install fishways on all five of the dams being relicensed, using the exact same design and sequenced timing for the fishways as demanded by the natural resource agencies in the FERC licensing process, as described below.[47] The 401 did not call for dam removal but was a significant step forward for FOPR/AR and river restoration. Section 401 of the Clean Water Act required FERC to incorporate the MDEP's decisions.[48] FOPR/AR were certain, due to our economic studies, that when the time came to actually install fishways at the three smaller dams, SDW/Sappi would choose instead to remove the dams, because the construction and operation of fishways would be very costly. This scenario is exactly what would later occur at Saccarappa.

SDW/Sappi would soon challenge the MDEP's authority to issue its 401 water-quality certification in a multiyear legal appeal process that would have national impacts and set precedent. FOPR/AR would be further wrapped up in intensive legal proceedings.

FERC Licenses Issued

FERC issued the federal licenses for the five Presumpscot River hydro projects on October 2, 2003, for a term of 40 years. The licenses laid out provisions for recreational enhancements, the protection of archeological sites, bypass minimum flows, drawdown restrictions, maintaining head ponds' water levels behind the dams, and provisions for upstream and downstream eel passage. FERC also ordered fishways for anadromous fish in a phased approach that included upstream and downstream passage provisions, mirroring the MDEP 401 water-quality certification.[49] The phased and ordered fishways at each project were based on a biological triggered approach; the passage of certain numbers of shad and blueback herring at one dam would trigger passage at the next dam, opening up additional habitats. This sequential fish passage marched up river from Saccarappa to Mallison Falls, Little Falls, Gambo and Dundee.

At the Saccarappa project, FERC ordered that a Denil fish ladder or other fish-passage facility that would pass at least 18,000 American shad, 109,000 blueback herring, and 273 Atlantic salmon annually be operational two years after fish passage was available or dam removal occurred at Sappi's non-hydro Cumberland Mills Dam. FERC also required a counting, trapping, and sorting facility at Saccarappa. When targeted species passing at the Denil exceeded the figures above, SDW/Sappi had to install a fish lift designed to pass 58,000 shad, 353,000 blueback herring, and 426 salmon annually.[50]

The fish-passage requirements for the next two dams, Mallison Falls and Little Falls, would be triggered within two years of at least 2,960 shad or 18,020 blueback herring passing in a single year at Saccarappa. At Mallison Falls, FERC ordered the passage requirements in two phases. In Phase One, a Denil fish ladder or other fish-passage facility would need to pass 4,200 shad, 26,000 blueback herring, and 32 Atlantic salmon annually. When those numbers were exceeded, Phase Two required a fish lift to replace the Denil that would pass up to 44,000 shad, 270,00 blueback herring, and 185 salmon annually.[51]

Phase One fish passage at Little Falls called for a Denil fish ladder or other passage facility to pass 3,100 shad, 19,000 blueback herring, and 15 Atlantic salmon. When these numbers were exceeded, Phase Two required

SDW/Sappi to replace the Denil with a fish lift that would pass 43,000 shad, 263,000 blueback herring, and 168 salmon annually. A counting, trapping, and sorting facility at Little Falls would determine when the fish counts were sufficient to trigger fish passage at the Gambo Dam: at least 620 shad or 3,800 blueback herring annually.[52] The "Draft Fisheries Watershed Plan for the Presumpscot River Drainage" produced during the development of the river-management plan, called for a two-phase approach to fisheries restoration. Phase One was from the Smelt Hill Dam (which was removed in 2002) to the base of the Gambo Dam. Restoration achievement in Phase One would trigger Phase Two restoration to the base of the Great Falls Dam.

The license for the Gambo project ordered SDW/Sappi to install upstream fish passage in the form of a fish lift that would pass up to 40,000 shad, 244,000 blueback herring, and 153 Atlantic salmon annually. FERC didn't order a Phase One fish ladder at this dam as it had at the other smaller projects; it went straight to ordering a lift. The Gambo project also had to have a counting, sorting, and trapping facility that would trigger passage at Dundee.[53] The Dundee project's license also ordered the installation of a fish lift or other comparable facility that would pass up to 20,000 shad, 122,000 blueback herring, and 64 American salmon annually and a sorting, counting, and trapping facility. The Dundee fish lift had to be operational when 4,020 shad or 24,460 blueback passed Gambo annually.[54]

Dundee Dam (source: Michael Shaughnessy)

The new licenses brought mixed emotions for Friends of the Presumpscot River. We didn't attain FERC orders for dam removal at Saccarappa, Mallison Falls, and Little falls, but, as stated previously, we also knew that SDW/Sappi would most likely surrender the licenses and remove the three smaller dams when faced with the costs of installing and operating fish passages.

Legal Challenges to the 401 Water-Quality Certification

On May 29, 2003, SWD/Sappi appealed the MDEP's 401 water-quality certification to the Maine Board of Environmental Protection, an appointed citizen board, just as FERC was issuing its licenses. The mill argued that water flowing through hydropower turbines did not constitute a discharge into navigable waters (the threshold for requiring certification under Section 401 of the Federal Clean Water Act)[55] and, therefore, did not require a water-quality certification from the MDEP. The company claimed that a discharge must contain pollutants or other substance to require a 401. SDW/Sappi further argued that the conditions imposed by the water-quality certification were beyond the MDEP's authority.[56] Ron Kreisman filed for intervenor status on behalf of FOPR/AR on June 30, 2003, in response to SDW/Sappi's appeal. We pointed out our long history of participating in the FERC process; the filings we made on the draft water-quality certification; the hundreds of pages of detailed expert information on fisheries, river geology, and economics; and the extensive historical information on the Presumpscot River. We argued that we had status to intervene, that the MDEP had authority under the Clean Water Act to issue a 401, and that the terms and conditions of the 401 were consistent with the terms of the FERC licenses.[57] On October 2, 2003, the MBEP held a public hearing and upheld the MDEP's certification.[58]

SDW/Sappi then appealed the MBEP decision to the Maine Superior Court, Cumberland County. Sean Mahoney, a pro bono attorney from the firm Verrill Dana of Portland, wrote the brief on behalf of FOPR/AR with support from Ron Kreisman. This brief, filed on February 5, 2004, stressed the same points that we had made in the MBEP appeal. Carol Blasi, then an attorney in the Office of the Attorney General, represented the MBEP in defending the issuance of the certification. The court upheld the MBEP's decision in May of 2004.[59]

The challenge continued, with SDW/Sappi appealing the decision of the Maine Superior Court to the Maine Supreme Judicial Court. Attorneys argued the case on November 16, 2004; in a decision on February 15, 2005, the court unanimously upheld the lower court's decision of the MDEP's authority under 401.[60]

After losing its appeal at the Maine Supreme Judicial Court, SDW/Sappi appealed to the United States Supreme Court. We were stunned to hear the news on October 11, 2005, that the judges agreed to hear the case. This small, 25-mile long Maine river, into which local FOPR and our national partner AR had poured our hearts and souls for over 10 years, would be at the center of a legal battle in the highest court in the land. It was "all hands on deck" again for our legal team. Local attorneys Kreisman and Mahoney and Daniel Squire and Patrick Van Der Voorn, DC Supreme Court litigators, would prepare a brief for FOPR/AR. Steven Rowe, Maine Attorney General, argued the case for the state on February 21, 2006. River-advocacy organizations and hydropower interests across the nation were watching this case. On May 15, 2006, in a 9-0 decision, the court upheld the Maine Supreme Court's judgement. WE HAD WON! The court affirmed that a hydropower owner must obtain a 401water-quality certification as part of the FERC process, that dams can cause changes in the chemical and biological character of rivers, that water released through the dams and turbines do constitute a discharge, and that states have the authority to issue 401 water-quality certifications with conditions to protect the water quality of these rivers.[61] It was an extraordinary win for the Presumpscot River and rivers across the nation!

The Quest for Fish Passage at Cumberland Mills

The next step for fisheries restoration on the Presumpscot River was to achieve fish passage or dam removal at the Cumberland Mills Dam, the non-hydro dam beneath the SDW/Sappi mill. The mill, situated at Cumberland Mills, is seven miles upriver from the estuary; with the removal of the Smelt Hill Dam, the dam at Cumberland Mills was the first impediment to fish passing. The complex consists of two river channels with dams at each. One channel was the old course of the river; the other was blasted after a significant flood in 1896 to relieve flooding issues. Because the Cumberland Mills Dam didn't generate power, it wasn't under FERC jurisdiction. The only option to obtain fish passage was to employ a Maine statute to initiate a state fish-passage proceeding, which had never before occurred. The statute gives the commissioner of the Maine Department of Inland Fisheries and Wildlife (MDIF&W) the ability to order fish passage.[62]

271

The Cumberland Mills project was the only first dam on a Maine coastal river located in inland waters without fish passage. FOPR/AR would be setting precedent again. We began another intensive legal and outreach effort. To trigger fish passage at Saccarappa and the other upstream dams in the FERC licenses, we needed to obtain fish passage at the Cumberland Mills Dam. On October 19, 2006, Mr. Kreisman filed a petition to initiate a fishway proceeding[63] to MIF&W Commissioner Roland Martin, who announced on January 10, 2007, that he was initiating a fishway proceeding.[64]

This continued advocacy, which was still very legalistic, required funding, so grant writing was again a major priority. The campaign coordinator's position was no longer funded by the early EFA grant, so we were back to an all-volunteer effort. Fortunately, Dusti Faucher, still president of FOPR, and I as treasurer were able to devote a great deal of time working with our attorney in this effort. We wrote grants for funding to continue the extensive legal work and to fund fish-passage experts. Board members and supporters stepped up to work on outreach to keep the public aware of what we were doing and why. The support of several Maine foundations like the Orchard Foundation, and the continued support of the Davis Foundation was invaluable to us during this time.[65]

Shortly after filing the latest petition, SDW/Sappi recognized the inevitable and reached out to FOPR/AR and fisheries agencies with an offer to begin negotiations on a settlement agreement (SA) on the Cumberland Mills Dam. Commissioner Martin stayed the fishway proceeding, and work began to see if Sappi, FOPR/AR, USFWS, and MDMR could reach terms on fish passage or dam removal. Ron Kreisman and board members again worked diligently to pursue a settlement. On July 10, 2007, SDW/Sappi, FOPR, AR, and MDMR announced at a press event at Westbrook's Riverbank Park, that Sappi would remove the Cumberland Mills Dam and regrade the river channels at the site by May 2011.[66] FOPR was guardedly optimistic with the settlement, but that optimism was short lived. In July 2008, SDW/Sappi quietly pulled out of the agreement without public comment, notice, or explanation; state officials believed that the cost of dam removal and river channel regrading was too great.[67]

Within a few weeks of the mill withdrawing from the dam-removal settlement, FOPR/AR requested that Commissioner Martin reinitiate the fishway proceeding that he had stayed while the groups tried to reach a settlement, which he did.[68] FOPR had anticipated the need to obtain information about the presence of various fish species below the Cumberland Mills Dam, so Friends of Casco Bay (FOCB) and the Maine Coastal Conservation Association (CCA Maine), which supported our goals for fisheries restoration, worked with us to obtain this information. Normandeau Associates, Inc. performed the fisheries survey in the lower river in the spring and early summer of 2003 and reported the presence of shad, river herring, and eels.[69]

As part of the proceeding, Commissioner Martin scheduled a two-day hearing in Westbrook in mid-December 2008.[70] SDW/Sappi, fisheries agencies, FOPR, and Conservation Law Foundation (CLF) fisheries consultants gave testimony. The legal teams from FOPR, CLF, and SDW/Sappi could cross examine those who testified. Ron Kreisman and Sean Mahoney, who previously had worked with FOPR as a pro bono attorney and was now with the CLF, led a very effective effort to not only discount some of SDW/Sappi's misrepresentations of its responsibility for damage to the river's fisheries but also to defend the information of the river's fisheries potential. Community members from around the Presumpscot attended an evening public hearing. Some testified in support of fisheries restoration and its benefit to the river and to Westbrook. A significant number of mill employees espoused a common concern that the cost of building a fish passage would cause layoffs or a mill closing.

Commissioner Martin issued the order for fish passage in June of 2009.[71] This order was a great success for the river and FOPR/CLF. The ruling for a fish passage at Cumberland Mills would mean that when fish passage was operational, it would trigger the FERC license requirements for the upstream dams. We again celebrated a significant step in the restoration of the river's fisheries. With the expertise of the legal team and commitment of our board, we had set another precedent: initiating and employing a state fishway proceeding, and doing so successfully. A process then began to design fishway plans, an effectiveness-testing plan, a fishway and channel-maintenance plan, and a construction schedule. FOPR had anticipated the need for expert information and had respected consultants complete a fish-passage study to use in the design process. Fish-passage consultants from SDW/Sappi, and the fish-passage engineering staff from USFWS—with input from Laura Wildman, a fish-passage engineer from American Rivers—all worked to ensure the design of a Denil fish ladder that would safely and effectively pass fish and a counting facility that would count the fish passing. Construction began in the spring of 2011 and was completed in the spring of 2013. The opening of the fishway at Cumberland Mills again brought local and state attention to the river and the fisheries restoration.

Saccarappa and Dam Removal

Because fish-passage requirements in the FERC licenses for the upstream dams were contingent upon fish passage at Cumberland Mills, the clock was ticking. Passage at the Saccarappa Dam had to be operational in 2015, two years after passage at Cumberland Mills. As with all prior efforts, the upstream march for fish passage would not be smooth.

In March of 2013, just before the celebration of the operational fish passage at Cumberland Mills, the City of Westbrook and SDW/Sappi publicly announced a joint effort to study the impact of dam removal at Saccarappa.[72] The city had applied for a $733,000 grant from the National Oceanic and Atmospheric Administration to study the environmental impacts of removing the dam.[73] SDW/Sappi offered to transfer eight acres along the river and the island in the middle of Saccarappa Falls to the city. FOPR and the Conservation Law Foundation were highly suspicious of the company's motivations in this effort to engage the city in the dam removal effort. City administration was interested in the island and other river properties and in opening up the river and falls for whitewater recreational opportunities.[74] FOPR and CLF's primary focus was always and would continue to be safe, effective, and timely fish passage at the Saccarappa site; the creation of whitewater amenities could jeopardize those goals. Was this agreement with the city an effort by SDW/Sappi to delay the FERC order or to benefit the company's bottom line somehow? FOPR and CLF also learned of efforts by SDW/Sappi to engage the city of Westbrook in an agreement wherein it would transfer the Saccarappa hydro project, its accompanying land, and other river properties to the city, which would then become financially responsible for preparing the FERC application to surrender the hydro license and removing the two spillways to provide fish passage: a huge liability for the city. If FERC denied the surrender application, the city would have the right to submit another application requesting FERC's permission to transfer the hydro license back to SDW/Sappi.[75] This effort was clearly to benefit the mill's financial bottom line. The Saccarappa site is very complex and has undergone significant blasting and rechanneling; the most significant change was the construction of a western channel that directs the water through the turbines at the powerhouse and exits at the base of the falls. The eastern channel has two sets of falls, an upper and lower, with a pool between them. The site has two dams or spillways to direct water to the western channel and the turbines. One dam sits at the top of the upper eastern falls near the Dana Warp mill. This dam blocks a significant amount of water from flowing over the eastern falls, because it directs water to the western side of the river, where another small dam forces the water to flow into the constructed channel to the turbines. Given the complexity of the site, the huge financial commitment for dam removal, and the 733,000 NOAA grant funding not materializing, the city ultimately decided to walk away from this project-transfer agreement effort.[76]

SDW/Sappi Files Surrender Application at FERC

On November 18, 2013, SDW/Sappi shared a draft application for license surrender of the Saccarappa Dam and removal of the hydro project with USFWS, MDEP, MDMR, the City of Westbrook, CLF, and FOPR.[77] Prior to distributing this draft application, SDW/Sappi, the City of Westbrook, USFW, and the MDMR had begun discussions on fishway design, construction, and maintenance. Sean Mahoney and Ron Kreisman, CLF and FOPR attorneys respectively, responded with comments to SDW/Sappi's draft surrender notice.[78] In these comments, FOPR/CLF brought forward the following concerns: (a) SDW/Sappi's design of a Denil fishway did not mention the Phase Two fish lift that was part of the 2003 FERC license; (b) the company had not gathered enough data about the bathymetry (river-bottom topography); (c) SDW/Sappi had not performed hydraulic modeling to demonstrate that shad, river herring, or salmon could pass up the Denil and the upper eastern falls with dam removal; (d) the mill's design in the upper falls was too steep for fish passage and was designed more as a recreational feature than a fishway; and (e) it had made no provision for who would operate and maintain the fishway.[79]

SDW/Sappi filed its final Surrender Application to FERC on December 31, 2013.[80] FOPR would be entering another legally intensive time and, again, renewed efforts to obtain significant grant funding. The Quimby Family Foundation and the Elmina B. Sewall Foundation ultimately provided multi-year funding for our legal advocacy.[81]

Meetings began among fisheries agencies, FOPR/CLF, the city of Westbrook, and SDW/Sappi to discuss a delay in the surrender to study more natural fishway alternatives. FOPR/CLF had significant concerns about inadequacies in the modeling and data provided by SDW/Sappi's consultants. FOPR/CLF again consulted Laura Wildman, now with Princeton Hydro, who helped us find data gaps and determine how to engage in a meaningful design process. We believed that fish would be better able to pass in a constructed nature-like series of pools and steps over the lower falls and proceed in more steps and pools up both the upper western channel and the upper eastern falls.

Extension Agreement, an Effort for Natural Fish-passage Designs

The discussions yielded an Extension Agreement, and, on March 28, 2014, SDW/Sappi filed the agreement with FERC and with the MDEP under the state's authority under the 401 process.[82] The MDEP issued approval on June 3, 2014, and FERC on July 30, 2014.[83] The city and SDW/Sappi reached a financial agreement to hire Laura Wildman to design a natural fishway,[84] and the mill withdrew its FERC Surrender Application in September 2014.[85] The Extension Agreement moved the timing for the fish passage to be operational from spring 2015 to spring 2017,[86] which gave FOPR/CLF and the fisheries agencies the opportunity to ensure that SDW/Sappi would get Saccarappa "right." The extension would provide time to gather appropriate data and to design a natural fishway. We wanted to look back at the Saccarappa process and know that we had done all we could to ensure safe, effective, and timely fish passage at the site. The triggering of fish passage or dam removal on the upstream dams all hinged on making sure that fish passed at Saccarappa in significant numbers. We had to get Saccarappa right.

The process ahead would be intensive, move quickly, and require timely decisions, so a segment of FOPR board members became the "Saccarappa team," comprised of seasoned, longtime board members: President Michael Shaughnessy; Treasurer Sandy Cort; and Dusti Faucher, who had served as our campaign coordinator during the early FERC process. The Saccarappa team, our legal team of Ron Kreisman and Sean Mahoney CLF, fisheries agencies, the City of Westbrook, SDW/Sapp, and their fish-passage consultants would spend hundreds of hours evaluating fish-passage options.

To explore these options, we needed SDW/Sappi and their consultants to provide additional information, which included flow rates and bathymetry. With that data, Laura Wildman produced a two-channel design that had a nature-like "rock-ramp" fishway in the western channel tail-race area over the lower falls to the middle pool between the upper and lower falls. Fish could continue up the upper western side into a "step-and-pool" constructed channel (or, as FOPR referred to it, "turning left") or leave the middle pool between the upper and lower falls, turn right, and head up the upper sculpted eastern-side falls. The Wildman rock-ramp design in the lower western channel had a switchback in the proposed design that later would raise concerns from the fisheries agencies. This initial two-channel design would guide further designs. In August 2015, SDW/Sappi held a public meeting in Westbrook to provide an update on the process and to explain the two Saccarappa fish-passage designs.[87] One had a Denil on the lower falls, and a "natural" step-and-pool fishway in the tail race in the western side; it did not provide opportunities for fish passage in the upper falls on the eastern side. The other design was Laura Wildman's, described above.

SDW/Sappi's Second Surrender Application

SDW/Sappi again filed at FERC a Surrender Application in December 2, 2015, proposing the Denil and western-channel design.[88] After spending hundreds of hours working with SDW/Sappi, USFWS, and MDMR, FOPR/CLF again had to respond to a SDW/Sappi application that was missing critical information for FERC to make an informed decision about fish passage at Saccarappa, even as the extension date to have it operational by the spring of 2017 was quickly approaching. This was another moment when FOPR's board members had to take a collective deep breath and remember that Saccarappa was the key to the rest of the river's fisheries restoration.

Our December 29, 2015, filing stated that we would not be averse to an extension of one year, from spring 2017 to May 2018, for operational fish passage. FOPR/CFL knew it was vital that we worked with MDMR and the USFWS to reach consensus on fish-passage issues as we negotiated with SDW/Sappi. An agreement between all the parties on these issues would go to FERC, which would then engage in a process to evaluate all possible consequences of granting a surrender order.[89] SDW/Sappi proposed a Denil at the lower falls; a reconstructed fish-passage channel with significant amounts of fill in the upper western channel; and a counting facility, which would be critical to triggering upstream fish passage. All three would need ongoing upkeep. The mill indicated that it would continue operations and maintenance (O&M) of the Denil, upper channel, and fish-counting facility as long as it owned the site[90] but did not set forth any

O&M plans, explain how it would fund these responsibilities, or specify how it would coordinate with the fisheries agencies. Moreover, the designs that the company proposed were only preliminary—what fisheries agencies call a 30% design stage—and the mill indicated no plans for intermediate or final design plans. It also didn't provide information on post-construction adjustments to the Denil and the constructed upper western channel if either did not pass fish. Nor did it list provisions for changes if the counting facility didn't work properly. FOPR/CLF and the fisheries agencies also shared another significant concern: after surrender of the federal license, FERC would lose oversight and legal or enforcement jurisdiction at the site for on-going operation and maintenance of the fishway should SDW/Sappi sell or abandon the site. We also felt that we needed to research the history of changes to the river at the Saccarappa site and who was responsible for those changes. We did not want SDW/Sappi to claim that it had no responsibility for changes to the river historically and thus no responsibility to make sure fish could pass above Saccarappa. FOPR hired Darien Brahms, a history scholar, who worked with me to find maps and historical documents that showed how and when this site had been altered, and by whom. This effort uncovered maps of the site from the mid-1700s to the mid-1900s. The earliest map was from 1729 that showed two islands and three channels at Saccarappa Falls.[91] SDW/Sappi had been involved in numerous and significant alterations to the site and river channels, especially in the late 1880s and early 1900s, and had benefited from some of these changes.

Pursuit of a Settlement Agreement

In early March 2016, the mill filed a letter to FERC requesting a stay on behalf of SDW/Sappi, the City of Westbrook, CLF, FOPR, MDMR, and USFWS of the surrender review process until July 1, 2016, so that the company, the fisheries agencies, the city of Westbrook, and FOPR/CLF could explore a settlement.[92] The request for a stay also asked FERC to extend the deadline for operational fish passage until May 2018. The MDMR, USFW, FOPR, CLF and Westbrook wrote in support of the request. More very intensive negotiations began to try to reach a settlement agreement. This process was not without its challenges, with changes occurring almost daily, and the Saccarappa team dedicated hours of time to participate with our attorney. FOPR and CLF felt that the extension would give us time to spell out the fishway-design process, test the effectiveness of designs, and assure funding for possible post-construction changes and operation and maintenance.

With much interest from the press and watershed citizens, the parties involved announced on November 15, 2016, that they had reached a Settlement Agreement.[93] Members of FOPR/CLF felt that we had reached a commonsense plan forward. SDW/Sappi proposed and received changes to the upstream licenses at Mallison Falls, Little Falls, Gambo, and Dundee (described in detail below), but we had won on important details: how the design development, construction, operation and maintenance, and effectiveness testing would take place at Saccarappa. Even with this sense of accomplishment, we knew that things could still fall apart.

In the SA, SDW/Sappi agreed to remove both spillways and the powerhouse and to pursue a two-channel design. At the lower falls, it would construct a double Denil fish ladder with a fish-counting facility at the Denil's exit, create a step-and-pool upper western channel, and remove the western side spillway. At the upper falls, the company would remove the spillway on the eastern side at the top of the falls and sculpt part of the upper eastern falls. The design plans would depict a 90% complete stage and require agreement by Sappi, MDMR, and USFW. The two-channel plan above the lower falls would be based on Laura Wildman's Princeton Hydro (PH) conceptual design drawings. During the negotiations, the USFWS and MDMR had raised concerns about the steepness of the rock ramp up the lower falls and the switchback in that section. Consequently, these fisheries agencies favored a double Denil fish ladder for the lower falls.[94] We were disappointed that a natural fishway would only occur in the upper falls, but the double Denil would pass significant numbers of fish and eliminate the need to replace a single Denil with a fish lift later, which was in the 2003 license. All parties to the SA, with the exception of the city of Westbrook, would participate in the fishway design process. The SA set out a process to select the fish-passage engineering firms that would receive a design request for proposal (RFP), a timeline for the bid process, and a total-cost cap for the design work. SDW/Sappi would consult with the other settlement parties but would have final authority in the selection of the design firm. The following SA condition would affect the fish-passage operational date: A selected bid from the fish-passage-design-firm that did not suggest the need for "Additional Data Gathering" (modeling, bathymetry or gauging) would be "Two-Channel Passage Design A"; the bid that did require "Additional Data Gathering," would be "Two-Channel Passage

Design B." The choice of Design B would add an additional year before the fish passage was operational.

The SA also set a process for selecting a small group of construction firms able to construct the two-channel natural fishway who would receive RFPs. It also set a construction timeline and a cap for SDW/Sappi's total construction cost. The SA laid out how the fisheries agencies would be involved in design planning and construction oversight, detailed SDW/Sappi's financial responsibility for effectiveness testing, and designated MDMR to conduct that testing. SDW/Sappi would be responsible for the operation and maintenance of the Denil, the counting facilities, and any structures supporting the Denil area. Under the operation and maintenance plan, SDW/Sappi would have no responsibility to maintain the two-channel passage. The SA did not require fish counting to begin at Saccarappa until 2024. MDMR would delay its fish stocking program on the river until 2025 but could stock limited amounts of alewives in Highland Lake, which connects to the Presumpscot by the Millbrook and had a significant run of the fish.

The upstream fish passage at Mallison Falls and Little Falls dams would still be trigged by the numbers of fish passing at the Saccarappa counting facility. When 2,960 shad or 18,020 blueback herring pass in any single season, SDW/Sappi would have to construct fish passage within two years at the Mallison Falls dam or surrender its FERC license and remove that dam within three years. At Little Falls, the company would have to either construct the fish passage per the current FERC license or surrender and remove the dam within three years of dam removal at Mallison Falls. The SA laid out that SDW/Sappi would request at FERC and MDEP, as part of the 401 water-quality certification, that fish- passage requirements not apply under the new licenses for the Gambo and Dundee dams and that a 10-year extension of the new license term, from 2043 to 2053 would apply. As part of the SA, the mill would request in its surrender application that FERC include the Saccarappa Denil as part of the Mallison Falls project so that SDW/Sappi surrenders the license for Saccarappa, FERC still has jurisdiction. This provision was very important to FOPR/CLF and the fisheries agencies.

The city of Westbrook maintained its desire to obtain land and incorporate whitewater recreation, so the SA included a retractable wave feature called an Obermeyer, which could sit flat along the river bottom during fish migrations, so it would not be an impediment, and raise to create waves for white-water kayaking during nonmigratory seasons. SDW/SAPPI would also transfer to Westbrook land to extend the city's river walk.

The SA gave SDW/Sappi a timeline of January 1, 2018, to file a new surrender application at FERC for dam removal at Saccarappa and license amendments for the other dams and request that MDEP extend the 401 requirement of fish passage to May 2020 or to 2021 if it chose the channel design that required "Additional Data Gathering."

Fish-Passage Design Work Begins

The agreement parties decided upon—and SDW/Sappi sent out RFPs to—several firms with experience in fishway design, and, in February 2017, SDW/Sappi chose Alden to model and create the design. The firm had the capacity and knowledge to create 3-D models and was familiar with the site. The Acheron firm that designed the Cumberland Mills fishway would now engineer the double Denil at Saccarappa. FOPR's Saccarappa team actively participated in design review.

The design process progressed with a 30% two-channel design that went to fisheries agencies' staff and all agreement parties for questions and input. The engineer used a three-dimensional Computational Fluid Dynamics (CFD) program to predict depth, velocities, and flow patterns. So much goes into this type of design, and the process was a steep learning curve for FOPR volunteers. We learned about river topography, how water-velocity rates affect potential designs, how the split of the river flow to each channel can shift in a design, the survivability of each fish species passing under different flow conditions, and the energy that each species expends in passing certain distances under various flows. In June 2017, the design moved to a 60% stage and, again, the fisheries agencies and FOPR received a detailed presentation and gave input, with Laura Wildman also providing feedback. The design work to that point had focused heavily on creating the western-channel design; FOPR, MDMR, and USFWS pushed to ensure that the necessary sculpting on the eastern falls also received attention. The design phase moved to 90% in August 2017. The design was a bedrock sculpted western channel that would be more stable than the originally proposed channel created by fill. The eastern falls would be sculpted to have a number of step pools for fish to ascend. Alden finalized the design, and, with the SA parties' support, Sappi sent out construction proposal requests with a late November 2017 bid deadline. All of the bids exceeded the financial cap. SDW/Sappi chose the firm that came closest, Sumco,

281

which had constructed a number of natural fish passages and was well respected by the fisheries agencies. All parties agreed on the construction firm and the processes and timing of the construction after obtaining needed regulatory permits. Experts from MDMR and USFWS would monitor the construction.

Intensive work began for FOPR/CLR, the City of Westbrook, and the fisheries agencies to hold the SA together in light of the higher construction costs from bids. FOPR President Michael Shaughnessy, in concert with our attorney Ron Kreisman and Sean Mahoney of CLF, spent significant time working with Westbrook, the agencies, and SDW/Sappi. This was a time of daily communications and major decisions for FOPR and the SA partners. Westbrook officials decided not to proceed with the Obermeyer but, as part of the settlement, would still work with SDW/Sappi to obtain land along the river, acquiring the island in the middle of the river at the falls, and a right of way to connect two river-walk sections. In the end, all parties had made compromises to hold the SA together.

SDW/Sappi filed at FERC an Application for a License Surrender at Saccarappa and amendments on licenses it held for Mallison, Little Falls, Gambo and Dundee.[95] It also filed with the MDEP for changes to the 401 water-quality certifications on the licenses.[96] SDW/Sappi's application to FERC and the MDEP laid out the following from the SA:

SDW/Sappi would finance, construct, operate, and maintain in perpetuity a FERC-approved double Denil fishway that would make a Phase 2 fish lift unnecessary. The company would also finance, construct, operate, and maintain a fish-counting facility until it became unnecessary for purposes of upriver license compliance (the triggering of Mallison and Little Falls fish passage or dam removal). The mill would finance and make changes and repairs to the tailrace area and other structures needed to support the operation of the Denil and counting facility and would maintain support structures in perpetuity. FERC would have ongoing regulatory jurisdiction and oversight of the Denil and counting facility, and settlement parties agreed to include these structures in the Mallison Falls license.

In the upper falls, SDW/Sappi would finance the two-channel plan, remove both spillways and the powerhouse in the western channel, and fill most of the tailrace. It would also finance and regrade both the eastern and western channels. MDMR and USFWS personnel would monitor construction of the channels. All parties agreed to a process for the financing of mid-course channel-sculpting changes and post-testing changes and set up a detailed and comprehensive post-construction, post-surrender effectiveness-testing program. The date for operational fish passage at Saccarappa would be May of 2021, due to the fact that the passage-design team gathered more data on the river topography (bathymetry) and made use of 3-D modeling; otherwise, the operational date would have been 2020. FOPR/CLF felt that having all the necessary information and a comprehensive design-modeling process would yield the best results; it was worth the additional year. The Saccarappa site is the key to the rest of upriver fisheries restoration; fish passage would need to be the best it could be at this heavily altered site.

SDW/Sappi didn't propose any changes to the fish numbers required to trigger fishways at the Mallison Falls and Little Falls hydro projects. If it decides to remove the Mallison Falls and Little Falls dams in the future, when the trigger numbers are met, a removal timeline was set out in the Surrender Application, which also proposed to extend the term of the Mallison Falls and Little Falls licenses by 10 years, from 2043 to 2053.

At the Gambo and Dundee dams, the application proposed that FERC suspend the requirement for fishway construction during the term of the licenses and would extend the licenses by 10 years to 2053.

FOPR/CLF filed individually as intervenors and provided joint supportive comments on SDW/Sappi's FERC Surrender Application.[97] This filing pointed to the support of all the signatories in the SA and the time and financial commitment necessary to reach the agreement. We expressed our belief that the approval by FERC of the Saccarappa Surrender Application and amendment applications for Mallison Falls, Little Falls, Gambo and Dundee would "save time and money, avoid prolonged litigation and would promote a healthy working relationship amongst the parties in the work ahead during the implementation of the surrender and accomplishing safe, timely and effective fish passage."[98] We also stated that removing the requirements for fish passage and extending the licenses for Gambo and Dundee were in keeping with what would occur biologically: that the numbers of fish needed to trigger these projects would not likely be met in the proposed license terms. The "Draft Fishery Management Plan for the Presumpscot River Drainage," formulated by three of Maine's fisheries agencies, laid out a two-phase fisheries restoration plan: Phase One restoration to the base of Gambo dam, followed by Phase Two restoration of the remainder of the river. We felt that the full restoration of Phase One would not take place before 2053.

As FOPR was deeply engaged in the process of reaching a final settlement agreement, members launched another grant-funded educational outreach effort. During the spring of 2016 and continuing to date, we've organized close to nine river talks/lectures and several film showings. Abigail Cioffi, coordinator of Discover Downtown Westbrook, has worked with FOPR consultants Jennifer Cook and Jennifer Christian on these events. The lectures and films have covered a variety of river-based topics, from the economic benefits of restored rivers to the Native American peoples of the Presumpscot River and Abenaki place names for areas around it. One talk spotlighted the history of mill building at Saccarappa Falls and plans for the revitalization of downtown Westbrook; another focused on fly-fishing tales and tips from a women's perspective; two other lectures were on anadromous fisheries restoration and anadromous fish biology. We also held two river-themed film nights.

FOPR board member Zack Anchor, owner of Portland Paddle, led the effort to have several river paddles each year, with a number featuring speakers for lecture/paddles. Zack also brought his fleet of kayaks, canoes, and paddleboards to the Brown Street Westbrook boat launch for a free family paddle followed by a cookout. Maine Path and Paddle and Community Partnership for the Protection of Children supported this effort. We've been thrilled to watch children venture onto the water for the first time, many of whom are new arrivals to this country and community.

After learning about the rich history of Chief Polin and the Abenaki People of the Presumpscot, FOPR embarked upon a tribute, an effort envisioned by our president, Michael Shaughnessy, whose family now calls home a property previously owned by of one of the earliest settling families, the Conants. A section of Portland Trails runs through the property along the Presumpscot River. Near the trail, on a rise above the river, now stands an upright granite plinth and several large horizontal stones. Plaques with facts about the Presumpscot and the history of Chief Polin and his people were erected in the fall of 2018 with a celebratory Three Sisters dinner featuring the three main agricultural crops of Native American peoples (squash, beans, and corn).

At this chapter's completion, the Maine Department of Environmental Protection has issued its Water Quality Certification and Water Quality Certification Amendments that supported the terms of the settlement agreement.[99] On April 18, 2019, FERC commissioners approved and authorized the decommissioning of the hydro project, ordered the removal of the Saccarappa Falls dams, and issued amended licenses for the Mallison, Little Falls, Gambo and Dundee hydro projects.[100] Removal of the spillways and construction of the double Denil and upper falls natural fishway at Saccarappa will take place in the summer construction season of 2019 and 2020, with fish passing in the spring of 2021. FOPR will continue to monitor the construction, and we look forward to working to restore this anadromous fishery further upriver.

This intensive, twenty-two-year process has been an extraordinary, time-consuming, and costly journey, with many victories and, at times, discouragement for our small and mostly volunteer local nonprofit group and our attorney and partner organizations. From beginning research on the FERC process in 1997 and filing as intervenors on June 21, 1999, through two precedent-setting actions—the US Supreme Court decision on the 401 water-quality certification, and the first use of Maine's fishway proceeding—to the dam removal order on April 18, 2019, this was and will continue to be a local river-restoration effort, although across the country and internationally, similar efforts are continuing. These words from our longtime attorney Ron Kreisman, after reaching one of many milestones, frames the effort well:

> We are a tenacious and determined bunch. I believe we kept our rendezvous with history as it has played out on this river, and the once in a lifetime opportunity we saw and seized. What a team. Has there ever been a closer and more cooperative, respectful, pulling-with-one-set-of-oars, we'll-work-out-our-different-viewpoints coalition of state-federal and NGO players? I doubt it."[101]

This successful quest for fish passage will open up a river that had been barred over with dams for almost 300 years, decimating the anadromous fish runs. Friends of the Presumpscot River hope that somewhere in the mists of time, Chief Polin and the Abenaki Peoples of the Presumpscot River are beginning to smile.

Looking Down (Mary Brooking, 2016, acrylic on paper, 16" x 24", print)

[1] United States Congress, *The Federal Power Act*. 16 U.S.C. § 791-828(c); United States Department of Energy (2018). *Federal Energy Regulatory Commission*. https://www.ferc.gov/about/ferc-does.asp?csrt=11920091696853246443

[2] Hydropower Reform Coalition (2018). *The Federal Power Act*. https://www.hydroreform.org/policy/fpa

[3] Ibid.

[4] S. D. Warren, 74 FERC ¶ 62,026 (1996).

[5] S. D. Warren Company, 74 FERC ¶ 62,026 (1996)

[6] S. D. Warren, 74 FERC 74 ¶ 62,026 (1996)

[7] U.S Army Corps of Engineers New England District (2001, January). *Presumpscot River aquatic ecosystem restoration project: Smelt Hill Dam Removal. Falmouth, Maine*. https://cw-environment.erdc.dren.mil/restore/fishpassage/pdfs/

NAE%20-%20Smelt%20Hill%20Dam% 20Removal%20EA.pdf

[8] Presumpscot River Plan Steering Committee, Presumpscot River Plan Fisheries Subcommittee, & Land & Water Associates. (2002). *A plan for the future of the Presumpscot River: Summary background of fisheries*. Portland, ME: University of Southern Maine, Muskie School of Public Service, Casco Bay Estuary Partnership. 20-21.

https://digitalcommons.usm.maine.edu/cgi/viewcontent.cgi?article=1167&context=cbep-publications

[9] SAPPI (1999, April 13). *Press release*. http://www.sharenet.co.za/v3/sens_display.php?tdate=19990413164419&seq=1278&scode=SAP

[10] S. D. Warren Company (1998, June). *Draft application for new license for major water power project projects under 5 MW*. Gambo Project (FERC No. 2931), Dundee (FERC No. 2942*); Draft application for subsequent license for minor water project*. Saccarappa project (FERC no. 2897), Mallison Falls project (FERC No. 2932), Little Falls project (FERC No. 2941). Prepared by Kleinschmidt Associates. Pittsfield, Maine.

[11] S. D. Warren Company (1999, January). *Application for subsequent license for minor power projects*. Saccarappa project (FERC No 2897), Mallison Falls project (FERC No 2932),

Little Falls project (FERC No 2941). *Major Power Project* - Gambo (FERC No 2931), Dundee project (FERC No 2942). Prepared by Kleinschmidt Associates. Pittsfield, Maine.

[12] Federal Energy Regulatory Commission, Office of Energy Projects (2001, September). *Draft environmental impact statement: Presumpscot River projects, Maine.* Dundee project (FERC Project No. 2942), Gambo project (FERC No. 2931), Little Falls project (FERC No. 2932), Mallison Falls project (FERS No. 2941), Saccarappa project (FERC No. 2897), 31.

[13] U. S. Environmental Protection Agency (2017). *National Environmental Policy Act review process,* 40 CFR 1508.18. https://www.epa.gov/nepa/national-environmental-policy-act-review-process

[14] Federal Energy Regulatory Commission (1999, July 23). *Scoping document 1 for the Presumpscot River Project;* Federal Energy Regulatory Commission (2000, March 16). *Scoping document 2 for the Presumpscot River Projects.*

[15] The Educational Foundation of America. https://theefa.org/about/

[16] The Davis Foundations. https://www.davisfoundations.org

[17] River Network (2001). Case Study: Mapping Your Watershed. *River Voices, 12*(1), 18, 19.

[18] Catama Productions. http://catama.net/about-us/ This video is available for viewing on the Friends of the Presumpscot River Facebook page.

[19] Bell, T. (2001, August 26). A paddle on the Presumpscot River day 1. *Maine Sunday Telegram,* 1A, 6A, &7A. Bell, T. (2001, August 27). A paddle on the Presumpscot River day 2. *Portland Press Herald,* 1A, 4A.

[20] Sappi letter to FERC regarding comments on Draft Environmental Impact Statement, December 4, 2001.

[21] The Presumpscot River Management Plan Steering Committee, Casco Bay Estuary Project, U.S. Environmental Protect Agency, Region 1, & Land and Water Associates (2003, August 18). *A plan for the future of the Presumpscot River.* https://static1.squarespace.com/static/57fef2d28419c2478111e0f8/t/5c7fccbbee6eb0788d91d018/1551879357115/Presumpscot+River+WMP+2003.pdf

[22] Whippelhauser, G. S., Squiers, T. S., Jr., Brautigam, F. C., Dube, N. R., & Christman, P. (2001, September). Draft fishery management plan for the Presumpscot River drainage. In *A Plan for the future of the Presumpscot River: Summary background of fisheries*, Appendix C. https://digitalcommons.usm.maine.edu/ cgi/viewcontent.cgi?article= 1167&context=cbep-publications

[23] American Rivers, (2000). *America's Most Endangered Rivers of 2000*, 30-31.

[24] Ibid., 30.

[25] Bowman, M., & Kreisman, R. (2001, February 2). *Comments, recommendations, terms and conditions by American Rivers and Friends of the Presumpscot River*. S.D. Warren Company Projects Nos.2942-005; 2931-002; 2941-002; 2932-003; & 2897-003, 1. United States of America. Filing before FERC.

[26] Ibid.

[27] The bypass reaches at the Presumpscot hydro projects were the original river channels. These areas were either partially or completely dewatered by the dams with the flows diverted through the tailrace channels and the powerhouses.

[28] S. D. Warren Company (1999, January). *Dundee project application for new license for major water power project under 5 MW*, vii-xi. Identical language is contained in the other four applications.

[29] Bowman & Kreisman, *Comments, recommendations, terms and conditions*, 6-8.

[30] S. D. Warren Company, *Application for subsequent license*. Dundee project (FERC No 2942). Identical language, except for substitution of appropriate hydro power capacity numbers, appears in each of the other five filings.

[31] Parker, R. B. (January 2001). Analysis of economic value of five hydropower projects to S. D. Warren Company's Westbrook mill. In Bowman & Kreisman, *Comments, recommendations, terms and conditions*.

[32] Dadswell, M. J. (January 2001). Fisheries Resources: Past, Present and Potential: The Presumpscot River, Maine. In Bowman & Kreisman, *Comments, recommendations, terms and conditions*.

[33] Northern Ecological Associates, Inc. (January 2001). Substrate Survey of the Mallison and Little Falls Impoundments and Preliminary Substrate Survey of the

Saccarappa Impoundment, Presumpscot River, Maine. In Bowman & Kreisman, *Comments, recommendations, terms and conditions.*

[34] Kreisman, R., American Rivers, Friend of the Presumpscot River, Friends of Sebago Lake, & Atlantic Salmon Federation (2001, July 5). *Filing of supplemental information.* Re: S. D. Warren, Projects Nos. 2942-005: 2931-002: 2941-002: 2932-003: & 2897-003

[35] S. D. Warren Company (2001, April 18). *Response to agencies' and non-governmental organizations' terms and conditions filings*

[36] Maine Department of Environmental Protection (1998, August 28). *EPA – New England's review of Maine's Presumpscot River TMDL.* https://www.maine.gov/dep/water/monitoring/tmdl/1998/presumpscot_rev.pdf

[37] Federal Energy Regulatory Commission, *Draft Environmental Impact Statement*, xvi.

[38] Ibid., xvii.

[39] Federal Energy Regulatory Commission, Office of Energy Projects (June 2002). *Environmental impact statement: Presumpscot River projects, Maine.* Dundee Project (FERC Project No. 2942), Gambo Project (FERC Project No. 2931), Little Falls Project (FERC Project No.2941), Mallison Falls Project (FERC Project No 2932), Saccarappa Project (FERC Project No. 2897).

[40] Hydropower Reform Coalition (2018). *E. FPA Section 18 Fishway Prescription.* https://www.hydroreform.org/ hydroguide/hydropower-licensing/e-fpa-section-18-fishway-prescription

[41] Federal Energy Regulatory Commission, *Environmental Impact Statement.*

[42] Hydropower Reform Coalition (2018). *H. water quality certification under CWA section 401 (a).* https://www.hydroreform.org/hydroguide/hydropower-licensing/h-water-quality-certification-under-cwa-section-401-a

[43] Kreisman, R., American Rivers, Friends of the Presumpscot River, & Friends of Sebago Lake, (2002, October 25) *Supplemental historic records related to anadromous fisheries of the Presumpscot River and Sebago Lake, Maine.* FERC Submittal No. 20021029-0010. https://elibrary.ferc.gov/idmws/common/downloadOpen.asp?downloadfile= 20021029%2D0010%2811018603%29%2Epdf&folder=8738959&fileid=10656445&trial=1

[44] Baxter, J. P. (Ed.). (1869-1916). Conference with Polin and Indians of Presumpscot—August 10, 1739. *Documentary history of the State of Maine* (Vol 23 of 24 volumes). Portland: Maine Historical Society, 257 (reformatted here for ease of reading). https://archive.org/details/documentaryhisto23main/page/n8

[45] Baxter, J. P. (Ed.) (1910) Resolve of the Massachusetts Legislature appointing a committee of three men to view the mill dams on the Presumpscot River to determine where sluice ways should be made at the dams for the passage of fish" Journals of the Massachusetts April 4, 1777 House of Representatives 1776-1777. *Documentary history of the State of Maine* (Vol. 15 of 24). Portland, ME: Lefavor-Tower Company, 72 & 73.

[46] Secretary of the Commonwealth, *The laws, acts and resolves of the Commonwealth of Massachusetts* (1780-1820). *Acts* (1784) January Session, Chapter 62, effective date March 14, 1785, An Act of the Massachusetts Legislature titled: "An Act for Opening Sluice Ways in the Mill Dam or Dams which Have or May Be Erected on the Presumpscot River, in the County of Cumberland, and Upon Any Stream or Streams Which Fall into the Same River," 62. *Acts* (1788) Chapter 73, effective date February 16, 1789, An Act of the Massachusetts Legislature requiring sluice ways at mill dams for the passage of Salmom, Shad and Alewives on the rivers of "Presumpscut, Androscoggin, Merrymeeting bay, Kennebec, Sheepscut, Bristol, Muscongus *alias* Medumcock, St. Georges & Penobscot, and also the stream of Negwaset," 157-163. *Acts* (1793) Chapter 45, effective date February 24, 1794, An Act of the Massachusetts Legislature requiring the mill dam owners on the Presumpscot River and its tributaries to provide "good & sufficient" sluice ways for fish between April 15 and July, annually, 461, 462. Available at the Maine Law Library, Augusta Maine.

[47] Maine Department of Environmental Protection (2003, April 3). *Water quality certifications conditions for S. D. Warren Company's Presumpscot River hydro projects.* #L-19713-33-E-N (Dundee), #L-19714-33-E-N (Gambo), #L-19715-33-E-N (Little Falls), #L-19716-33-E-N (Mallison Falls), #L-19717-33-E-N (Saccarappa).

[48] Hydropower Reform Coalition (2018). *H. Water Quality Certification.*

[49] Federal Energy Regulatory Commission (2003, October 2). *Order issuing subsequent license re SD Warren under P-2897 et al.* Nos. 2897-003; 2932-003; 2941-002; 2931-002; 2942-005. 105 FERC ¶ 61,013. United States of America. Issuance 20031002-3076.

[50] Federal Energy Regulatory Commission (2003, October 2). *Order issuing subsequent license re SD Warren Project under P-2897* Nos. 2897-003, 2932-003, 2941-002, 2931-002, 2942-005. 105 FERC ¶ 61,013. United States of America. Issuance 20031002-3076.

[51] Federal Energy Regulatory Commission (2003, October 2). *Order issuing subsequent license. S. D. Warren, Project No. 2932-003.* 105 FERC ¶ 61,011. United States of America.

[52] The Presumpscot River Management Plan Steering Committee, Casco Bay Estuary Project, U.S. Environmental Protect Agency, Region 1, & Land and Water Associates, *A plan for the future.*

[53] Federal Energy Regulatory Commission (2003, October 2). *Order issuing subsequent license.* S. D. Warren, Project No. 2931-002.105 FERC ¶61,010. United States of America.

[54] Federal Energy Regulatory Commission (2003, October 2). *Order issuing subsequent license.* S. D. Warren, Project No. 2942-005. 105 FERC ¶61,009. United States of America.

[55] Hydropower Reform Coalition, H. *Water Quality Certification.*

[56] Maine Board of Environmental Protection (20003, May 29). *Appeal of water quality certification order for S. D. Warren Company's Presumpscot River Hydro Projects.* Re: #L-19713-33-E-N (Dundee), #L-19714-33-E-N (Gambo), #L-19715-33-E-N (Little Falls), #L-19716-33-E-N (Mallison Falls), #L-19717-33-E-N (Saccarappa).

[57] American Rivers & Friends of the Presumpscot River (2003, June 10). *Apprise the commission of certain developments regarding S.D. Warren Company's appeal of the Maine Department of Environmental Protection under P-2942 et al.* FERC Submittal 20030619-0080.

[58] Maine Board of Environmental Protection (2003, October 2). *Water quality certification findings of fact and order on appeal for S.D. Warren Company's Presumpscot River Hydro Projects.* Re: #L-19713-33-E-N (Dundee), #L-19714-33-E-N (Gambo), #L-19715-33-E-N (Little Falls), #L-19716-33-E-N (Mallison Falls), #L-19717-33-E-N (Saccarappa) (Oct. 2, 2003).

[59] *S. D. Warren Company. v Maine Department of Environmental. Pro*tection. No. AP-03-70, 2004 Me. Super. LEXIS 115 (May 4, 2004). http://files.mainelaw.maine.edu/library/SuperiorCourt/decisions/CUMap-03-70.pdf

[60] *S.D. Warren Company v Maine Board of Environmental. Pro*tection. 868 A.2d 210 (2005, May 27). https://www.courts.maine.gov/opinions_orders/opinions/2005_documents/05me27s d.htm

[61] *S.D. Warren Company v. Maine Board of Environmental Pro*tection. 547 U. S. 370 (s006) (2006, May 15). https://www.justice.gov/osg/brief/sd-warren-co-v-maine-bd-envtl-prot-amicus-merits

[62] Maine Legislature (2003). *Fishways in dams and other artificial obstructions.* 12 M.R.S.A § 12760 (4). https://legislature.maine.gov/statutes/12/title12sec12760.html

[63] Maine Department of Inland Fisheries and Wildlife (2009, June 29). *In the matter of Cumberland Mills Dam fishway proceeding: Finding of fact and decision.* https://static1.squarespace.com/static/57fef2d28419c2478111e0f8/t/59075ac9db29d650783caf7a/1493654218248/decision_on_cumberland_mills.pdf

[64] Ibid.

[65] Orchard Foundation https://www.orchardfoundation.org; Davis Foundations https://davisfoundations.org

[66] Lane, G. (2007, July 11). Sappi to Remove Westbrook Dam. *Keep Me Current.* http://news.keepmecurrent.com/ sappi-to-remove-westbrook-dam/

[67] Associated Press (2008, July 9). Sappi Pulls Out of Dam Agreement. *Lewiston Sun Journal.* https://www.sunjournal.com/ 2008/07/09/sappi-pulls-dam-agreement/

[68] Maine Department of Inland Fisheries and Wildlife, *In the matter of Cumberland Mills.*

[69] Normandeau Associates, Inc. (2004, February). *Diadromous fish survey of the Presumpscot River.* Prepared for Coastal Conservation Association, Friends of Casco Bay, and Friends of the Presumpscot River.

[70] Bridges, L. (2009, November 12) Design for dam at issue. *Keep Me Current.* 1, 13.

Maine Department of Inland Fisheries and Wildlife, *In the matter of Cumberland Mills.*

[72] Bridges, L. (2013, March 6) Westbrook paper mill changes course, may remove dam. *Portland Press Herald.* https://www.pressherald.com/2013/03/06/sappi-alters-course-may-remove-dam_2013-03-07/

[73] Ibid.

[74] Rice, A. (2015, July 23). River at critical juncture. *American Journal.* 1,13,16.

75 *State of Maine Department of Marine Resources Comments on Draft Surrender Application Saccarappa Hydroelectric Project* (FERC No. 2897). Email communication from William Baker (2013, December 18).

76 S.D. Warren Company (2013, December 31). *Application for license surrender for the Saccarappa project*, 4-9. (FERC No. 2897). FERC Submittal 20131231-5175.

77 Ibid.

78 Ibid., 4-8.

79 Conservation Law Foundation and Friends of the Presumpscot River (2013, December 31). *Saccarappa hydroelectric project; Comments on draft surrender application.* Contained in Ibid.

80 S. D. Warren, *Application for license surrender for the Saccarappa project.*

81 Quimby Family Foundation, https://quimbyfamilyfoundation.org; Elmina B. Sewall Foundation, https://www.sewallfoundation.org

82 S. D. Warren Company (2014, March, 28). *Application for amendment of licenses and motion to stay processing of license surrender application.* Project Nos. P-2897, 2932, 2941, 2931 and 2942. United States of America. Before the Federal Regulatory Commission.

83 Federal Energy Regulatory Commission (2014, July 30). *Order amending fishway prescriptions, incorporating revised water quality certification conditions, amending fish passage plan and placing surrender application in abeyance.* S. D. Warren Company Project No. No. 2897-039, -041, 2932-041, 2941-034, 2931-036, 2942-047). 148 FERC ¶ 62,086. United States of America. Issuance 20140730-3036; Maine Department of Environmental Protection (2014, June 3). *Department order in the matter of S.D. Warren Company Westbrook, Cumberland County.* Saccarappa Project L-19717-33-G-M (approval) Maine Water Quality Program Federal Clean Water Act Water Quality Certification Minor Revision.

84 *Agreement to request extension of fish passage deadline and stay of license surrender application for the Saccarappa project* (FERC 2987). (2014, March 14). By and Between: S. D. Warren Company, U.S. Department of the Interior and U.S. Fish and Wildlife Service, Maine Department of Marine resources, City of Westbrook, Friends of the Presumpscot River, Conservation Law Foundation. United States of America Before the FERC. S. D. Warren Company (2014, March 28). *Application for amendment of licenses and motion to stay processing of license surrender application.* Project Nos. P-2897, 2932, 2941, 2931 and 2942. Tab. Table A2.3, p. 7.

[85] S. D. Warren Company (2014, September 4). *Withdrawal of surrender application under P-2897.* Submittal 20140904-5179.

[86]*Agreement to request extension of fish passage deadline and stay of license surrender application for the Saccarappa project* (FERC 2987). (2014, March 14). By and Between: S. D. Warren Company, U.S. Department of the Interior and U.S. Fish and Wildlife Service, Maine Department of Marine resources, City of Westbrook, Friends of the Presumpscot River, Conservation Law Foundation. United States of America Before FERC. S.D. Warren Company (2014, March 28). *Application for amendment of licenses and motion to stay processing of license surrender application,* Table A3.1.1, p. 9. Project Nos. P-2897; 2932, 2941; 2931 and 2942.

[87] Rice, River at critical juncture.

[88] S. S. Warren Company DBA Sappi North America & Acheron Engineering Services (2015, December 2) *Application for license surrender for the Saccarappa project.*

[89] Conservation Law Foundation & Friends of the Presumpscot River (2015, December 29). *Comments by Conservation Law Foundation and Friends of the Presumpscot River on additional information needs, and lack of readiness for environmental analysis for application.* Before FERC Project- 2897, p. 2.

[90] Conservation Law Foundation & Friends of the Presumpscot River, *Comments,* 3.

[91] Jones, P. (1729). *This is the plan of Sacarappy Falls being the third falls on Presumpscot river which was grated to Benjamin Ingalls, Robert Pierc, Benjamin Larraby and John Baiey / and surveyed by Phineas Jones January 10, 1729.* Maine Historical Society Map FF87.

[92] S. D. Warren Company (2016, March 7). *Letter re; Multiple Party request for Stay Proceeding to Enable Settlement Discussion under P-2897.* FERC Submittal 201060307-5208.

[93] *Settlement Agreement for the Saccarappa Project* (FERC No. 2897), License Surrender, By and Between: S.D. Warren Company, U.S. Department of the Interior and U.S. Fish and Wildlife Service, Maine Department of Marine Resources, Conservation Law Foundation, Friends of the Presumpscot River, City of Westbrook, Maine. (November 15, 2016).

[94] United States Department of the Interior, & U.S. Fish and Wildlife Service (2018, June). *Modifications of fish passage prescription provisions for S. D. Warren minor projects,* 5, 6. Saccarappa Project No. 2897; Mallison Falls Project No. 2932; Little Falls Project No.

941; Gambo Project No. 2931; and Dundee Project No, 2942, Presumpscot River, Cumberland County, Maine.

[95] S. D. Warren Company (2018, March 23). *Application for license Surrender for Saccarappa.* (FERC No. 2897); S. D. Warren Company (2018, March 23). *Application for amendment of license for minor project-existing dams, initial statement,* (Pursuant to 18 CFR § 4.201), Mallison Falls Project No. 2932; Little Falls Project No. 2941; Gambo Project No. 2931; Dundee Project No. 2942. United States of America. Before FERC.

[96] Maine Department of Environmental Protection (2018, March 23). *Water quality certification and water quality certification amendments for S. D. Warren Company's Presumpscot River hydro projects.* Re: #L-19713-33-N-M (Dundee), #L-19714-33-G-M (Gambo), #L-19715-33-G-M (Little Falls), #L-19716-33-G-M (Mallison Falls), #L-19717-3D-M-N (Saccarappa) #L-19717-33-N-M (Saccarappa) (Approval March 23, 2018).

[97] Friends of the Presumpscot River (2018, May 30). *Motion to intervene by Friends of the Presumpscot River.* S. D. Warren Company Project Nos. 2897-048, 2932-047, 2931-042, 2941-043, 2942-051. FERC Submittal 20180530-5231. United States of America. Before FERC; Conservation Law Foundation (2018, May 31). *Motion to intervene by Conservation Law Foundation.* FERC Submittal 20180531-5311; Conservation Law Foundation, & Friends of the Presumpscot River (2018, June 11). *Comments of conservation law foundation and friends of the Presumpscot River under 2897 et. al.* FERC Submittal 20180611-5038

[98] Conservation Law Foundation, & Friends of the Presumpscot River, *Comments, 3.*

[99] Maine Department of Environmental Protection (2018, October 18). *Water quality certification and water quality certification amendments for S.D. Warren Company's Presumpscot River hydro projects: Findings of facts and order new permit and certifications.* Re: #L-19713-33-N-M (Dundee), #L-19714-33-G-M (Gambo), #L-19715-33-G-M (Little Falls), #L-19716-33-G-M (Mallison Falls), #L-19717-3D-M-N (Saccarappa) #L-19717-33-N-M (Saccarappa). https://elibrary.ferc.gov/idmws/common/downloadOpen.asp?downloadfile=2018101 0%2D5126%2833180804%29%2Epdf&folder=8740252&fileid=15065717&trial=1

[100] Federal Energy Commission (2019, April 18). *Order Approving Surrender of the Saccarappa Project License and Authoring Decommissioning of Project Features; and Amending the Mallison Falls, Little Falls,Gambro and Dundee Projects Licenses re Sappi North America, under P-2897 et al. Issuance 20190418-3033*

[101] Ron Kreisman, personal email correspondence to FOPR, October 2, 2003. Used with permission.

Chapter 12   Rachel Bouvier

The Economic Value of a Restored Fishery on the Presumpscot River

Introduction

Within the past several years, towns in Maine and elsewhere in New England have begun to rediscover and restore once-overlooked assets: native fish runs. The rivers and streams of New England were once teeming with alewife, American shad, and blueback herring, and communities living alongside the river, including those bordering the Presumpscot, benefited significantly from them. These sea-run fish brought in revenue for the harvesters, served as lobster bait for local fishermen, and were plentiful sources of protein upon which town residents relied. In fact, widows and orphans may still ask for a bushel of alewives during the harvest in many Maine towns![1]

During the Industrial Revolution, New England's rivers served another purpose, as a source of hydropower energy to mills, which heavily dammed them—especially the Presumpscot–and all but eradicated the once mighty native fish runs by the mid-twentieth century. Yet today, runs of native species are returning to some Maine and other New England rivers that have undergone ecological restoration efforts. Although these restored fish runs are still a trickle compared to their former abundance, towns located alongside these rivers are again recognizing the importance of native fish, albeit in some new and significant ways. Towns are discovering that both residents and people "from away" are eager to reconnect with nature and natural history. Families with children are actively seeking out activities that bring them closer to the natural world. Tourists from more urban areas who do not interact with nature on a day-to-day basis are rediscovering the beauty of Maine rivers and wildlife, without having to travel too far from comfortable amenities. And, increasingly, businesses and their workers are realizing the value–monetary and otherwise–of natural features near downtown areas.

Damariscotta Mills, ME

Damariscotta Mills is home to the oldest fish ladder in Maine and a very productive alewife fishery. The restored fish ladder at Damariscotta Mills attracts thousands of visitors every year. Educational programs bring in busloads of children (and their parents). The Maine Eastern Railroad's passenger train, which runs between Brunswick and Rockland, makes a special stop in Damariscotta Mills for the annual alewife festival. Until 2009, "trains hadn't stopped in Damariscotta Mills for fifty years, says Dick Chase, Newcastle resident, train fan, and fish-ladder restoration committee member. We're very excited to have trains stop for the festival."[1] Other activities include smoked alewife demonstrations, an alewife puppet show, fish-science-discovery centers, and live music. For more information, visit the Damariscotta Mills Fish Ladder Restoration Project at https://damariscottamills.org/

The benefits occurring from a restored fishery are varied and wide-reaching:

- Corporate Relocation and Increased Property Values
- Increased Tourism Revenue from Water-Based "Passive" Recreation (including Birding and other Wildlife Viewing, Hiking, and Photography)
- Increased Angling Revenues (both commercial and recreational)
- Community Revitalization, Quality of Life, and Civic Pride
- Ecological Values

That small and mid-size New England towns are seeing the value of a restored fishery comes as no surprise to resource economists and community planners.

Corporate Relocation and Increased Property Values

Recently, community planners have become aware of the importance of "amenity migration"—the idea that as the structure of the economy changes, businesses (especially those that employ a relatively high percentage of professionals) are more likely to consider the importance of amenities such as natural scenery, environmental quality, recreational opportunities, climate, and "cultural richness."[2] Surveys of new residents and businesses in rural counties with high levels of natural features found that these amenities were actually more important reasons for relocation than job opportunities or cost of living.[3] Literature on amenity migration suggests that people want to live within an hour's drive of good fishing, skiing, and hiking.[4] All of this information suggests that natural amenities within close proximity to more urban activities, such as shopping and cultural offerings, are well poised to bring about economic development.

Amenity Migration

Gosnell and Abrams define "amenity migration" as "the movement of people based on the draw of natural and/or cultural amenities."[2] Amenity migrants "may be part-time or full-time residents to their new communities; they may be retirees, professionals able to telecommute; or entrepreneurs looking to serve the other new residents."[3] Globalization, telecommunication, and the rise of the "footloose worker" have all led to a shift in the places where Americans live and work. No longer tied to urban areas or large industrial centers, workers are free to move to more attractive areas endowed with natural amenities such as forests, open space, lakes, rivers, the ocean, hills, and mountains.[4]

The economic benefits of a restored fishery can extend to current residents as well. Unlike other parts of the country, where having a house located on a river is a boost to its property value, until recently, the same was not true for a house situated on one of Maine's badly polluted rivers. Yet that is changing. Economist Lynne Lewis of Bates College and ecologist Curtis Bohlen of the Casco Bay Estuary Project found that, in the past, proximity to the Kennebec River was associated with a "penalty," a vestige of its industrial history. However, when Lewis and Bohlen investigated housing prices after the removal of the Edwards Dam and the beginning of river restoration, they found that the penalty had decreased. Given that the study is from 2008, the penalty may have completely reversed itself as of this writing, as it takes time for current events to capitalize into housing prices.[5]

Alison McDeedy, executive director of the Blackstone Valley Community Pollution Prevention Project in Massachusetts, echoes that sentiment about her community's restoration efforts:

When I began working in 1992, people were very derogatory about the river. Back in those days, people would build houses and make sure they faced away from the river. Now we field questions all the time from people interested in the river and interested in spending time on it. It seems that everything is snowballing.[6]

Increased Tourism Revenue from Birdwatching and Wildlife Viewing

In a time when more active outdoor recreation activities are declining, wildlife-associated activities, such as wildlife watching, are actually increasing. According to senior research scientist H. Ken Cordell at the USDA Forest Service, "viewing, photographing, and studying nature in all its forms, for example, wildlife and birds, have grown strongly."[7] In fact, wildlife watching is one of the fastest growing outdoor experiences in Maine. Statistics show that of all outdoor activities in the state, wildlife watching attracts the widest demographic—from the very young to the very old, and all walks of life in between.[8]

Woolwich, ME

The Bath Water District owns and maintains a fish ladder on the Nequasset Dam in Woolwich. By 2011, the fish ladder was in disrepair. Woolwich, the Bath Water District (BWD), the Kennebec Estuary Land Trust (KELT), the Woolwich Fish Commission, and the Woolwich Historical Society all joined forces to replace the crumbling structure. BWD was especially interested in the removal of phosphorus by the alewives, helping to keep Nequasset Lake, a reservoir, clean. Today, hundreds of individuals sign up for volunteer fish counts, and KELT leads school groups and scouts on educational trips. According to Ruth Indrick, Project Manager at KELT, "There are people who have lived over 50 years in the town and never come down to see the fish. Now they're hearing a lot more about it, and they're coming!"[5] And from Bill Potter, Chairman of the Woolwich Fish Commission: "The project has given people something to rally around. The fish count gave people a sense of ownership. You see the eagles flying overhead and the osprey sitting there. It gave people a way to be involved. A way that they could contribute."[6] Visit the Nequasset Dam Fish Ladder Restoration Project Facebook page, or http://kennebecestuary.org

In 2006, Maine had the second highest birdwatching participation rate in the nation,[9] and birdwatching contributed approximately $346 million to the Maine economy in 2000 alone.[10]

The Downeast Birding Festival, for example, draws people from all over the country. In 2014, at least half of the registered participants were from outside Maine and as far away as California, Texas, and Florida.[11] William Kolodnicki, supervisor of the Moosehorn Wildlife Refuge (part of the festival), says that the revenue and visitors the festival attracts are meaningful, especially during late May, a time of year when the more active outdoor season has not yet begun. "This is really pretty significant for Maine at this time of year," he said.[12]

Birds of prey are actually the second-most-watched bird type in the country, second only to waterfowl, implying that a restored fishery is good news for Maine's birdwatching industry.[13] Although no studies have directly measured the impact of a restored fishery on the growth of bird-watching, we know that eagles, osprey, and other birds of prey concentrate where food items like alewife, blueback herring, and shad are seasonally abundant and accessible.

Camouflaged Along the River (Barbie DelCamp, 2017, Digitally Enhanced Photo)

After removal of the Fort Halifax Dam on the Sebasticook River in 2008, and the subsequent explosion of river herring occurred, Maine's Department of Inland Fisheries & Wildlife (IF&W) began tracking the numbers of eagle and osprey on the river. On a single day in June 2011, officials counted 35 eagles on the portion of the river upstream of the former Fort Halifax Dam site.[14] In 2014, during the river-herring run, IF&W "consistently observed 40-50 eagles" in the same stretch of river, with a single-day peak of 64 eagles. The department official in charge of these counts believes that the true eagle numbers are likely greater, but the estimate still constitutes "the largest observed aggregation of eagles . . . in all of New England." The influence of the river-herring run on the eagle population, she believes, "extends well beyond the summer months, and benefits several hundred eagles over the course of an entire year."[15] IF&W officials had earlier recorded a cluster of nearby osprey nests related to the restored river-herring run.

Middleborough, MA

Middleborough, a mid-size town in eastern Massachusetts, held its first herring run festival in 2014, although it has had an established fish run for centuries. The run brings in 8,000 visitors a year, even before the festival, says Leilani Dalpe, Vice Chairman of the Board of Selectmen and Chair of the Tourism Committee. But the first festival brought in 3,000 people, just for the weekend, from as far away as Maine and New Jersey. "We had vendors who sold out two, three times during the two-day festival. They couldn't keep food in their trucks, they couldn't keep stuff on their tables. . . . People just bought everything," says Ms. Dalpe. In 2015, in addition to participating restaurants offering a "Herring Run Fish Special" (a discount on fish dinners), participating hotels in town offered a discount. Attendance at the 2015 festival more than doubled, to 6,415, and the 2019 festival had 7,745 attendees. "The fish have put us on the map," says Ms. Dalpe. "We weren't on the map before. We are now."[7] For more information, visit https://www.discovermiddleborough.com/

According to David Cavanaugh, chairman of the Middleborough-Lakeville Herring Fisheries Commission in Massachusetts (see textbox 4), an increase in birds of prey along the Presumpscot from a restored fishery will translate into economic value:

> Obviously, since the ban [on the commercial harvest of herring], people who usually take herring for bait aren't there. But the tourist traffic has been just as busy. People like to see the wildlife come for the fish that they wouldn't normally see, like a mink or an eagle. The kids can dip their hands in and grab a fish. It's great.[16]

Increased Angling Revenues

The town of Benton, in possession of a harvesting license, received $13,000 in alewife sales in just one week in 2013, a meaningful percentage of its overall budget.[17] However, this amount only constitutes a small portion of the economic benefits that the alewife run has brought to the community. Benton held its sixth Annual Benton Alewife Festival in 2017 (organizers cancelled the 2018 festival due to rain).[18] The festival has sold out several years in a row. Although a good portion of those individuals and families may live in town, more and more are coming from "away" as Benton achieves a place on the map. Those families are traveling to an event that not only puts them close *to* nature but actually allows them to interact *with* nature.

Benton, ME

The Benton Alewife Festival began in 2012, after the Fort Halifax Dam on the Sebasticook River was breached in 2008. The event features a live underwater camera feed of the migrating alewives, a fly-fishing demonstration, an Alewife Chowder contest, and an alewife fish smoker demonstration.

The festival also incorporates characteristics unique to Benton's history, such as the ringing of the Paul Revere Bell at the Benton Falls Congregational Church. Benton selectman Antoine Morin says that the festival, which drew 400 attendees in its first year, is a way to "build a sense of community among residents, increase traffic to local businesses, and showcase Benton's appeal to prospective residents."[8]

For more information, visit the festival's Facebook page, or the Benton, Maine, website: www.bentonmaine.info.

A 2008 study on the Kennebec River (post-removal of the Edwards Dam) found that the restored recreational fishery in the freshwater section of the river generated over $27.6 million annually in angling revenue alone. This study, the first to compare results of angler surveys both pre- and post-dam removal, found that freshwater anglers are paying more to visit the enhanced fishery than they were before the dam removal. Furthermore, survey respondents indicated a willingness to pay for increased fishing opportunities. The authors note that the study underestimates the total value of the restored fishery, as it did not include non-use value.[19] Total revenue from the sale of river herring in Maine averaged over $300,000 annually from 2009 to 2014, and numbers are strongly rebounding from their low in 1995.[20]

Community Revitalization, Quality of Life, and Civic Pride

Less measurable than the impacts on tourism, relocation, or property values is the impact of a restored fish run on a community's sense of civic pride. In their study on the social and economic benefits of the restored alewife run in Maine, a research team at Colby College found that civic pride was one of the most common themes that residents and town officials alike mentioned in interviews.[21]

Connecting Urban Rivers

"Rivers connect us. They link our cities and towns; create opportunities to be outside, fishing and swimming with our families and friends; and shape a sense of place that ties people together."[9] Even though many of our cities and towns were founded on the banks of rivers, those same cities turned their backs on the rivers during their industrial era. Now, towns are rediscovering that rivers can be key economic-development tools. Urban river revitalization and "daylighting" (literally uncovering streams that were forced underground) can provide residents with access to much-needed green space and, at the same time, help to manage water flows and improve water quality.[10]

Carrie Kinne, executive director of the Kennebec Estuary Land Trust, says of the ongoing efforts to restore the fish ladder on the Nequasset Dam (see textbox 3):

This restoration project has not only effectively improved this historic fishery and retained an important local economic asset, but has galvanized the local community. Hundreds of concerned citizens and a wide array of conservation organizations have been involved, and we've increased the awareness of and pride in this critical natural and cultural resource.[22]

Although community pride in sustainably using and managing a natural resource, increasing its natural beauty, and deepening residents' awareness of their own natural history does not immediately translate into dollar figures, it does translate into a sense of place–and, perhaps, nurtures deeper human needs.

Ecological Values

Scientists are just beginning to fully appreciate the value of river herring to the ecology of Maine. Researchers at Bowdoin and Bates Colleges and the University of Maine, for example, can connect the decline of New England's groundfish population to the disappearance of the alewife in Maine rivers. Ted Ames, 2005 recipient of the MacArthur Award (better known as the "Genius Grant") and 2011 Coastal Studies Scholar in Residence at Bowdoin College, believes that "if you look at alewives as a major reason why large coastal populations of cod, pollock and haddock were here, then you're looking at a powerful economic engine and an opportunity to . . . create a sustainable fishery." He adds, "It may mean that managers have a new tool to rebuild populations of cod, pollock and haddock in areas where they haven't had any in decades, even centuries."[23]

Undervaluing Nature

Despite all of our gadgets designed to increase connectedness, a recently published study profiled in Psychology Today observes that "our hunger for the natural world still endures." Psychologists Elizabeth Nisbet and John Zelenski found that study participants who took a short outdoor walk in an urban park showed a statistically significant decrease in stress level and increase in positive affect, compared to those who took a similar walk indoors. However, participants *expected* no difference in the two experiences, indicating that perhaps people fail to appreciate the beneficial effects that "nearby nature" can have on their own well-being. Research shows that experiences in nature increase our attention span, reduce stress, and speed recovery from illness. These attributes suggest that spending more time connecting with nature may be beneficial for our health![11]

Saccarappa Lower Falls (source: Michael Shaughnessy)

Conclusion

Rarely do we get a second chance at something from an ecological perspective; rarer still is a second chance that is a "win-win" for all. Restoring native fish runs on the Presumpscot River will have multiple benefits: increased revenue for local businesses from tourism and fishing, heightened quality of life and civic pride for residents, and enhanced natural beauty and ecological quality. No other river-based activity has such appeal to such a wide variety of users: old and young, families and individuals, wildlife lovers and nature enthusiasts. The return of the small, humble, native fish could mean big things for the Presumpscot![24]

---

[1] Bouvier, R. (2015, May). *The economic value of a restored fishery on the Presumpscot River.*
https://static1.squarespace.com/static/57fef2d28419c2478111e0f8/t/
59075bd0bebafb87ca428648/1493654483470/ Economic+Impact+Study.pdf

[2] National Park Service. (1995). *Economic impact of protecting rivers, trails, and greenway corridors.* Washington, DC: National Park Service.
http://www.nps.gov/pwro/rtca/econ_index.htm

[3] Johnson, J., & Rasker, R. (1995). The role of economic and quality of life values in rural business location. *Journal of Rural Studies, 11*, 405-416.
https://www.researchgate.net/publication/ 222506565_The_Role_ of_Economic_ and_Quality_of_Life_Values_in_Rural_Business_Location

[4] Hansen, A. et al. (2002). Ecological causes and consequences of demographic change in the New West/ *BioScience, 52*(2), 151-162.
https://academic.oup.com/bioscience/article/52/2/151/341204

[5] Lewis, L., Bohlen, C., & Wilson, S. (2008). Dams, dam removal, and river restoration: A hedonic property value analysis. *Contemporary Economic Policy, 26*(2), 175-86. https://www.researchgate.net/publication/
4989047_Dams_Dam_Removal_and_River_Restoration_A_Hedonic_Property_Value_Analysis

[6] Wyss, B. (2000, September 17). Upstream fight: We've spent millions on the Blackstone River. Will it ever pay off? *The Providence Journal*, p. A-01.

[7] Cordell, H. K. (2008, Spring). The latest on trends in nature-based outdoor recreation. *Forest History Today,* 4-10. https://www.srs.fs.usda.gov/pubs/ja/ja_cordell021.pdf

[8] U.S. Fish and Wildlife Service. (2009). *Birding in the United States: A demographic and economic analysis.* Arlington, VA: USFW. https://www.fws.gov/southeast/pdf/report/birding-in-the-united-states-a-demographic-and-economic-analysis.pdf

[9] Ibid.

[10] Mack, S. K. (2010, May 28). Birding festival boosts economy. *Bangor Daily News.* https://bangordailynews.com/ 2010/05/28/news/birding-festival-boosts-economy/

[11] Cox, T. (2014, May 21). Participants nationwide flocking to annual Down East Birding Festival. *Bangor Daily News.* https://bangordailynews.com/2014/05/21/news/down-east/participants-nationwide-flocking-to-annual-down-east-birding-festival/

[12] Mack, Birding festival.

[13] U.S. Fish and Wildlife Service, *Birding.*

[14] Todd, C. (2011, June 6). Sebasticook River BAEA aggregation in Benton/Winslow (electronic mail message). Augusta, Maine.

[15] Call, E. (2015, April 15). Sea run fish = Raptors? (electronic mail message). Augusta, ME.

[16] Conroy, E., & Rizer, G. (2007, May 6). In pursuit of the herring. *Boston Globe,* GS1.

[17] Hongoltz-Hetling, M. (2013, May 20). Sebasticook to the Sea: Alewives' perilous lives crucial to ecosystem, economy. *McClatchy-Tribune Business News,* p. A1. https://www.centralmaine.com/2013/05/19/sebasticook-to-the-sea-alewives-perilous-lives-crucial-to-ecosystem/

[18] Ellis, C. (2018, May 18). Despite millions of alewives rushing up Sebasticook River, Benton cancels alewife festival. *Kennebec Journal.*

https://www.centralmaine.com/2018/05/17/despite-millions-of-alewives-rushing-up-the-sebasticook-river-benton-cancels-alewife-festival/

[19] Robbins, J., & Lewis, L. (2008, December). Demolish it and they will come: Estimating the economic impacts of restoring a recreational fishery. *Journal of the American Water Resources Association, 44*(6), 1488-1499. https://www.midcoastconservancy.org/wp-content/uploads/2018/02/Robbins_et_al-2008-JAWRA_Journal_of_the_American_Water_Resources_Association.pdf

[20] Maine Department of Marine Resources. (2015, February 25). *Historical Maine fisheries landings data.* http://www.maine.gov/dmr/commercialfishing/historicaldata.htm

[21] McClenachan, L., Lovell, S., & Keaveney, C. (2014). *Community benefits of restoring historical ecosystems and fisheries: Alewives in Maine.* Waterville, ME: Unpublished report.

[22] Kennebec Estuary Land Trust. (2015). *Nequasset fish ladder restoration.* https://www.kennebecestuary.org/ nequasset-restoration

[23] Bowdoin College, Academic Spotlight (2011, March 6). *Scientist, fisherman Ted Ames: 'Can't believe we've stumbled on something as important as this'.* http://www.bowdoin.edu/news/archives/1academicnews/008268.shtml

[24] Acknowledgements: This chapter was adapted from a 2015 report prepared by the author for the Friends of Presumpscot River (FOPR). In writing the original report, the author appreciates the support and review of Ron Kriesman, Esquire, and members of FOPR.

Textbox Notes

1. Celebrating the return of the alewives in Damariscotta Mills (2011, May 26). *The Free Press.* https://freepressonline.com/Content/Features/Features/Article/Celebrating-the-Return-of-the-Alewives-in-Damariscotta-Mills/52/78/12906

2. Gosnell, H., & Abrams, J. (2009). Amenity migration: Diverse conceptualizations of drivers, socioeconomic dimensions, and emerging challenges. *GeoJournal, 76*(4), 303-322. https://www.researchgate.net/publication/225606168_Amenity_Migration_Di-verse_Conceptualizations_ofDrivers_Socioeconomic_Dimensions_and_E merging_Challenges

3. Donoghue, E., & Sturtevant, V. (2010). *Forest community connections.* New York: Routledge.

4. Marcouiller, D., Clendenning, J., & Kedzior, R. (2002). Natural amenity-led development and rural planning. *Journal of Planning Literature, 16*(4), 515-542. https://www.researchgate.net/publication/245381477_Natural_Amenity-Led_Development_and_Rural_Planning

5. Indrick, R. (2015, March). Personal interview with author.

6. Potter, B. (2015, April). Personal interview with author.

7. Dalpe, L. (2015, March). Personal interview with author.

8. Hongoltz-Hetling, M. (2013, May 16). Benton festival to be held Saturday in honor of alewives," Kennebec Journal. https://www.centralmaine.com/2013/05/16/hail-hail-the-alewives-are-here_2013-05-16/

9. American Rivers. (2014). *Restoring urban rivers, Revitalizing communities.* http://www.americanrivers.org/

10. Patten, G. (2012, December 14). *A watershed era for urban river restoration.* http://greatecology.com/ watershed-era-urban-river-restoration/

11. Nisbet, E., & Zelenski, J. (2011). Underestimating nearby nature: Affective forecasting errors obscure the happy path to sustainability. *Psychological Science, 22*(9), 1101-1106.

Chapter 13

Why Paddle the Presumpscot When the Allagash is in Your Backyard?

The river redirected for canal/power generation purposes.

An exploration of the Presumpscot River by canoe or kayak will reward any paddler many times over. Furthermore, anyone who cares deeply about this river should surely become acquainted with it from both land and water. The purpose of this chapter is to help you do just that by introducing you to the benefits, the sights along the way, and the potential hazards and difficulties of boating here. So, first let's take a broad-brush look at the watershed to explore some options.

Like much of Maine, the Presumpscot basin is peppered with lakes and streams. These waterways are truly some of the state's greatest natural

311

resources yet, in some ways, are still abused and underappreciated for their long-term economic, social, and environmental value. Much of the Presumpscot basin lies northwest of Sebago Lake, which acts as a collecting basin prior to discharging these waters into the Presumpscot River. Between Sebago Lake's outlet and tidewater, the river drops 267 feet. Sadly, construction has converted much of that elevation loss into impoundments (small artificial lakes) formed from dam creation. These dams have made travel on the river difficult (although not impossible). . . getting around the papermill in Westbrook being an excellent case in point.

It's not always easy to carry a canoe around a dam.

312

But the determined paddler can still: a) travel the Presumpscot from source to mouth, and b) easily find other opportunities for recreational paddling elsewhere in the watershed.

So, where to begin? A survey of existing literature for the paddler doesn't turn up anywhere near the material that exists for, say, the Allagash, various branches of the Penobscot, the Machias, or several other Maine rivers. Why? The short answer to that question lies in the industrial uses and history of the river. Following are a few examples of that literature.

Joe's Log: The Story of a Canoe Trip on Lake Sebago, Maine, September 1900 is a little-known account of two young men who embarked on an exploration of Sebago Lake by canoe at the same time that one of the worst hurricanes of all time blew through. The Galveston hurricane of September 1900 had already wreaked havoc (approximately 10,000 deaths) in the southern US; its vestiges, by the time they reached Maine, were still strong enough to sink two youthful and exuberant canoeists only looking for a few days of rest and relaxation. *Joe's Log* is a reproduction of the diary kept by Joseph Warren Smith (1879-1900) found after the tragedy.[1]

Quick-Water and Smooth: A Canoeist's Guide to New England Rivers (1935), the first true guidebook for canoeing Maine rivers, only included one river from the Presumpscot watershed: the Crooked River, Sebago Lake's largest tributary. The authors recommend the Crooked highly, characterizing it as steep, beautiful, and wild in its upper sections and with handsome meadows and good views as one progresses downstream.

A view of Babb's Covered Bridge from the river—originally built 1864, burned 1973, rebuilt shortly thereafter.

Overall, the authors of *Quick-Water and Smooth* were looking for excitement, attractive rivers, and whitewater—and, in the 1930s, not unlike today, most paddlers didn't turn to the Presumpscot to find these attributes.[2]

Some thirty years later, in1965, the Appalachian Mountain Club (AMC) published its first *AMC New England Canoeing Guide* and did write about the Presumpscot as well as the Crooked but says this in introducing it to prospective paddlers:

Despite the number of dams the canoeing is pleasant down to Cumberland Mills [Westbrook]. Below here the river is sometimes smelly from the paper mill effluvium. Summer canoeing on the upper river is less pleasant because of the sewage discharged from the smaller towns. The July 4th week should be avoided as the water is often drawn down for maintenance work on the dams.[3]

This perception hardly constitutes an endorsement for the Presumpscot as a first choice for one's summer vacation plans.

A few years ago, this boom caught foam, etc. from a point downstream of the two discharge pipes—one municipal, one industrial.

The fourth edition of the *AMC River Guide: Maine*, published in 2008, also includes a good description of the Presumpscot and encourages paddling the river, even with its many portages around dams. But this trip is not for the faint of heart. An aside: anyone planning a trip on the Presumpscot would be well advised to read and carry along this write-up on the river. In speaking of the river's history, the 2008 edition minces no words: "at its worst, the Presumpscot became so polluted that no measurable oxygen was found in the river at all. The water in the lower river resembled a 'root beer float' and was considered dead."[4] Fortunately, this is no longer the case, due in part to the good work of the Friends of the Presumpscot River (FOPR).

In addition to these descriptions of canoeing on the Presumpscot, people have written up a handful of other trips. For example, I took a trip from my then residence near Back Cove; out through Portland Harbor; up the Stroudwater River about four miles; overland to the Presumpscot at Westbrook; and down it to tidewater, making a complete circumnavigation of Portland by canoe.[5]

Where water exists, people will boat on it. A quick look at any map of Maine will reveal that not only does the state have vast water resources, but these waterways are also sometimes connected or, if not actually connected, very close to one another. For example, much commercial boat traffic travelled on the Cumberland and Oxford Canal (a.k.a. the C & O)— running between Long Lake, Sebago Lake, and tidewater at Portland.

Some of the rock and timber work that created a lock on the C & O Canal. Note the sneaker for scale.

Long Lake is connected to Sebago via a small stream and the Songo Lock. And the source of the Crooked River (which is arguably the *upper* Presumpscot) is Songo Pond, a body of water within walking distance of Bethel, a town on the Androscoggin River. Maine is so well watered, in fact, that a determined person could almost certainly get from any Maine town to any other Maine town by following rivers and streams instead of roads.

Another possible factor in the Presumpscot's less than average canoeing literature for a river of its size is that river travel requires a specialized skill—among boaters called "reading the water"—which isn't difficult to learn, but one must first form the necessary respect for currents, rapids, and falls. One learns to go *with* the river—never to fight it—for a river, particularly one in flood, will outpower any paddler. A canoe in unskilled hands in a difficult rapid can bring dire consequences for both the people and the boat. Historically, Native Americans and, after them, sporting guides facilitated the ascent or descent of Maine's rocky rivers. Thoreau hired a Native American (1840s-1850s); Teddy Roosevelt hired local guides in northern Maine (1880s); and Eisenhower ditto near Rangeley (1950s). All benefited from local knowledge, more specifically, river knowledge. Even today, people are frightened by rivers—their currents and mystery. Certainly, many people drive their cars blithely over bridges, not even realizing that they've crossed what used to be a "road" in a vast network of roads that Native Americans used. In those days, the rivers *were* the roads. A glance at the map of Maine points to the vastness of this network.

View on the Presumpscot.

A 19th-century bucolic rendering of life along the Presumpscot River.

Imagine for a moment that the year is 1491, and not a single dam exists on the Presumpscot (except for very small weirs used by Native Americans to trap fish and eels). The Presumpscot would have been a lively river, indeed—with falls after falls all the way from Sebago Lake down to the ocean: Whitney Falls, Island Falls, Dundee Falls, and many others you'll never see—all now submerged by dams built by industrial users of the river.[6] Other falls, like Saccarappa and Steep Falls (also known as Eel Weir Falls), have been either so altered by development as to be unrecognizable from what they originally were or are inaccessible due to re-channeling of the river. In the case of Steep Falls, for example, the Presumpscot's redirection to an artificial C & O channel has made the natural riverbed run nearly dry compared to its original robust descent through this area.[7] The canal served industry well—during the nineteenth century, it carried boats up and down the river valley; in the twentieth century, the same canal, in places, carries practically the entire flow of the river into a hydroelectric generating facility.

Canoeing some of the exciting whitewater on the Crooked River, a tributary of Sebago Lake. This river is generally paddled in April and May on spring high water. For the experienced.

Incidentally, either an aerial or a Google Earth view of Sebago Lake's outlet vicinity is very instructive: the natural river channel is more winding and roundabout, whereas the artificial channel, once the C & O Canal, is almost perfectly straight, now carrying Presumpscot River water directly to a power plant. Both the artificial channel and the natural riverbed are clearly visible from Route 35, approximately one mile southwest of the Routes 35 and 302 intersection at North Windham.

So, what's the meaning of all this for the person who wants to explore the Presumpscot River? And, truly, why bother to paddle in the Presumpscot basin when other paddlers come perhaps thousands of miles to paddle Maine's famed Allagash River? The reasons are numerous. Here are a few:

1. If you live in or within 50 miles of Portland, the Presumpscot *is* in your backyard. You will continue to hear about it for years to come, so why not get acquainted?

2. Although, generally speaking, these waters (both lakes and river) are developed lands (e.g. houses, camps, dams, motor boats, etc.), you'll be pleasantly surprised at how often you'll feel isolated and appreciative of the natural beauty that remains.

3. Who doesn't love to travel? The price of fuel isn't likely to decrease, so travel, particularly long-distance travel, is increasingly expensive. It makes sense to turn a "problem" into an opportunity by poking around the Presumpscot.

4. A canoe or kayak is the *ideal* boat for getting to know Maine. Most of the lakes just northwest of Portland have some form of public access available, and it's always easier to get a canoe or kayak to the water than a larger motorboat with its cumbersome trailer.

When in a small boat on any lake, keep in mind that the wind may be both your friend and your enemy. The informed paddler always keeps abreast of weather forecasts. On large lakes like Sebago or Long Lake, high winds bring big waves and trouble. Generally speaking, crossing large expanses of water is asking for trouble. A little common sense goes a long way on Maine waters.

Here's a sampler of ideas for trips in the Presumpscot watershed, exclusive of the Presumpscot River itself, which we'll discuss later (note: please be respectful of private property):

1. The Pleasant River in Windham. Mixed rapid water and smooth with at least one short portage. Best for people with at least some whitewater experience. "Put in" at the Route 302 bridge. Generally best run in spring, but can sometimes be run following substantial rains at other times of year.

2. Long Lake from Harrison to Naples. Prevailing winds will usually blow you down the lake toward Naples. Easy shuttle (or even ride a bike!) back to your car in Harrison.

3. An exploration of Little Sebago Lake . . . which has countless tiny islands.

4. Lower Crooked River near Sebago Lake State Park. Very, very serpentine! Learn where the river got its name!

5. The Dingley Islands on the northeast side of Sebago Lake. Poke around on a calm day, not a windy one. Note: Sebago is prone to having numerous large, high-speed motorboats. They're noisy, and their drivers are sometimes careless . . . even dangerous. Do your best to avoid them by staying in shallow, rocky areas.

6. Explore the mouth of the Presumpscot River. Although close to 295, it has beautiful wetlands, nooks and crannies to explore, abundant birdlife, and possibly some deer. Suggestion: go at or near high tide; at low tide, you'll find much mud! You may also want to paddle upriver to the point where the Presumpscot River actually meets tidewater. For many years, Smelt Hill Dam operated here. Its recent removal has revealed the very beautiful "Lower Falls," which the public hadn't seen for well over 100 years, as it had been submerged by the artificial pond created by the Smelt Hill Dam. In addition to the dam, this lower portion of the river and its estuary have been the sites of much commercial activity at various times through history: shipyards, brickyards, fishways, Native Indian trails, ferry slips, a target-practice area, an iron company, and boathouses to name a few. Now the area is largely wild except for the presence of 295.

Those are but a few suggestions for trips in the region. Most importantly, use your Maine Atlas or other maps and start wondering about what lurks here and what there. One of the greatest aspects of kayaking or canoeing is that you find a discovery around every corner!

An admirable goal for any Presumpscot lover would be to paddle the river from source to mouth. These days, it's much more common for paddlers to choose a small portion of a river and paddle it repeatedly. Perhaps that section has a great reputation for scenery or rapids, or it's easy to shuttle cars from the ending point back to the beginning. People who invest the time and energy to paddle a river from source to mouth, however, will almost always be handsomely rewarded. But, they could also encounter a few headaches along the way, too. Following are some general comments on paddling from Sebago Lake to tidewater.

Paddling the Presumpscot from source to mouth is not an easy proposition. This difficulty is less due to the severity of the whitewater (there is little) than the number of portages around dams. They're so frequent and come so closely after one another that they'll surely wear you down. For this reason, it's sensible to paddle the river in *two separate day trips* rather than trying it in a single day or as a camping trip (hauling camping gear over portages is possible but gets tedious with multiple carries).

Before paddling the river, you'd be well advised to read (and take with you on the river) a copy of either a) *AMC River Guide: Maine.* 4th edition, or b) *The Presumpscot River Watch Guide to the Presumpscot River.*[8] Each has detailed descriptions of the river, portages, and more. Both point out the challenges, hazards, and rewards associated with travel on this river.

Looking at a map, you might conclude that starting your trip at White's Bridge would make sense, but this area is badly congested with no trespassing signs, commercial motorboat operations, and almost completely private property.[9] No good options exist here for the no-octane crowd. Better to start some four miles north, at the north end of Jordan Bay, and proceed south along the eastern shore of the bay.

The river was originally diverted near North Windham to build the Cumberland & Oxford Canal, later for power-generation purposes. Here is the original (natural), often nearly dry riverbed.

If it's windy, particularly from the northwest, you'll have your first problem. So, hope for a calm day. As you progress south on Sebago Lake, you'll see large boats, homes, camps, etc., much of which will disappear once you're on the river. Progress south through the basin—which is really nothing more than a small pond alongside the much larger Sebago Lake. At its south end, you'll encounter your first significant obstacle: a dam. At this (basin) dam, you could go down the left (natural) river channel IF you encounter sufficient water to float your boat.

Given that the bulk of the water is generally diverted into the artificial channel (originally the C & O Canal) toward the power station, you'll need to assess your best option. Also, paddling in the artificial channel is discouraged, so you may be faced with a bit more than a mile of canoe or kayak carrying. If you're fortunate enough to paddle the natural channel, it, too, has complications: about a mile downstream, you'll come to Steep Falls, a drop over which most people do not run boats. Carry your boat around it on the right.

If you've managed to survive the Sebago Lake outlet vicinity, the real fun begins! The next six miles of the Presumpscot is best suited to true lovers of the Presumpscot, diehards, or those with a penchant for agony, as they will encounter *five dams within these six miles*! You're barely back in your boat from one portage, when you're out of it for the next. Not to be discouraging—it's interesting, indeed, to see the river in this region, but it's a dramatically altered river from the one that Native Americans knew prior to its industrial development. Standing at the Great Falls Dam in North Gorham, your mantra for getting around these several dams should be: right, right, right, left, right. Those are the sides of the river you should be on for each progressive dam.

But better than your mantra would be some useful guidelines for getting around any dam on any river:

1. As you approach a dam, proceed with caution. Any dam can pose hazards and/or headaches for paddlers but often don't. Just be on guard.

2. Scan *both* shores. Often (but not always) these days, you'll see some sort of marker (e.g. a portage sign, obvious path, brightly colored surveyor's tape marking a trail, etc.). In other words, you're not likely to be the first one to portage around the dam— look for the places where others before you have gone.

321

3. It's often necessary to make more than one trip along the portage trail to get all your gear around the dam. When this is the case, make your first load a light one while you assess the trail to find the easiest and, if possible, shortest route.

After you've survived carrying around your fifth dam, consider how the river may have looked with NO dams! Imagine: beautiful falls, rapids, and vistas quite unlike most other metropolitan areas.

Because carrying around so many dams in such rapid succession can be trying, you might think about "cheating" and skip this section of the river, putting in at the next bridge downstream of South Windham. From this point down to Westbrook is a calm stretch of roughly five miles of river and, most times, you'll see little other boat traffic. By bypassing all the dams, however, you will miss seeing: a) what an industrial workhorse this river is, and b) Babb's Bridge, one of Maine's few remaining wooden covered bridges.

Babb's Covered Bridge near South Windham. The view of the bridge from a canoe is even better than this!

Originally built in 1864, it burned in 1973 and was rebuilt shortly thereafter. In the early-twentieth century, about 1500 wooden truss bridges graced New England.[10] Today, the bulk remain in New Hampshire and Vermont, but Maine has a few that are popular with artists and photographers. So . . . even if you skip this section of the river, you should consider a side trip to Babb's covered bridge, which is only about three miles from South Windham.

Let's assume that you've paddled the five miles of flatwater from South Windham and are approaching Westbrook. As you get closer to the large, brick Dana Warp Mill (built in 1881) on the left, you should be on the *right* side of the river. As you approach the first of three dams in Westbrook, look along the right shore for a very small gravel beach—it's very close to the dam, so be careful. Saccarappa Falls has had dams since 1729 (a sawmill). From this small gravel beach, things get complicated, because the river is hemmed in by city, mill, and private property for nearly the next three miles. Although, technically, you could put a boat back in the river to paddle a portion of one mile between dams two and three, you must remove your boat again to get around the mill. The river actually passes through (beneath) part of the mill at one point.

The river passes *through* the Sappi paper mill in Westbrook.

Briefly, you have two options at Westbrook:

1. Remain on the southeast side of the river, carrying, wheeling, or cartopping your boat through downtown Westbrook (yes, you get stares when carrying a canoe down city streets, but you

aren't likely to be arrested . . . in Maine, anyway). Find your way to Warren Avenue and go about a half mile along it until you reach "Gate 9," the Sappi papermill "scale entrance." According to the main office at Sappi, the guards at this gate will allow you to cross private Sappi property to get to the river just downstream of the mill. But even by doing this, your portage will be more than one and a half miles long. By the way, alerting the mill and asking permission to go through the gate might save you some time and headaches later: 856-4000 or 856-4100.

Dams at Westbrook divert the river, leaving the natural river channel nearly dry much of the year.

2. Another option bypasses the mill and its property entirely. Gist: same as above, but continue on Warren Avenue to Riverside Street, where you turn left. Go down Riverside one and a half miles to Route 302 and put in at nearby Riverton Trolley Park. This option entails about three miles of carrying, so car support or wheels for your boat are advised.

Again, the city of Westbrook and, particularly, its three dams and papermill are the largest impediments to paddling the Presumpscot. They and the many dams upstream of Westbrook are why you rarely hear of source-to-mouth boat trips on the Presumpscot River. Having said that, paddling the river from Sebago to the sea would provide you with stories galore!

Let's assume that you've survived the difficulties of Westbrook and made your way past the outfalls of both a Portland sewage-treatment plant and the Sappi one, too.

A view of the Sappi mill (formerly known as S.D. Warren) from the river in Westbrook.

Surely, you'll notice diminished water quality by now. When you arrive at the Route 302 bridge at Riverton, you should look up underneath the bridge to see the flotsam and jetsam that floods have lodged there. Ponder how many feet above you the water level was at that time. Rivers go on rampages now and again, and this debris is clear evidence of the Presumpscot having done so.

Although few vestiges of it remain, Riverton Trolley Park once occupied the site that now consists of a few footpaths. In the 1920s here, you could have gone roller skating, bowling, dancing, or pony riding or had dinner, gone to the theater, or ridden on a merry-go-round. You also could have taken a steamer boat ride up or down the river, leaving from the Riverton wharf. No more, though. It's all grown up to trees.

From the Route 302 bridge, you'll have one more pleasant section of the river to paddle—with only one complication at Presumpscot Falls— more on that in a moment. During these five miles, more or less, of mostly flatwater with current, you'll pass beneath several bridges, including that of the Maine Turnpike, as you progress toward tidewater. Here, you're paddling parallel to an industrial part of Portland and, again, you can't help but notice the poor water quality. It's definitely worthwhile to see Portland from the water, though, and if you paddle this section of the Presumpscot, you'll join an exclusive club of paddlers!

The paddling is relatively uneventful until you approach Presumpscot Falls. Background: this vicinity has had dams since 1734, but, in 2002, the dam (damaged by a 1996 flood) was removed, exposing the falls that the impounded dam waters had covered. The "new" falls are a marvelous addition to the Portland area's catalog of natural areas. But it's a place to exercise considerable caution if you're a paddler. Most people will want to portage their boats around. Paddlers would generally rate this rapid a Class Three or Four, which means difficult. Beginners or intermediate paddlers definitely should not attempt to negotiate it.

So, as you approach the falls, you'll notice the riverbanks closing in on you, the current increasing, and the noise of the rapid. Stay to the *right* side of the river and proceed very slowly. Nearly to the brink of the falls, you'll see a short but steep stairway going up the bank. As you near the falls, a large orange sign appears on the right bank, telling you to portage. Carry a short way around the falls on the right side. This trail is part of a larger network of trails in greater Portland and is managed by a nonprofit organization called Portland Trails. Be sure to stop and take in the beauty of this special place on the Presumpscot. Once you've put your boat back in the water below the falls, you've reached tidewater.

99.999999999% of the people who see this Presumpscot River sign read it from the Maine Turnpike. But 99.999999999% is not everyone.

You may opt to take your boat from the water at nearby Walton Park (left shore) or continue out through the Presumpscot estuary and take out at East End Beach, which adds about another three and a half miles of paddling best attempted on a calm (not windy) day.

Now it's time to pause and reflect on a few major themes of a descent of the Presumpscot River from Sebago Lake or even points beyond.

1. It's a wonderful trip and highly recommended but also somewhat complicated due to dams, a city, and a mill.
2. You can divide the trip into parts, some of which exclude carries around dams (e.g. South Windham to Westbrook).
3. You'll see a part of greater Portland that few have seen and from a radically different perspective than that of a footpath or automobile.
4. You'll see how we as a people and as a culture have treated and still treat our rivers. It's often not pretty, but it is instructive.

So, what about that question, "Why paddle the Presumpscot when the Allagash is in your backyard?" Each river has its own merits, supporters, history, special places, problems, and more. Both the Allagash and Presumpscot have seen extensive use by Native Americans and industry (primarily lumbering/paper), and, in more modern times, for recreational and artistic purposes (photographers, artists, etc.). Both are Maine rivers. The Presumpscot happens to be in an area where greater concentrations of people live . . . so those people should get to know, appreciate, and use that which is in their backyards. Consider paddling the Presumpscot!

The lovely lower Presumpscot River, near tidewater. You'll feel remote even though less than five miles from downtown Portland, Maine's largest city.

[1] Smith, J. W. (1900). *Joe's log: The Story of a canoe trip on Lake Sebago, Maine, September 1900.* Andover, MA: Andover Press.

[2] Phillips, J. C. & Cabot, T. D. (1935). *Quick-Water and smooth: A canoeist's guide to New England rivers.* Brattleboro, VT: Stephen Daye Press.

[3] Appalachian Mountain Club. (1965). *AMC River Guide: Maine* (1st ed.). Boston: Author, 426.

[4] Fiske, J.(Ed.). (2008). *AMC River Guide. Maine* (4th ed.). Boston: Appalachian Mountain Club, 225. Has a good, brief write up on the Presumpscot that will get you safely down the river. Important to read if you plan to get on the water.

[5] Kellogg, Z. (2008, April/May). Around Portland by canoe. *Maine Boats, Homes, & Harbors 21*(2), issue 99, 66-71. https://issuu.com/maineboats/docs/mbhh99_v15; See also Bell, T. 2001, August 26). A paddle on the Presumpscot. [Part 1 of 2] *Maine Sunday Telegram*, p. A1; Bell, T. (2001 August 27) A paddle on the Presumpscot. [Part 2 of 2] *Portland Press Herald*, p. A1.

[6] Willis, S. C. (1974, February). Dundee Falls. *Maine Life* 6A. A look back at the construction of Dundee Falls in 1913.

[7] Knight, E. H. (1976). *A guide to the Cumberland & Oxford Canal.* NY: Cumberland & Oxford Canal Association. A 38-page mimeographed booklet with bibliography; Milliken, P. I. (1975).

[8] Presumpscot River Watch (2009). *The Presumpscot River Watch Guide to the Presumpscot River: Its History, Ecology, and Recreational Uses.* Portland, ME: Author. See also Presumpscot River Watch. (1994). *River use map.* Portland, ME: Author. This map shows various landmarks from Sebago Lake to tidewater, including inset maps of several portage trails around dams.

[9] Dole, S. T. (1895). White's Bridge. *Collections and Proceedings of the Maine Historical Society* (2nd Series, Vol. 6), 252-255. A brief article about the history of the bridge on the southeast side of Sebago Lake.

[10] State of Maine Department of Transportation (n.d.). *Covered bridges.* http://www.maine.gov/mdot/ historicbridges/coveredbridges

Chapter 14   Robert Kuech

Education Along the Presumpscot: Developing a Sense of Place

A place is a piece of the whole environment that has been claimed by feelings.

Alan Gussow *A Sense of Place*, 1971

Photograph courtesy of author

Introduction

Throughout time, humans have been drawn to and gathered within distinct areas that provide a feeling of special attachment or a sense of place. These areas may be where two thoroughfares cross, or where important resources are present that provide for the needs of the individuals within the group. One resource that has played a particular role in human endeavors on Earth is water. It logically follows that one of the major thoroughfares forming a distinct crossroad would be a river or long lake that provides transportation and critical natural resources for people's prolonged sustainability. The Presumpscot River corridor is that kind of place-forming thoroughfare. For just as long, and certainly longer than recorded history, countless individuals have gathered and developed a strong sense of place around rivers.

Knowing the essence of the place you inhabit or in which you participate is part of knowing where you are and who you are. In general terms, a sense of place is how one perceives, relates to, feels about, experiences, and/or gains knowledge of one's local environment. A person compiles these emotions and experiences over time, and they bring about an attachment of that person to the area in which he or she lives. Becoming a member of the local environment, i.e. developing a strong sense of place, is an important part of developing a healthy respect for preserving and protecting those areas that have particular meaning for each individual.

Involvement in the environment and local community promotes not only respect but also deeper learning of science/environmental concepts. Part of this endeavor involves engaging learners in educational activities and providing authentic learning experiences. Engaging learners is the first step of the "Five E's" of the science educational teaching strategy (engage, explore, explain, elaborate, and evaluate) promoted by nationally recognized educational programs at the University of Southern Maine, Duke University, and the Biological Science Curriculum Study to name a few. It is a very important step in furthering deeper learning and a more complete conceptual understanding that national educational organizations advance.

When individuals are engaged in their learning experiences, they are willing to spend increased time and effort on solving problems and understanding material that their teacher/instructor requires of them to help develop science literacy. This engagement makes developing a sense of place and placed-based learning important aspects of today's educational experience for students, especially in learner-centered schools. Sense of

331

place and place-based education make learning more meaningful and authentic, as students are observing and collecting data that can contribute to many other researchers' work in the broader community of scientists. Involving students in authentic experiences that promote thinking like a scientist is a central tenet in the Next Generation of Science Standards (NGSS) Three Dimensions of Learning (science and engineering practices, disciplinary core ideas, and crosscutting concepts). Authentic learning experiences involve students directly with the NGSS Science and Engineering Practices, which include Constructing Explanations and Designing Solutions. Authentic experiential learning exposes students to the Crosscutting Concepts of the NGSS listed here:

- Cause and Effect
- Scale, Proportion, and Quantity
- Systems and System Models
- Energy and Matter
- Structure and Function
- Stability and Change

Observing and collecting data to serve as empirical evidence allow students to differentiate between cause and correlation and make claims about specific causes and effects. These abilities accurately connect to the High School Life Science Standard that expects students to "develop logical and reasonable arguments based on evidence" (NGSS: HS-LS2-8) or "construct and revise an explanation" based on valid and reliable evidence obtained from a variety of sources (including students' own investigations) (HS-LS2-3) (part of Science and Engineering Practices).[1]

In addition to direct connections to the new iteration of national science standards, other research-based reasons exist for adopting place-based education in schools. A recent study determined that outdoor experiential education provides opportunities for students to become informed about the environmental necessities of the places surrounding them and the communities they are part of as a way of improving their "engagement and participation."[2] Again, we are reminded that student engagement is an important part of educational practices that lead to improved understanding and retention of science concepts.

This engagement may be why students benefit from outdoor learning, as they perform better on academic tests after their outdoor learning experience compared with peers who learned the same topic in a typical classroom situation. It then follows that well-structured outdoor educational experiences would positively impact the retention of learned facts and concepts.[3] Rozenszayn & Ben-Zvi Assaraf conducted a study demonstrating that collaborative outdoor ecology learning has a positive effect on students' knowledge construction and long-term knowledge retention.[4] Other research on the effectiveness of place-based learning has focused on elementary- and secondary-school programs and has yielded positive but indirect results that include:

- Significantly improved student performance on standardized achievement tests[5]
- Significantly improved student motivation[6]
- Significantly improved critical-thinking skills.[7]

Learning along the Presumpscot

Fresh Water (Michelle Stuckey, 2006, 18" x 24", oil on canvas)

Although the Presumpscot River is well known for recreational activities, including powerboating, canoeing, kayaking, swimming, and fishing, people generally know less about the research and educational activities that occur almost constantly along the full length of the river and its tributaries. These observational and data-collection activities cover not only the river water itself and the abundant flora and fauna within it but also take place throughout the Presumpscot River watershed that serves to protect the quality of the aquatic environment. Such local educational opportunities help students and other participants develop an increased sense of place, which promotes greater engagement, achievement, motivation, and long-term knowledge retention, to name a few advantages. They provide students, adult volunteers, and scholarly researchers with chances to monitor all the parameters that indicate a healthy aquatic ecosystem and watershed. Researchers from every field collect, identify, and quantify benthic macro-invertebrates (bottom-living animals without backbones visible to the naked eye) to determine a biological quality index that demonstrates the long-term health of the river system. Chemical analysis covers all of the standard tests, including dissolved oxygen, biological oxygen demand, dissolved carbon dioxide, nitrogen, phosphorus, pH, total dissolved solids, turbidity, etc. These initiatives provide a shared longitudinal database of important water-quality parameters that scientists can use to determine trends in the Presumpscot's overall health.

Now that we have a brief overview of the research-supported benefits of place-based outdoor learning experiences, let's take a look at some opportunities currently available along the Presumpscot River, its tributaries, and its watershed. Although the benefits of outdoor place-based science education are well known, a barrier remains to the implementation of this kind of instruction. Many elementary educators have a minimal science background and are less than ideally prepared to conduct science activities in general, and place-based lessons in particular.[8] Many organizations are providing assistance to overcome this barrier, however, by supporting educators through training programs and making available standards-based learning materials. Many of the organizations below provide information, training, and other opportunities for interested people to become citizen scientists. These organizations include but are not limited to:

- The Presumpscot Regional Land Trust
- Friends of the Presumpscot River
- Cumberland County Soil and Water District
- Casco Bay Estuary Partnership
- Portland Water District
- Maine Department of Environmental Protection
- Gulf of Maine Research Institute

Often known as "citizen scientists," members of the general public receive proper training in how to collect and report observations and scientific data. These enlightened individuals not only sate their own curiosities but also provide a meaningful and necessary service to their communities. Once they become properly trained—and often supplied with necessary equipment—these volunteer scientists monitor and report valuable data that support the work of various agencies that are too overwhelmed to gather this data on their own. We cannot overstate the importance of citizen scientists, as they are most closely associated with the community and experience the data first hand on a daily basis and, thus, are first to notice a significant change in their observations.

Closely related to the work of citizen scientists are the service-learning projects that students may undertake as part of their educational experience. These projects require student learners to become directly involved in a problem that they have identified in their communities. They research the issue, gather data, and make observations to determine the root cause of the problem. Participants must learn all of the related science, history, civics, and math and present the information in a well-written report to their facilitating educators. After thoroughly investigating the problem and its causes, students then collaborate with community members to develop possible solutions. When all parties have agreed upon the best possible solution, students will then—again, often in collaboration with locals—implement their solution. Through service learning, students are not only researching and learning about problems in their communities, they are learning the politics of how to collaborate with others to implement needed change.

As part of their established curriculums, the Environmental Science Department and Science Education programs at the University of Southern Maine conduct yearly water quality monitoring activities in Alden Pond and Tannery Brook, whose waters ultimately flow into the Presumpscot River. Outfitted with knee-boots, nets, collecting pans, and various water-sampling apparatus, students from these programs collect samples from the two distinct water environments to analyze chemical parameters such as carbon dioxide, dissolved oxygen, nitrates, phosphates, pH, and turbidity. These chemical/nonorganic parameters provide an instantaneous snapshot of the water quality for that moment when they took the samples. This type of water sampling has recently entered the digital age, so students also use small computers connected to digital probes and meters that collect water samples and feed the information directly into a larger database. For the real hands-on part of their analysis, they also collect and identify living individual macro-invertebrates in the pond or brook waters. To accomplish this, students must catch the larval organisms and use pictures, diagrams, and a dichotomous key to identify them down to their genus and, in some cases, their species. Using the number and kinds of organisms with a pre-determined algorithm, students calculate the biological index that demonstrates the health of the aquatic environment. This type of analysis, which has been a multi-year program, provides a longitudinal look at the health of these waters.

The Cumberland County Soil and Water Conservation District developed an outreach program in cooperation with the Environmental Science Department at the University of Southern Maine that led to a CD resource guide containing several lessons and activities intended specifically for preparing teachers interested in providing high-quality educational water-resource-related activities. In conjunction with the distribution of this CD, the developers provided face-to-face, hands-on workshops that demonstrated how to efficiently and accurately use this resource in the classroom.[9] By preparing teachers with the proper training to go back to their classrooms and lead the activities with their students, the program provided a rapidly expanding network of community-based, environmentally conscious citizens.

The Maine Department of Environmental Protection (MDEP) conducts an extensive program of biomonitoring water quality throughout the state, including Sebago Lake and the Presumpscot River. The biomonitoring program takes samples of benthic macro-invertebrates and algae that demonstrate the quality of water in these important aquatic environments. As part of this program, the MDEP publishes many educational materials that support parties interested in studying the health of rivers and watersheds in Maine.[10] The department's website provides a full array of bio-monitoring publications that includes program standards, sampling methods, field sheets (see Figure 2), technical reports on stream factors affecting water quality, standard operating procedures, and quick reference guides. Figure 2 offers a look at the kind of documents that the MDEP provides and the type of data that many citizen scientists collect to provide valuable information to publicly accessible databases. Interested school groups and volunteers can access the many free publications. They are also important resources for educators who are often looking for materials that can engage their students in authentic experiences; that serve as service learning; and may, in the future, lead to their students becoming citizen scientists. By using these standard sampling methods, collectors can upload the data to any of several websites that scientists and lay people alike use to continually keep track of the water quality in the Presumpscot River and its tributaries. Key geneses of benthic macro-invertebrates that are common in Maine rivers and streams are those of stone flies, may flies, and caddis flies. The larvae of these insects live in the water for extended periods of time and are the most sensitive to pollution and habitat disturbances. Finding the larval stages of these insects in the aquatic environment is a reliable indicator that the quality of the water is quite good.

Figure 2:

Example of Citizen Scientist Data Collection Form available from the Maine Department of Environmental Protection.
Location: _____
Potential Stressor: _____
Maine DEP Biological Monitoring Unit Stream Macroinvertebrate Field Data Sheet
Log Number _____
Station Number_____Waterbody_____
River Basin_____   Town_____
Stream Order_____
Directions_____
Lat-Long Coordinates (WGS84, meters) Latitude_____
Longitude_____
Type of Sampler_____
Date Deployed_____
Number Deployed_____
Date Retrieved_____
Number Retrieved_____
Agency/Collector(s) Put-In: Take-Out:

1. **Land Use** (surrounding watershed) ☐Urban ☐Cultivated ☐Pasture ☐Upland hardwood ☐Upland conifer ☐Swamp hardwood ☐Swamp conifer ☐Marsh	2. **Terrain** (surrounding watershed) ☐ Flat ☐ Rolling ☐ Hilly ☐ Mountains	3. **Canopy Cover** (surrounding view) ☐Dense (75-100% shaded) ☐Partly open (25-75% shaded) ☐Open (0-25% shaded) (% daily direct sun)

4. **Physical Characteristics of Bottom** (estimate % of each component over 12 m stretch of site; total = 100%)
- [ ] Bedrock [ ] Cobble (2.5" – 10") [ ] Sand (<1/8") [ ] Clay
- [ ] Boulders (>10") [ ] Gravel (1/8" – 2.5") [ ] Silt [ ] Muck [ ] Detritus

5. **Habitat Characteristics** (immediate area)
- Time _____ AM PM Wetted Width (m)____ Bank Full Width (m) _____ Depth (cm) _____ Velocity (cm/s) ____ Diss. O2 ___ (ppm) ___ (%) Temp (°C) _____ SPC (μS/cm) _____ pH _____ DO Meter #_____ Cal? Y / N SPC Meter # _____ Cal? Y / N
- Time ____ AM PM Wetted Width (m) _____ Bank Full Width (m) _____ Depth (cm) _____ Velocity (cm/s) _____ Diss. O2 ___ (ppm) ___ (%) Temp (°C) _____ SPC (μS/cm) _____ pH _____ DO Meter #_____ Cal? Y / N SPC Meter # _____ Cal? Y / N

Temperature Probe # _____ ☐ deployed ☐ retrieved

6. Observations (describe, note date)

7. Water Samples
   ☐ Standard ☐ Other Lab Number:

8. Photograph #
   Put-In Up Down Take-Out Up Down

9. Landmarks of Sampler Placement (illustrate or describe landmarks to be used for relocation).[11]

Vital Signs is another active program that lends its help to the study of the local environment and offers participants authentic science experiences. This program furnishes the necessary instructions, data-collection forms, and a web-based database for educators, students, and citizen scientists to become valuable participants in providing quality data accessible to all interested researchers. The program is operated through the Gulf of Maine Research Institute, with a physical presence on the waterfront in Portland and a well-designed website to which program participants can upload the data they collect. An important program of Vital Signs is finding, identifying, and documenting the presence of invasive species. Such species affect both the aquatic environment and watershed land areas of the Presumpscot River. The data, collected and uploaded using the instructions outlined in Figure 3, help to form a database that researchers of all abilities use. The activity is an example of the kind of training that takes place to ensure that citizen scientists are collecting and uploading accurate and valuable data for the scientific community.

 Explore. Share. Learn.   www.vitalsignsme.org

Activity Title
Data Quality Hunt

Author(s)
Sarah Morrisseau and Christine Voyer

Gulf of Maine Research Institute
Vital Signs Program
Questions
What makes great data?

Overview

Vital Signs data is used by students, the public, and professional scientists to better understand invasive and native species in Maine. For that reason, observations need to be of a certain quality to ensure their usefulness. Before students do their own data collection, they take time to explore and decide what good quality data looks like.

Activity Type
Exploratory

Learning Objectives
Students identify high-quality data that are usable by the scientific community

Grade Level
7 and 8

Setting
Classroom

Materials
Computers with web access
Student handout

Time Needed
40 minutes

Set-up:
Students work individually or in small groups at computers, exploring the data on the Vital Signs website.

Activity Procedure:

1. Give students time to explore the Vital Signs database, using the student handout to collect their observations about data quality.

2. Have a guided discussion with students about why data quality is important.

3. Students use their observations from the website to brainstorm what makes good and great data, and how to improve data; have them share their findings.

4. Make lists of characteristics of great data and okay data.

5. When students disagree, offer them opportunities to state their case using evidence and examples from the database.

6. Come to an agreement on the lists of characteristics and post them in the room or agree to disagree.[12]

In addition to this example of lesson plans, the Vital Signs website provides more than a dozen "Missions" in which students/educators can participate. Each mission contains lesson plans and directions that guide learners through steps and activities that require the gathering of scientific data. After they collect the data, the site has instructions on how to upload them to a database that others can access if they are interested in the same content. The website is constantly adding new content, including a space where educators can add new missions as they develop them, as long as the format matches that of the Vital Signs program.

These programs and organizations provide accessible ways for educators, students, volunteers, and citizen scientists to experience the benefits of place-based or nature-based education along the Presumpscot River and its tributaries and within its watershed. Children and adults are naturally curious about the world, especially when that world is alive and moving. Place-based experiential learning promotes critical thinking and problem solving, which correlate with increased standardized test scores and improved academic achievement. As service-learning and community-based education gain acceptance as ways to increase student engagement—which leads to increased achievement and the integration of subject matter—programs like those above will become ever more important.

People tend to cherish and protect what they know, what is familiar. Thus, if we, as interested citizens, wish to maintain the quality of the river and its watershed, it is important to have our fellow community members experience the Presumpscot River corridor along with us and become involved in its educational opportunities. Only through prolonged exposure and increased familiarity can a community develop feelings that make the local area a place.

[1] National Research Council. (2013). *Next generation science standards: For states, by states.* Washington, DC: The National Academies Press. https://www.nextgenscience.org/pe/hs-ls2-8-ecosystems-interactions-energy-and-dynamics; http://www.nextgenscience.org/pe/hs-ls2-3-ecosystems-interactions-energy-and-dynamics

[2] McInerney, P., Smyth, J., & Down, B. (2011). Coming to a place near you?' The politics and possibilities of critical pedagogy of place-based education. *Asia-Pacific Journal of Teacher Education 39*(1), 3-16.

[3] Rickinson, M., et al. (2004). *A review of research on outdoor learning.* Shrewsbury, UK: Field Studies Council/National Foundation for Educational Research.

[4] Rozenszayn, R., & Ben-Zvi Assaraf, O. (2010). When collaborative learning meets nature: Collaborative learning as a meaningful learning tool in the ecology inquiry-based project. *Research in Science Education, 41*(1), 123-146.

[5] Lieberman, G. A., & Hoody, L. L. (1998). *Closing the achievement gap: Using the environment as an integrating context for learning.* San Diego, CA: State Education and Environment Roundtable.

[6] Athman, J., & Monroe, M. (2004). The effects of environment-based education on students' achievement motivation. *Journal of Interpretation Research, 9(*1), 9-2. http://www.seer.org/pages/research/ AthmanandMonroeJIR2004.pdf

[7] Ernst, J. A., & Monroe, M. (2004). The effects of environment-based education on students' critical- thinking skills and disposition toward critical thinking. *Environmental Education Research, 10,* 507-522.

[8] Kuech, R. (2014, November). Using concept maps to assess science knowledge of pre-service elementary methods students. *European Scientific Journal, Special Edition, 1,* 290-294. https://eujournal.org/ index.php/esj/article/download/4781/4586

[9] Sanford, R., Plummer, S., Mosher, R., & Craig, M. (2009). *Presumpscot River watershed CD resource guide for teachers.* Windham, ME: Cumberland County Soil and Water Conservation District.

[10] Maine Department of Environmental Protection. (2018). *Materials.* https://www1.maine.gov/ dep/water/monitoring/biomonitoring/material.html

[11] Maine Department of Environmental Protection. (2018). *Materials*
https://www1.maine.gov/dep/water/monitoring/biomonitoring/materials/fieldsheet_s
tream_macro2017.pdf

[12] Vital Signs. (2018). *Data quality hunt.* http://vitalsignsme.org/data-quality-hunt

Chapter 15   Tracy S. Michaud

We Now Face the River:
Tourism on the Presumpscot River,
A View from Westbrook, Maine

Maine Rivers: A Natural Source of Community and Economy
Rivers have always been a distinctive part of Maine's landscape, economy, and community life. The Native tribes of Maine, who located many of their communities along rivers, appreciated them as food sources, transportation corridors, and trade routes. In fact, most Maine rivers retain their Native names, showing their intimate knowledge of and connection to this landscape. The European settlers who took over most of the land in Maine between the 1600s and 1800s, however, saw some Maine rivers primarily as power sources and dumping grounds for the manufacturing economy that dominated until the end of the 1900s.

Although it is true that nature tourism—fishing, canoeing, swimming, and camping—are part of the heritage of Maine's rivers, and we have many interesting stories of Maine guides and intrepid tourists on the waterways of Maine history, they tend to focus on remote and rural rivers. Note Thoreau's journey on the Allagash Waterway in Northern Maine that inspired the famous book *The Maine Woods*. In the cities and large towns, however, where mills processed raw materials, rivers became industrial tools for economic gain. Tourism became almost non-existent on these rivers.

In Maine, mill-towns' rivers were necessary for the economy but were not attractive parts of a community due to smelly pollution and other manipulations of the waterway, such as dams. Many people who complained about the unpleasant smell of the rivers in these towns remember hearing the old adage "That is the smell of money." An interesting dichotomy developed: these rivers were important, but no one wanted to associate with them. We turned our backs to the dirty, polluted commodities that moved materials into and out of industrial mills. They were not something to recreate on or even touch. People built facing away from them and did not orient most landscaping and infrastructure to necessarily capture the best views of the rivers or give people access to them. The Clean Water Act passed by Congress in 1972, under the leadership of Maine's Senator Edmund Muskie, began to change this history.

Clean Water Act

Senator Muskie's Clean Water Act was vital legislation for the redevelopment of river-based recreation and tourism. It was inspired by the horrifically polluted rivers in Maine's mill towns. The Androscoggin River in Rumford, Maine, where Senator Muskie grew up, was one of the most polluted in the country by the 1960s.[1]

Oxford Paper Company Mill at Rumford on the Androscoggin River (source: Charles Steinhacker (1973) *Documerica* U.S. National Archives)

Muskie's legislation protected rivers by severely restricting factories from dumping toxic waste, called point-source pollution, into the rivers. His environmental work was groundbreaking in that it recognized the human element in the preservation and conservation of natural resources. He helped the nation realize that clean water was just as important for people and communities as it was for Mother Nature. In the 2000s, due to this protective legislation and the decline in Maine's manufacturing industry, most of its rivers were open to clean up, and we are now rediscovering and recognizing them for their economic potential as community (workforce) attractions and for building a tourism economy. In fact, The Maine Development Foundation's *Measures of Growth 2018 Update* notes Maine's high water quality in its rivers, streams, and lakes.[2] It is well above the national average and is a stand-out gold-star indicator of quality of life in the state. We are once again engaging with rivers as lovely oases for recreation and as draws for tourist revenue worthy of protection. We now face the river.

Maine Rivers and the Tourism Economy

Today, as pressures of the manufacturing age are relieved, rivers are still focal points of the economy but in different ways: through an improved quality of life that reclaimed, natural, healthy waterbodies provide a community, and for new recreation opportunities for locals and visitors alike. Building tourism into community economic-development plans is important, as the tourism industry is a major driver of the Maine economy. This sector is growing throughout the world, and Maine has a strong tourism brand on which to build, especially in the nature, adventure, and eco-tourism sector. The travel and tourism industry is a large employer in Maine and across America, with travel-dependent leisure the largest small-business employer in the USA. In this multi-billion-dollar industry, from 2010-2017, travel jobs increased 20% compared to 12% in the rest of the private sector.[3]

Many Maine communities are looking at the rivers that run through them as ways to bring in more visitors, which fits within the Maine Office of Tourism's marketing strategy to entice visitors to other parts of Maine to "Discover Your Maine Thing."[4] The goal is to help spread out the large number of tourists who visit only Maine's Southern Coast. It is interesting how this transition is happening on the Presumpscot River in Westbrook. We will review suggestions for capitalizing on the opportunities this river holds for tourism development here and in other similar communities.

Presumpscot River History in Westbrook

The Presumpscot River in Westbrook, named by the Abenaki for its "many falls," is a prime example of a river once controlled and dominated by the manufacturing industry. Originally known, in part, as Saccarappa—after Saccarappa Falls on the Presumpscot River—Westbrook incorporated as a city in 1891. The river and its dams built the town. On a darker note, one of the original dams on the Presumpscot in the mid-1700s was built to stop the food supply to the Native Abenaki upriver and drive them out in order to make way for white settlers.[5] Most initial dams, though, were for passing logs and for water power. In Westbrook, Saccarappa Falls and Congin Falls provided power for the early mills. The papermill at Cumberland Mills, once Indian horticultural fields referred to as Ammoncongin, produced 1,000 tons of paper annually by 1859.[6] In 1867, the factory would be known as the S. D. Warren Paper Mill and then change to Sappi Fine Paper North America in 1994. Currently, the river runs through the city, connecting two business districts in Westbrook.

In the past, some recreation and tourism did occur on the river. Canal boats with parties on them were towed up the canals from Westbrook, and a steamboat took excursions on the Presumpscot River and stopped at Riverton Trolley Park in Westbrook in the 1800s. Along with the trolley park, a theme park opened in 1896. However, S. D. Warren's interests dominated the hydroelectric use, water supply, and wastewater dumping on the Presumpscot. Although the mill provided electricity and jobs for the region and built homes for its workers, the Presumpscot became so polluted in the process that no measurable oxygen remained in the river at all. It was filled with sludge and dredge from industrial waste and considered dead. Due to its many dams and long impoundments, by the early 1900s it was arguably the most dammed river in the country. A quote from the 2001 *Presumpscot River News* states:

> By all accounts, the Presumpscot River was once healthy, with thriving and robust populations of migratory birds and residential fish, which provided food, recreation and income to surrounding communities. Yet for almost all of the last century, two major forces combined to decimate this river and its fishery, and to cause the communities situated along the river to "turn their backs" on it. Water pollution and the presence of nine dams, with no fish passage or environmental restrictions, were the cause of the abandonment of the Presumpscot for nearly 100 years.[7]

Although this quote indicates that people metaphorically turned their backs to the river by not protecting it from destruction, the building structures on Main Street in Westbrook show how the community literally turned its back on it. These older buildings do not engage with the river, having few windows and little but backdoors and dumpsters on their river sides.

Examples of the back of buildings facing the Presumpscot River in Downtown Westbrook (source: Michaud 2018)

New Vision for the Presumpscot River

Although Westbrook has been associated for more than a century with the Maine paper and wood-pulp industry, and Sappi Fine Paper North America and its predecessors employed thousands, the industry eventually changed and jobs decreased. Today, Sappi manufactures a range of products but with only a few hundred employees.[8] The decrease in mill-tax dominance by the early 2000s allowed Westbrook to envision a new use for the river that included recreational tourism. As the perception of Westbrook changed from a pulp-mill town and finances for the town shifted from a 40% reliance on Sappi for taxes to less than 10%, Westbrook diversified its vision.[9] Without being so dependent on the mill for tax revenue, a realignment of priorities took place. The mention of the Presumpscot River in the Land Use Ordinances of the City of Westbrook document indicates this realignment.

Chapter I Preamble: 101 Purpose.

Now, as the mills' role in the community has decreased, Westbrook has a unique opportunity to reinvent itself. No longer dependent on processes that often polluted the environment, Westbrook citizens can now look forward to development and activity that is sensitive to the needs of its families and children, respective of its neighborhoods . . . and sensitive to its environment. To achieve these goals, this ordinance will accomplish the following:

A. Promote and conserve the health, safety, and general welfare of its residents.

B. Promote a safe and sensitive use of the environment that respects our unique resources: The Presumpscot and Stroudwater Rivers.[10]

Today, the Presumpscot River is transitioning to be a focal point of the community, a lovely recreational area offering new economic opportunities for nature, adventure, and eco-tourism. It is becoming an asset to local community members. In an interview with Abigail Cioffi, Executive Director of Discover Downtown Westbrook, she pointed out that the first downtown building built specifically facing the river was constructed in 2014.[11] Businesses are now adding signage and encouraging entrance from the river side as well as from Main Street.

Ethos/Vont Building built in 2014 with lovely river views (source: Michaud, 2018)

View from Ethos/Vont Building (source: Michaud 2018)

Arabic Market with signage on River Walk as well as facing the street (source: Michaud 2018)

According to community activist Michael Shaughnessy, "Attracting visitors to Westbrook and the Presumpscot River has always been in the background, but now that Westbrook is coming out of the shadow of the mill town, it is looking for a new self-identity, which could bring tourism to the forefront."[12]

Historic Mill now a part of the River Walk experience (source: Michaud 2018)

The Bright Side of "Turning our Backs"

Interestingly enough, by turning our backs to the industrialized river, "modern development" skipped much of the Presumpscot River corridor. One can argue that locals and tourists not regularly seeking access to the river over the last century actually helped to preserve the rural nature of the Presumpscot River and the authenticity of the Westbrook community. No major developments exist on the river from Mallison Falls to Saccarappa Falls—five miles with only a handful of structures and no roads. Westbrook is unique in having an unobstructed river corridor this close to an urban center. People can quickly be in what feels like wilderness without going too far from the city center. This combination is attractive to the nature tourist seeking a "softer" adventure and good for the local community. As Cioffi mentions:

Westbrook's charm is still there, with many local businesses in the downtown having been around for a long time and not taken over by big box stores or national chains. Young people that are craving authenticity and a connection to the heritage of a place can still find it in Westbrook.[13]

We Now Face the River

The opportunity for tourism development on the Presumpscot River, especially in Westbrook, is now prime. Tourism development that takes into consideration the protection of the natural asset, the wants and needs of the local community, and the development and maintenance of infrastructure and policy to make it accessible to locals and visitors alike is a sustainable approach that gives the community the best chance to reap the economic and social benefits of tourism.

Protect the Asset

To sustain nature, adventure, and eco-based tourism businesses, it is critical that industry not denigrate the natural resource on which it is based to the point where no one will want to visit it. The federal Clean Water Act was the first step and an important policy that allowed for the protection and better treatment of rivers in Maine and the USA. Today, it is vital to have organizations like Friends of the Presumpscot River (FOPR) and the Presumpscot Regional Land Trust (PRLT), which can continually focus community volunteers on giving voice to the landscape and keeping the best interests and protection of the river corridor in the public's and policymakers' minds.

Friends of the Presumpscot River

Formed in 1992 around the opposition, and eventual defeat, of a planned pulp mill in the upper river, FOPR has been the primary advocate for the Presumpscot River. As an all-volunteer organization, Friends of the Presumpscot River has a mission that touches on recreation, water quality, fishery restoration, and preserving the natural character of the river. Shaughnessy states that FOPR has been the driving force on issues such as dam removals (Smelt Hill, Saccarappa), five Federal Energy Regulatory Commission licenses (Saccarappa, Mallison, Little Falls, Gambo, and Dundee), state-ordered fish passage (Cumberland Mills), and river-classification upgrades.[14] This work has not been easy. Opponents have challenged FOPR in court at all levels, up to and including the U.S. Supreme Court, where it gained a unanimous decision upholding section 401 of the Clean Water Act.[15] According to Shaughnessy:

This group, with the legal support of Ron Kreisman and the Conservation Law Foundation, have, for many years, worked steadily for the river. In addition, it is committed to and active in outreach efforts related to education in schools; talks for organizations; and lectures and films focused on a public understanding of the river, its history, and fisheries issues.[16]

Today's visitors want "experiences" with places; therefore, river access is vital, and dam removal is important to gaining that access. An excerpt from the April 2001 Friends of the Presumpscot River publication, *Presumpscot River News*, talks about the benefits of dam removal:

> A restored Presumpscot River, running through the most populated county in Maine, would bring innumerable aesthetic, recreational and economic benefits to all the communities surrounding it. The lower river features rocky sides that form a small gorge; its shoreline is relatively undeveloped and would provide nearly seven miles of beautiful canoeing, kayaking, and fishing, only 15 to 20 minutes from downtown Portland. While there are some small segments that flow through developed areas, the entire length of the river has many runs of natural shoreline that still exist, providing a mostly rural experience when on the river. Fishing opportunities would dramatically increase with the re-population of many historic species, plus improved circumstances for the species that already exist in the Presumpscot. Along with this increased diversity of fish life, comes the increased activity of other marine life, birds, and mammals that thrive with a healthy ecosystem.[17]

Presumpscot Regional Land Trust

The Presumpscot Regional Land Trust oversees 1,600 acres of conserved lands and 14 free public-access preserves, including trails and water access. Safe recreation and a robust wildlife habitat require clean water; therefore, the land trust works to conserve the land and clean water while also engaging the public by providing recreational access throughout the watershed and beyond. It has a Water Stewards Program that regularly tests the water to help identify health issues and important places on the river to conserve and restore. It also engages visitors by coordinating the Sebago to the Sea Trail, a 28-mile trail from Standish to Portland.[18] The maps and the public events that the trust and others hold are important ways to encourage people to experience the river, to teach them the importance of caring for the river, and to help develop a caring connection to the river from the community and visitors.

Engaging Local Community

Although it is important for tourism development to preserve natural assets, it is equally important that some organizations think about the community's wants, needs, heritage, and sense of place in order to preserve the authenticity of the place and create tourism development that includes and benefits locals. Most modern nature tourists want the same. Many tourists crave authentic natural and cultural experiences that make them feel like they are participating in an activity or partaking of a site just like a local would. Creating activities and developing sites on rivers that locals actually use and appreciate will usually also attract tourists. More tourists mean increased revenue, which allows small Maine towns and cities to sustain attractions for their citizens that they normally could not with revenue from just the local population. Case in point is the City of Portland's numerous excellent restaurants. They could not flourish on the relatively small number of local diners only. Tourist dollars are vital to the survival of these businesses.

Having a vibrant and healthy river also speaks to the well-being of the community that surrounds it. The community's sense of stewardship and the degree to which it values the natural environment promote a positive legacy for future generations. The health of a river can strengthen how citizens and others perceive a city. It builds a quality sense of place and desirability to new residents and businesses. The perception of Westbrook is improving due in part to the change in the health of the river.

Discover Downtown Westbrook

Discover Downtown Westbrook is an organization focused on engaging local citizens in improving the downtown. It received its official National Main Street accreditation from the Maine Downtown Center in 2017. The Presumpscot River flows through the downtown and is a major factor in the work of this organization. Abigail Cioffi, Executive Director of Discover Downtown Westbrook, said that community members mentioned the river at every visioning session they held in 2016 for the organization's strategic plan. It is telling that everyone chose the river as the focal point of revitalization in Westbrook and had hopes that it would bring the community together. The City of Westbrook has already committed to a

353

river-focused development strategy by creating Riverbank Park and part of a pedestrian river walk in the early 2000s. Ideas from the visioning sessions that could build and support river-based tourism on the Presumpscot River in Westbrook and benefit the local community include:

- Creating kayak rental businesses
- Completing the River Walk loop
- Creating a park amidst the rapids and falls on Saccarappa Island
- Developing a river festival[19]

Docks and swimmers in Presumpscot River in Westbrook (source: Michaud 2018)

Kayaks on the Presumpscot River in Westbrook (source: Michaud 2018)

According to Cioffi, the hurdles of doing this work include a poor sense of place with many residents who still think of Westbrook as an old mill town rather than a destination. After such a long history of the Presumpscot River being polluted, and fear of it making people sick, even decades after the Clean Water Act led to the cleanup of most of the pollution, only recently have docks appeared on the Presumpscot River in downtown Westbrook and more people have regularly begun to seek access to it. Some still say that they will not touch the river. Discover Downtown Westbrook is working to change that attitude so that anyone local can list at least one thing to do for fun on the river. Cioffi believes that fighting the "dirty-river" perception is key. Although more work could make the river even cleaner, the city tries to allay people's fears that citizens cannot safely engage with the river. Its website has the following statement:

> Presumpscot and Stroudwater Rivers: These water bodies are suitable for human use (recreation, industrial process and cooling water supply and hydroelectric power generation). This state rating reflects their location in an urban setting with long term development and agriculture along the water bodies. They are fishable and swimmable and provide habitat for fish, plants and other aquatic life.[20]

Infrastructure, Policy, Planning

In the end, in order for locals and visitors to enjoy the Presumpscot River, organizations, community members, and business must all work together with planners in town and state governments to create and maintain access and quality experiences through infrastructure, policy, and planning. City policy on the Presumpscot River is moving in a positive direction of collaboration, protection, and access:

- Westbrook will encourage landowners involved in agricultural and wood harvesting to protect water quality.
- Westbrook will continue to work with regional partners such as the Cumberland County Soil and Water Conservation District, Friends of the Presumpscot River, and the Presumpscot Regional Land Trust to preserve the health of the water resources in Westbrook and to provide recreational opportunities for the public.[21]

Riverfront Master Plan

Good planning creates community goals, focuses policy, and defines infrastructure needs. The City of Westbrook has undertaken and continues to engage in some good planning. Much of the above policy and river-based improvements in Westbrook came out of the *Westbrook Riverfront Master Plan* of 2000. The mission of this plan was to bring new life to downtown and the Presumpscot River. It revolved around making downtown a destination. Goals of the *Riverfront Master Plan* include:

- Reconnect neighborhoods to downtown
- Create economic development
- Preserve natural settings on river
- Expose the beauty of Saccarappa Falls and Island
- Upgrade parks
- Increase safety
- Repair erosion
- Keep maintenance affordable
- Create pedestrian access on safe walking paths.

A number of plan components specifically relate to tourism development, including:

- A fully linked walking system on the banks of the Presumpscot for recreation
- Saccarappa Boardwalk and Park
- Saccarappa Boating Center (along with the creation of a whitewater rapid system at Saccarappa Falls with rentals to attract canoe and kayak enthusiasts to the Presumpscot).[22]

In order to continue this work, the City of Westbrook intends to complete the Downtown Riverwalk North project, a bicycle and pedestrian trail on the north side of the Presumpscot River. According to Shaughnessy, this and other proposed trails are possible due to a strategic agreement between the city, private business, and non-profit organizations, leading to fish passage, removal of the Saccarappa Dam, and the acquisition of other lands.[23]

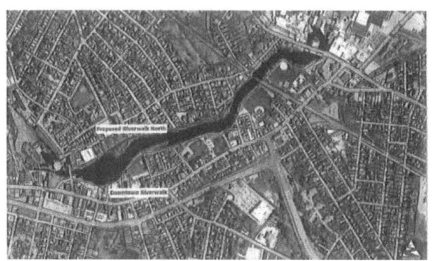

Riverwalk North Plan—red line indicates walking loop—(source: City of Westbrook)

Destination Development

To build a destination, a city needs to put in place the proper infrastructure and create attractions and activities to both entice and handle an influx of people. For the Presumpscot, Westbrook is discussing and acting upon the following infrastructure needs:

- Creating boat launches, docks, and swimming areas
- Beautifying the River Walk with façade improvements, signage for businesses on both Main Street and the river side, and mitigating dumpsters on the river side of Main Street businesses
- Creating activities on or near the Presumpscot to develop the downtown as a destination.

Attractions and Activities
Nature Tourism—Fishing AND Fish Viewing
Fishing is a traditional Maine recreation and has always drawn nature tourists to our Maine rivers. However, less adventurous nature tourists and families who want a "softer" experience of nature are looking for other options. Wildlife viewing versus wildlife hunting is a way to cater to these visitors. The Mill Brook Preserve is a five-mile trail system that is an excellent location for such an experience. Owned by the Presumpscot River Land Trust, it is noted for the annual migration of alewife fish from Casco Bay to Highland Lake. The brook connects into the Presumpscot River in central Westbrook. Up to nine different fish species used to

357

migrate to and from the ocean via the brook, before industrial waste and dams all but eradicated them here. The first step in restoring that ecology is fostering the return of alewives to the brook. [24]

The removal or modification of dams with fish ladders to restore natural fish habitats is important to habitat recovery and recreational fishing. The Friends of the Presumpscot River have long led the way to make this recovery happen. Some dams are already gone, and others are slated for removal in the next few years. More fish in the river also means more wildlife to view. Trails along Mill Brook that opened in 2016 provide views of alewife migration in late May and early June and could be potential tourism draws. The Presumpscot Regional Land Trust website promotes "viewing alewives" and the feeling of being in a remote area but close to an urban center. [25] As dams disappear and further habitat restoration occurs along the main stem of the Presumpscot River, these viewing opportunities could occur in downtown Westbrook as well.

Events
Events can bring awareness to the river and allow people to experience it, helping to build it as a destination. Trail races in unique places are popular and could be good events along the Presumpscot, as could a special alewife-migration-viewing event as the alewife population increases. Currently, the Friends of the Presumpscot River offers free guided river-kayaking tours. These family-friendly activities are important, as family-based adventure travel is increasing, and people consider Maine a good place for families.

Younger families do not necessarily recognize the stigma that the rivers are untouchable; because they did not grow up with mills dominating the landscape, they are more likely to seek out river experiences. The Presumpscot Regional Land Trust offers family-friendly summer programs such as "Introduction to Paddling the Presumpscot for Families," for children 6-15, with canoes to rent, lessons on paddling, and guided boat trips on the river. The Friends of the Presumpscot River have many annual "floats," including the free Brown Street Float with Portland Paddle (a local business) in one of Westbrook's underserved neighborhoods, which allows many in this community to get out on the water for the first time. These types of events tend to bring people back year after year.

Trails, Tours, and Interpretation

Providing maps, trails, and guided or self-guided tours is a great way to attract visitors. Maintaining safe trails with clear directions will help people have a good experience with a place. A number of trail maps have come out about the Presumpscot River, especially pertaining to paddling: *The Presumpscot River Paddling Map and Guide,*[26] the *Presumpscot River Paddling Trail,*[27] and the *Sebago to the Sea Trail*[28] are good examples.

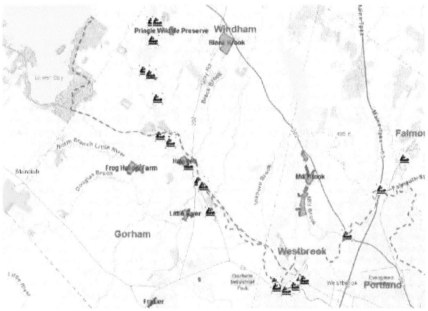

Sebago to Sea Trail Map (source: Presumpscot Regional Land Trust)

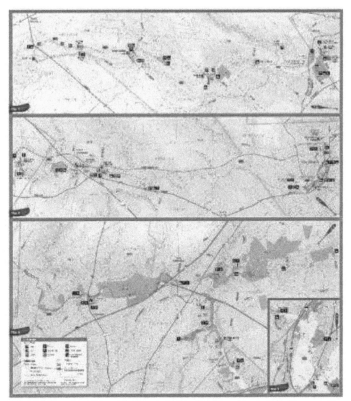

Presumpscot River Paddling Map and Guide (source: Casco Bay Estuary Partnership)

Another good example of providing interpretation to enhance the visitor experience is a proposed informational Memorial to Chief Polin and the First Peoples of the Presumpscot along Portland Trails' Conant Trail. FOPR is establishing this interpretative stop on donated land.[29] It will be the only memorial of its sort and will serve to both offer a moment of contemplation and to educate those visiting about those who came before, the river itself, and its restoration. Westbrook and other places along the river can replicate this type of interpretative signage to focus on various topics, even the manufacturing heritage of the river, to invite visitors to stop and engage. Likewise, trails for walking, hiking, bird and fish viewing, or other recreational activities, along with guided tours, would attract a wider range of visitors to the river, enhance the experience of those who already come, and connect them all more strongly to the Presumpscot and its communities. Once that happens, other types of complementary development can more easily take place.

Shopping and Eating

Complementary to most tourism activities are eating and shopping. Encouraging such business development along or near the river will support the visitor economy, especially when those establishments are locally owned and use locally produced goods when possible. According to a news article in *Keep Me Current*, a new state law "permits the sale and consumption of alcohol in an area that doesn't directly border a licensed premise." This relaxation of previous laws allows the City of Westbrook to amend municipal liquor licenses so that restaurants can serve alcohol on city-owned property (like the River Walk). The city just needs to post accurate signage and rope off an area for seating. A policy like this will allow the several downtown restaurants with access to the River Walk to have seating and serve food and drink. City officials hope that this addition will bring more people to the downtown.[30] Policies like these are important in encouraging businesses to engage with the river for economic gain. Increases in the quality and abundance of activities along the river will also foster business development.

Conclusion

Rivers remain vital to Maine's economy and, today more than ever, are assets in improving residents' quality of life. Rivers are becoming focal points for community recreation and growing attractions for tourists. As we now "face the river," locals and visitors seek personal engagement with these defining waterbodies of Maine. Tourism is an economic sector that is growing and providing jobs in Maine and the USA, and many new opportunities for tourism along rivers are emerging. Important to fostering tourism on the Presumpscot in Westbrook, and in any community along a river, is first to protect and conserve the natural asset and give voice to the local community through the cooperative work of conservation and community-based organizations, businesses, and government. Also vital are new and softer nature, adventure, and eco-tourism activities and attractions, such as creating areas for fish viewing, putting in place infrastructure to give locals and visitors access to the river in safe and sustainable ways, and developing policy to support complementary businesses growth. Westbrook is creating new opportunities on the Presumpscot River through completing and expanding use of the River Walk Loop; gaining public access to Saccarappa Island; connecting the River Walk to the

Conant Trail; removing Saccarappa Dam and restoring the fishery; beautifying the river side of Main Street businesses with signage and façade improvements; creating and marketing trails, tours, interpretation, and events that engage local people and businesses; and updating policy to support sustainable business development on the river. Taken together, this work will help the Presumpscot River continue to grow to be a place that locals and visitors all love to face.

Visitor facing the Presumpscot River in Westbrook (source: Michaud 2018)

[1] Collins, S. (2017, October 18) Androscoggin River, once full of toxic chemicals, now clean after 45 years of Clean Water Act. *Portland Press Herald.* https://www.pressherald.com/2017/10/18/androscoggin-river-once-full-of-toxic-chemicals-now-clear-after-45-years-of-clean-water-act/

[2] Maine Development Foundation. (2018). *Measures of growth 2018 update.* http://www.mdf.org

[3] U. S. Travel Association (2017, August 28). *Travel: America's unsung hero of job creation.* https://www.ustravel.org/research/travel-americas-unsung-hero-job-creation

[4] Maine Office of Tourism. (2018). *Discover your Maine thing.* https://visitmaine.com/

[5] Brooks, L. T. & Brooks, C. M. (2010). The reciprocity principle and traditional ecological knowledge: Understanding the significance of indigenous protest on the Presumpscot River (pp. 11-28). *International Journal of Critical Indigenous Studies, 3*(2). http://www.isrn.qut.edu.au/publications/internationaljournal/documents/ Final_LCBrooks_IJCIS.pdf

[6] City of Westbrook. (2018). *Westbrook, Maine.* https://www.westbrookmaine.com/471/History-of-Westbrook

[7] Friends of the Presumpscot River. (2001, April). *Presumpscot River news, 10*(1), 1. https://static1.squarespace.com/static/57fef2d28419c2478111e0f8/t/59075c0715cf7 d64e06152dd/1493654536718/newsletter2001-04.pdf

[8] City of Westbrook, (2018). *Westbrook, Maine.* https://www.westbrookmaine.com/471/History-of-Westbrook

[9] Orcutt Associates, PA. (2000) *The Westbrook riverfront master plan, 8.* file:///E:/Publications/ Presumpscot%20River%20Book/ 2000%20Riverfront%20Master%20Plan.pdf

[10] City of Westbrook. (2018). *Land use ordinances of the City of Westbrook.* (Adopted 2004, February 9, amended 2018, February 7), 429. http://www.westbrookmaine.com/DocumentCenter/View/1170/Appendix-A-Land-Use-Ordinance--2070207

[11] Cioffi, A. (2018, May 9). Personal interview with author.

[12] Shaughnessy, M. (2018, May 9). Telephone interview with author.

[13] Cioffi, A. (2018, May 9). Personal interview with author.

[14] Shaughnessy, M. (2018, May 9). Telephone interview with author.

[15] S.D. Warren Co. v. Maine Board of Environmental Protection, 126 S. Ct. 1843 (2006).

[16] Shaughnessy, M. (2018, May 9). Telephone interview with author.

[17] Friends of the Presumpscot River. (2001, April). *Presumpscot River news, 10*(1), 6. https://static1.squarespace.com/static/57fef2d28419c2478111e0f8/t/59075c0715cf7d64e06152dd/1493654536718/newsletter2001-04.pdf

[18] Presumpscot Regional Land Trust. (2018). *Presumpscot Regional Land Trust strategic plan 2018-2022.* https://www.prlt.org/about-us/

[19] Cioffi, A. (2018, May 9). Personal interview with author.

[20] City of Westbrook. (2018). *Westbrook, Maine.* https://www.westbrookmaine.com/468/Water-Resources

[21] Ibid.

[22] Orcutt Associates, *Westbrook riverfront master plan.*

[23] Shaughnessy, M. (May 9, 2018, May 9). Telephone interview with author.

[24] Presumpscot Regional Land Trust. (2018). *Mill Brook Preserve—Westbrook, 130 acres.* https://www.prlt.org/mill-brook-preserve/

[25] Ibid.

[26] The Presumpscot River Watershed Coalition & The Casco Bay Estuary Partnership. (2015, September 24). *The Presumpscot River paddling map and guide.* https://www.cascobayestuary.org/presumpscot-river-paddling-map-guide/

[27] Center for the Community GIS. (2018). *Presumpscot River paddling trail.* https://www.mainetrailfinder.com/ trails/trail/presumpscot-river-paddling-trail

[28] Center for the Community GIS. (2018). *Sebago to the sea trail: Presumpscot River paddling route.*https://www.mainetrailfinder.com/trails/trail/sebago-to-sea-trail-paddling-route

[29] Friends of the Presumpscot River Website. (2018). http://www.presumpscotriver.org

[30] Kelley, M. (2018, July 5) Change in law could allow cocktails along river walk. *Keep Me Current.*http://news.keepmecurrent.com/change-in-law-could-allow-cocktails-along-river-walk/

The Water Road

All journeys begin here, Madawamkeetook.
Home, beside the good river, rocky at its mouth.
Stone shards, bone stratum buried deep,
our ancient cenotaph,

Old Meductic Fort, traceless memorial on
the shores of Wolastoq.
Now St. John, the naming taken,
baptized in ink and parchment.
They say he knew water transformation;
it gives life.

A thousand years and more, we paddled
the Old Meductic Trail; the water road.
Nomads, they called us, citing
'most ancient evidence' of our passage;
'the solid rocks have been furrowed
by the moccasins of the native tribes."

The signpost, our chalcedony flesh.
Blue veins you call Nature's highway,
a map flowing inside our bodies.
The Thoroughfare; Chepneticook lakes to
Mattawamkeag and onward to the
Penobscot, where a girl became a woman.

Her body craves the past, its water seeks the
cool flow, ancestral memory, where tributaries meet,
flood undernourished roots that cling to her edges,
eroded year by year with forgetting.

Remember Meductic and the Water Road.
Birch bark, chert and bone melded with riverbank clay,
merging in the rippling shallows where canoes slide,
silent, among water lilies and pickerel grass.

First published at The Abbe Museum *Look Twice: The Waponaki in Image and Verse* 2009. 2nd printing in *20th Century PowWow Playland* 2012 Greenfield Review Press.

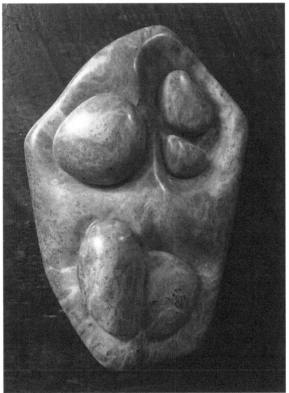

Riverbed (Pam Slaughter, 2018, 3 H x 8 L x 5.5 W, Soapstone)